The Economic Regulation of Broadcasting Markets

New technology is revolutionising broadcasting markets. As the cost of bandwidth processing and delivery fall, information-intensive services that once bore little economic relationship to each other are now increasingly related as substitutes or complements. Television, newspapers, telecoms and the internet compete ever more fiercely for audience attention. At the same time, digital encoding makes it possible to charge prices for content that previously was broadcast for free. This is creating markets where none existed before. How should public policy respond? Will competition lead to better services, higher quality and more consumer choice – or to a proliferation of low-quality channels? Will it lead to dominance of the market by a few powerful media conglomerates? Using the insights of modern microeconomics, this book provides a state-of-the-art analysis of these and other issues by investigating the power of regulation to shape and control broadcasting markets.

PAUL SEABRIGHT is Professor of Economics at the University of Toulouse-1.

JÜRGEN VON HAGEN is Professor of Economics at the University of Bonn.

The Economic Regulation of Broadcasting Markets

Evolving Technology and the Challenges for Policy

Edited by

PAUL SEABRIGHT AND
JÜRGEN VON HAGEN

CAMBRIDGE
UNIVERSITY PRESS

CAMBRIDGE UNIVERSITY PRESS
Cambridge, New York, Melbourne, Madrid, Cape Town, Singapore, São Paulo

Cambridge University Press
The Edinburgh Building, Cambridge CB2 8RU, UK

Published in the United States of America by Cambridge University Press, New York

www.cambridge.org
Information on this title: www.cambridge.org/9780521696340

First published 2007

Printed in the United Kingdom at the University Press, Cambridge

A catalogue record for this publication is available from the British Library

ISBN 978-0-521-874052 hardback
ISBN 978-0-521-696340 paperback

Cambridge University Press has no responsibility for
the persistence or accuracy of URLs for external or
third-party internet websites referred to in this publication,
and does not guarantee that any content on such
websites is, or will remain, accurate or appropriate.

Contents

Part III   Institutional approaches in various jurisdictions

Figures

Tables

Boxes

Notes on contributors

PETER J. ALEXANDER is a senior economist at the Federal Communications Commission in Washington D.C. where he conducts research on media and international communications and advises policymakers on economic issues. His work has been published in numerous scholarly journals, including the *Journal of Economic Behavior and Organization*, *Economics Letters* and the *Journal of Public Economic Theory*. The views and ideas expressed are those of the author and do not reflect the ideas, views and opinions of the Commissioners or staff at the Federal Communications Commission.

SIMON P. ANDERSON is Commonwealth Professor of Economics at the University of Virginia. He recently finished a term of almost a decade as co-Managing Editor of the *International Journal of Industrial Organization*. He has worked extensively on the economics of product differentiation. His current research interests include advertising, the media and political parties.

ELENA ARGENTESI obtained a PhD in Economics at the European University Institute, Florence and is now Assistant Professor of Economics at the University of Bologna. Her main research interests are in empirical industrial organisation and competition policy, with a focus on the media industry and on two-sided markets.

MARK ARMSTRONG is Professor of Economics at University College London. He has previously held positions at the universities of Oxford, Cambridge and Southampton. His research focuses on industrial economics and he has published papers on topics which include price discrimination, regulation, access pricing, telecommunications and broadcasting.

KEITH BROWN spent five years working as an economist for the Federal Communications Commission before joining the Center for Naval Analysis. Dr Brown has had articles published/accepted in

Economics Letters, *Applied Economics* and the *Review of Industrial Organization*, among other journals.

PIERRE BUIGUES is Professor in the Solvay MBA programme (Université Libre de Bruxelles) and Professor at Toulouse Business School. He is also the Law and Economics Consulting Group's European competition policy special consultant. Before joining LECG at the end of 2004 he was Economic Adviser to the Chief Economist at the Directorate-General for Competition of the European Commission and before 2003 head of the unit for the application of antitrust law in the telecommunications and internet sector.

EINAR HOPE is Professor Emeritus at the Norwegian School of Economics and Business Administration (NHH) in Bergen, Norway. He was Statoil Professor of Energy Economics at the NHH from 1999 to 2004 and Director General of the Norwegian Competition Authority from 1995 to 1999. Prior to that he headed three research organisations for applied research affiliated with the NHH and has also chaired a number of governmental committees on industrial policy and other economic policy issues in Norway. His publications are primarily within industrial organisation, competition policy and energy economics.

MARC IVALDI is Professor of Economics at Toulouse School of Economics, Researcher at Institut d'Economie Industrielle (IDEI) and Industrial Organization Programme Co-Director at CEPR. He specialises in applied industrial organisation, particularly of network industries, and is one of the leading European experts on empirical methods for competition policy. He has published several articles in the leading academic journals in industrial organisation. He holds a PhD in Economics from the University of Pennsylvania.

MICHELE POLO is Professor in Economics at Bocconi University in Milan. His research interests are in industrial organisation, regulation, antitrust and economics of the media industries. He is an economic advisor of the DG Competition, European Commission. He has published several papers in books and in international journals.

VALÉRIE RABASSA is a member of the Chief Economist Team, DG Competition, European Commission. She was case officer in AOL/ EMI/Time Warner, Vivendi/Universal and Canal+/RTL/Groupe

Jean-Claude Darmon/JV. She represented the Chief Economist in Lagardère/Editis and in the Football Association Premier League.

COLIN ROWAT is a microeconomist at the University of Birmingham. He received his PhD in 2001 from the University of Cambridge. His research has concentrated on dynamic commons problems. He has taught at New York University and writes on Iraq for the Economist Intelligence Unit.

PAUL SEABRIGHT is Professor of Economics at the University of Toulouse-1, a member of the Institut d'Economie Industrielle and a research fellow of CEPR. He was formerly a Fellow of All Souls College, Oxford and of Churchill College, Cambridge. He has written widely on topics in microeconomics, especially on competition policy. He is a member of the European Commission's Economic Advisory Group on Competition Policy. His most recent book is *The Company of Strangers* (2004, Princeton University Press).

JÜRGEN VON HAGEN is a professor of economics at the University of Bonn and a research fellow of the Center for Economic Policy Research (CEPR). His research, which has been published in numerous articles in leading scholarly journals and several books, covers various aspects of economic policy. He has been a consultant to the International Monetary Fund (IMF), the World Bank, the European Commission and other international organisations as well as governments in Europe and beyond.

HELEN WEEDS is a lecturer in economics at the University of Essex. She specialises in industrial organisation and has published papers on research and development (R&D), investment and utility regulation. She currently holds an Economic and Social Research Council (ESRC) grant to pursue a research project entitled 'The economics of broadcasting in the digital age'.

PART I
Introduction

1 Introduction: the future of economic regulation in broadcasting markets

JÜRGEN VON HAGEN AND
PAUL SEABRIGHT

THIS book is about how the dramatic technical changes impacting the nature of broadcasting are affecting, and should affect, our ideas on the role of public economic regulation of the markets in which broadcasting transactions take place. Broadcasting used to be considered a classic public good, in that it was impossible to exclude viewers who had not paid.[1] There were two solutions to the public good problem: one was public provision, nearly always by a publicly owned and funded organisation such as the BBC; the other, often coexisting with the former, was private provision funded by advertising revenue. In addition, scarce spectrum capacity and high fixed costs of programme making ensured that in many countries there was little competition between channels. And there was little direct competition, likewise, between broadcasting and other forms of information transmission, such as newspaper publishing or the commercial cinema.

The rapid evolution of broadcasting technology, and especially the move from analogue to digital means of processing and transmission, has transformed the landscape of broadcasting beyond recognition. The main features of the new landscape are as follows:

- Broadcasting signals can now be encrypted, meaning that exclusion of non-payers is possible for the relatively small cost of a set-top box. Radio broadcasting remains free but that is because of listeners' relatively low willingness to pay; television broadcasting has to all intents and purposes ceased to be a public good, except where the authorities (or private benefactors) choose to supply it on terms appropriate to a public good.
- Digitisation of the signal has enabled much greater compression of content into the available spectrum. Spectrum scarcity is no longer a significant constraint upon entry into broadcasting markets.
- Digitisation has also enabled the characteristics of the content that viewers care about – quality, timeliness, richness of multi-media representation and so forth – to depend less on the particular

3

platform by which the content has been transmitted. Satellite transmission competes directly with cable; the same content can be transmitted to television receivers, to computers and increasingly to mobile telephones. Internet sites make available multi-media content that is increasingly similar to that available from traditional broadcasters – and indeed more and more broadcasting channels use their websites as portals both to attract viewers and to provide them with complementary sources of content.

- Processing and transformation of content by final consumers has become much more sophisticated as computers and other kinds of digital processing equipment (DVD recorders, for instance) have become widely available to households. This means that copying is easier, which raises issues about piracy (so that just as exclusion of non-paying viewers at time of first transmission is becoming easier, exclusion of non-paying viewers at subsequent times is becoming more difficult). It also means that some kinds of bundling of content are becoming harder – specifically those that rely on bundling attractive content with unattractive content such as advertising. Consumers who wish to view a programme without viewing the advertising can increasingly find ways to do so, which renders infeasible certain ways of financing content production and transmission.

- Finally, the falling costs of computing and other forms of information processing have dramatically lowered the purely technical costs of programme making – those that arise from the cost of equipment required to take and manipulate sounds and images. This does not mean that the total costs of making programmes of a given type have necessarily fallen, since the total includes two other kinds of costs: first, the remuneration of the artists and the other subjects (such as the locations) and second, the costs of special effects and other programme elements whose novelty often requires an escalation of sophistication that compensates for the falling costs. However, it does mean that the basic entry barriers to certain kinds of programme making (art-house movies, quiz shows) have fallen significantly.

These changes have important implications for regulators. First, there is no longer any case for treating broadcasting as a pure public good. If certain kinds of broadcast (radio, for instance) are still provided like public goods, it is because the broadcasters have not thought it worth investing in technologies of encryption; when the value of the content to consumers is high enough, encryption technologies will be used. Second, due to the fall in certain kinds of entry barriers (the technical cost of making basic programmes and the cost of spectrum acquisition) and to the increasing substitutability between content delivered by different platforms, all countries can expect to see a more competitive and diverse market for broadcast content than has been possible at any previous time. However, this does not mean that regulators now have nothing to worry about. There are several reasons why they should be concerned:

1. Encryption works well for some kinds of content but not for all. Specifically, encryption works well for content whose value to the consumer decays rapidly with time: football matches between leading clubs, for instance. The longer the content retains its value, the more likely it is that consumers will find ways to copy it and re-transmit it to others. This is likely to reduce the rents that can be appropriated by the producers of content with lasting value and increase the value that can be appropriated by producers of ephemeral content.

2. The fact that it is increasingly difficult for producers to exploit market power arising from the ownership of physical means of transmission does not mean that market power is no longer an issue; rather, it may be an issue when it concerns producers that can corner the market in certain kinds of scarce content – the kinds that consumers are willing to pay for. Also, some kinds of content are strongly complementary to others (for instance, it is said that the willingness of viewers to pay high subscriptions to cable services depends on the bundles containing a certain amount of such premium content as top-league football matches and recently released Hollywood movies), which can give the owner of the complementary content a good deal of market power. These considerations mean that the authorities may need to be vigilant about market power coming from different sources to those that have traditionally been of concern.

3. Even though producers may be able to use exclusion technologies to appropriate more of viewers' willingness to pay, their customers' viewing decisions may have significant consequences for other producers due to scale economies, or for other consumers due to a broad range of externalities (which we consider in point 4 below). Scale economies may imply that when a large number of consumers choose to watch a certain broadcast or subscribe to a certain

channel, its producers can invest more in certain quality components (such as special effects) which make it harder for small-scale
producers to compete. As a result, it may be difficult for more than a
few producers to have a conspicuous presence in the market, even if
technically it is possible for many producers to be present in it. In
turn this can lead to the emergence of some new kinds of market
power – for instance, viewers may have a large choice of programmes, but the fact that they bunch in their choices may mean
that advertisers have few channels to choose between.

4. The viewing decisions made by consumers may have all kinds of
external effects on behaviour and welfare of society at large. They
may affect how consumers vote, take part in political debates,
approach their education and their absorption of other sources of
information, behave towards each other on an everyday level, contribute to the broader welfare of their communities or nations, or
feel about outsiders (such as immigrants or residents of foreign
countries with whom their own country has important commercial,
political or military relations). These kinds of effects are potentially
very important but extremely hard to pin down in a specific empirical way. There is no shortage of convinced and often convincing
advocates of theories about the systematic effects of broadcasting
viewers' decisions (see Sunstein, 2001, for one particularly influential argument to the effect that the internet and the increasing
competition among information media are breaking down the sense
of community that is necessary to the happy functioning of political
and social life). These arguments will no doubt continue for a long
time, though there is too little hard evidence about the nature of
such external effects for anything like a system of broadcasting
regulation to be based upon them. The best we can say is that
their likely importance, as well as the high degree of uncertainty
surrounding them, means that the evolution of broadcasting markets, and the nature of broadcasting regulation, will be watched and
discussed in our political and social life with an enthusiasm and a
passion that exceeds what we can expect from almost all of the other
markets in which economic regulation is a concern.

This book makes a contribution to that discussion. Without any
pretence to comprehensiveness, we have collected essays from a range
of distinguished contributors, both academic researchers and competition policy practitioners, on important topics relating to the future of

broadcasting regulation. The focus is upon economic regulation rather than the regulation of other aspects of broadcasting such as regulation of content. We have not sought to cover all of the externalities mentioned in item 4 above – not because we believe them to be unimportant but because we ourselves do not have the evidence that would enable us to deal with them adequately.

Chapter 2, by Colin Rowat, undertakes a comparative summary of the state of broadcasting regulation in the OECD, considering both economic and non-economic criteria. It then outlines some of the heterogeneity in adoption rates of new communications technologies across the OECD (such as the penetration of broadband internet access and high-definition television). Finally, it offers some hypotheses to explain the substantial variation in both investment and penetration observable across OECD countries. The chapter underlines just how much variety there is in the regulation experience of different countries and, therefore, how much we can learn from the experience of those countries about the merits and shortcomings of the various approaches to the regulation of this complex and fast-evolving sector.

The remaining chapters are divided into two broad groups. The first consists of chapters examining questions of principle in broadcasting regulation. Chapter 3, by Paul Seabright and Helen Weeds, considers where the scarce assets are located in the broadcasting sector and what are the lessons for public interventions to prevent the abuse of market power. It focuses on what makes broadcasting different from other sectors and on the way in which recent technological developments such as digitisation may be changing the nature and distribution of scarcity rents. The chapter goes on to look at a number of challenges for competition policy, including such issues as market definition, exclusionary practices and bundling, matters that have been brought to the fore in recent antitrust developments. It suggests that the risks attendant on these practices may be somewhat different from those that have traditionally been emphasised and proposes rules of thumb to help identify the circumstances under which they are most likely to lead to a consolidation of market power.

Chapter 4, by Mark Armstrong and Helen Weeds, looks at the impact of technological changes in broadcasting on the rationale for public service broadcasting, along the lines exemplified by the traditional Reithian model for the BBC. It argues that the case for this model of public service broadcasting has largely disappeared. This is partly because there is less need for public service broadcasting in a world where encryption enables broadcasters to appropriate more of the benefits created by their activity. It is also because even if it would be desirable for viewers to watch a different mix of programmes from those a competitive market would provide, public service broadcasting may be an increasingly ineffective means of making them do so. Public provision may ensure that programmes are made but it cannot ensure that anybody watches them. Nevertheless, the chapter identifies a number of areas in which market competition may fail to deliver desirable outcomes in broadcasting and discusses public service broadcasting and some alternative policies as responses to such failures.

Chapter 5, by Michele Polo, considers a particular source of concern about the outcomes of unregulated market competition – namely whether this process does enough to ensure pluralism in the viewpoints represented in the media. It proposes a double definition of pluralism with respect to political opinions and viewpoints: there is *external* pluralism, when the market as a whole displays a sufficiently diverse set of views, and *internal* pluralism, when individual media firms provide access to a sufficient diversity of views. The chapter concludes that unregulated competition may fail to provide adequate safeguards for pluralism under either definition and discusses some possible regulatory mechanisms that may compensate for this failure. It argues that authorities independent of the government are necessary to ensure pluralism.

Chapter 6, by Simon Anderson, looks at the role of advertising in funding broadcasting and examines the nature of and rationale for regulation of television advertising. Such regulation typically covers both the time devoted to commercials and restrictions on the commodities or services that can be publicised to various audiences (stricter laws often apply to children's programming). Time restrictions (namely advertising caps) may improve welfare when advertising is overprovided in the market system. Even then, such caps may reduce the diversity of programming by curtailing revenues from programmes. They may also decrease programme net quality (including the direct benefit to viewers). Restricting advertising of particular products (such as cigarettes) probably reflects paternalistic altruism, but restrictions may be less efficient than appropriate taxes. Overall, Anderson's chapter is a timely reminder that even if advertising may be perceived by some as a nuisance, it exists in a market framework because it makes possible other benefits (such as investment in programming quality).

Proposals to limit advertising therefore need to consider alternative ways of funding investment or at least to examine carefully the consequences for overall quality and quantity of programming if such revenue sources are no longer to be relied upon.

Chapter 7, by Elena Argentesi and Marc Ivaldi, is the last in the section on general principles of broadcasting regulation. It considers the issue of how to define markets (and consequently how to evaluate the effect of the presence of substitute products on the existence of market power) when the markets in question are what is sometimes called *two-sided*. Many broadcasting markets are two-sided in the sense that the attraction of a programme to advertisers depends on how many viewers are likely to be watching, just as the attraction of a programme to viewers may depend (probably negatively) on how many advertisements there are. The chapter presents an econometric methodology which will be of considerable importance in enabling competition authorities to define markets and assess market power. Though the particular data are drawn from the print media, the methodological issues are broadly similar to those in broadcasting and the chapter will be an important reference for future empirical work in this area.

The last section of the book, on institutional approaches, contains three chapters. Chapter 8, by Peter Alexander and Keith Brown, examines broadcasting regulation in the United States, with particular reference to the role of the Federal Communications Commission in pursuing public interest objectives. It has interpreted this role as implying the balancing of three, sometimes conflicting, objectives: competition, localism and diversity. The authors illustrate with a rich range of cases the kinds of conflict that can arise between these objectives and the authorities' different responses to these conflicts over recent years.

Chapter 9, by Pierre Buigues and Valérie Rabassa, examines the role of the European Union in regulating the media, focusing particularly on the way in which the European Commission regulates competition in the media, subject to various public interest objectives which concern the Member States. The Commission has been particularly alert to concerns about exclusionary conduct in the market for certain kinds of content and the history of Commission intervention illustrates a significant evolution in the arguments and justifications that have been advanced for regulatory action.

Finally, Chapter 10, by Einar Hope, looks at the relationship between general competition regulation and sector-specific regulation at a national level, with particular emphasis on the approach adopted by the authorities in Norway. The chapter presents a broadly optimistic view arguing that general competition regulation can gradually replace many of the diverse interventions that have historically been undertaken in pursuit of objectives that are specific to the broadcasting sector. Whether or not its readers are persuaded, this chapter focuses on what is at stake when considering whether the general tools of competition regulation can do what is needed for broadcasting regulation.

What exactly *is* needed for broadcasting regulation remains, of course, one of the important unsettled questions in this area. There is much less agreement about what would constitute a healthy broadcasting sector than there is about other sectors of the economy such as manufacturing industry, financial services or even agriculture. In fact, of all the sectors in which questions of economic regulation arise, perhaps only the health care sector is characterised by as much fundamental questioning of aims and values as is routine in discussions of broadcasting. We have not done more than scratch the surface of these questions in this volume, but we hope to have illustrated that even the modest tools of economic analysis can yield real insights when applied carefully and rigorously to this important area of social activity.

This book presents the results of a research project that was made possible by a grant from the Center for European Integration Studies at the University of Bonn, which we gratefully acknowledge. We also thank the Center for Economic Policy Research (CEPR) for its technical support of the project and the Institut d'Economie Industrielle at the University of Toulouse for organising a conference on media regulation in October 2004 at which preliminary versions of this work were presented. We are grateful to Cambridge University Press, and in particular to Chris Harrison, Lynn Dunlop, Jackie Warren and Vivienne Church, for excellent editorial work. We hope that this book will stimulate a lively policy debate about the future of media regulation in Europe and beyond.

Reference

Sunstein, Cass (2001) *Republic.com*, Princeton, Princeton University Press.

Note

1. In principle the authorities could prosecute those who had purchased a television set without a licence, but exclusion by programme was not possible.

2 Technological and regulatory developments in broadcasting: an overview

COLIN ROWAT*

2.1 Introduction

I coined the word cyberspace in 1981 ... At the time, I didn't have a very clear idea of what I was going to try to make it mean ... Actually I think it was probably more fun for me when I was still able to look at it and wonder what it meant ... When I started writing ... the absolute top of the line professional writing machine in the world was an IBM Selectric with a couple of type balls, and that's what everybody aspired to. But I could never have afforded one of those things. Today those things are like landfill. Literally. I've seen fifty working Selectrics piled up like dead cockroaches in the back of a university clearance warehouse. (Gibson, 1996)

William Gibson's achievement – discovering cyberspace from a 1933 typewriter while dreaming of a Selectric – is nothing more than that constantly required of those regulating communications today. When a sexually explicit film made on a mobile phone in Delhi is sold over the Indian subsidiary of eBay and burned onto CDs around the world, who is responsible for its regulation and what standards should they apply?[1] And this is an easy question: we can describe it; it involves technology already in existence. Regulators have always faced the problem of regulating for a future that does not yet exist, but that future is upon them much more quickly than it has been in the past.

One particular challenge for regulators has been platform convergence – the increasing substitutability between platforms for data delivery, whether 'plain old telephone service' (POTS) lines, cables originally laid for television or even mobile platforms. This has obvious implications for regulators: regulation that is stricter for one platform will simply be ignored by users, who will switch to more leniently regulated platforms. It also raises the threat that a monopolist on one platform may be able to dominate a unified market as well.

This chapter first surveys telecommunications and broadcasting regulation across the Organisation for Economic Co-operation and

Development (OECD). It then turns to the extent to which new technologies have been adopted across the OECD and attempts to explain these by reference to their regulatory environment.

2.2 Broadcasting regulation

Regulatory issues arising in broadcasting may be divided into economic issues, often related to competition, and non-economic issues of public policy. These latter include issues of content (e.g. promotion of public service or cultural messages, protection of minors, controls on advertising) as well as access (typically universal access). This section outlines key features of each within the OECD. In both cases, in spite of considerable national variation, two international organisations have been driving harmonisation within the OECD, the European Union and the WTO.

Within the EU,[2] three bodies of law are relevant: generic competition law, sector-specific competition regulation and content regulation. This last is particularly relevant to broadcasting.

The principal basis for the EU's generic competition law is Articles 81 and 82 of the EC Treaty. These are largely reactive *ex post* instruments designed to be applied to market conduct. As such, they are 'hands-off', light regulatory instruments. The exception to this are the merger control provisions: given the huge costs associated with mergers, these contain more interventionist *ex ante* provisions.

Article 81 disallows any agreements which, either by design or otherwise, restrict or distort trade. These include agreements on pricing, exclusionary or shared access to facilities (including technical standards) and market sharing. The Article also allows exemptions, as well as for the Commission to assess the merits of individual cases. For example, in 2002, T-Mobile and VIAG Interkom successfully appealed to the Commission to allow them to share infrastructure in order to help them more rapidly provide new services to consumers.

Article 82 prohibits the anti-competitive abuse of a dominant market position. In addition to prohibiting pricing strategies such as predatory pricing and cross-subsidisation, Article 82 requires that access to 'essential facilities' – those without close substitutes – be granted. This, clearly, is particularly relevant to broadcasters, often dependent on expensive infrastructure.

In addition to these generic rules are *ex ante* sector-specific provisions for fostering competition. These develop from a process begun in the 1980s to foster a single, competitive telecommunications market in Europe. At the time, only the UK had taken even partial steps to liberalise a sector otherwise dominated by national monopolies. Thus, from the 1987 Green Paper on Telecommunications, the EU has issued directives on harmonisation and liberalisation that have transformed the industry. Responsibility for these goals has largely fallen within the ambit of the Information Society and Competition Directorates-General, respectively.

Liberalisation was then introduced a sector at a time over the next decade. This gradualism was designed to maintain both stability within the liberalising sectors and universal service provision. This process ended with full liberalisation on 1 January 1998; the directives passed to this point formed the regulatory framework (RF). Structurally, one of their key elements was the establishment of national regulatory authorities (NRAs), independent of the operational bodies that they regulated.

More recently, in March 2002, existing directives on liberalisation and harmonisation were consolidated as the new regulatory framework (NRF). As these came into force in July 2003, they are also referred to as the '2003 regime' (Walden, 2005b). Recognisant of rapid technological change, one of the objectives of the NRF was to regulate in a technologically neutral fashion.

A second objective was the rolling back of the *ex ante* provisions of the RF: once the state monopolies were broken up, it was argued, the need for more interventionist *ex ante* controls would be reduced, allowing competition to be maintained by generic *ex post* competition law. However, consultations with new entrants led the Commission to conclude that entrants still faced entrenched incumbents, thus warranting the retention of *ex ante* controls (Walden, 2005a). Nevertheless, the expectation remains that periodic reviews of the *ex ante* controls will lead to their gradual roll-back in favour of pure competition law.

As the *ex ante* and *ex post* measures to foster competition have developed separately, the NRF also sought to align their operational terms. The NRF therefore redefined the concept of 'significant market power' (SMP), which serves as the threshold for *ex ante* regulatory intervention, in terms of competition law's concept of 'dominance'.

Structurally, the NRF consists of a Framework Directive and four more specific directives. The Access Directive is of most interest from the point of view of competition law. It specifies more detailed measures to guarantee access to essential facilities, thus complementing the provisions of Article 82. These are broadly defined to include:

access to network elements and associated facilities, which may involve the connection of equipment, by fixed or non-fixed means (in particular this includes access to the local loop and to facilities and services necessary to provide services over the local loop); access to physical infrastructure including buildings, ducts and masts; access to relevant software systems including operational support systems; access to number translation or systems offering equivalent functionality; access to fixed and mobile networks, in particular for roaming; access to conditional access systems for digital television services; access to virtual network services. (Art. 2(a))

The Access Directive therefore limits vertical concentration. In spite of its breadth, the development of new technologies prevents the Directive specifying an exhaustive list (Schulz, 2004).

Alongside this, the Framework Directive provides the interpretative framework for interpreting and implementing the Access Directive, including whether an undertaking possesses SMP. Its scope explicitly includes wholesale broadband access, unbundling of the local loops to do so and broadcasting transmission services (McCormack, 2005).

In spite of these common provisions, the degree of competition still varies across EU countries. In December 2004, the EU's Communication Commission expressed concerns that 'competition in broadband access is still weak in certain countries', so that 'broadband penetration varies considerably' (Commission of the European Communities, 2004).

One platform capable of providing broadband internet services is the public switched telecommunications network (PSTN); the form of broadband then provided is generally referred to as xDSL (digital subscriber line, where x indicates the particular technology used).

As the infrastructure for the PSTN was typically developed by monopolists, there has been a hope that, in the long run, entrants would compete by investing in their own infrastructure. In the short run, regulators have sought to open the existing PSTN to competition. These efforts have focused on granting entrants access to incumbents' 'local loop' – the copper wires running between subscribers' premises and the incumbents' distribution frame (Umino, 2003).

Nevertheless, the Commission noted that 'developments ... relating to rollout of local loop unbundling are patchy across the [EU15] member states' (Commission of the European Communities, 2004). Table 2.1 shows how entrants access the local loop. Under full local loop unbundling (LLU), the incumbent retains ownership over the local loop and responsibility for its maintenance; otherwise, it is the entrant's to use as desired. Line sharing is slightly more restrictive for the entrant, which now shares the line with the incumbent, which retains ownership. Bitstream access is more restrictive yet, granting the entrant only the right to transmit over the local loop, but not to use

Table 2.1: New entrants' DSL lines by type of access

	Full LLU	Line sharing	Bitstream	Resale
Austria	41%	0%	59%	0%
Belgium	1.70%	1.30%	57.50%	39.60%
Cyprus				
Czech Republic			0%	100%
Estonia	71%	0%	0%	29%
Denmark	31%	25%	44%	0%
Finland	47%	19%	34%	0%
France	3%	45%	49%	4%
Germany	79%	0%	0%	21%
Greece	7%	3%	90%	0%
Hungary	0%	0%	100%	0%
Ireland	1%	5%	94%	0%
Italy	38%	3%	59%	0%
Latvia	11%	2%	52%	34%
Lithuania	0%	0%	100%	0%
Luxembourg	0%	0%	0%	0%
Malta	0%	0%	0%	100%
Netherlands	10%	90%		0%
Poland				
Portugal	19%	0%	81%	0%
Slovak Republic				
Slovenia	0%	0%	100%	0%
Spain	10%	5%	86%	0%
Sweden	7%	52%	1%	40%
United Kingdom	0%	1%	13%	86%

Source: Communications Committee (2005)

its own hardware (Umino, 2003). Finally, under resale the entrant can retail only services purchased wholesale from the incumbent.

Bitstream access has therefore been the most popular means of entry for new DSL service providers: in eleven of the EU25 countries, a majority of entrants' DSL lines were supplied this way. Resale has been heavily used in the large UK market, while new German operators have entered with full LLU and the Dutch have shared lines.

Finally, the third body of EU regulation relevant to broadcasting concerns not its competitive provision but its content. The goals associated with this regulation tend to be non-economic, such as fostering a pluralistic discourse while protecting national identity, protecting minors and guaranteeing universal access to services. As some of these are 'cultural activities', they fall outside the aegis of Community legislation.

Nevertheless, some Community legislation applies to broadcasting.[3] For the most part, the NRF has little relevance for content regulation, as its scope excludes services that provide content, such as radio and television. Instead, EU activity has largely come under the heading of the Television Without Frontiers (TWF) Directive.

TWF was initially adopted in 1989 and was subsequently revised in 1997. It sought to apply harmonised standards to television broadcasting intended for European audiences. Thus, TWF is platform independent, applying equally to cable, free-to-air and satellite television (as broadcasting refers to the provision of a predetermined schedule of programmes simultaneously to more than one recipient, it does not apply to video on demand).

Key features of the TWF are as follows. First, it allows national authorities to ensure that 'major events' (often sporting events) are carried on free-to-air television. Second, it requires a majority of the discretionary transmission time on national networks to be reserved for 'European works'. Similarly, at least a tenth of the discretionary time is to be devoted to independently produced European works, particularly recent works. In both cases, the requirements do not apply to local television, can be gradually attained and are qualified by the term 'where practicable', which has allowed latitude to Member States. Third, the TWF Directive controls advertising and teleshopping, including content restrictions (e.g. no tobacco or prescription medicines, controls on alcohol) and provisions to protect minors. Finally, Member States may apply more stringent controls to protect minors or prevent incitement to hatred than those adopted at the Community level.

The European content requirements, however flexible, are in conflict with the most favoured nation (MFN) requirements of the General Agreement on Trade in Services (GATS), which prohibit discrimination against foreign members. Thus, the European Union notified the World Trade Organisation (WTO) of its intention to exempt itself, for unlimited duration, from these requirements when they clash with the TWF Directive. Negotiations during the TWF's revision left the content requirements largely unchanged. Such exemptions are not uncommon: the WTO Services Database generates a 72-page list of exemptions for the film, radio and television sectors.

Since the WTO's establishment in 1995, it has come to play an important role in spurring liberalisation internationally. As regards communications and broadcasting, its fourth protocol (adopted in 1997), the Agreement on Basic Telecommunications (ABT), is the most relevant. The ABT, however, was largely limited to statements of principle. Thus, while it has spurred an agenda to reform in many countries, it has not served as a good model of regulation. Buckingham and Williams (2005) therefore claim that the EU's approach to encouraging competition has become the *de facto* global standard.

The US model is perhaps the most obvious alternative. US regulation is dominated by the country's federal structure. This has both divided jurisdiction for sector-specific regulation between the Federal Communications Commission (FCC) and state bodies and led to the granting of local rather than national broadcast licences. To guard against concentration, the FCC has imposed limits on the ownership of licences. However, demonstrating a further feature of the US federal structure, responsibility for competitive practices also falls within the domain of both the Department of Justice and the federal courts; the latter frequently overturn FCC decisions and indeed have struck down the FCC's concentration limit (Speta, 2004). US programme suppliers are also restricted in their ability to dictate broadcast affiliates' programming decisions.

In general, Buckingham and Williams conjecture that judicial intervention has done more to promote competition in the USA than has the FCC. In consequence, they conclude that there has been less progress both in fostering competition and in adopting technology-neutral reforms in the USA than in the EU. Speta (2004) agrees that US regulation has been lighter than the EU's Access Directive but believes that this may be justified: platform convergence may allow cross-platform competition rather than regulation to address the problem of bottle-necks in essential facilities; when this does not, the discretionary ability to intervene remains.

Finally, the FCC has adopted measures with respect to international programme suppliers. In an example of 'second-best' regulation, its 1997 Benchmark Order for International Settlements established a country-by-country payment schedule that removed from US operators the right to negotiate their international settlements themselves. Against this disadvantage, it aimed to ensure that foreign monopolists could not extract surplus from US operators and consumers (Walden, 2005a).

Another alternative model is that pursued by New Zealand until 2001. This relied exclusively on its general competition law regulator, spurning sector-specific controls. This approach was not regarded as a success: dispute resolution through the courts was slow and did not indicate appropriate forms of behaviour. Thus, in 2001, a sector-specific regulator was created. Nevertheless, Buckingham and Williams note that the level of liberalisation achieved compares well with that in other jurisdictions. This approach obviously requires efficient generic competition institutions, something that more newly industrialised countries are still developing.

Competition in Japan's communications sector is the joint respon-sibility of the Fair Trade Commission (JFTC) and the sector-specific Ministry of Internal Affairs and Communications (MIC).[4] The former upholds Japan's general *ex post* rules, while the latter applies sector-specific *ex ante* regulations, largely under the Telecommunications Business Law (TBL) and the Nippon Telegraph and Telephone Corporation (NTT) law (Moussis, Ishida and Shiroyama, 2004). Relative to the EU, Moussis et al. report that Japan makes more use of *ex ante* regulation. It also relies more heavily on structural measures, such as the 1999 division of NTT into three entities. Overall, Japan has had less success in fostering competition than has the EU in spite of its early start; Moussis et al. attribute this in part to the JFTC's quasi-ministerial status, which forced it to negotiate with other ministries with different agendas.

In Korea, responsibility for competition is also divided between the Fair Trade Commission (KFTC) and the Korea Communications Commission (KCC) in the Ministry of Information and Communications. The WTO's most recent trade policy review of Korea concluded that 'KCC therefore appears to fall short of being an independent regulator ... The precise anti-competitive and regulatory roles of the MIC and the KFTC are unclear' (WTO, 2004). In broadcasting, Korean content requirements are more stringent than those in the EU: free-to-air television is limited to 20 per cent foreign content; on cable, the limit is 50 per cent.

Domestic or other public service content requirements are fulfilled in a number of different ways across the OECD. Historically, the most popular means has been for the national state broadcaster to deliver the required content directly. The development of commercial broadcasters has opened up new possibilities. Armstrong and Weeds (2006) distinguish between two ways of compensating commercial broadcasters for carrying public service content. The first, licensing, grants broadcasters concessions on spectrum in return for carrying public service content; the UK has adopted this approach. The second, commissioning, is more targeted, commissioning individual programmes on the basis of competitive bidding; New Zealand and Singapore both commission. As Armstrong and Weeds note, the arguments for public service broadcasting weaken as spectrum becomes less scarce, as occasioned by the growth of digital. Digitisation also has implications for protection of minors regulation: whereas countries like the UK previously used 'watersheds', allowing material deemed unsuitable for children only after 9pm, digital television allows content to be labelled in advance and access to it controlled. This possibility has driven recent interest in harmonising content labelling across platforms as diverse as video games, internet pages, broadcast television and film.

A brief overview of regulatory authorities in OECD countries is presented in Tables 2.2 and 2.3. Both show considerable diversity. Even nominally, Table 2.2 shows that nine telecommunications regulators also retain postal services. Another eleven use the more modern 'communications' title, including the US FCC which – founded in 1933 – is the oldest of them. Increasingly, both telecommunications and broadcasting authorities are the same: this is the case for ten of the countries listed.

More significantly, regulators may be structured as autonomous quasi-judicial commissions (as the US FCC), independent office inside or outside of a government ministry (as in Sweden and France, respectively) or non-autonomous government ministries (Walden, 2005a). Among the OECD countries, only Denmark and Japan indicate that their telecommunications regulators are not autonomous.

In Belgium, separate bodies regulate broadcasting to the Flemish and Walloon communities; in New Zealand this is the case with English

Table 2.2: Regulatory authorities in OECD countries

Country	Telecommunications regulator	Broadcasting authority (if different)
Australia (2004)	Australian Communications and Media Authority[a]	
Austria (2004)	Austrian Regulatory Authority for Broadcasting and Telecommunications (RTR-GmbH)	
Belgium (2003)	Belgian Institute for Postal Services and Telecommunications	Conseil Supérieur de l'Audiovisuel, Vlaams Commissariaat voor de Media
Canada (2005)	Canadian Radio-television and Telecommunications Commission	
Czech Republic (2005)	Czech Telecommunication Office	Council for Radio and Television Broadcasting
Denmark (2004)	National IT and Telecom Agency	Radio and Television Board (Ministry of Culture)
Finland (2004)	Finnish Communications Regulatory Authority (FICORA)	
France (2003)	Autorité de Régulation des Communications électroniques et des postes	Conseil Supérieur de l'Audiovisuel
Germany (2004)	Regulatory Authority for Telecommunications and Posts	State media authorities, broadcasting councils
Greece (2005)	National Telecommunications and Post Commission, Greece	Ministry of Press and Mass Media
Hungary (2005)	National Communications Authority	National Radio and Television Commission
Iceland (2001)	Post and Telecom Administration	Broadcasting Commission (Útvaprsréttarnefnd)
Ireland (2005)	Commission for Communications Regulation	Broadcasting Commission of Ireland
Italy (2002)	Autorità per le Garanzie nelle Comunicazioni (AGCOM)	
Japan (2004)	Ministry of Internal Affairs and Communications	
Korea (2003)	Korea Communications Commission	Korean Broadcasting Commission
Luxembourg (2004)	Institut Luxembourgeois de Régulation	Conseil National des Programmes
Mexico (2004)	Comisión Federal de Telecomunicaciones	Secretaría de Comunicaciones y Transportes

Netherlands (2004)	Onafhankelijke Post en Telecommunicatie Autoriteit	Commissariaat voor de Media
New Zealand (2004)	Commerce Commission	Broadcasting Standards Authority (Ministry for Culture and Heritage), Te Puni Kōkiri, Ministry of Economic Development
Norway (2004)	Norwegian Post and Telecommunications Authority	Mass Media Authority (Statens medieforvaltning)
Poland (2005)	Office of Telecommunications and Post Regulation	National Broadcasting Council
Portugal (2004)	National Communications Authority (Anacom)	
Slovak Republic (2005)	Telecommunication Office	Council for Broadcasting and Retransmission
Spain (2005)	Comisión del Mercado de las Telecomunicaciones	Ministerio de Ciencia y Tecnología, councils in Catalonia, Navarra
Sweden (2003)	National Post and Telecom Agency	Radio and TV Authority (licensing), Swedish Broadcasting Commission (content)
Switzerland (2005)	Office Fédéral de la Communication (Ofcom)	
Turkey (2005)	Telecommunications Authority	Radio and Television Supreme Council (RTÜK)
United Kingdom (2004)	Office of Communications (Ofcom)	
United States (2004)	Federal Communications Commission	

Note: [a] formed July 2005 from the ACA and the ABA

Sources: ITU World Telecommunication Regulatory Database, Leonardi (2004), European Audiovisual Observatory IRIS MERLIN database

Table 2.3: Sources of telecommunications regulatory authorities' budgets, in percentages

Country	Mobile licences	Licence fees	Government appropriation	Numbering fees	Spectrum fees	Contributions from regulated telecoms based on turnover	Regulatory fees	Fines, penalties	Financial income	Other
Australia (2004)										
Austria (2004)						70.5				29.5
Belgium (2003)	2	7		6	81					4
Canada (2005)							100			
Czech Republic (2005)			100							
Denmark (2004)			65							35
Finland (2004)		18		13	22					47, 34, 9, 4
France (2003)			100							
Germany (2004)			100							

	C1	C2	C3	C4	C5	C6	C7	C8
Greece (2005)	0.48		4.71	8.55	12.34	0.41	0.64	72.87
Hungary (2005)	1		12	56	13			18
Iceland (2001)	2, 19			44				35
Ireland (2005)	61							2, 4
Italy (2002)		60			30			
Japan (2004)					39			
Korea (2003)		100					1	
Luxembourg (2004)								
Mexico (2004)	35		10	41	0.2–0.3			14
Netherlands (2004)		100						
New Zealand (2004)				97				
Norway (2004)								
Poland (2005)		100						
Portugal (2004)	0.0014					0.0004	0.0007	2.9

Table 2.3 (cont.): Sources of telecommunications regulatory authorities' budgets, in percentages

Country	Mobile licences	Licence fees	Government appropriation	Numbering fees	Spectrum fees	Contributions from regulated telecoms based on turnover	Regulatory fees	Fines, penalties	Financial income	Other
Slovak Republic (2005)										
Spain (2005)			100			0.15				
Sweden (2003)	56		7			37				
Switzerland (2005)			100							
Turkey (2005)					88	9				3
United Kingdom (2004)	19		59			15				7
United States (2004)			3.6				96.4			

Source: ITU World Telecommunication Regulatory Database

and Maori. In federal Germany, responsibility for broadcasting is decentralised; public service broadcasters ZDF and ARD each have their own independent management council. The former's is composed exclusively of state representatives while the latter's also involves members of civil society (Leonardi, 2004).

Table 2.2's focus on national regulators should be qualified by noting 'a shift to self-regulation' arising partly from increasing technical complexity in the broadcasting sector (Leonardi, 2004). In practice, this involves higher-level authorities establishing general guidelines to be followed by independent lower-level bodies – often those responsible for the content itself. For example, the regulatory framework adopted by Australia in 1997 encouraged 'self-regulation . . . in all areas, including access, technical standards, interconnection standards, and consumer and customer service standards'. If self-regulation was not 'working effectively', government could intervene (Australian Communications and Media Authority, 2005). In the UK, the Internet Service Providers' Association (ISPA) and the Association for Television on Demand (ATVOD) are self-regulating.[5]

Outside the OECD, Buckingham, Bustani, Satola and Schwarz (2005) note that most poor countries that have yet to reform their communications sector use a 'PTT' office – for posts, telegraph and telecommunications. This tends to be a parastatal or state entity, that serves both to set policy and to provide services. Some of the exceptions to this rule were English-speaking Caribbean islands, which had given a private monopoly to Cable & Wireless.

Table 2.3 shows that funding for regulatory authorities is also diverse. The most common funding model is that in which the telecommunications regulator receives a majority of its budget from a direct government appropriation; this is the case for eleven OECD countries. The only other two countries receiving any direct appropriations, Sweden and the USA, receive very small sums.

The only funding source responsible for shares as high as direct government appropriations is regulatory fees. Canada's Radio-television and Telecommunications Commission (CRTC) and the USA's FCC both receive almost all their income this way; the FCC's share is estimated to have climbed to 99 per cent in 2005 (FCC, 2005). Austria's RTR receives all of its income directly from the organisations that it regulates, in this case as turnover-based fees. The income under 'other' refers to regulated broadcasters.

Other regulators report their revenues in a more disaggregated fashion. Belgium, Hungary, Portugal and Turkey depend on spectrum fees for the bulk of their income. This may grow in other countries as spectrum auctions gain popularity: the UK's Ofcom aims to allocate 70 per cent of its spectrum by market mechanisms by 2010, up from 6 per cent in 2004 (Foster, 2005).

In Sweden and Ireland, a majority of the regulator's budget comes from licence fees; Finland, Iceland and the UK each receive about a fifth of their income directly from licence fees. Other countries receive licence fees which are not indicated in the ITU database; these include Germany and Finland, whose FICORA received almost half its income as a refund for collecting television licence fees. (A further third came from domain name fees.)

Greece is unusual in receiving almost three-quarters of its income from previous years' reserves. Luxembourg's Institut Luxembourgeois receives a seventh of its income from energy and postal regulation.

To close this section, we present two measures of telecommunications regulation in the OECD. The first is constructed by editing the International Regulation Database.[6] The second is taken from the European Competitive Telecommunications Association (ECTA).

The OECD regulation database used a survey to produce sixteen low-level regulatory indicators, each ranging from 0 (least regulated) to 6 (most). These were then weighted to produce a single measure of product market regulation (PMR) with the same range (Conway, Janod and Nicoletti, 2005). We edit this to focus on telecommunications by removing information specific to other sectors. Thus, the result still reflects general product market regulation but has been purged of information specific to other sectors, especially the road freight and airline industries.

Table 2.4 displays the high-level indicators resulting from this modification. A plot of the original and modified PMR scores is depicted in Figure 2.1. The figure also includes the best-fit line, defined by

$$\text{mod} = (1.02 \times \text{PMR}) + 0.05$$

Thus, on the whole, the modified regulation score is higher than the original one. This suggests that telecommunications and broadcasting across the OECD are slightly more highly regulated than the economy as a whole. Further, as the coefficient on the original PMR indicator is just greater than 1, the modified score varies more than does the

Table 2.4: Modified high-level product market regulation indicators

	Product market regulation		Inward-oriented policies		Outward-oriented policies		Administrative regulation		Economic regulation	
	PMR	mod	PMR	mod	PMR	mod	PMR	mod	PMR	mod
Australia	0.9	1.3	0.9	1.1	0.9	1.5	1.0	1.2	0.9	1.3
Austria	1.4	1.6	1.8	2.0	0.8	1.1	1.9	1.5	1.5	2.1
Belgium	1.4	2.0	2.0	3.3	0.5	0.2	1.9	1.9	1.8	3.7
Canada	1.2	0.8	1.2	0.8	1.2	0.8	0.8	0.7	1.4	1.6
Czech Republic	1.7	2.2	2.2	2.8	1.1	1.2	2.4	2.4	2.0	3.4
Denmark	1.1	0.8	1.3	1.0	0.9	0.5	1.1	1.3	1.4	0.7
Finland	1.3	1.4	1.7	1.6	0.8	1.1	1.3	1.3	1.9	2.1
France	1.7	2.1	2.1	2.6	1.1	1.4	1.6	1.6	2.3	3.6
Germany	1.4	1.4	1.9	2.1	0.8	0.5	1.9	2.0	1.8	3.0
Greece	1.8	2.3	2.2	2.7	1.3	1.6	1.9	1.7	2.2	2.5
Hungary	2.0	2.1	2.4	2.4	1.5	1.7	1.5	1.4	2.7	3.1
Iceland	1.0	1.4	1.4	1.8	0.4	0.8	1.8	1.8	1.1	2.5
Ireland	1.1	1.4	1.4	2.2	0.6	0.2	1.1	1.3	1.5	1.3
Italy	1.9	1.0	2.3	1.2	1.3	0.7	1.6	1.5	2.6	1.3
Japan	1.3	2.0	1.5	2.5	1.0	1.4	1.7	1.5	1.4	2.1
Korea	1.5	1.0	1.7	1.0	1.3	1.0	1.8	1.8	1.6	0.7
Luxembourg	1.3	1.4	1.6	1.6	0.8	1.1	1.6	1.9	1.5	1.9
Mexico	2.2	1.8	2.1	1.8	2.3	1.8	2.0	1.7	2.1	1.6

Table 2.4 (cont.): Modified high-level product market regulation indicators

	Product market regulation		Inward-oriented policies		Outward-oriented policies		Administrative regulation		Economic regulation	
	PMR	mod	PMR	mod	PMR	mod	PMR	mod	PMR	mod
Netherlands	1.4	1.6	1.8	1.8	0.8	1.1	1.9	2.1	1.6	1.8
New Zealand	1.1	0.9	1.3	1.1	0.9	0.5	1.4	1.5	1.1	0.8
Norway	1.5	1.5	1.9	1.7	0.9	1.1	1.0	1.1	2.3	3.1
Poland	2.8	2.7	2.9	2.8	2.5	2.7	2.9	2.6	2.7	2.7
Portugal	1.6	1.5	2.0	1.8	0.9	1.2	1.5	1.4	2.2	3.2
Slovak Republic	1.4	1.7	1.3	1.4	1.5	2.1	1.5	1.4	1.1	1.9
Spain	1.6	1.6	2.1	2.3	0.9	0.7	2.0	1.8	2.1	1.7
Sweden	1.2	1.6	1.5	1.9	0.9	1.2	1.1	1.2	1.7	1.9
Switzerland	1.7	1.8	2.1	2.2	1.1	1.2	2.2	2.5	2.0	2.8
Turkey	2.3	3.0	2.6	3.7	1.8	1.9	3.0	3.0	2.1	3.7
United Kingdom	0.9	0.6	1.2	0.8	0.5	0.3	0.8	0.9	1.4	0.9
United States	1.0	0.5	1.2	0.7	0.8	0.2	1.1	1.1	1.3	0.5

Sources: OECD PMR (Conway, Janod and Nicoletti, 2005) and author's calculations

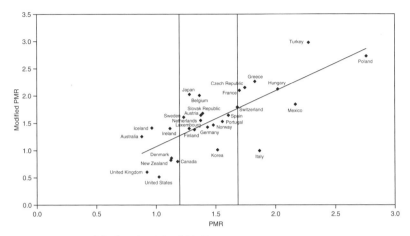

Figure 2.1. Modified and original PMR

original. Unsurprisingly, regulation in newer, high-technology sectors such as telecommunications and broadcasting seems to vary more than that in the economy as a whole.

The two vertical lines in Figure 2.1 roughly divide the countries into the 'relatively liberal', 'middle of the road' and 'relatively restrictive' groups identified by Conway et al. (2005). These are on the left, middle and right of the graph, respectively. The differences between these groups have decreased since 1998 when the data were first collected. Changes between 1998 and 2003 allowed Iceland to join the common law countries and Denmark among the 'relatively liberal'.

The second regulatory measure, provided by ECTA, was tailored to the telecommunications sector from the outset. It divided sixty-six criteria into five sections: 'general powers of the NRA, effectiveness of the dispute settlement body, application of access regulations, availability of key access products and implementation of the NRF' (ECTA, 2004). The ECTA's disadvantage is that it provides a measure for only ten European countries. Of these, the UK, Denmark and Ireland score highest.

2.3 Results of regulation: investment and access

Figure 2.2 displays the association between these two regulatory measures and per capita investment by public telecommunications

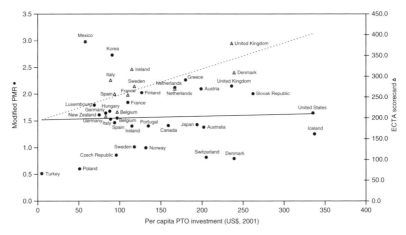

Figure 2.2. PTO investment and regulation

operators (PTOs) in 2001.[7] The solid circles plot the modified PMR measure while the hollow triangles plot the ECTA scorecard measure. The solid line is a best-fit line for the PMR measure and the dashed line for the ECTA measure. Thus, it may be seen that the general measure of product market regulation, even tailored as it is, trends only weakly with investment. Regressing the PMR measure, gross domestic product (GDP) per capita and population density on per capita investment shows all three regressors to be insignificant. Replacing the PMR measure with the ECTA measure reduces the sample to ten countries but makes the competition measure significant at the 5 per cent level and with the expected sign; adjusting for the number of regressors, these explanatory variables account for just over 60 per cent of the variance in investment.[8] As few of the countries in the sample are multi-lingual, we do not explore the role of a common language on investment.

Fostering competition while still allowing returns on the massive investments required to adopt new broadcasting technologies, such as digital, is not a trivial task. Thus, while Figure 2.2 shows that some countries seem to be doing this successfully, throughout Europe 'most of the digital platforms and thematic channels are still heavily loss-making', although concentration may reverse this (Lange, 2003).

Penetration of new technologies may be a more relevant outcome of regulatory effectiveness than is expenditure. Table 2.5 displays the

Table 2.5: Percentage of population subscribing to technologies

Country	Standard access lines (2001)	Dial-up internet (2001)	DSL lines (2002)	Cable TV (2001)	Cable modem internet (2002)	Other broadband (2002)	Widescreen (as per cent of TV households) (2001)
Australia	51.4	21.0	0.9	3.9	0.9	0.9	
Austria	35.7	17.0	2.2	15.4	4.0	3.6	5.9
Belgium	39.0	9.6	5.0	37.2	3.2	4.2	14.4
Canada	65.2	13.8	5.3	25.3	6.5	8.8	
Czech Republic	37.4	4.3	0.0	9.4	0.2	0.1	2.0
Denmark	51.7	33.3	5.7	20.1	2.5	4.5	2.3
Finland	54.0	17.0	4.4	19.2	1.0	1.3	3.1
France	53.8	10.8	2.4	5.7	0.5	1.0	11.3
Germany	37.2	15.7	3.9	26.5	0.1	2.4	5.5
Greece	52.8	3.3	0.0	0.0	–	0.0	2.2
Hungary	36.7	2.7	0.3	15.3	0.3	0.3	2.0
Iceland	49.2	55.3	8.3	1.8	–	3.7	
Ireland	41.4	15.6	0.1	16.0	0.1	0.0	2.9
Italy	38.8	13.7	1.5	0.2	–	0.7	2.8
Japan	40.1	16.7	4.4	10.2	1.5	2.2	
Korea	57.0	31.4	13.5	22.9	7.8	17.2	
Luxembourg	43.4	17.9	1.3	27.4	0.0	0.3	14.5
Mexico	13.9	2.0	0.1	2.5	0.2	0.0	

Table 2.5 (cont.): Percentage of population subscribing to technologies

Country	Standard access lines (2001)	Dial-up internet (2001)	DSL lines (2002)	Cable TV (2001)	Cable modem internet (2002)	Other broadband (2002)	Widescreen (as per cent of TV households) (2001)
Netherlands	42.4	21.7	2.2	38.8	5.0	3.4	17.1
New Zealand	45.8	16.0	1.4	0.7	0.1	0.7	
Norway	34.4	25.5	3.3	18.6	1.1	1.9	3.4
Poland	29.5	7.7	0.0	11.1	0.1	0.0	0.6
Portugal	35.4	17.2	0.5	11.1	2.1	1.0	5.1
Slovak Republic	28.9	1.9	–	13.5	0.0	0.0	0.6
Spain	43.3	7.9	2.4	1.4	0.6	1.2	5.3
Sweden	63.7	26.6	4.8	23.7	1.7	5.4	3.4
Switzerland	44.8	28.9	2.7	37.1	3.6	1.9	11.7
Turkey	27.6	4.9	0.0	1.3	0.0	0.0	
United Kingdom	53.0	22.1	1.0	6.0	1.3	0.6	15.2
United States	63.1	22.7	2.3	24.2	4.0	4.5	
OECD	45.6	15.8	2.6	14.3	2.0	2.9	

Sources: OECD DSTI/ICCP/TISP(2003)1/FINAL – http://www.oecd.org; OECD Telecommunications Database 2003; OMSYC, 'World Audiovisual Market' (2002)

Table 2.6: Explaining broadband subscription rates

	Coefficient	Standard error	t Stat	P-value
Modified PMR	−0.0607	0.0245	−2.48	0.0206
PTO investment/ capita ($US)	2.82×10^{-5}	1.73×10^{-4}	0.163	0.872
GDP/capita ($US)	-1×10^{-6}	1.31×10^{-6}	−0.802	0.430
Population density (cap/km^2)	3.28×10^{-4}	9.89×10^{-5}	3.31	0.00291
Heating degree days	2.16×10^{-5}	1.05×10^{-5}	2.06	0.0503
Constant	0.0741	0.0652	1.14	0.267
	$R^2 = 0.467$	adj. $R^2 = 0.356$	$F = 4.21$	Significance of F: 0.007

Source: World Resources Institute (heating degree days)

penetration of various technologies in the OECD. The first six columns indicate the number of subscribers as a fraction of the total population rather than the fraction of the population with access to a particular technology. The final column is normalised by television-owning households.

The top adopters of broadband are a mixed bag: Korea leads the pack with 39 per cent of its population subscribing to some form (DSL line, cable modem and 'other' broadband), followed by Canada (21 per cent), Denmark (13 per cent) and Sweden and Belgium (12 per cent each). Some of the factors associated with broadband adoption are indicated by the linear regression presented in Table 2.6.

The modified PMR indicator is now seen to be significant and of the expected sign: a one-unit decrease in a country's regulatory burden is associated with a 6 per cent increase in its broadband adoption rate. Due to the modified PMR measure's negative correlation with per capita investment in PTOs and per capita GDP (−0.46 in both cases), its inclusion leaves the income and expenditure measures insignificant in this regression. The significant positive sign on population density may be interpreted as a measure of returns to investment: a kilometre of cable connects more subscribers in a densely populated country. Practically, however, this effect is very small.

Table 2.7: Global distribution of Skype users

	Per cent of overall/ bn pop	Per cent of overall users
Israel	375.98	2.36
Taiwan	340.69	7.8
Denmark	318.46	1.73
Netherlands	211.49	3.47
Poland	203.70	7.87
Switzerland	189.60	1.42
Belgium	188.14	1.95
Sweden	179.96	1.62
France	92.65	5.62
Germany	73.48	6.06
Australia	70.18	1.41
Canada	67.67	2.22
Spain	61.10	2.64
United Kingdom	57.91	3.5
Italy	32.87	1.91
Brazil	31.43	5.85
United States	30.76	9.13
Japan	24.88	3.17
Turkey	22.82	1.59
China	5.17	6.75

Source: Euro Telcoblog, 12 April 2005

Heating degree days (HDD) are calculated by first determining how much colder (in °C) a daily average temperature is than 18°C and then summing over the whole year. Thus, colder countries have higher HDD scores. This too helps explain broadband uptake, although interpreting the effect is more complicated: a 365-degree increase in HDD is associated with just under a 1 per cent decrease in its broadband prevalence. However, increasing HDD by 365 degrees generally requires more than a 1°C daily temperature increase as temperature rises on days warmer than 18°C do not increase HDD. This effect seems consistent with harsh winters decreasing the – literal – outside option. While television viewing might also be expected to become more attractive as the weather became harsher, HDD is negatively correlated with average viewing across the OECD. Even so, there is some international evidence that viewing increases during cold seasons (CSM Media Research, 2001). Market research does suggest that broadband internet use and television viewing are substitutes (BBC, 2004).

Within Europe, broadband adoption has been the subject of concern since at least 2000, when the EU saw itself as falling behind the USA (McCormack, 2005, pp. 230–231).

As to widescreen television adoption in Europe, countries with a high level of 16:9 widescreen broadcasting output also have high levels of widescreen television ownership, and vice versa. The Netherlands, the UK, Belgium and Luxembourg all enjoy high adoption rates; in the first three cases this reflects pro-active policy by, largely, public service broadcasters to encourage adoption (Eurostrategies, 2004).

Finally, more recent technologies yet enjoy still different patterns of adoption. The global distribution of users of Skype, the voice-over-internet (VoIP) software, is displayed in Table 2.7. While adoption rates are positively correlated with 2001 broadband access, other factors are clearly also at work: the list's top two countries are famously 'high tech'; the advantages of free internet telephony depend on the cost of standard telephony. A feature of VoIP technology is that it requires no further infrastructure than that already provided for an internet connection, whether dial-up or broadband.

2.4 Conclusion

Lessons for students: what have we learned?

In spite of the size and maturity of some parts of the broadcasting industry, and the drive towards harmonisation within the EU, a single standard for broadcasting regulation has yet to arise. This is true even as regards competition policy: the communications sector is, on average, more heavily regulated than other sectors within the OECD, but also displays higher variance. While Buckingham and Williams (2005) argue that the EU approach to competition has become a *de facto* standard globally, the US federal model – with its divided jurisdictions – is an important alternative.

As regards content and access regulation, there is less international consensus on the appropriate criteria than there is for competition regulation. This lack of a shared normative framework and the rapidity of change in the sector make it unsurprising that a uniform regulatory model has yet to develop. By contrast, within the power sector in the OECD, an agreement on the goals of regulation is accompanied by a trend to using generic competition regulation, at least for large customers (Al-Sunaidy and Green, 2006).

Lessons for researchers: what do we still need to know?

One of the tasks for researchers in this area may be to help define the appropriate criteria for effective regulation. Can, for example, the relative merits of the US federal and the European Access Directive approaches be more precisely compared? How robust are the results suggested above about the importance of regulation for investment by telecoms operators and in explaining broadband and high-definition television penetration? Does the investment result hold on a larger set of countries? Do these results persist if the regulatory process is seen as endogenous? If these results are robust, what explains them? The chapters to follow outline yet more open questions for researchers.

Lessons for policymakers: what are the priorities for policy in this area?

Finally, policymakers should be aware that there is a real choice between regulatory models, with the jury still out on which better serves citizens. Further, even within the framework of EU directives, much scope remains for tailoring regulation. Finally, the absence of consensus on non-economic regulatory goals does not imply that a competitive sector is not a high priority. The results presented here suggest that a competition measure designed for the communications sector helps explain most of the variance in per capita investment by telecommunications operators, albeit in a small sample. Even the general-purpose competition measure helps explain the penetration of broadband. Thus, a more competitive economy will adopt new communications technologies more quickly – requiring vigilance from policymakers to ensure that their definitions of competition are not left behind by the rapid changes in this sector.

References

Al-Sunaidy, A. and R. Green (2006) 'Electricity deregulation in OECD countries', *Energy*, 31(6), 769–787.
Armstrong, M. and H. Weeds (2006) 'Public service broadcasting in the digital world', Chapter 4 of this volume.

Australian Communications and Media Authority (2005) 'The Australian telecommunications regulatory environment', http://www.acma.gov. au/ACMAINTER.2293898:STANDARD::pc=PC_1593, 6 August.

BBC (2004) 'Broadband challenges TV viewing', http://news.bbc.co.uk/1/hi/technology/4065047.stm, 3 December.

Buckingham, A., C. Bustani, D. Satola and T. Schwarz (2005) 'Telecommunications reform in developing countries', in I. Walden and J. Angel (eds.) *Telecommunications Law and Regulation*, 2nd edition, Oxford University Press.

Buckingham, A. and M. Williams (2005) 'Designing regulatory frameworks for developing countries', in I. Walden and J. Angel (eds.) *Telecommunications Law and Regulation*, 2nd edition, Oxford University Press.

Commission of the European Communities (2004) 'European Electronic Communications Regulation and Markets 2004', Tenth Implementation Report, SEC(2004)1535, 2 December.

Communications Committee (2005) 'Broadband access in the EU: situation at 1 January 2005', European Commission DG INFSO/B2, COCOM05-12 FINAL.

Conway, P., V. Janod and G. Nicoletti (2005) 'Product market regulation in OECD countries: 1998 to 2003', *OECD Economics Department Working Paper 419*, ECO/WKP(2005)6.

CSM Media Research (2001) 'TV in Korea and China over 2001', http://www.csm.com.cn/en/download/ratingchina05.html, 7 March.

European Competitive Telecommunications Association (2004) 'Regulatory scorecard: report on the relative effectiveness of the regulatory frameworks for electronic communications in Belgium, Denmark, France, Germany, Ireland, Italy, the Netherlands, Spain, Sweden and the United Kingdom', mimeo.

Eurostrategies (2004) 'Implementation of wide-screen and high definition television in the context of digital broadcasting', mimeo, 17 December.

Federal Communications Commission (2005) 'Regulatory fees', http://www.fcc.gov/fees/regfees.html, 8 February.

Foster, R. (2005) 'Competition and the public interest: a more transparent approach – a paper for the OECD/Ofcom Roundtable on Communications Convergence, 2 June 2005', http://www.oecd.org/dataoecd/16/10/34982282.pdf

Garzaniti, L. J. H. F. (2003) *Telecommunications, Broadcasting and the Internet: EU Competition Law and Regulation*, 2nd edition, Sweet and Maxwell.

Gibson, W. (1996) 'The William Gibson interview', *Playboy*, www.playboy.com/gibson/gibson.html; telephone interview.

Lange, A. (2003) 'The financial situation of the various branches of the European Union audiovisual industry', mimeo.

Leonardi, D. A. (2004) 'Self-regulation and the broadcast media: availability
and mechanisms for self-regulation in the broadcasting sector in countries of the EU', http://www.selfregulation.info/iapcoda/0405-broadcast-
report-dl.htm, 30 April.

McCormack, E. (2005) 'Access and interconnection', in I. Walden and
J. Angel (eds.) *Telecommunications Law and Regulation*, 2nd edition,
Oxford University Press.

Moussis, V., H. Ishida and Y. Shiroyama (2004) 'Japan: telecoms regulation
and competition rules', *Asia Pacific Antitrust Review 2004*, Global
Competition Review.

OMSYC (2002) 'World Audiovisual Market', http://www.omsyc.fr/index.html

Palzer, C. (2003) 'Co-regulation of the media in Europe: European provi-
sions for the establishment of co-regulation frameworks', in *IRIS Plus
Collection: Key Legal Questions for the Audiovisual Sector*, European
Audiovisual Laboratory, 8–15.

Schulz, W. (2004) 'Extending the access obligation to EPGs and service
platforms?', in *IRIS Special: Regulating Access to Digital Television:
Technical Bottlenecks, Vertically-integrated Markets and New Forms of
Media Concentration*, European Audiovisual Laboratory, 47–58.

Speta, J. (2004). 'Vertical regulation in digital television: explaining why the
United States has no Access Directive', in *IRIS Special: Regulating
Access to Digital Television: Technical Bottlenecks, Vertically-integrated
Markets and New Forms of Media Concentration*, European
Audiovisual Laboratory, 69–78.

Umino, A. (2003) 'Developments in local loop unbundling', OECD *Working
Paper on Telecommunication and Information Service Policies*, DSTI/
ICCP/TISP(2002)5/FINAL.

Walden, I. (2005a) 'Telecommunications law and regulation: an introduction', in I. Walden and J. Angel (eds.) *Telecommunications Law and
Regulation*, 2nd edition, Oxford University Press.

Walden, I. (2005b) 'European Union communications law', in I. Walden and
J. Angel (eds.) *Telecommunications Law and Regulation*, 2nd edition,
Oxford University Press.

World Trade Organisation (2004) 'Korea: trade policy review', WT/TPR/
S/137.

Appendix 2.1: Editing the product market regulation (PMR) database

We use ten of the sixteen low-level indicators without modification (see
Table 2.8). One, a measure of administrative burden in the road freight
and retail distribution industries, we delete as irrelevant. We also delete

the measures specific to other sectors from the 'use of command and control regulation' and 'price controls' indicators, scaling up the remaining questions proportionately. As no OECD country is recorded as maintaining price controls in the telecommunications sector, this measure becomes unable to explain variance in adoption of new technology within the OECD.

In the original dataset, the 'scope of public enterprise sector' and the 'legal barriers to entry' indicators average over a number of sectors. As that of most relevance to this study is ISIC (Rev 3.1) 642, which covers telecommunications (including broadcasting, but not the production of radio or TV programmes), we exclude the others, reducing this indicator to a dummy variable.

We modify the 'foreign ownership barriers' indicator in two steps. First, we have inferred weights and rescaling in cases in which the PMR dataset contains qualified information without explaining how it is to be scored. This yields an interim indicator. Second, we exclude the airline sector, producing our final indicator.

France and Spain have ownership caps in the telecommunications sector that apply only to non-European investors. While PMR does not explain how it takes this into account, halving the value usually assigned to majority ownership restrictions in the airlines sector replicates their results. Thus, we follow this practice for France and Spain's ownership restrictions. Japan restricts foreign ownership only in NTT rather than in telecommunications more generally. Reducing by one the regulation score that would result were the restriction applied to the whole sector replicates the PMR results; we therefore do so as well. Countries whose governments do not have special voting rights ('golden shares') are not concerned by the question of whether those rights can be exercised in the event of share purchases by foreigners; these countries receive a zero score. The above allows us to produce our interim indicator of foreign ownership regulation; this matches the PMR measure in sixteen of the thirty countries and exceeds the PMR measure by between 0.2 and 0.5 in the remaining fourteen.

Finally, we remove the airlines measure for the 'foreign ownership barriers' indicator by scaling up the remaining questions and replacing the government ownership weight with the 'scope of government ownership' dummy mentioned above.

To form the medium- and higher-level indicators PMR derived weights using principal components analysis (see Table 2.9). While the

Table 2.8: Low-level product market regulation indicators

	State control							Barriers to entrepreneu
	Scope of public enterprise sector		Size of public enterprise sector	Direct control over business enterprise	Use of command and control regulation		Price controls		Licence and permits system	Communicat and simplific of rules and procedures
	PMR	mod			PMR	mod	PMR	mod		
Australia	2.8	6	0.1	0.0	0.4	0	0.0	0	2.0	0.2
Austria	3.5	6	4.0	0.0	2.2	3	1.3	0	0.0	0.5
Belgium	1.8	6	3.3	1.5	4.5	6	1.0	0	4.0	0.3
Canada	2.8	0	2.1	0.8	1.3	0	2.0	0	0.0	1.0
Czech Republic	3.8	6	3.2	2.3	2.3	3	1.3	0	4.0	0.5
Denmark	2.5	0	2.3	0.8	1.4	0	0.0	0	4.0	0.0
Finland	3.5	6	3.2	2.9	1.4	0	0.3	0	2.0	0.3
France	4.5	6	4.1	1.9	3.0	3	0.3	0	2.0	0.3
Germany	3.3	6	3.2	2.3	1.8	0	0.5	0	4.0	0.3
Greece	3.0	6	3.8	0.9	5.1	6	2.3	0	0.0	1.1
Hungary	3.5	6	3.0	4.8	2.3	3	2.0	0	0.0	0.5
Iceland	2.3	6	2.8	0.7	0.0	0	0.3	0	4.0	0.7
Ireland	2.5	0	2.6	0.8	3.8	6	0.8	0	4.0	0.2
Italy	4.5	0	3.7	3.5	1.9	0	2.0	0	0.0	0.5
Japan	2.0	6	0.0	0.6	3.0	6	2.5	0	2.0	0.3
Korea	2.0	0	2.8	1.0	1.1	0	2.0	0	2.0	0.0
Luxembourg	3.5	6	1.2	2.9	1.5	0	0.0	0	2.0	0.0
Mexico	3.0	0	3.6	0.9	1.7	3	1.0	0	0.0	0.3
Netherlands	2.8	6	2.8	2.0	1.7	0	0.3	0	4.0	0.9
New Zealand	2.3	0	0.8	2.6	0.8	0	0.0	0	4.0	0.3
Norway	4.8	6	4.0	2.4	2.2	0	0.8	0	2.0	0.2
Poland	5.8	6	4.6	3.0	3.5	3	1.6	0	2.0	0.8
Portugal	3.8	6	1.7	3.8	2.0	0	1.8	0	0.0	2.6
Slovak Republic	1.6	6	0.0	3.5	0.0	0	0.4	0	0.0	1.4
Spain	3.5	0	2.5	2.3	4.4	6	0.8	0	0.0	0.6
Sweden	3.7	6	2.7	0.7	2.3	3	1.0	0	2.0	0.0
Switzerland	3.8	6	0.9	2.6	1.2	0	2.6	0	6.0	0.0
Turkey	4.8	6	4.3	1.0	4.4	6	0.6	0	6.0	0.5
United Kingdom	0.8	0	1.6	2.9	2.3	0	0.4	0	2.0	0.2
United States	2.5	0	0.6	0.8	1.5	0	0.8	0	2.0	0.4

* = estimated indicator due to too many missing data points

ministrative dens for poration	Administrative burdens for sole proprietor firms	Legal barriers		Antitrust	Outward-oriented policies				
					Foreign ownership barriers		Discriminatory	Regulatory barriers	Tariffs
		PMR	mod		PMR	mod	exemptions	procedures	
1.3	1.3	1.6	0	1.5	2.4	4.0	0.0	0.0	1.0
3.0	2.5	0.3	0	1.0	1.5	2.7	0.3	0.0	1.0
1.8	1.5	1.6	6	0.0	0.3	0.0	0.0	0.0	1.0
0.8	1.3	0.9	6	0.6	2.9	1.7	0.5	0.0	1.0
3.0	2.0	1.4	6	0.0	2.0	2.7	0.7	0.0	1.0
1.0	0.0	1.4	0	1.9	1.2	0.0	0.5	0.7	1.0
1.3	1.8	1.4	0	0.0	1.5	2.7	0.0	0.0	1.0
2.0	2.0	2.2	6	1.1	2.3	3.5	0.5	0.0	1.0
2.3	1.3	1.4	6	0.0	0.3	0.0	0.7	0.7	1.0
2.3	3.3	1.6	0	0.0	1.3	2.7	2.0	0.7	1.0
2.3	3.0	1.6	0	0.9	1.9	2.7	1.2	0.0	3.0
1.3	1.3*	2.3	6	0.0	1.1	2.7	0.0	0.0	0.0
0.8	0.3	0.9	0	0.0	1.2	0.0	0.0	0.0	1.0
2.8	2.8	1.9	0	0.0	2.8	1.3	0.7	0.0	1.0
1.5	2.3*	1.4	0	0.3	2.4	3.7	0.3	0.0	1.0
2.7	2.3	1.9	0	0.6	2.2	1.0	0.0	0.0	3.0
2.5	3.0	0.3	0	0.0	1.5	2.7	0.3	0.0	1.0
3.3	3.3	1.9	0	3.5	2.8	1.0	1.4	0.0	6.0
2.0	1.3	1.9	0	0.0	1.2	2.7	0.5	0.0	1.0
1.0	0.8	0.3	0	0.4	2.3	1.0	0.0	0.0	1.0
1.0	1.0	2.2	6	0.0	1.9	2.7	0.3	0.7	0.0
4.3	3.3	0.6	0	0.0	3.7	4.0	0.3	1.6	4.0
1.5	1.8	1.4	6	0.0	1.6	2.7	0.7	0.0	1.0
2.0	2.3	0.6	0	0.0	2.3	4.0	1.1	1.6	1.0
2.8	4.0	1.1	0	0.0	0.8	0.7	0.3	0.7	1.0
1.0	1.8	2.0	0	0.0	1.5	2.7	0.7	0.0	1.0
2.3	1.8	2.2	6	0.0	2.0	2.7	1.1	0.0	1.0
2.3	3.0	1.4	6	0.0	3.1	3.7	0.7	0.0	3.0
0.8	0.5	1.4	0	0.0	0.3	0.0	0.3	0.0	1.0
0.8	1.3	1.4	0	1.6	1.8	0.0	0.0	0.0	1.0

Table 2.9: Medium-level product market regulation indicators

| | Domain | | Sub-domain | | Sub-domain | | Domain | | Sub-domain | | Sub-domain | | Sub-domain | | Domain | | Sub-domain | | Sub-domain | |
| | State control | | Public ownership | | Involvement in business operation | | Barriers to entrepreneurship | | Administrative burdens on startups | | Regulatory and administrative opacity | | Barriers to competition | | Barriers to trade and investment | | Explicit barriers to trade and investment | | Other barriers | |
	PMR	mod	PMR	mod	PMR	mod	PMR	mod	PMR	mod	PMR	mod	PMR	mod	PMR	mod	PMR	mod	PMR	mod
Australia	0.6	1.0	0.8	1.8	0.3	0.0	1.1	1.2	1.0	1.3	1.2	1.2	1.5	1.1	0.9	1.5	1.4	2.1	0.2	0.0
Austria	1.9	3.0	2.2	3.0	1.6	3.0	1.6	1.1	2.8	2.8	0.4	0.2	0.8	0.7	0.7	1.1	1.0	1.6	0.2	0.0
Belgium	2.4	4.5	2.2	3.4	2.6	6.0	1.6	2.0	1.7	1.6	2.2	2.3	0.6	1.8	0.3	0.2	0.5	0.3	0.1	0.0
Canada	1.7	0.5	1.7	1.0	1.5	0.0	0.8	1.0	0.9	1.0	0.5	0.5	0.7	2.2	1.1	0.8	1.7	1.2	0.4	0.0
Czech Republic	2.5	3.4	3.0	3.7	1.9	3.0	1.9	2.3	2.3	2.6	2.3	2.4	0.5	1.8	0.9	1.2	1.4	1.7	0.3	0.0
Denmark	1.3	0.5	1.7	1.0	0.8	0.0	1.2	1.5	0.5	0.6	2.1	2.2	1.7	1.3	0.8	0.5	1.0	0.4	0.7	0.7
Finland	2.3	2.2	3.2	3.9	1.3	0.0	1.1	1.0	1.3	1.5	1.2	1.2	0.4	0.0	0.6	1.1	1.0	1.5	0.2	0.0
France	2.7	3.4	3.3	3.8	1.9	3.0	1.6	1.8	1.9	2.0	1.3	1.2	1.4	2.6	1.0	1.4	1.5	2.0	0.3	0.0
Germany	2.2	2.0	2.8	3.7	1.5	0.0	1.6	2.1	1.6	1.8	2.2	2.3	0.5	1.8	0.6	0.5	0.6	0.5	0.7	0.7
Greece	2.0	4.5	2.4	3.3	3.3	6.0	1.6	1.0	2.6	2.7	0.6	0.5	0.5	0.0	1.2	1.6	1.4	2.0	1.0	0.7
Hungary	3.3	3.9	3.8	4.6	2.6	3.0	1.4	1.0	2.3	2.6	0.4	0.2	1.1	0.6	1.4	1.7	2.1	2.4	0.6	0.0
Iceland	1.1	1.6	1.8	2.9	0.3	0.0	1.6	2.0	1.4	1.3	2.4	2.5	0.7	1.8	0.3	0.8	0.5	1.2	0.1	0.0
Ireland	2.0	3.2	1.8	1.1	2.1	6.0	0.9	1.2	0.5	0.5	2.1	2.3	0.3	0.0	0.5	0.2	0.8	0.3	0.2	0.0
Italy	3.2	1.4	3.8	2.5	2.3	0.0	1.4	0.9	2.4	2.8	0.4	0.2	0.6	0.0	1.1	0.7	1.7	1.1	0.4	0.0
Japan	1.5	3.8	0.8	2.0	2.4	6.0	1.4	1.2	1.9	1.8	1.2	1.2	0.6	0.2	0.9	1.4	1.4	2.0	0.3	0.0

Korea	1.7	0.7	1.8	1.2	1.5	0.0	1.7	1.4	2.2	2.5	1.2	1.1	1.0	0.4	1.3	1.0	1.9	1.4	0.4	0.0
Luxembourg	2.0	1.9	2.6	3.3	1.2	0.0	1.2	1.3	1.8	2.7	1.1	1.1	0.1	0.0	0.7	1.1	1.1	1.6	0.2	0.0
Mexico	1.9	2.1	2.3	1.4	1.4	3.0	2.2	1.6	3.1	3.3	0.4	0.1	2.9	2.4	2.4	1.8	3.4	2.6	1.0	0.0
Netherlands	1.9	1.9	2.5	3.5	1.2	0.0	1.6	1.7	1.6	1.7	2.5	2.6	0.6	0.0	0.7	1.1	1.0	1.6	0.3	0.0
New Zealand	1.4	0.7	1.9	1.3	0.8	0.0	1.2	1.5	0.8	0.9	2.2	2.3	0.4	0.3	0.8	0.5	1.3	0.8	0.2	0.0
Norway	2.8	2.2	3.5	4.0	1.8	0.0	1.0	1.3	1.0	1.0	1.2	1.2	0.6	1.8	0.8	1.1	0.9	1.3	0.6	0.7
Poland	3.6	3.8	4.2	4.4	2.8	3.0	2.3	1.8	3.7	3.8	1.5	1.4	0.3	0.0	2.4	2.7	3.0	3.1	1.7	1.6
Portugal	2.7	2.1	3.1	3.8	2.2	0.0	1.3	1.4	1.7	1.6	1.2	1.2	0.5	1.8	0.8	1.2	1.2	1.7	0.3	0.0
Slovak Republic	1.4	1.8	1.9	3.2	0.8	0.0	1.2	0.9	1.9	2.1	0.7	0.6	0.3	0.0	1.6	2.1	1.6	2.4	1.5	1.6
Spain	2.7	3.6	2.7	1.7	2.7	6.0	1.6	1.1	2.8	3.3	0.4	0.3	0.4	0.0	0.7	0.7	0.7	0.7	0.6	0.7
Sweden	1.9	2.9	2.2	2.9	1.6	3.0	1.1	0.9	1.2	1.3	1.1	1.1	0.6	0.0	0.8	1.2	1.2	1.7	0.3	0.0
Switzerland	2.2	1.7	2.4	3.1	2.1	0.0	1.9	2.6	1.7	2.0	3.1	3.3	0.7	1.8	1.0	1.2	1.5	1.8	0.4	0.0
Turkey	2.8	4.6	3.1	3.5	2.5	6.0	2.5	2.9	2.7	2.6	3.4	3.5	0.5	1.8	1.7	1.9	2.5	2.7	0.6	0.0
United Kingdom	1.7	0.9	1.9	1.6	1.6	0.0	0.8	0.8	0.7	0.6	1.2	1.2	0.4	0.0	0.4	0.3	0.5	0.4	0.2	0.0
United States	1.2	0.3	1.2	0.5	1.2	0.0	1.2	1.2	1.0	1.0	1.3	1.3	1.5	1.1	0.7	0.2	1.1	0.3	0.2	0.0

modified data presented here are a subset of the PMR dataset, we nevertheless use its weights when possible; this facilitates both calculation and comparability. Exceptions to this rule are as follows. First, as there is no variation in the modified 'price controls' low-level indicator, we give all the weight in the 'involvement in business operation' measure to the remaining low-level indicator. Second, as we have deleted the low-level sector-specific administrative burden indicator, we maintain the relative weights on the remaining two components of the medium-level 'administrative burdens on startups' indicator.

The summary measures of 'economic regulation' and 'administrative regulation' are also formed by adopting the PMR weights and rescaling to compensate for omitted low-level indicators.

Notes

* The author thanks Rob Elliott, Esperanza C. Magpantay, Becket McGrath, Paul Seabright and Helen Weeds for generously sharing their time and expertise.
1. In May 2005, Australia issued content codes applying classifications from film and computer games to mobile phone content as well.
2. Unless otherwise specified, our discussion of EU regulation relies on Garzaniti (2003).
3. See Garzaniti (2003), Chapter II.
4. In September 2004, the English name of the Ministry of Public Management, Home Affairs, Posts and Telecommunications was changed to the MIC.
5. The term 'co-regulation' is also used (Palzer, 2003).
6. See Appendix 2.1 for details.
7. A public telecommunications operator is public in the sense of being licensed to offer services to the public.
8. ECTA reports that the fit is best for investment as a share of gross fixed capital formation, 90 per cent of which is explained by scorecard performance and the inflation rate.

PART II

Questions of principle in broadcasting regulation

3 | Competition and market power in broadcasting: where are the rents?

PAUL SEABRIGHT AND HELEN WEEDS*

3.1 Introduction

This chapter considers where the scarce assets are located in the broadcasting sector and what are the lessons for public interventions to prevent the abuse of market power. It focuses on what makes broadcasting different from other sectors and on the way in which recent technological advances such as digitisation may be changing the nature and distribution of scarcity rents.

It considers two hypotheses in particular: first, that falls in the cost of reproducing and transmitting information have greatly reduced entry barriers in broadcasting, meaning that market power is less of a concern, and second, that rents in broadcasting will increasingly come from control of scarce content rather than from control over means of transmission. Both hypotheses contain elements of truth but the situation is more complex than either implies on its own. The chapter goes on to look at a number of challenges for competition policy, including such issues as market definition, exclusionary practices and bundling, matters that have been brought to the fore in recent antitrust developments. It suggests that the risks attendant on these practices may be somewhat different from those that have traditionally been emphasised and proposes rules of thumb to help identify the circumstances under which they are most likely to lead to a consolidation of market power.

We begin with a summary of technological changes in broadcasting and an assessment of their impact on the nature of competition in broadcasting markets.

3.2 The changing nature of broadcasting

'Digitisation' is a broad term encompassing a number of technological changes. Replacing analogue signals with digital format economises on processing, storage and transmission capacity, reducing costs and expanding capabilities. The impact of digitisation is felt across the broadcasting industry, with the following developments:

- digital recording and production techniques;
- use of digital compression in transmission, alongside proliferation in transmission platforms (terrestrial, cable, satellite and broadband);
- digital set-top boxes and encryption technologies; and
- digital personal video recorders.

Digital production lowers the cost of recording and editing television content and permits major quality improvements. With video footage in digital format, scenes can be edited and modified using computer-aided imaging techniques; backgrounds can be altered easily and characters may even be created. Such modifications can be achieved more cheaply, and with better results, than using older production techniques. Moreover, digital video equipment is relatively inexpensive, assisting the growth of small, independent movie producers. Digital recording and transmission, including the use of satellite video links, improves the speed and quality of news gathering and sports reporting. Other things being equal, digitisation reduces the cost of programme production – although in recent years greater spending on special effects and higher costs of certain content rights (e.g. popular sports) may have offset this trend.

Digital compression allows many more channels to be transmitted for a given bandwidth allocation, reducing the unit cost of transmission. With analogue technology, limited transmission capacity (resulting from the scarcity of spectrum or other transmission media) constrains the number of channels that can be broadcast. By allowing much more information to be transmitted over a given bandwidth, digital format greatly increases the number of channels that can be broadcast: digital terrestrial transmission (DTT) supports several dozen channels, while digital satellite and cable platforms can support hundreds. Alongside this development, the number of transmission platforms available to viewers has proliferated with the rollout of satellite and cable (where this did not previously exist) and the growth in broadband connections.[1]

With the distribution of digital set-top boxes containing decoder slots, encrypted television signals can be used, overcoming the non-excludability property of traditional broadcasting. Viewers can then be charged directly for watching television, by means of subscription or pay-per-view. Sophisticated charging schemes, such as channel bundling and tiering, may be tailored to viewer demands, boosting subscription and increasing revenues.[2] With viewer charging, broadcasters show programmes that match the viewers' desires rather than maximising the audience available to advertisers and sponsors. Although pay-TV might not be used for all programmes – it may remain desirable for some material to be provided free-to-air – it is likely to be the dominant model for highly valued, 'premium' programming such as movies and popular sports.

Digital personal video recorders (PVRs) such as TiVo and the Sky+ box give viewers far greater control over their viewing than older video recorders did. As well as recording huge quantities of programming, PVRs allow the viewer to pause and rewind live TV and to skip unwanted material such as advertising. Although uptake of PVRs is low at present, as their use becomes widespread this development has two important implications. First, viewer avoidance behaviour is likely to undermine advertising as a dominant source of revenue, increasing the trend towards pay-TV. This does not mean that advertising will disappear entirely, however: broadcasters are likely to find that viewers are prepared to watch some advertisements if these are sufficiently entertaining or if they are sufficiently unobtrusive, as with product placement. But it will change the exclusive dependence on advertiser revenues that has been the dominant broadcasting model up to now. Second, greater time-shifting ability increases the degree of competition between programmes shown at different times, replacing head-to-head competition between contemporaneous channels.[3]

In analogue broadcasting, transmission capacity forms a major barrier to entry. Most viewers have access to a single transmission platform, which has limited capacity. The number of channels is restricted by spectrum availability, with commercial broadcasters earning large scarcity rents as programme revenues (typically from the sale of advertising airtime) far exceeding costs. Depending on national broadcasting regulation and spectrum licensing policies, rents do not always appear as excess profit: broadcasters may be required to meet costly public service obligations, implicitly funded out of spectrum rents, or rents may be extracted through licence fees levied on broadcasters for their use of spectrum.[4] Moreover, if the available transmission capacity is controlled by a small number of operators (perhaps even a single broadcaster), competition will be weak.[5] Exploitation may then occur upstream, where buyer power results in low prices for content producers, and downstream, where monopolisation of output markets leads to high prices and poor service to consumers (both viewers and advertisers). With digital transmission, however, spectrum constraints on the number of channels are effectively removed and scarcity rents are eliminated. Existing transmission capacity is sufficient to meet demands (at current and anticipated future levels) and there is a strong incentive to utilise spare capacity that militates against using access to transmission as a barrier to entry.

This discussion would seem to imply that following digitisation, barriers to entry are eliminated and competition concerns fall away. However, other parts of the broadcasting value chain must also be considered before such a conclusion can be drawn. In particular, it is unclear how the economics of programme production are affected by digitisation. Although film recording and processing costs are reduced, production involves a number of other inputs – and in these areas expenditure may rise. Costs may be endogenous: for example, producers can decide how much to spend on high-quality locations and special effects, with more authentic sets and spectacular effects raising costs substantially. If producers compete by raising quality and spending more on special effects, total production costs may not fall by as much as would be implied by the fall in filming costs *per se* and might even rise, and entry may be correspondingly reduced.[6]

In addition, the cost of premium content rights and talents, such as popular sports events and top movie stars, is determined by economic processes that are affected by industry structure and technology. Alongside the growth in multi-channel television, the price of key broadcasting content – for example the right to televise live Premier League football matches in the UK – has increased dramatically. If rights acquisition is included in the cost of programming, total expenditure has increased significantly in these premium niches. Moreover, if key content rights are scarce, these rather than transmission capacity accrue scarcity rents and become potential sources of market power.[7] If so, competition concerns in the industry do not fall away but simply change in their origin and nature, raising new and different issues for regulators. To assess this question, the next section addresses the economics of content creation and the impact of digitisation on this process.

3.3 Content, superstars and the impact of digitisation

If the scarcity of means of production and transmission of information is being rapidly overcome due to digitisation, what can be said of the scarcity of content? Two very different views have been expressed about the impact of digitisation on content creation. One is that content is becoming more abundant as it becomes easier to create and transmit, so that rents to scarce content are falling. The scarcity is rather on the side of viewers, listeners and readers, who are submerged in content, not all of which they want and which they are increasingly able to avoid – as a consequence of this, advertisers find it more and more difficult to gain viewer attention.[8] Furthermore, it is becoming easier for viewers with niche interests to find content that corresponds to their preferences, since falling costs of worldwide transmission mean that a film or programme can reach more easily the critical mass of viewers that makes it economically viable.

The second view is that digitisation, far from reducing rents to scarce content, is increasing them, a development attested by the rising real prices paid for such premium content as top-flight football broadcasting rights. For example, annual payments for live rights to Premier League football matches in the UK rose from £38.3 million over the period 1992–1997 to £167.5 million in 1997–2001 and £370 million in 2001–2004 – almost a ten-fold increase – although annual payments for 2004–2007 are slightly lower at £341 million and cover a larger number of matches. Relatedly, certain kinds of popular programme are growing to dominate broadcasting markets at the expense of less popular but arguably higher-quality programmes. Hollywood and Bollywood movies are driving out arthouse movies and those in languages other than English and Hindi; *Big Brother* and other reality-TV shows are not only taking vast audiences but are spawning copy-cat initiatives that further reduce the variety of available programmes. Bestsellers are driving quality books off the shelves and superstars – bland and omnipresent – are driving out mere stars.

Which of these two views is more accurate? The first thing to note is that they are not in fact incompatible. Indeed, it is quite possible that there are more types of content available in total than ever before and simultaneously that viewer attention is more concentrated upon a narrow range of content types than before. For these things both to be true would require only that the viewers' attention be increasingly skewed towards a small subset of the types of available content, so that the increasing numbers of content types are available but all except a very few of these have to share a decreasing proportion of total viewers (or, strictly speaking, of viewer time). Likewise, it is possible for the rents to some kinds of premium content to be increasing while the rents to the remaining kinds are falling: all this means is that the distribution of rents is becoming more skewed over time.

Evidence on this is patchy and hard to evaluate on a consistent basis, though this possibility seems consistent with at least the bulk of the anecdotal evidence. Robert Frank describes the process in his book *Luxury Fever*:

> Winner-take-all markets have proliferated in part because technology has greatly extended the power and reach of the planet's most gifted performers. At the turn of the century, when the state of Iowa alone had more than 1,300 opera houses, thousands of tenors earned adequate if modest livings performing before live audiences. Now that most music we listen to is prerecorded, however, the world's best tenor can be literally everywhere at once. And since it costs no more to stamp out compact disks from Luciano Pavarotti's master recording than from a less renowned tenor's most of us now listen to Pavarotti. Millions of us are each willing to pay a little extra to hear him rather than other singers who are only marginally less able or well known; and this explains why Pavarotti earns several millions of dollars a year even as most other tenors, many of them nearly as talented, struggle to get by.[9]

Can we say anything systematic about the economic mechanisms involved? Several different economic models explain some of these developments, though there is as yet, to our knowledge, no encompassing model that can explain them all. The first and best-known model is that developed by Sherwin Rosen (1981) in 'The economics of superstars'. This is a model of vertical differentiation between producers – that is, producers are located along a continuous measure of quality or 'talent' and all consumers agree as to their ranking by this measure. Both price and the amount sold at that price are functions of a producer's talent, with the more talented selling more in equilibrium even though their price is higher. Indeed, it is the fact that price and quantity sold can both be increasing in talent that gives rise to the potential skewness of revenue as a function of talent, whereby small differences in talent are magnified into large differences in income. For instance, if both price and quantity sold are linear, then revenue is a quadratic function of talent.

This result is due to a property of imperfect substitutability in preferences: low talent is an imperfect substitute for high talent. Thus a viewer who might wish to watch a high-quality programme but finds the price too great would not be consoled with the offer of three lower-quality programmes instead. Technically this is ensured by assuming a fixed cost of consuming each unit of consumption (this can be interpreted as the time that has to be devoted to watching each programme). On its own this is enough to yield skewness in revenues, though it does not by itself explain the concentration of output in the hands of a few sellers. This comes from an assumption about technology, namely that there are economies of scale in production. If the technology were one of pure public good production, with zero marginal cost, then in equilibrium only one seller would serve the entire market.

So, to capture greater realism, Rosen supposes that there are sources of positive (and increasing) marginal cost even while average costs of production fall with scale. The first source is an internal diseconomy: there are costs to the seller of producing higher output. The second is an external diseconomy: the quality of the service produced by the seller declines (as perceived by the buyer) when more units are sold. Rosen uses as an example a famous opera singer giving a concert in a football stadium: this is bound to be of lower quality than in a concert hall. This decline in quality compensates for the fact that low-quality producers are otherwise unable to produce substitutes for high-quality output. However, Rosen assumes the decline in the quality of the output with quantity is smaller when the output is of higher quality (a high-talent opera singer is less challenged by singing in the Yankee Stadium than one of lesser talent would be), so that in equilibrium low- and high-quality output substitute for each other only at greatly asymmetric levels of output. These assumptions together ensure that sellers of higher talent charge only slightly higher prices than those of lower talent, but sell much larger quantities; their greater earnings come overwhelmingly from selling larger quantities rather than from charging higher prices.

The model has interesting and intuitive comparative-static properties, beginning with the fact that increases in demand (or in the size of the overall market) tend to raise incomes but do so proportionately more for high-talent producers. Reductions in internal and external diseconomies tend to reduce prices, which makes consumers better off but has ambiguous effects on sellers' incomes, these being positive if demand for the service is sufficiently elastic. However, the distribution of rents between sellers is highly sensitive to whether the reductions in internal or external economies are more important. If it is mainly internal economies, low-talent sellers benefit and more sellers enter the market. If it is predominantly external economies, high-talent sellers become even more dominant and some low-talent sellers can even exit.

Applying the Rosen model to broadcasting, the fact that programmes are typically bundled into channels, and channels into larger packages, means that prices for individual programmes or genres cannot generally be observed. However, the hypothesis that the higher return to talent results much more from a quantity than from a price effect can be tested by examining relative values and audience sizes for programmes of different qualities. In the UK, both Premier League (top division) and Football League (lower divisions) football matches are broadcast live on the Sky Sports channels and thus have the same potential audience. At the time of writing, payments per live match are around £2.5 million and £0.3 million for Premier League and Football League respectively – an eight-fold difference – while viewing figures differ by a factor of between three and four.[10] Thus the greater earnings of the Premier League are partly, but not entirely, accounted for by higher consumption; the implicit price paid per viewer for Premier League matches is at least double that for the lower divisions.

Moreover, as a representation of broadcasting markets the Rosen model is not entirely suitable. There are three main respects in which the fit is imperfect. First of all, the significance of both external and internal diseconomies seems negligible in broadcasting. The quality of the broadcast perceived by the ten millionth viewer is surely no lower than that perceived by the millionth viewer (so no external diseconomies), while the technical cost of broadcasting to the ten millionth is surely no higher (so no internal diseconomies). In fact, broadcasting appears to display something close to a pure public goods production technology (though it differs from the case of pure public goods by being able to exclude non-paying consumers through encryption technology). Yet, though there is striking concentration in production, it is far from being dominated by a single producer.

The explanation lies in the second way in which the model fails to fit the circumstances of broadcasting. This is that consumer preferences involve a great deal of variety in tastes, covering a range of genres including news and current affairs, drama, movies, comedy, arts and sport – what industrial economists call 'horizontal' rather than 'vertical' product differentiation. Technically, products are vertically differentiated if, at identical prices, all consumers can agree which they prefer and variety persists in equilibrium only because consumers find they can afford different levels of quality. Products are horizontally differentiated, in contrast, when different consumers would make different choices even in the absence of any difference in price – some like classical music, some prefer rock. The impact of technical changes such as digitisation on market concentration will depend importantly on the relative significance of these two types of differentiation in broadcast programmes. In the presence of vertical differentiation, cost reductions create a strong tendency towards market concentration to the extent that they enable sellers to produce at higher quality without a significant increase in price. But in the presence of horizontal differentiation, cost reductions allow new entrants into the market to offer services that more closely match the preferences of particular niches of viewers. The latter is the conclusion of the well-known model of Steven Salop (1979), for instance.

A third important feature of broadcasting markets that is not adequately captured by the Rosen model is that quality is not just a matter of talent. As we discussed in Section 3.2, it is also a matter of investment – of the amount that producers spend.[11] They may spend to improve programme quality partly by paying directly for more attractive content (better writers and actors, or broadcast rights to more popular films and sporting events) and partly by investing in expensive techniques such as special effects, location shooting, larger networks of correspondents for news gathering and so on. The important thing about such investments is that they typically add to the fixed costs of programme making and so are more attractive the larger the audience the programme can expect to attract. For this reason, reductions in the cost of reaching additional viewers that increase potential audience size – such as when more people take up cable or broadband – may thereby lead to increases in endogenous *fixed* costs, thus increasing market concentration (or causing it to fall by less than might otherwise be expected). Furthermore, this may be true even in the presence of horizontal differentiation, thereby complicating the effects shown in the Salop model.

In order to compare the effects of vertical and horizontal differentiation, and of the endogenous character of product quality due to investment in programming, we present in Appendix 3.1 an extension of Salop's model. This allows for both vertical and horizontal product differentiation and allows the vertical dimension to depend endogenously on investment. The equilibrium number of firms in the market is determined by a free-entry (zero-profit) condition, on the assumption that firms position themselves at equal intervals around a unit circle representing the ideal preferences of viewers for horizontally differentiated programme types. The 'distance' of a consumer from any given producer can be interpreted as how different is the type of programme broadcast from the type that the viewer would ideally prefer: this distance imposes a reduction in utility that behaves analytically just like a transport cost.

In this model, we show that reductions in costs of programme making have an ambiguous effect on the number of firms in equilibrium and hence on variety, depending on whether they take the form of reductions in the exogenous fixed cost per programme or in the cost of investments in programme quality. The former tend to increase the number of firms (lower fixed costs raise the number of firms which can enter and still make non-negative profits), while the latter tend to lower the number of firms (since firms invest more in raising quality and therefore spend higher fixed costs overall). It is important to note, though, that variety and quality are inversely related in equilibrium: when variety increases, average quality declines and vice versa.

Furthermore, in this model reductions in variety increase not just quality but the overall utility of both average consumers and marginal consumers (the latter being those furthest away in tastes from what is provided by firms and therefore most likely to lose out from reduced variety).[12] The reason is that increases in quality benefit consumers not only directly but also indirectly, as a fall in the number of firms reduces the extent of duplication of fixed costs – and competition ensures that these cost savings are passed on to consumers, thereby benefiting them by more than the decline in variety has harmed them (although prices nonetheless rise overall, reflecting higher quality). This conclusion is important as it suggests that some of the suspicion with which digitisation is viewed may be misplaced: reductions in variety, if they occur,

may be an important means by which quality improvements take place
to the benefit of viewers. Conversely, high levels of variety can sometimes coexist with poor quality of individual programmes.[13]

What about the effect on content rents? With its variable quality,
programme content contributes to the vertical differentiation element in
the model: greater expenditure on quality translates into higher content
rents, as the return to talent is bid up.[14] Once again this effect depends
on the source of the cost savings. Reductions in the fixed costs of
programme making reduce expenditure and hence rents, but reductions
in the cost of making quality improvements increase them. Under the
latter circumstances, programme prices are higher, though this reflects
quality improvements: consumers (of all tastes) are better off overall.

We also explore the effect of reductions in the transport cost of
horizontal differentiation – the cost to consumers of having to consume
varieties that do not perfectly match their own preferences. Such
reduced costs might come from two sources. First, they might represent
intrinsic shifts in preferences that occur, typically as a by-product of
habituation (itself a product of trade and globalisation), as consumers
who initially find a type of broadcast culturally unfamiliar come to
familiarise themselves with it and to enjoy it more. Second, they may
result from reduced costs to producers of adapting their broadcasts to
match the preferences of certain groups of consumers – for instance, by
dubbing or subtitling movies, or making versions of situation comedies
for foreign audiences using local actors. What the model shows is that
reductions in these costs have qualitatively the same impact as a reduction in the cost of improving quality: this reduces the equilibrium
number of firms while raising quality, prices and viewer utility.

It is worth noting also that different types of programme have
different intrinsic transport costs: action movies, for instance, appeal
more easily across cultural and linguistic boundaries than do those that
depend on subtleties of social and linguistic observation. This fact has
been used to account for the strong dominance of Hollywood movies in
world markets, as well as for the fact that the leading challenger to
Hollywood's dominance, at least in terms of sheer audience numbers, is
the Indian film industry. Tyler Cowen cites a Bombay movie producer,
Romu Sippy, on the reasons why India produces mostly action movies:

Mythological films are not popular, because they offend the Muslim people.
Regional films are okay, but they cannot appeal to people who do not speak

the language. If you make a *dacoit* [bandit] movie, you miss out on the south, where they don't have *dacoits*. Westernized movies may be popular among the educated people of the cities, but what about the rickshaw wallah, the small vendor, the villager? If you get an adult certificate you miss out on the young audience. If you make a good clean film, it may be well received by the critics but commercially it will do nothing. Even a little sex is likely to offend the orthodox Hindu in Uttar Pradesh who goes to see a film first to find out if it is suitable for his daughters. The only thing that all people can relate to and understand is *action*.[15]

Our model has clear findings, therefore, but it has significant limitations too, though these are not the same as those of the Rosen model. First, and most obviously, we do not incorporate differences in talent, so the question of whether rents to talent are changing does not arise. Indeed, the framework of the Salop model has the important limitation that firms are symmetric: they all use the same technology and in equilibrium they are all the same size and charge the same price. Incorporating the insights of the Salop and Rosen models into a single encompassing framework has not been achieved to date to our knowledge and remains an important task for further research.

Second, our model ignores the distinction between the number of firms and the number of programme types. Indeed, we simply equate the two, meaning that each programme type is produced by just one producer. This may be a disadvantage in portraying a world in which there may exist multiple studios producing rather similar types of content; once again, an adequate model of such a process awaits further research.

Finally, we assume that viewers pay for individual programmes, ignoring the fact that programmes are typically bundled into channels and channels are sold together in larger packages. To the extent that channels bundle together a variety of types of content, and different channels do so to different degrees (some channels being very specialised, while others incorporate substantial variety in programme types), this is a significant limitation. As traditional modes of broadcasting are replaced by video streaming over the internet, however, our model might be more suitable. We discuss some issues to do with bundling in Section 3.4, but note again that a proper model of broadcasting market interactions that incorporates this distinction has yet to be undertaken.

In practice, and with all respect for these limitations of the available models, what kinds of change do we expect to predominate in broadcasting markets? The effect of falling reproduction and transmission costs seems likely to lead to market consolidation and possibly to the emergence of rents to certain kinds of premium content, while probably encouraging an increase in overall variety of content types available. The result is likely to be more niche programmes, with a smaller audience share for each, and an increasing dominance of a minority of 'superstar' content that gains very large audience shares – i.e. greater skewness of returns to talent.

However, these changes will probably be tempered by simultaneous technological developments that have increased both the number of platforms (terrestrial broadcasting, cable, satellite, broadband) and the number of channels within each platform. These relax the constraint of spectrum scarcity, make it cheaper to enter the market and fragment the available audience. As we noted above, this problem already concerns advertisers, who struggle to gain audience attention, and it will increasingly preoccupy superstars and would-be superstars as well. In effect, it underlines that there is more to gaining an audience than transmission and reproduction costs of programming; gaining attention requires increasing amounts of ingenuity and novelty. If audiences fragment, there is likely to be less investment in quality and the return to premium content may fall. However, if the cost of investing in quality is itself reduced by digitisation, this effect may be mitigated or even reversed.

Another possible countervailing factor may be the presence of network externalities in viewer preferences. It has long been a commonplace that stardom in the film and musical world is driven to an extent by social network effects – individuals have a preference for viewing and listening to those who are already popular with others, either out of simple conformism or because this aids social interaction. (The latter is known as the 'water cooler' effect, since it appeals to the fact that stars provide a topic of conversation when individuals meet.) Broadcasting has traditionally played an important role by making it common knowledge what programmes or stars are likely to have been watched by others. It remains to be seen whether these network effects will survive an era of channel proliferation.

It must be emphasised, however, that content is not homogeneous. Different programme types have different features, including the nature of their costs of production and the strength of associated network effects. It seems likely, therefore, that there will be a wide range of outcomes – more 'niche' content and more premium content too – lower rents for most producers of content, but lower costs of production too, and the possibility of a very lucrative stardom for a fortunate few. A further point to be stressed is that few conclusions can be drawn from current observations: being in a period of transition between analogue and digital, it is unlikely we are observing an equilibrium outcome. For example, high returns to certain types of programming might be a temporary phenomenon, to be eroded in the future by entry and audience fragmentation, or could be a lasting feature of the market. At this stage predictions are highly speculative.

What does all this imply for competition in broadcasting? What are the implications for competition policy?

3.4 Challenges for competition policy

This section discusses the challenges facing competition authorities and regulators as the broadcasting industry is reshaped by technological change. We consider a number of propositions, assessing their validity and drawing out implications for policy.

Content rights replace transmission bottlenecks as sources of market power

The introduction to this chapter raised two hypotheses concerning market power in the broadcasting industry:

- first, that the falling cost of reproducing and transmitting information has greatly reduced entry barriers, lessening market power; and
- second, that rents increasingly come from control of scarce content rather than from control over means of transmission.

Starting with the first hypothesis, the enormous expansion in transmission capacity and the rollout of multiple broadcasting platforms have relaxed transmission bottlenecks. With plentiful capacity, there is little reason for this to be concentrated in the hands of just a few broadcasters. Nonetheless, concern remains that control over certain key assets might confer market power over broadcasting platforms: terrestrial transmission sites,[16] satellite conditional access services[17] and electronic programme guide (EPG) listings.[18] These assets display economies of scale and are expensive to duplicate (often prohibitively so), akin to essential facilities. Regulators appear concerned that platform operators may exploit control over these assets by raising prices to (other) channel operators or excluding them entirely. Thus, concern over transmission bottlenecks has not fallen away; merely, their location has shifted from transmission capacity itself to related areas.

In expressing these concerns, regulators tend to consider each platform on its own, regarding control over a single platform as conferring dominance in a distinct economic market. This approach may become more questionable in the future as uptake grows and households become familiar with multiple platforms. In time, these trends may result in platform convergence, with different transmission methods forming part of the same economic market. The precise extent of substitution between platforms is a matter for empirical investigation and further evidence is needed on this point before firm conclusions can be drawn. However, inter-platform competition – if and when this develops sufficiently – lessens concerns on the viewer side of the market and provides strong incentives for platform owners to bring attractive content on board, constraining incentives to restrict access. In view of this, access regulation might no longer be required and competition authorities might adopt a more relaxed approach to intra-platform mergers than has historically been the case.[19]

Broadcasting is a two-sided market and competition authorities need to consider both sides. Although viewers may in future benefit from inter-platform competition, it does not necessarily follow that the other side of the market – e.g. advertisers seeking access to audiences – cannot be exploited. If each viewer joins just a single platform, then each platform holds a monopoly over access to its subscribers, thus gaining a degree of market power vis-à-vis advertisers and programme makers.[20] It should be noted that such a monopoly does not necessarily benefit platform owners: the result will be fiercer competition for viewers – the eyeballs that generate advertising profits – and it is viewers, not platforms, that gain rents. Although this situation may be desirable from the perspective of viewers, it is unlikely to achieve allocative efficiency. When there is multi-homing – each viewer joining several platforms – the monopoly problem is mitigated; this outcome may become more prevalent as viewers become accustomed to multiple platforms. Nonetheless, conditions on each side of the market, and interactions between them, must be carefully assessed before any conclusion is reached.

We now turn to the second hypothesis, that rents in broadcasting increasingly come from control of scarce content, with this becoming the new source of monopoly power. High returns to premium content rights might suggest market power, but the discussion in Section 3.3 would query whether this is a permanent phenomenon. Depending on the precise nature of cost savings from digitisation, competition in programme production may either become more intense or may fall and returns to talent may become more or less skewed. The long-run outcome of these changes is unpredictable and observations at an intermediate stage may be misleading. Although control over live top-flight football matches has been an important part of the development of pay-TV in several countries, with high revenues being generated for broadcasters and football clubs, market power conferred by these rights may be weaker in the future.

Viewer markets replace advertiser markets

In analogue free-to-air broadcasting, economic markets are typically defined in relation to advertisers – the paying customers – not viewers.[21] Advertising-funded broadcasting is one example of what economists describe as a two-sided market. A broadcaster shows attractive programmes to build an audience; access to this audience is sold to advertisers, thus generating the revenues out of which broadcasts are funded. The two sides of the market – viewers and advertisers – are interdependent and the broadcaster must get both sides on board. These network effects complicate the estimation of demand elasticities and market definition is not straightforward (for such an analysis of printed media see Chapter 7 in this volume). Moreover, regulation of one aspect must take into account effects on the other (e.g. advertising restrictions affect the quality of programming offered to viewers, an effect emphasised in Chapter 6 by Simon Anderson in this volume).

With the growth of pay-TV, competition must be assessed in relation to subscribers as well as, or even instead of,[22] advertisers. Substitutes are very different for the two groups: in place of one programme or channel, an advertiser would switch to any other (perhaps a combination) that delivers an audience of a similar size, but this need not consist of the same individuals. Thus, to an advertiser, popular soaps and comedies would substitute for a football match. From the viewer's perspective, however, these programmes are unlikely to be close substitutes: notably, premium programming such as live football matches and Hollywood movies appear to form narrow product markets.[23] Furthermore, substitutes outside television also differ: while an advertiser might instead advertise on a billboard or in newspapers, a television viewer would seek alternative entertainment, perhaps going to a pub or reading a book.

In advertising-funded broadcasting, network effects resulting from the two-sided nature of the market are important. If advertising declines, such concerns may fall away – only to be replaced in a viewer-driven market by social network externalities. As noted in Section 3.3, individuals benefit from the social interactions that are made possible when they watch the same programmes and can discuss them 'around the water cooler'. Even in a world of channel proliferation, network effects may permit some programmes to retain a large audience share and gain a higher return.

Exclusivity over premium content may be anticompetitive

In a viewer-defined broadcasting market, programming with particular appeal to viewers and few, if any, substitutes forms a narrow product market which is extremely valuable to broadcasters. Live top-flight football matches might form such a class: fans are willing to pay large sums to watch live matches and regard other sports, and even lower football leagues, as poor substitutes. Competition authorities have in recent years expressed great concern over the sale of premium content rights on an exclusive basis.[24] With the value of a monopoly exceeding the sum of oligopoly profits, broadcasters will be willing to pay a premium for exclusivity, making this attractive to the seller.[25] Even when rights are sold as several packages so that multiple winners are possible, these may nonetheless be bought by a single bidder.

Complementarities are important in broadcasting. When programmes form part of a series, such as a soap or sporting championship, watching one episode or event raises the attraction of watching the next. Values increase when the programmes are offered and consumed together, generating super-additivity.[26] Even when values are merely additive, bundling – of programmes into channels and of channels into packages – is more profitable than supply on a stand-alone basis, generating economies of aggregation.[27] For these reasons, broadcasters are typically willing to pay more for combinations of rights than the sum of their stand-alone values: thus, a premium may be offered for multiple or exclusive holdings. Such bidding tends to result in more concentrated holdings – in the limit, full exclusivity.

The challenge for competition authorities is that combinatorial bidding may reflect either intrinsic complementarities or market power. On the one hand, if exclusivity maximises viewer surplus or allows pricing efficiencies to be realised, it is socially as well as privately beneficial. But these values are difficult to quantify. If such bidding reflects the higher value of a monopoly, on the other hand, a concentrated outcome is detrimental to consumers. With true motivations being hidden from the competition authority, the two are observationally equivalent, making policy difficult to formulate.

Exclusionary behaviour is difficult to identify

Like other information industries, broadcasting has a distinctive cost function. Fixed costs – of programme production, transmission, encryption and reception – are high, but once a programme has been made and broadcast the cost of supplying an additional viewer is zero. Although revenues must of course be raised in some way, any price above zero is profitable at the margin.

This characteristic makes exclusionary behaviour difficult to identify and prosecute. The Areeda–Turner test[28] states that a price below marginal cost is exclusionary, while prices above this level are permissible. In broadcasting, this rule carries no weight at all. Yet by charging very low prices for additional channels within a bundled pricing scheme, a multi-channel broadcaster may exclude a single-channel competitor (this firm being unable to match the incremental price and operate profitably) while still recouping its own costs overall. The likely outcome is that competition in pay-TV will primarily be between multi-channel operators which compete in offering attractive bundles of channels to subscribers, with competition constraining average prices so that excess profits are curtailed.

Bundling is essential to broadcasting

Although in some contexts competition authorities are intrinsically suspicious of bundling – the sale of two products for a single price lower than the price at which the products may be purchased separately, if they are available separately at all – in broadcasting markets bundling is inescapable. Indeed, bundling is the source of much of the value added produced in the sector: different scenes are bundled in one programme, different programmes are bundled in one series, different series are bundled in one channel and different channels are bundled in one subscription. The reasons that may lead broadcasters to bundle content in this way are many and various, and some have a clearer role in creating value than others.

For instance, the broadcaster may put together material for reasons associated with artistic or thematic creativity. The sequence of scenes in a drama, of episodes in a series or matches in a tournament may aim at creating suspense, attachment to characters or situations, an interesting degree of variety, a growing familiarity on the part of the viewer with the material (such as the setting of a drama or the characteristics of a sporting tournament) or simply aesthetic unity in a complex story. This kind of bundling creates value added from complementarity and typically presupposes that viewers watch all the bundled material. Another possibility is that the types of content bundled together are alternatives and are therefore substitutes rather than complements – much as a chef will bundle together meals in a menu to create an interesting and varied selection for the diner. Moreover, with a huge quantity of programmes competing for viewer attention, a trusted broadcaster plays an important role in making an initial selection from which the viewer may then choose. This reduces search costs for the viewer, as well as the cost of making mistakes (which are not the same thing). Such benefits may arise either from the reputation of the broadcaster (which, for familiar reasons, tends to display scale economies) or from the presence of positively correlated preferences for the elements of the bundled material.

There is some uncertainty as to what the impact of digitisation is likely to be on the extent of bundling in the broadcasting sector. Lower filming and editing costs increase the volume and range of programme content from which broadcasters may select in creating their channel output. Meanwhile, greater transmission capacity increases the amount of programming that they are able to distribute to viewers. In one sense this may strengthen the role of broadcasters in selecting and packaging material to make it attractive and accessible to viewers, for example as themed channels. The need for efficient means of revenue generation, which channel bundling tends to be, could heighten this role. However, other developments would seem to reduce the need for broadcasters to act as intermediaries between programme creators and viewers. Producers can make their outputs directly accessible to viewers, for example by posting them on websites, while viewers can use search engines to find programmes of interest and make their selections.

Two distinct issues arise in considering the competition impact of such bundling. First there is the question of *selection*: a broadcaster chooses what material to include in the bundle, which implies choosing not to include certain potential alternative material. Selection is both desirable and inescapable and indeed is one of the principal ways in which broadcasters exercise their judgement and creativity for the benefit of viewers. However, selection entails refusing to carry other content. Imagine if every broadcaster of films were obliged to allow viewers to choose among alternative competing endings for the films supplied by rival film makers, and every series to allow viewers to choose among competing episodes at each stage. More bizarrely still, imagine if every news programme were obliged to allow viewers to choose between rival news stories filed by competing correspondents – the very suggestion highlights the fact that selecting news and enforcing the quality and reliability of reporting is one of the central functions of news organisations.

The issue of selection extends beyond the choice of film endings and the composition of news bulletins. The selection of programmes to form a channel, whether this is varied or themed, and the combination of channels into a bundle that appeals to a large number of subscribers are important parts of a broadcaster's role. As a channel packager, the broadcaster must exercise creative and commercial judgement to decide which programmes and channels to include in its offering. Although anticompetitive motives might sometimes be present, it is almost impossible to regulate vertical relations between broadcasters and content providers in such a way as to rule out the possibility of exclusionary foreclosure. Such foreclosure may happen, but no realistic rules could prevent it from happening without stifling quality and creativity in broadcasting. Indeed, it is doubtful that workable rules could even be specified. Obliging platform owners to grant equal access to (other) broadcasters is a policy that sometimes made sense when platforms were the bottleneck in broadcasting. But it is neither practical nor realistic to impose analogous obligations on channel

packagers, giving equivalent rights to independent producers and channels, now that it is bundles of content that increasingly represent scarce
assets in the industry.

The second issue is *pricing*. As Mark Armstrong and Helen Weeds
emphasise in Chapter 4 in this volume, bundling implies charging a
low or even zero price for additional components of a bundle to a
viewer who is already consuming the rest of the bundle. This can be
efficient, though it need not always be so, and even when efficient is
likely to make it difficult for new channels to enter the market (and may
even create a tendency towards natural monopoly or oligopoly). At any
rate, without detailed knowledge of viewer preferences of the kind that
is typically unavailable to competition authorities, there is no way to
formulate rules that adequately track the difference between efficient
and exclusionary bundling practices.[29] The best that can be hoped for is
that in certain circumstances where complementarities between components are widespread (as between some components of transmission
rights for sporting events, as in the TPS–Canal Plus case discussed in
Box 3.1), competition authorities will adopt an approach that is more
favourable to bundles that embody these natural complementarities
than to those that deny them. In other words, the presence of plausible
natural complementarities of viewer preference should be considered a
sufficient defence against suspicion of exclusionary intent.

To summarise, bundling is ubiquitous and in many circumstances
entirely desirable. Elements of market power that arise through ownership of scarce physical assets (such as broadcasting platforms) may
indeed provide an argument for regulatory intervention, for example to
ensure access to third parties. But it is likely that through digitisation
physical assets will become less scarce over time, while scarcities deriv-
ing from the ownership of content assets are much less susceptible to
interventions of this kind. The easiest cases to deal with may be in
acquisitions markets, where mergers (for example) may be motivated
purely by the wish to establish a monopoly over certain kinds of
content. A restrictive attitude to mergers of this kind will be just as
warranted as for mergers where more traditional, physical assets are at
stake. But competition authorities need to be careful not to adopt
overly restrictive attitudes to other industry practices, such as bundling
(or other forms of non-linear pricing), that may have a pro-competitive
rationale in terms of either the creativity of the broadcasting sector or
its role in providing trusted content for viewers in an age that is

---

Box 3.1: The TPS–Canal Plus case

In 2002 the French Football League organised a first-price sealed-bid auction for the transmission rights for matches in the First Division. There were two main participants in the auction: the broadcaster TPS (a subsidiary of the private broadcaster TF1) and Canal Plus (a subsidiary of Vivendi Universal). Three main lots were up for auction and bidders could specify whether they wanted the lots exclusively or non-exclusively, the value of the latter being significantly lower. The lots were:

• the live broadcast to all subscribers of the first-choice match in each week and the third-choice match in each week;
• the live broadcast to all subscribers of the second-choice match in each week and the weekly magazine, consisting of a round-up of all the highlights of the previous week; and
• all matches broadcast on a pay-per-view basis.

In the event TPS submitted bids of €260 million, €238 million and €113 million for the three lots, with an additional €9 million if the second and third lots were on an exclusive basis. Canal Plus submitted bids of €150 million, €20 million and €20 million, plus a large bonus of €290 million if it could obtain all three lots exclusively (all sums represented annual payments). Canal Plus was awarded the contract, but TPS complained that this bid was effectively exclusionary and would drive it out of the pay-TV market. The case was referred to the French Competition Council and after arbitration the parties agreed to annul the auction.

An important feature of the case was that Canal Plus had previously enjoyed the rights to the first-choice live broadcast and to the magazine (which it had pioneered). It argued that these two components were strongly complementary, since many football fans derived much greater pleasure from following the league systematically than from watching isolated matches. It further argued that this complementarity (rather than any exclusionary intent) was what justified the large bonus bid for all three lots together.

An interesting question arises if it is true that such complementarities exist (which there is no reason to doubt). For in that case, if the League had divided the lots differently, with the first-choice match and the magazine allocated to the same lot and the second- and third-choice matches together in a different lot, Canal Plus could have bid for the former and TPS for the latter. But the prices would almost certainly have been much lower, since the bidders would have had different target lots and would not have been strongly competing against each other. The result of the auction can be seen as the direct consequence of the

> **Box 3.1 (cont.)**
> League's decision to divide up the rights among lots in such a way as to set the bidders competing fiercely against each other. There is no reason to think that the League was unaware of the consequences of its method of dividing the lots, innocent as it may have looked at the time.

increasingly characterised by information overload rather than information scarcity.

3.5 Conclusion

We conclude with some key messages from this analysis for students, researchers and policymakers.

Lessons for students: what have we learned?

- Technological changes in broadcasting will lead to diminishing scarcity of physical assets (such as transmission platforms), but may increase the scarcity of certain kinds of premium content.
- Lower entry costs mean that the overall number of channels and types of programme in the market can increase, broadening diversity of provision, while the audience share (and income) of the leading channels and programmes also increases. Thus niche programming can coexist with an increasing dominance of superstars.
- The ability to raise quality at lower cost, resulting from digitisation, may increase investment in endogenous programme costs, an effect which tends to limit the expansion of channel numbers.

Lessons for researchers: what do we still need to know?

- We need to understand better the effect of differences in talent among producers in a world in which there is also horizontal differentiation of viewers' tastes. A comprehensive model encompassing the Rosen (1981) and Salop (1979) models has yet to be developed.
- We need to develop a better understanding of the circumstances in which bundling can be exclusionary and to establish rules of thumb for recognising such circumstances in practice, especially when possible efficiency and exclusionary motives coexist.

Lessons for policymakers: what are the priorities
for policy in this area?

- Scarcity of transmission capacity is diminishing in importance. Combined with competition between platforms, this reduces the need to regulate platform access.
- Viewer markets are likely to grow in importance relative to advertiser markets for competition policy.
- Control over scarce content may be a means of anticompetitive conduct, but aside from concentration of content via mergers, authorities should be wary of adopting a restrictive attitude to practices such as bundling and non-linear pricing, which play an important part in the creation of value in the broadcasting sector.

Appendix 3.1: Digitisation and entry

In Section 3.2 we described the impact of digitisation in reducing fixed costs of programme provision (such as video storage, editing and transmission) and generating cheaper and more effective ways of raising a programme's appeal to viewers (better special effects, speedier news reporting, etc.). Then, in Section 3.3, we argued that digitisation might reduce the 'transport cost' of horizontal differentiation – the cost to consumers of having to consume varieties that do not perfectly match their preferences. These changes can be characterised as: (i) a fall in the exogenous fixed cost of programme provision, (ii) a reduction in the cost of raising programme quality, which affects endogenous costs, and (iii) a reduction in the unit transport cost.

The appendix presents a model that combines these features.[30] The Salop (1979) model of entry into a differentiated product market is augmented by incorporating endogenous programme quality, where higher quality increases viewer surplus and raises programme costs. Using this framework we examine the impact of the three features noted above on the equilibrium number (and hence diversity) of programmes,[31] programme quality and the prices paid by consumers.

Salop model with endogenous quality

Viewers (with measure 1) are uniformly distributed around a circle of circumference 1 and incur a per-unit transport cost t. Viewer utility (ignoring transport costs) from watching programme i is given by

$$u_i = v_i - p_i \qquad [1]$$

where

$v_i \geq 0$ is programme i's quality and

$p_i \geq 0$ is the price charged for programme i.[32]

Each firm provides a single programme type. Once a programme has been made, the marginal cost of supplying an additional viewer is zero. The cost C of providing a programme of quality v has two elements, an exogenous cost K and an endogenous, quality-related term

$$C = K + \frac{1}{2}\gamma v^2 \qquad [2]$$

where

$K > 0$ is a fixed cost (for a programme of minimal quality) and

$\gamma > 0$ is a parameter representing the cost of raising quality.

Firms are located at equal intervals around the circle and entry occurs until it is no longer profitable. Existence of competitive equilibrium with a positive number of firms requires $2t\gamma > 1$; this is assumed henceforth. For the market to be covered, the marginal consumer (located equidistant between two firms) must obtain non-negative utility, which requires $3t\gamma \leq 2$ (this can be seen from expression [9] below).[33] Together these conditions entail the following parameter restriction:

$$6t\gamma \in (3,4]. \qquad [3]$$

Equilibrium

Solving the model, the equilibrium number of firms (and hence programme diversity) is given by[34]

$$N = \sqrt{\frac{2t\gamma - 1}{2\gamma K}}. \qquad [4]$$

Equilibrium quality and price, respectively, are given by

$$v = \frac{1}{\gamma N} \qquad [5]$$

and

$$p = \frac{t}{N}.$$ [6]

Comparative statics

We can now study the impact of a reduction in (i) the exogenous programme cost, K, (ii) the cost of raising quality, γ, and (iii) the unit cost of transport, t.

(i) Exogenous programme cost, K

From expression [4], a reduction in K increases the equilibrium number of firms, N, increasing diversity; this is the same result as is found in Salop (1979). Greater competition entails a reduction in equilibrium quality per programme, v, and a lower equilibrium price, p (from expressions [5] and [6] respectively). This is the 'audience fragmentation' effect, whereby greater entry shrinks each programme's audience share and quality falls.

(ii) Cost of raising quality, γ

From [4], a reduction in γ reduces the equilibrium number of firms, lowering diversity.[35] From [6], the reduction in competition increases equilibrium price, p. Equilibrium quality provision increases, both via the direct effect of lower γ and indirectly through the reduction in N. Substituting for N we can write

$$v = \sqrt{\frac{2K}{\gamma(2t\gamma - 1)}}.$$ [5']

It can be seen from this expression that a reduction in γ increases equilibrium quality. So: a reduction in the cost of raising quality results in a smaller number of programmes in equilibrium, each of which charges a higher price and provides higher quality. Note that higher quality raises endogenous programme costs, increasing C.

(iii) Unit transport cost, t

From [4], a reduction in t reduces the number of firms, N, and therefore (from [5]) raises quality, v. Its impact on price is ambiguous since it lowers both the numerator and the denominator of [6]. For parameter values within the range given by [3], however, p is decreasing in t, so we can conclude that a reduction in t increases the price. Note that the directions of the comparative static results are the same as those in γ.

Viewer welfare

In addition to considering the impact of these changes on the number of firms, we may be interested in their impact on the welfare of consumers.[36] Noting that utility of a given consumer is given by the equilibrium quality minus the price and transport cost, we can write

$$u_i = v_i - p_i - \frac{t}{2N} \qquad [7]$$

for the utility of the marginal consumer – the one furthest in preferences from the varieties supplied by the firms. This is the consumer with 'niche' tastes who is often cited as the most likely to lose out from the homogenisation of market standards brought about by digitisation. The most 'mainstream' consumer is the one whose tastes are precisely equal to the variety supplied by the firm and whose utility is therefore just equal to $u_i = v_i - p_i$. The average consumer therefore has a utility given by the mean of these two types. Substituting equations [5] and [6] we can therefore write

$$\bar{u} = (4 - 5t\gamma)\sqrt{\frac{K}{8\gamma(2\gamma t - 1)}} \qquad [8]$$

for the utility of the average consumer and

$$u' = (2 - 3t\gamma)\sqrt{\frac{K}{2\gamma(2\gamma t - 1)}} \qquad [9]$$

for the utility of the marginal consumer.

The Salop (1979) model exhibits excess entry and a similar result is found in this model. Thus, any change in parameter values that reduces the number of firms increases utility, with both average and marginal utility displaying the same qualitative responses. A reduction in K reduces the utility of both marginal and average consumers because the increase in the number of firms reduces quality by more than it reduces prices and (marginal or average) transport costs. However, a reduction in either γ or t increases utility because the reduction in the number of firms gives them an incentive to invest in higher quality that

Table 3.1: Comparative statics

| | Equilibrium outcome | | | |
Variable	N	v	p	u
K	−	+	+	+
γ	+	−	−	−
t	+	−	−	−

more than offsets the increase in price and (marginal or average) transport costs.[37]

Comparative static results for the key variables are summarised in Table 3.1.

The impact of digitisation

The analysis demonstrates that digitisation may have very different effects according to the precise mechanism through which it works: a fall in exogenous programme costs and a fall in the cost of raising quality have very different effects, for instance. The impact of digitisation on programme diversity, quality and prices is sensitive to the precise nature and degree of the changes it induces, making it difficult to anticipate.

If digitisation reduces both K and γ,[38] the overall impact depends upon which of the two mechanisms dominates. If the exogenous cost effect is stronger, the number of channels increases and price falls, while programme quality may decrease, remain unchanged or increase.[39] If the endogenous cost effect dominates, programme numbers fall while both prices and quality increase.

The analysis also demonstrates that a change resulting in a reduction in programme numbers is typically good for viewer welfare, even the welfare of those niche consumers whose preferences are furthest from what the remaining programmes provide. This is because quality improves and there is less duplication of programme costs – savings that are passed on to viewers through the effect of competition (although prices rise overall due to higher-quality provision). However, one caveat should be noted: these welfare results are linked to the excess entry property of equilibrium, which arises in this model as in Salop (1979). The excess entry result is not always present in other models of horizontal differentiation;[40] thus, it is unclear whether these results would carry over to alternative formulations.

References

Adams, William and Janet Yellen (1976) 'Commodity bundling and the burden of monopoly', *Quarterly Journal of Economics*, 90, 475–498.

Areeda, Phillip and Donald F. Turner (1975) 'Predatory pricing and related practices under Section 2 of the Sherman Act', *Harvard Law Review*, 88, 697–733.

Armstrong, Mark (1999a) 'Price discrimination by a many-product firm', *Review of Economic Studies*, 66, 151–168.

Armstrong, Mark (1999b) 'Competition in the pay-TV market', *Journal of the Japanese and International Economies*, 13, 257–280.

Armstrong, Mark and Helen Weeds (2005, revised 2006) 'Subscription Versus Advertising-Funded Television: the case of programme quality', University of Essex, Mimeo.

Bakos, Yannis and Erik Brynjolfsson (1999) 'Bundling information goods: pricing, profits and efficiency', *Management Science*, 45, 1613–1630.

Bakos, Yannis and Erik Brynjolfsson (2000) 'Bundling and competition on the internet: aggregation strategies for information goods', *Marketing Science*, 19, 63–82.

Cowen, Tyler (2002) *Creative Destruction: How Globalization is Changing the World's Cultures*, Princeton University Press.

Crampes, Claude, Carole Haritchabalet and Brune Jullien (2004, revised 2006) 'Advertising, Competition and Entry in Media Industries', University of Toulouse, CESifo Working Paper no. 1591.

Dixit, Avinash K. and Joseph E. Stiglitz (1977) 'Monopolistic competition and optimum product diversity', *American Economic Review*, 67, 297–308.

Frank, Robert (1999) *Luxury Fever*, Princeton University Press.

Frank, Robert H. and Philip J. Cook (1996) *The Winner-Take-All Society: Why the Few at the Top Get So Much More Than the Rest of Us*, Penguin.

McAfee, Preston, John McMillan and Michael Whinston (1989) 'Multiproduct monopoly, commodity bundling, and correlation of values', *Quarterly Journal of Economics*, 104, 371–384.

Motta, Massimo and Michele Polo (2003) 'Beyond the spectrum constraint: concentration and entry in the broadcasting industry', in M. Baldassarri and L. Lambertini (eds.) *Antitrust, Regulation and Competition*, Palgrave Macmillan.

Rosen, Sherwin (1981) 'The economics of superstars', *American Economic Review*, 71, 845–858.

Salop, Steven C. (1979) 'Monopolistic competition with outside goods', *Bell Journal of Economics*, 10, 141–156.

Sutton, John (1991) *Sunk Costs and Market Structure*, MIT Press.

Notes

* The authors would like to thank Mark Armstrong for helpful comments. The views expressed and any errors are those of the authors.

1. In the UK, for example, terrestrial coverage is near universal, satellite is accessible to the majority of households and cable networks pass around 50 per cent. If broadband becomes ubiquitous, virtually all households will have access to at least two platforms and many will have the possibility of four.

2. For literature on the use of bundling and price discrimination to reduce allocative inefficiency see Adams and Yellen (1976), McAfee, McMillan and Whinston (1989), Armstrong (1999a) and Bakos and Brynjolfsson (1999). Bundling is considered at length in Section 3.4.

3. This trend is further increased when television programmes are made available for internet download.

4. For example, ITV plc, the largest of the UK's commercial public service broadcasters, estimates the cost of its public service obligations at around £250 million per annum. This consists of programming costs of £180 million plus the opportunity cost of not showing more popular programmes, which ITV plc estimates to be £70 million (cited in *The Independent*, 9 March 2006). The other public service broadcasters – the BBC, Channel 4 and Five – also incur costs. In addition, the UK's commercial analogue broadcasters (the Channel 3 licensees, the largest of which is ITV plc, and Five) collectively paid £230 million in licence fees in 2004. This amount is falling, however, with total licence payments in 2005 estimated to be around £90 million, reflecting falling spectrum rents as digital competition intensifies.

5. Monopoly control of transmission platforms has given rise to detailed regulation to open up access and prevent excessive pricing, such as the EU regulatory framework for electronic communications networks and services introduced in 2003. In some countries terrestrial transmission networks are publicly owned (though this does not necessarily imply open access) or capacity is franchised to a number of broadcasters.

6. Sutton (1991) develops the endogenous sunk costs paradigm, which explains the persistence of high concentration in food and beverage industries, for example. Motta and Polo (2003) apply a similar framework to consider concentration and entry in the broadcasting industry.

7. Our analysis focuses on reallocation of rents between broadcasting platforms and holders of content rights. With the advent of pay-TV, rents may also shift from viewers – who now pay directly rather than indirectly by watching advertisements – to rights-holders, such as top-flight football leagues. Evidence on whether viewers gain or lose overall is unclear: they pay more for certain programmes but receive additional ones that were previously unavailable, and quality may also rise. Moreover, in practice wide-scale intervention in the market, such as the historic role of public broadcasters and the 'listing' of major sporting events to ensure free-to-air availability, further complicates the picture. The model in the appendix draws implications for viewer welfare within the context of pay-TV.

8. This may increase advertisers' willingness to pay for forms of advertising that are effective in reaching a large audience, although empirically this effect, if present, is difficult to distinguish from broader trends and influences. For example, the UK Competition Commission's 2003 report on the merger of Carlton Communications and Granada, forming ITV plc, commented that ITV's share of television advertising revenue had held up relatively well as its audience share had fallen since the mid-1990s, resulting in a widening 'ITV premium'. Alongside this, concern has been expressed that television 'impacts' are falling, especially with the growing use of PVRs (such as TiVo and Sky +) and some advertisers are abandoning television advertising in favour of other media such as the internet and mobile phones.

9. Frank (1999), p. 38. A previous book by the same author and Philip Cook (Frank and Cook, 1996) was devoted entirely to such markets and their effects on society.

10. Estimate based on Broadcasters' Audience Research Board (BARB) TV viewing figures for September–October 2005.

11. In the Rosen model, quality is also strictly speaking endogenous in the sense that it depends on the extent of external diseconomies. However, it does not depend on investment – it is just a function of talent and demand.

12. This result is a consequence of the excess entry property, which is found here as in the Salop model. Other models of horizontal differentiation, such as Dixit and Stiglitz (1977), have ambiguous results.

13. Those nostalgic for the supposed former glories of public service broadcasting bodies such as the BBC often overlook how poor, by contemporary standards, was the quality of much of the day-to-day programme making (sceptics might like to consider viewing some of the very first episodes of that science fiction classic *Dr Who*, to say nothing of run-of-the-mill situation comedies and quiz programmes from the 1950s and

early 1960s). It is not appropriate to compare the average quality of contemporary programming with only the best of the past.

14. The model simplifies vertical differentiation into a single term. In reality quality has many dimensions and outcomes may differ depending on how digitisation affects the cost of each element. This extension is left for further research.

15. Cited in Cowen (2002).

16. The UK communications regulator Ofcom found "significant market power" (SMP) arising from the site and mast networks of terrestrial transmission operators and imposed access requirements.

17. Oftel (the former UK telecoms regulator, now merged into Ofcom) imposed a 'fair, reasonable and non-discriminatory' (FRND) condition on the pricing of technical platform services (including conditional access) offered by SSSL, a subsidiary of BSkyB. Ofcom (which replaced Oftel in 2003) published its draft guidelines on interpretation of the FRND condition in April 2006. Regulated platform access was among the remedies imposed in the merger of Italian satellite operators Stream and Telepiù to create Sky Italia, approved by the European Commission in 2003.

18. EPG listing arrangements have been the subject of several disputes, with independent channels arguing for greater prominence.

19. The merger of the Italian satellite broadcasters, Stream and Telepiù, to form Sky Italia in 2003 was permitted only in view of the enormous losses being incurred by both operators and the likelihood that one would imminently exit; even then it was subject to a wide-ranging set of undertakings. In Germany, where cable is the major means of transmission, the Bundeskartellamt prohibited the acquisition by Kabel Deutschland (KDG) of three other regional cable operators, Ish, Iesy and Kabel Baden-Württemberg (KBW), in 2004, although it subsequently permitted the proposed merger of (the smaller operators) Ish and Iesy in 2005.

20. A similar issue concerns the 'competitive bottleneck' in call termination on telephone networks: even with strong retail competition, each network controls access to its own subscribers for incoming callers.

21. For example, in the UK Competition Commission's 2003 inquiry into the merger of two free-to-air terrestrial broadcasters, Carlton Communications and Granada, the analysis focused primarily on the impact on advertisers.

22. As PVRs become widespread, avoidance behaviour may eliminate advertising altogether.

23. In its investigation of the UK satellite broadcaster BSkyB in 2002, the Office of Fair Trading (OFT) defined premium sports and movie

channels as distinct product markets, separate from other programming. See *Decision of the Director General of Fair Trading, BSkyB investigation: alleged infringement of the Chapter II prohibition*, 17 December 2002.

24. The UK Office of Fair Trading challenged collective selling of football rights by the Premier League but lost this case at the Restrictive Practices Court in 1999. Under pressure from the European Commission, the League agreed to offer the rights as several packages so that there might be multiple winners, but successive auctions in 2000 and 2003 ended with all live packages being acquired by BSkyB. In March 2006 the Premier League agreed to a rule change that would prevent a single bidder from winning all packages of live rights, up until June 2013. In May 2006 the outcome of the first auction held under the new rules was announced. Of six packages, each conferring live rights to twenty-three matches for the three seasons from 2007–2008, two were won by Setanta, an Irish pay-TV channel, for a total payment of £392 million. The other four were won by BSkyB, with payments totalling £1.3 billion.

25. Armstrong (1999b) discusses private and social incentive for signing exclusive contracts.

26. Super-additivity entails that the combined value of two goods exceeds the sum of their individual values.

27. Bakos and Brynjolfsson (2000) discuss the role of bundling in creating economies of aggregation for information goods, such as those distributed on the internet, and assess their competitive implications.

28. Areeda and Turner (1975).

29. In its Competition Act investigation of BSkyB in 2002, the UK's Office of Fair Trading applied an 'incremental price' test which compared the incremental price of an additional channel in a bundled pricing scheme to its incremental cost of supply, regarding an incremental price below incremental cost as anticompetitive. This approach is not entirely robust, however, as it ignores additional revenues from new subscribers who are brought into the market by the larger bundle, not merely upgrading from the smaller one.

30. This model is the same as one developed by Helen Weeds in joint ongoing work with Mark Armstrong (2005), though the implications of digitisation for cost parameters and the distinction between niche and mainstream viewers are new to this chapter. Another paper which independently endogenises quality in the context of a Salop-type model, albeit with a different focus, is Crampes et al. (2004).

31. We refer to 'programmes' throughout: these are best thought of as distinct series or genres (e.g. the soap *EastEnders* or FA Premier League football matches) which are differentiated from one another

rather than individual programmes that are very similar in content (e.g. a single *EastEnders* episode or football match).

32. This assumes that the programme is financed from viewer subscription alone. Advertising funding (and the viewer disutility it causes) can be incorporated without altering the results presented here.

33. Alternatively v_i could be regarded as the viewer's valuation of quality above some base level v_0, conferred by the minimum investment K, where this is sufficient to ensure participation.

34. Note that taking the limit as $\gamma \to \infty$ the expression collapses to $N = \sqrt{t/K}$, the usual Salop formula.

35. As long as the existence condition $2t\gamma > 1$ continues to hold.

36. Note that welfare outcomes are identical to consumer outcomes since, with free entry, profit always equals zero.

37. Note that a reduction in t nonetheless increases both average and marginal transport costs (given by $t/4N$ and $t/2N$ respectively), as the indirect effect via lower N more than offsets the direct effect of lower t.

38. Or t, which has a similar impact to γ.

39. There are parameter values for which N increases, yet the combined effect (of higher N and lower γ) results in higher v.

40. For example, Dixit and Stiglitz (1977).

4 | Public service broadcasting in the digital world

MARK ARMSTRONG AND HELEN WEEDS*

4.1 Introduction

The concept of public service broadcasting (PSB) is for many people summed up by the mission given to the BBC by its first Director General, John Reith, in the 1920s: to 'inform, educate and entertain'. This broad statement encompasses several elements, some clearly appealing to viewers themselves (to entertain), others with wider social purposes (to educate and inform).[1,2] The aims of public service broadcasting would therefore appear to encompass two main strands: that television should give people the programmes that they want to watch and that it should also satisfy wider social purposes such as education and the promotion of 'citizenship'. Reflecting these strands, in this chapter we discuss two broad questions concerning the provision of television broadcasting:[3]

- Will the television broadcasting market give people what they want to watch?
- Should people be allowed to watch only what they want to watch?

The first question investigates the traditional 'market failure' arguments for public intervention in broadcasting. These hold that the commercial broadcasting market will fail to meet viewers' demands in a number of important respects. Advertising-funded broadcasters will produce a bland diet of low-quality programmes, appealing to mass-market tastes and ignoring niche interests. We explore the basis for these arguments by assessing market provision of television broadcasting. Specifically, we consider whether audience numbers will be efficient, whether the level of advertising is appropriate and whether the right mix of programmes, in terms of diversity and quality of content, will be produced.

The second question relates to issues that go beyond the desires of the individual viewer. It encompasses two broad concerns. First, that (some) viewers do not necessarily choose what it is in their best interests to watch. Second, television viewing may have effects on the wider population that are ignored by the individual viewer (this is sometimes described as the 'citizen' rationale for PSB).[4] The first concern might justify controls on the broadcasting of certain harmful content, especially to protect children, while the latter would provide a basis for intervention to promote socially beneficial programmes and to restrict those causing social detriment. We examine the possible foundations of these concerns and their relevance in the modern broadcasting environment.

It is particularly important to subject the basis for public intervention in television to rigorous economic analysis at the present time. The sector is changing enormously due to the adoption of digital technologies. Digital signals relax spectrum constraints, greatly increasing the number of channels that can be broadcast. Encryption technologies facilitate charging of viewers, rather than (just) advertisers, making commercial broadcasters directly responsive to viewer demands. In addition, devices such as the personal video recorder give viewers greater control over what they watch. These developments have critical and wide-ranging impacts on television broadcasting.

In light of these developments, the rationale for public intervention needs to be re-examined. Regulation that was appropriate to the earlier, analogue era may become unnecessary, and even undesirable,[5] in the digital world. Although everyone would presumably agree that the mission to 'inform, educate and entertain' is a highly laudable one, and in this sense supports public service broadcasting,[6] it needs to be questioned whether public intervention is still required to fulfil these aims. As was well expressed by Gavyn Davies (who subsequently served as chairman of the BBC from 2001 to 2004):[7]

Some form of market failure must lie at the heart of any concept of public service broadcasting. Beyond simply using the catch-phrase that public service broadcasting must 'inform, educate and entertain', we must add 'inform, educate and entertain in a way which the private sector, left unregulated, would not do'. Otherwise, why not leave matters entirely to the private sector?

We argue that digital broadcasting greatly mitigates traditional market failures and, in this context, the market will give people broadly what they want to watch. In this sense, the 'market failure' basis for public service broadcasting falls away. A coherent rationale remains for more limited intervention to control the broadcasting of harmful material and to promote educational and other programmes generating social benefits.

The implementation of public service broadcasting also calls for re-examination in light of digital broadcasting. Funding sources for existing systems of provision come under serious pressure in the digital world, threatening their long-term viability. At the very least, these systems need to adapt to survive. Moreover, in this world of viewer sovereignty, with a vast and varied range of programmes to choose from, the ability of 'worthy' public service content to gain audience attention is greatly diminished. This challenge calls for more innovative techniques to be used in reaching viewers if public service messages are to be conveyed. An alternative view is that, given declining benefits and major costs of intervention, the time has arrived when wide-ranging intervention is no longer appropriate.

The chapter proceeds as follows. In Section 4.2 we describe the structure and characteristics of the broadcasting industry. Section 4.3 investigates the first question posed above: will the market give people what they want to watch? Section 4.4 explores the second question: should people be allowed to watch only what they want? Alternative systems of provision are described in Section 4.5. Drawing on this analysis, we then assess the rationale for, and provision of, public service broadcasting in the analogue era (Section 4.6) and in the digital world (Section 4.7). A case study of the UK's system of provision and challenges for its future is given in Section 4.8. Section 4.9 concludes with a set of messages for students, researchers and policymakers.

4.2 The broadcasting industry

The broadcasting industry consists of a number of vertical stages, by means of which television programming is created, packaged and trans-mitted to viewers and revenue is generated. Broadcasters are typically vertically integrated,[8] with some outsourcing of programme production.

The four main elements of the broadcasting supply chain can be described as follows:

- *programme production*, e.g. making a movie or drama, filming a sports event and news reporting;
- *channel packaging*: scheduling programmes into channels, packages and pay-per-view offerings;

- *transmission* to the viewer via terrestrial, satellite, cable or other platforms;
- *revenue generation* through licence fee collection, subscription and/ or the sale of advertising airtime.

We examine the features of each stage in turn.

Programme production

Programme production incurs costs that do not vary with the number of viewers: once a programme has been created, it can in principle be viewed by an unlimited number of viewers. Television content is highly differentiated, consisting of a wide range of programme types (or 'genres') such as news and current affairs, documentaries, coverage of sports and cultural events, movies, dramas, comedies and so on. Production of higher-quality programmes typically incurs greater expenditure (e.g. better special effects in movies, authentic period dramas, comprehensive news reporting), though production costs also vary considerably between genres.[9]

Channel packaging

Individual programmes are usually packaged into channels that are broadcast as a continuous television feed. A channel might focus on a single type of programming that appeals to a specific interest group or it may contain a range of genres. Channels may themselves be combined into packages (or 'bouquets') that are supplied as a bundle. Alternatively, programmes may also be shown on a 'pay-per-view' basis rather than as part of a channel.

In the future, programme downloads from the internet may become a popular viewing method. Video download departs from the traditional model of 'linear' broadcasting by giving the viewer, rather than the broadcaster, control over the timing of reception. In this case the role of channel packaging, as such, becomes redundant since the viewer, rather than the provider, determines the selection and timing of viewed content. Instead, the organisation and presentation of content libraries becomes an important role for providers.[10]

Transmission

Programmes can be transmitted to the viewer using many technologies. Historically in the UK and many other countries, radio and television broadcasters used terrestrial (airwave) transmission,[11] but recent decades have seen the emergence of cable and satellite distribution platforms. Analogue broadcasting requires each channel to have a dedicated frequency band. In digital broadcasting signals are converted into a digital format and, by means of compression and multiplexing techniques, this allows many more channels to be transmitted in the same bandwidth. Broadband networks, based on fixed or mobile telephone connections or emerging wireless technologies, may be used to deliver services similar to broadcasting (e.g. video downloads). With the growth of broadband, broadcasting, traditionally a one-way, one-to-many, passive activity, is likely to become increasingly interactive and personalised.

Transmission systems have substantial set-up costs, to build the transmission network and enable viewers' reception capability.[12] Once infrastructure is in place, costs do not increase significantly with the number of programmes delivered, consisting only of the power required to broadcast the signal. Moreover, once broadcast, a signal can be picked up by anyone with the necessary receiving equipment: there is no incremental cost of transmitting a programme to an additional viewer. The viewer makes an initial investment in receiving equipment, after which no additional cost is incurred in receiving further broadcasts. Effective transmission capacity varies with signal type. Analogue transmission is relatively inefficient in its use of spectrum,[13] placing a tight constraint on the number of programmes that can be broadcast simultaneously, while digital signals are much more efficient.

Revenue generation

In principle, four methods of revenue generation may be used to fund broadcasting activities:

- direct government grant funded from taxation;
- a compulsory licence fee levied on all television viewers;[14]
- direct viewer charges on a subscription or pay-per-view basis ('pay-TV'); and
- the sale of airtime to advertisers.

Broadcasting services funded from a licence fee or the sale of advertising alone are often described as 'free-to-air'. Government grants draw on funds raised from a wide tax base, but the amount given will be subject to political acceptability and budgetary priorities. Throughout this chapter we mostly ignore government grants as a source of funding for broadcasting.

A licence fee appears straightforward but, in the absence of an effective exclusion mechanism, incurs significant enforcement costs.[15] Pay-TV requires the installation of a conditional access system to exclude non-payers: the signal is broadcast in an encrypted format and authorised viewers use a set-top box containing a decoder (or 'smart card') to convert it for viewing.[16] Subscriber acquisition and management services, including a sophisticated billing system for levying charges that vary according to the channels taken, must also be set up.

Television advertising is a two-sided market in which the broadcaster shows attractive programming to draw in viewers, and access to this audience is sold to advertisers and sponsors. Although viewers may receive the programmes for free, they must tolerate, and be responsive to, advertisements placed between and within programmes. Disutility from the presence of adverts can be regarded as the implicit 'price' to viewers of advertising-funded broadcasting. Viewers can adopt a number of measures to reduce this disutility: switching channel during advertising breaks – the invention of the remote control was a major step in this direction – or skipping adverts during playback from a VCR. The ability to eliminate adverts is further heightened by the invention of the personal video recorder. This is a new type of recording device offering high-quality recording, much larger capacity and greater sophistication than the VCR.[17] Such avoidance behaviour, however, reduces the impact of adverts and, if widespread, ultimately undermines the sale of advertising airtime as a source of funding for broadcasters.[18]

4.3 Will the market give people what they want to watch?

In this section we address the question, 'will market provision give people the programmes they want to watch?' There are several aspects to this. First, taking the set of programmes as given, will the efficient level of viewing be achieved? Revenue is needed to cover broadcasters' production and transmission costs and so must be generated somehow, while viewing is sensitive to the method used. We assess the efficiency of market outcomes, considering in turn the television licence fee, advertising funding and pay-TV. A strand of this analysis concerns advertising: advertisers, as well as viewers, are consumers of television services, and the two sides of the market are interdependent although not always aligned in their interests. Viewer and social welfare are affected by the level of advertising as well as programme viewing, and both aspects must be assessed.

Turning next to production, we examine whether this is likely to be efficient. For production of a programme to be efficient the surplus it generates must exceed its cost. We note the role played by market prices in this context. A further aspect is whether the market will deliver the 'right' set of programmes, in terms of diversity and quality, that viewers want to watch. We examine programme selection under alternative funding systems to assess the diversity of genres produced in each case. Finally we assess quality provision and investment in innovation.

Throughout this section market outcomes are assessed against viewers' demands, ignoring any effects of television viewing beyond the individual viewer. Thus, 'social optimality' refers here to outcomes that maximise viewers' utility in the absence of externalities. In addition, the viewer is taken to be capable of determining what is in his or her own interests and making this selection for themselves; thus the possible concern that (some) viewers do not choose what is in their best interests to watch is ignored. These two issues are deferred until Section 4.4.

Charging and consumption

As described above, the broadcasting industry is characterised by substantial fixed costs while marginal, per-viewer costs are negligible. Programme production costs are independent of the number of viewers and, once transmission and reception capacity are in place, the marginal cost of transmitting the programme to an additional viewer is zero. Television viewing is a non-rivalrous form of consumption: viewing by one individual leaves unaffected the ability of others to view the same output. These characteristics are fundamental to the economics of broadcasting, with important implications for efficient production and consumption.

Efficient viewing of programmes
Once produced, allocative efficiency dictates that a programme should be viewed by all individuals whose consumption generates positive surplus. Since an existing programme can be supplied to an additional viewer at no incremental cost, this requires the programme to be

provided to all viewers with a positive valuation of it, however small. Such an outcome can be achieved by setting the price of viewing equal to marginal cost – i.e. at zero. At this price all individuals with a positive valuation view the programme and consumption is at the efficient level. A source of revenue is needed, however, since production and transmission costs must somehow be covered for the industry to be viable. Appeals to allocative efficiency are often used to support funding in the form of a licence fee or out of the public purse (though taxation elsewhere typically also creates distortions).

However, the zero price argument applies only to an existing set of programmes. It ignores the effect of such a policy on the incentive to develop desirable programmes in the future. A production function with high fixed and very low marginal costs is found in many other creative and innovative industries – books, software and pharmaceuticals, for example – yet these products are not supplied at marginal cost. Marginal cost pricing (even with a subsidy to cover fixed costs) gives poor incentives for high-quality provision, innovation and cost efficiency. Balancing these arguments, some means of revenue generation must be found that minimises allocative inefficiency while also allowing costs to be covered and providing good incentives to producers.

Efficient level of advertising
The issue of allocative efficiency also arises on the advertising side of the market. However, the interests of advertisers and viewers are somewhat opposed. Advertisers benefit from the viewing of their advertisements, while viewers typically suffer some disutility from the disruption and delay imposed on the viewing of their desired programme.

The extent to which advertiser surplus enters into the social welfare function is important here. The welfare effect of advertising is a contentious issue. Advertising may be designed to provide information, change preferences or steal business from rivals, and the welfare assessment varies according to its purpose. In the case of informative advertising without business stealing, the advertiser's surplus should count fully in social welfare. Then, if an advertiser is willing to pay an amount w per viewer to reach an audience while each viewer incurs a disutility d from the presence of the advert, the advert should be provided whenever w exceeds d. If this condition is violated, allocative inefficiency arises on the advertising side of the market. If advertising is socially wasteful, however, welfare is closer to viewer surplus plus broadcaster profits.

We now assess the efficiency of alternative methods of revenue generation, taking account of both viewing and advertising levels.

Television licence fee

Once the licence fee has been paid any programme may be viewed at no further charge.[19] The fact that viewing is free at the point of consumption is often taken to entail that allocative efficiency is always achieved. However, allocative inefficiency may nonetheless arise in a number of ways.

The licence fee excludes consumption of all television services by individuals whose willingness to pay for television as a whole is less than this amount (and who do not simply evade the fee). Although this could in principle be a source of allocative inefficiency, almost universal coverage implies that such exclusion is not significant in practice (and some of those who choose not to have a television set may actively dislike television, thus their failure to watch is not inefficient).

More significant inefficiency can arise if a commercial broadcaster (say, pay-TV)[20] operates alongside the licence fee-funded (public) broadcaster. The uptake and revenues of pay-TV are likely to be distorted, to the detriment of social welfare. Note that this would also be the case if the public broadcaster's channels were provided for free (e.g. if it is funded from taxation): even the availability of public television affects viewer choices, to the detriment of commercial operators.[21]

An individual who wants to watch any television – even pay-TV alone – must pay the licence fee. This alters his or her choice set by removing the option of taking only pay-TV. If choices were unconstrained, the pay-TV operator would gain a subscription from any viewer whose valuation of its offering, taken either on its own or in addition to the public channels, exceeds its subscription charge. But with a compulsory licence fee the viewer's choice is restricted to either paying the licence fee and watching only public channels or paying a subscription charge in addition to the licence fee and having both services. With this constrained choice, the viewer subscribes to pay-TV only if his or her net surplus from the second option exceeds that of the first.

Box 4.1: Pay-TV and the licence fee

Case (i): Exclusion of pay-TV

Consider a situation in which a single pay-TV operator (for simplicity) offers a single bundle of channels. Suppose that a viewer's ranking of net surplus (gross surplus minus the relevant charges) is given by:

$$S(pay) - P > S(public) - L > S(public + pay) - L - P > 0$$

where $S(.)$ denotes gross surplus from viewing public and/or pay-TV, P is the subscription charge for pay-TV and L is the licence fee. This viewer prefers pay-TV to the public broadcaster's service and has diminishing marginal utility of additional channels such that it is even less desirable for him to take both services given the charges involved.

The viewer's unconstrained choice would be to take pay-TV alone. But with the compulsory licence fee this choice is unavailable. Since his incremental valuation of pay-TV is negative – i.e. his net surplus from taking both services is less than that of having the public broadcaster's channels alone – he will not subscribe to pay-TV.

Case (ii): Diversion of surplus

Suppose that a viewer has a strong preference for pay-TV and a negative net surplus from public broadcasting, such that:

$$S(pay) - P > S(public + pay) - L - P > 0 > S(public) - L.$$

Again, the unconstrained choice would be pay-TV alone, but the constrained choice is to take pay-TV in addition to public broadcasting. The viewer pays the licence fee simply in order to take pay-TV, even though her valuation of the public broadcaster's output implies that she would not choose this under a voluntary system. Part of the viewer's surplus is diverted to the public broadcaster, even though her net valuation of its channels is negative.

Some simple representations of preferences and choices are given in Box 4.1. The first example suggests that subscription to pay-TV may be inefficiently low in the presence of the compulsory licence fee. In the second example, subscription is unaffected but the licence fee diverts part of the viewer's surplus to the public broadcaster. In fact, the actual situation may be more complicated than this, since the subscription charge is likely to be lower when the pay-TV operator competes against the compulsory licence fee.[22] If so, pay-TV revenue (as well as viewer surplus) is diverted to the public broadcaster.[23] With lower revenue and tougher competition for viewers, it is likely that the output and quality of programming offered by pay-TV will be lower.[24]

Advertising funding

Advertising funding avoids the need to levy subscription or licence fees on viewers to cover broadcasting costs. In the direct, monetary sense the price of a programme equals its marginal cost and allocative efficiency would appear to be achieved. However, advertising imposes on viewers a kind of 'hedonic' price given by their disutility from seeing adverts. Viewers must tolerate advertisements placed between and within programmes, imposing on them the disutility of disruption and delay. Given that the programmes have already been made and could be viewed without interruption, this is inefficient from the viewers' perspective. When transmission capacity is limited, advertising takes up valuable airtime that could otherwise be used to show more desirable programming.[25]

To the extent that broadcasters have market power over providing access to their audience, advertising rates may be set above the efficient level, but this is not necessarily so. Anderson and Coate (2005) analyse whether too much or too little advertising is supplied in equilibrium, for both free-to-air and pay-TV.[26] In the case of free-to-air, the welfare outcome is ambiguous: advertising may be either overprovided (if its nuisance cost is high) or underprovided (if this cost is low).[27] As the market for viewers becomes competitive, advertising may be underprovided since broadcasters compete for viewers by lowering advertising levels.

If viewers can avoid advertisements, e.g. by switching channel or using recording devices to skip over them, the scope for inefficiency is greater. A viewer will avoid adverts as long as the average cost incurred in doing so is less than d, the disutility of watching adverts. Even if the value to advertisers of viewer attention exceeds d, and advertisers would therefore be willing to compensate viewers for their disutility, no effective mechanism exists to pay viewers to watch. If widespread, avoidance behaviour could undermine advertising as a funding source for commercial television. The only viable advertising strategies would then be ones that are intertwined with the programme itself, e.g. programme sponsorship, product placement and advertisements captured by the programme (e.g. logos on Formula 1 cars, billboards in football stadiums).

Pay-TV

With conditional access, viewers may be charged directly for their consumption. However, even if feasible, direct viewer charges at the level necessary to recoup broadcasting costs may exclude a number of individuals whose consumption would be efficient. In particular, uniform average cost pricing, levied on a per-programme or per-channel basis, could be expected to exclude many viewers.

Price discrimination is the key to combining fixed-cost recovery through viewer charging with relatively efficient consumption. By charging different amounts to heterogeneous viewers, reflecting individual willingness to pay, surplus can be extracted from high-valuation viewers to cover fixed costs while achieving (close to) the efficient level of consumption.[28] Perfect (or first-degree) price discrimination achieves allocative efficiency, but its implementation requires the supplier to know each viewer's willingness to pay, to be able to set charges individually and to prevent resale. These conditions are rarely met in practice and instead mechanisms must be found by which to identify groups of viewers with different valuations (third-degree price discrimination) or to induce them to self-select between different charging schemes (second-degree price discrimination).

Price discrimination in broadcasting is typically achieved by two means: 'windowing' and channel bundling. Windowing, whereby a movie or other content is released through a sequence of distribution outlets at successively lower prices, is a form of intertemporal price discrimination. Viewers with a strong preference for seeing a movie immediately, who tend to value the programme more highly than other individuals, pay a high price to see it at the cinema, while less time-sensitive viewers view it later at a lower price through video release or on television. Pay-per-view, pay-TV and free-to-air broadcasting each form a separate stage in this process. Windowing allows surplus to be extracted while most viewers with positive valuations view the programme eventually. Nevertheless, a real form of allocative inefficiency remains: there is no additional cost to providing the programme to everyone immediately, yet delay is imposed on many viewers.

The packaging of individual programmes into a channel supplied as a single offering is a form of product bundling, as is the combining of several channels into a bouquet. Pure bundling occurs when two or more products are supplied only as a bundle.[29] Mixed bundling allows the components also to be sold separately, but the price of the bundle gives a discount on the sum of component prices. 'Tiering' – a form of mixed bundling in which channels are supplied as a hierarchy of packages between which subscribers select – is commonly used by pay-TV operators.

When two or more channels are supplied and viewer valuations are heterogeneous, channel bundling can be used as a price discrimination device to improve allocative efficiency.[30] A simple, two-channel example of pricing and consumption with no bundling, pure bundling and mixed bundling is given in Box 4.2; this demonstrates how bundling may improve allocative efficiency, as well as facilitating channel provision. The key mechanism underlying bundling is that the dispersion in valuations across viewers is lower for the bundle than for an individual channel. This is especially true if component values are negatively correlated, as in Box 4.2, but holds even for independent and positively correlated distributions. The benefits of bundling increase as the number of channels rises, due to the homogenising effect of the 'law of large numbers'. When the number of channels is large, pure bundling may achieve (almost) universal consumption while also covering the costs of channel provision.[31]

Mixed bundling increases the number of instruments available to the broadcaster and hence increases its revenue compared with pure bundling.[32] The welfare comparison between pure and mixed bundling is ambiguous. A danger inherent in pure bundling schemes is that individuals may inefficiently consume some components that they value at less than cost.[33] With the marginal cost of supply equal to zero, however, this inefficiency does not arise in broadcasting. Nevertheless, mixed bundling may induce viewers to select smaller bundles (perhaps even a single channel) while forgoing channels for which they have a small but positive valuation; if so, allocative efficiency will be lower than under pure bundling.[34] For this reason schemes that are closer to pure bundling, consisting of large packages and with few channels made available individually, are a particularly efficient form of pricing in the broadcasting industry.[35]

In Box 4.2 it is assumed that the channel provider is a monopolist. In a monopoly context, bundling increases profits compared with pure component pricing. In competitive situations, however, this result may no

Box 4.2: Channel bundling

Suppose that two television channels, 1 and 2, can be supplied by a monopoly broadcaster to three viewers, A, B and C. The per-channel cost of production and transmission is £10, but once this is incurred the marginal cost of supplying an additional viewer is zero. Viewer valuations of the channels are shown in the table below; if an individual receives both channels, the combined valuation is simply the sum of component valuations. For each channel the sum of viewer valuations exceeds its cost, thus provision of both channels is socially desirable. With all viewers having positive valuations of viewing each channel, allocative efficiency is achieved through universal consumption.

	Channel 1	*Channel 2*
Viewer A	£10	£1
Viewer B	£1	£9
Viewer C	£7	£7

Denoting the prices of the individual channels as P_1 and P_2 respectively and the price of the bundle as P_B, profit-maximising prices can be calculated for three cases: no bundling, pure bundling and mixed bundling. Together with the sales of each channel (Q_1, Q_2), revenue raised and consumer surplus (CS) generated, these prices are as follows:

- no bundling: $P_1 = P_2 = £7$; $Q_1 = Q_2 = 2$; revenue = £28; $CS = £5$
- pure bundling: $P_B = £10$; $Q_1 = Q_2 = 3$; revenue = £30; $CS = £5$
- mixed bundling: $P_1 = £10$, $P_2 = £9$, $P_B = £14$; $Q_1 = Q_2 = 2$; revenue = £33; $CS = 0$.

Pure bundling achieves allocative efficiency: each channel is consumed by all three viewers. Mixed bundling and no bundling, however, do not (in this case) achieve allocative efficiency.

Bundling raises broadcaster revenues, with mixed bundling extracting the most consumer surplus (here, all of it) and yielding the highest revenue. With a larger channel cost, bundling may be necessary to ensure provision. If the per-channel cost is raised to £15, the firm cannot break even without some form of bundling. With a cost of £16 per channel, mixed bundling is then necessary.

longer hold. In a duopoly model of bundling, Matutes and Regibeau (1992) and Armstrong and Vickers (2006) show that bundling can act to reduce profits since it intensifies price competition. Strategic use of bundling is possible: for example, in the face of competitive entry bundling can be an exclusionary device.[36] In a competitive broadcasting market the analysis of channel bundling is far from straightforward.[37]

When pay-TV broadcasters sell advertising airtime as well as levying charges to viewers, fewer adverts are shown compared with a pure advertising regime.[38] Thus, advertisers are worse off under pay-TV, though viewers may benefit. In a model of informative advertising, Anderson and Coate (2005) show that advertising is underprovided by pay-TV, the reason being that, in their model, viewers watch a single channel, giving channels a monopoly over providing access to their viewers. The model in Appendix 4.1 shows that advertising avoidance behaviour (e.g. skipping adverts using a PVR) in a pay-TV regime typically makes viewers worse off, as they pay a higher subscription charge that outweighs the benefit to them of avoiding adverts.

Programme production and asymmetric information

In the preceding discussion the set of programmes was taken as given, considering only the need to cover programme costs which were treated as fixed. We now go back a stage and ask whether production will be efficient. We start by noting the role of the price mechanism in revealing information about viewer preferences. We then turn to the questions of diversity, quality and innovation.

In general terms, a good should not be produced unless total surplus generated exceeds its production costs. Each viewer's valuation is known to the individual themselves but unknown to the producer; in other words, viewer valuations are asymmetric information. In a typical market the price mechanism reveals much of this hidden information: by purchasing the good at a given price, consumers reveal that their valuations are at least this amount. Since production is not profitable unless revenues exceed costs, inefficient overproduction is avoided, although efficient production may not always take place (unless price discrimination is close to perfect).

In pay-TV, viewer charges reveal information about viewers' preferences, assisting efficient production decisions.[39] In free-to-air broadcasting, however, this guide to viewer preferences is lacking.[40] Viewer surveys might be conducted instead.[41] However, such results are inferior to market data: questionnaires pose artificial choices, while market transactions are real ones, and statements about programme desirability are costless to make. Viewing patterns may reveal some information about relative valuations: analysis of choices between head-to-head combinations can yield some programme rankings. Even so, without an indication of willingness to pay, the broadcaster cannot determine whether surplus generated by a programme exceeds its cost of provision and hence whether its production is efficient.

Diversity of programmes

Television content is a highly differentiated product class, including sports coverage, news and current affairs, movies, comedies, documentaries and so on. Viewer tastes are heterogeneous, with preferences differing across individuals and each viewer typically enjoying many genres. Provision of a diverse range of programme genres, other things being equal, tends to raise viewer surplus. Diversity in broadcasting is also important for the political process, with expression of a plurality of opinions being vital to the functioning of democratic systems.[42]

Market provision of diversity depends on the means of revenue generation, as this may give broadcasters an incentive either to focus on a limited number of tastes or to differentiate themselves across a range of genres. Outcomes under pay-TV and advertising funding have been studied at length by economists. We summarise these findings next.[43]

Advertising funding

With pure advertising funding the broadcaster's broad aim is to maximise audience size, as this increases advertising revenues, while the amount of surplus accruing to viewers is unimportant.[44] Steiner (1952) assesses provision of diversity by competing single-channel broadcasters in a market with a set of distinct programme types, each with a distinct set of viewers. Welfare is maximised by having just one channel per genre, up to the point where the number of channels equals the number of genres. If two or more channels target the same genre then its audience is divided equally between them. Steiner finds that duplication tends to arise: a broadcaster will duplicate an existing programme type, taking part of the audience from a competing channel, rather than produce one that is as yet unserved whenever its share of the audience for the former exceeds the total audience for the latter.

A simple example of channel diversity for a varying number of competing channels, based on Steiner's approach, is presented in Box 4.3. With limited channel numbers, less popular genres tend to be left unserved while popular ones are duplicated. The precise extent of duplication depends on the distribution of viewer preferences, with a greater disparity in audience size raising the extent of duplication. As the number of channels increases, genres with successively smaller audiences are served. This analysis suggests that with a small, fixed number of channels, competition performs worse than multi-channel monopoly since business stealing between broadcasters results in duplication.

The Steiner model is special in a number of ways and its conclusions regarding the impact of competition do not necessarily carry over to more general models. Beebe (1977) allows viewers to have a second-choice programme that is preferred to not watching at all and shows that competition might produce more desirable outcomes than suggested by Steiner. Anderson and Coate (2005) explicitly model viewers' disutility of advertising and allow free-to-air broadcasters to decrease the amount of advertising shown in order to compete for viewers. They show that with competition, two free-to-air broadcasters would never duplicate a programme type since they would then compete fiercely by restricting advertising, which would eliminate advertising revenues. Relaxing the capacity constraint on the number of channels, Spence and Owen (1977) find that, since a monopolist supplies fewer channels and has the same biases, monopoly provision is worse than competition.

These models assume that programme genres have identical production costs. In reality this is not the case (see footnote 9) and relative profitability of genres depends on profit margins, i.e. advertising revenues (which depend on audience, or 'reach') minus production costs (which do not). For example, drama series attract many viewers but are costly to produce and so have a low profit margin.[45] Soaps also attract a large audience but are cheaper to make so have a high margin. If a cheap quiz show draws the same audience as an expensive period drama, an advertising-funded broadcaster will not find it worthwhile to spend extra resources on the latter. Thus, in the absence of regulation we would expect high-margin programmes – soaps, entertainment, movies and national news – to be produced while low-margin genres – arts and religion, regional programming and current affairs – would be largely ignored.

Box 4.3: Programme diversity under advertising funding

There are three programme genres, A, B and C. Viewers have exclusive preferences, each consuming only one genre, while intensity of preference is uniform. Total audiences for the three genres number 100, 45 and 30 respectively.

Programme production incurs a fixed cost that is independent of the number of viewers and the genre chosen. Channels are purely advertising funded; advertising revenues are proportional to audience size and independent of genre.

Competing single-channel broadcasters each choose a single genre. If two or more channels offer the same genre, the audience for that type is shared equally between them. In non-cooperative equilibrium each broadcaster selects the genre that maximises its audience given the choices of the others.

Equilibrium choices for markets with different numbers of channels (between two and five) are shown in the table below. The first column gives the total number of channels and the body of the table shows the number of channels for each genre.

No. of channels	A $(V_A = 100)$	B $(V_B = 45)$	C $(V_C = 30)$
2	2	0	0
3	2	1	0
4	3	1	0
5	3	1	1

Duopoly duplicates a single, popular programme genre. With three channels a second genre is served, while five channels are required before all three tastes are met. In the last case viewer preferences are fulfilled but there is duplication of production costs.

Under multi-channel monopoly provision, by contrast, each channel serves a different genre until the point where all three tastes are served (no more than three channels will be offered as this would increase programme costs with no increase in revenue). This outcome is the same as the welfare optimum.

Pay-TV

With viewers being charged directly, pay-TV is more responsive to their preferences than advertising-funded broadcasting. Spence and Owen (1977) compare the two systems in a model with heterogeneous intensity of preferences and unconstrained channel numbers, considering both monopoly provision and competition. They find that, in both systems, programme types with low elasticity of demand (i.e. minority tastes) are underprovided, as are more costly programmes (for a given contribution to total surplus). Pay-TV outperforms advertising funding regarding provision of diversity, due to its ability to take account of intensity of preferences, although it remains biased unless price discrimination between viewers is feasible. With a tight constraint on channel numbers, however, pay-TV may not be desirable since high subscription prices reduce audience size compared with advertising funding.

Quality and innovation

What is meant by programme quality?

Before discussing quality provision under alternative funding systems it is important to define what is meant by programme quality. Economists regard product A as being of higher quality than product B if all consumers value A more highly than B. Thus, when offered at the same price, all consumers choose A over B. In other words quality, or 'vertical' differentiation, refers to an *agreed ranking* over products. By contrast, diversity or 'horizontal' differentiation reflects *differences* in individual rankings.

In the broadcasting context quality needs to be distinguished from value judgements between genres whereby certain programme types are regarded by some people as being intrinsically more worthwhile or edifying than others – for example, the view that period dramas are 'quality' programmes while soaps are not. Although it is possible that all viewers have a higher willingness to pay for period dramas than for soaps, audience behaviour when the two are placed head to head in free-to-air schedules suggests that this is not the case. Although there may be some agreed rankings across genres, it is more straightforward to think of higher quality as referring to improvements *within* a genre. It is likely that all viewers would prefer, for example, more spectacular special effects in a movie, better camera angles for a football match, speedier news reporting, more illuminating discussion of current affairs and so on.[46] In practice, measuring quality is far from straightforward[47] and this has implications for the ability to regulate quality.

Quality provision

Higher programme quality typically requires greater production expenditure. For the broadcaster to have an incentive to provide higher quality, it must be able to extract a sufficient proportion of the additional viewer surplus to cover the extra costs. The impact of funding mechanisms on quality provision is examined next; Appendix 4.1 contains a stylised duopoly model that illustrates some of the results.

With advertising-funded television, profitability depends not on how strongly viewers like a programme but only on how many of them watch it. Although higher-quality programming draws in more viewers and hence increases advertising revenues, an advertising-funded broadcaster's incentive to provide quality depends only on its impact on viewer valuation at the margin, not its effect on infra-marginal viewers. As illustrated by the model in Appendix 4.1, with a fixed number of channels quality provision is typically too low.[48] It is possible that advertiser targeting of more affluent viewers, or of those with a greater propensity to spend on advertised goods, might result in some bias towards the viewing preferences of those groups. However, unless those viewers have a particularly strong desire for quality and, in addition, the elasticity of their expenditure with respect to advertising is sufficiently high, this effect is unlikely to guarantee the provision of high-quality programmes.

In a pay-TV system, part or all of the surplus from higher quality can be extracted from infra-marginal viewers by raising viewer prices. This generates incentives for quality provision and outcomes at or close to the social optimum can be achieved. In the duopoly model in Appendix 4.1, where all viewers have the same preference for quality,[49] a pay-TV operator provides the socially optimal level of quality given its market share. Quality is higher in pay-TV than under advertising funding. Viewer welfare may be higher or lower: in the pay-TV regime viewers pay more, but they view higher-quality programmes and fewer adverts. If programme quality is difficult to affect, viewer welfare is higher in a free-to-air regime than in pay-TV.

As the number of channels increases, loss of market share per channel reduces quality levels. Hence, other things being equal, more fragmented audiences reduce quality provision. For this reason there is a trade-off between quality and diversity, both of which are desirable to viewers. The optimal number of channels balances the two properties: if excess entry occurs, quality is too low and diversity too high, while insufficient entry limits diversity but provides higher quality.

In passing, the conceptual framework in Appendix 4.1 can be used to shed light on a claim that is sometimes made about the benefits of a public broadcaster: that raising the programme quality of one (regulated) broadcaster forces other (commercial) broadcasters to follow suit.[50] In this model, at least, the opposite result is found. If the quality of one broadcaster is increased then, all else being equal, this decreases the audience of rival broadcasters. Since a pay-TV broadcaster's return to investing in quality is increasing in its audience size, this implies that the commercial broadcaster responds by reducing its programme quality. The same point applies if the public broadcaster offers its programmes for free: this decreases the market share that commercial broadcasters can achieve and hence lowers the quality they provide.

Investment in innovation

Investment in innovation is closely related to quality provision. Whereas quality might often be thought of as deterministic, innovation involves stochastic (unpredictable) improvements. With the return to innovative programmes being risky, the incentive to invest derives from the high returns accruing to successful projects and the return to success must be sufficiently high to offset the possibility of failure. Hence the ability to gain a high return from successful programmes is crucial for innovation, in broadcasting as in any other sector.[51]

Free-to-air broadcasters cannot directly capture additional viewer surplus generated by a successful programme, so the incentive to innovate is weak. As noted above, an advertising-funded broadcaster's incentive is determined by the impact on the valuation of the marginal viewer rather than viewer surplus as a whole; for this reason innovation, like quality, will be underprovided. Pay-TV, by contrast, stimulates innovation by providing a mechanism through which (high) viewer surplus generated by successful innovation can be captured by broadcasters.

4.4 Should people be allowed to watch only what they want?

Public policy towards broadcasting encompasses concerns that go beyond simply meeting viewer demands as currently expressed. The view has long existed that, rather than simply 'giving the public what they want', broadcasters should provide the programmes that they ought to watch (for some reason) and withhold or restrict the material that they ought not to watch.

These concerns were stated explicitly in the early days of (radio) broadcasting in the UK, when the idea that a public broadcaster should control what people received was more widely accepted than it is today. John Reith, the first Director General of the BBC, wrote,[52] 'the preservation of a high moral tone is obviously of paramount importance', although he conceded that '[t]here is no harm in trivial things; in themselves they may even be unquestionably beneficial, for they may assist the more serious work by providing the measure of salt which seasons'. Ronald Coase remarked that public service broadcasting matched the preferences of some listeners more than others: 'Though the programme policy of the [BBC] gave the lower social classes what they ought to have, it gave the educated classes what they wanted.'[53] Moreover, at this time competition in broadcasting was seen as potentially dangerous since it might undermine the ability of the BBC, through its programme monopoly, to control what was received.[54]

There exist a number of possible reasons for the view that, in the broadcasting sector, merely meeting viewers' current demands is not sufficient to maximise social welfare. The arguments can be divided into two broad rationales:

- viewers do not necessarily choose what it is in their own best interests to watch; and
- television viewing has effects on the wider population that are not taken into account by the viewer themselves.

In Section 4.4 we examine the possible arguments in each case.

Do viewers make the 'right' decisions for themselves?

Textbook economics assumes that the consumer is able to assess the contribution of each of the available goods to her utility and make the choice that maximises her welfare. However, this ability may sometimes be less than perfect. There are three reasons why the consumer's choice may sometimes fail to achieve the best outcome for her:

- *experience goods*: the consumer's utility function is fixed and represents what is in her best interests, but she cannot determine all of the relevant characteristics of the good prior to consumption. The consumption experience reveals these characteristics, allowing sub-sequent decisions to be based on better information;

- *merit goods*: characteristics of the good are known in advance of consumption, but the consumer's utility function is not fixed. When a previously untried good is consumed, preferences change such that greater utility is derived from its future consumption; and
- *paternalism*: the consumer's utility function may not represent what is in her best interests, thus utility-maximising choices do not necessarily maximise her welfare.

We start by discussing the arguments surrounding experience and merit goods, then turn to possible justifications for paternalism.

Experience and merit goods

It is likely that there are elements of both experience and merit goods in television programming. The attractions of a new series are not entirely apparent prior to viewing – whether a new comedy will be amusing, for example – and certain tastes develop only with experience. However, these features are true of many other goods, including restaurant meals, music albums and leisure activities. It is unclear why they are deemed (by some) to be so problematic as to justify intervention in broadcasting but not in other sectors.

Moreover, although more complex than the standard case of a fully informed consumer exercising a static utility-maximising choice, rational decisions regarding both experience and merit goods can be taken by consumers. A hypothetical rational consumer anticipates that trying a new product might cause her assessment of its value to go up, either because her knowledge of its characteristics improves (experience goods) or because her tastes are developed by the experience (merit goods). Taking potential future benefits into account, she will consume the good. In addition, consumers frequently learn about product characteristics and the possibility of developing new tastes from the experiences of others: this diffusion process works well for restaurants, holidays and sporting activities and surely also for television programmes.

It might be argued that the consumer could be short-sighted and ignore, or fail to realise, the fact that his tastes or knowledge may change as a result of actions within his control. For anyone with a reasonable level of experience, however, this would imply that he disregards, or perhaps forgets, similar experiences of learning and development in the past; the former would be irrational, while the latter seems implausible. Of course, trying out a new product involves some risk: consumption might turn out not to be desirable after all. But this needs to be balanced against the possibility of higher utility in the future. In this sense sampling is similar to other forms of investment: the consumer incurs a cost now (by consuming a product that does not maximise immediate utility) for the prospect of an attractive return in the future (consumption of the product when it yields high utility). Consumers are capable of undertaking such decisions in other dynamic contexts and moreover, the impact of a poor viewing selection would be rather less severe than a bad choice of mortgage or pension, for example.

Commercial suppliers have an incentive to facilitate learning and the development of new tastes, e.g. through promotions and introductory offers, since they benefit from higher future consumption. To encourage sampling, broadcasters adopt a number of strategies: launch a series on a free-to-air channel then move it to pay-TV, show short excerpts of a programme as a trailer or (with pay-per-view) levy the charge after a portion of the programme has elapsed.[55] The broadcaster could also build a reputation for high-quality programming, increasing viewers' confidence in it and making them more likely to purchase its programmes in the future.

Even if there were a case that experience and merit goods are particularly prevalent in broadcasting and that these problems cannot be overcome as described above, the idea that a broadcaster can make optimal decisions for them is implausible.[56] Viewers are heterogeneous and both the actual preferences and potential tastes of a large number of individuals would need to be assessed. Note that, in the case of merit goods, since what is at issue are tastes that are not yet developed, viewer surveys will be uninformative. Nevertheless, merit good arguments are often put forward as a justification for directing public broadcasters to provide 'challenging' programmes and to stimulate rather than follow viewer tastes.[57]

Paternalism

The paternalistic view is that (some) people are unable to take decisions that are in their best interests and that, left to their own devices, they will fail to achieve the optimal outcome for themselves. In economic terms this implies either that the consumer is for some reason unable to take actions that maximise his utility or that his utility function, both now and in the future, does not represent his true welfare. Even if this were the case, for intervention to make sense it must also be believed that the public authority (here, a public broadcaster or regulator) is able to make better decisions and get closer to achieving consumer welfare.

As illustrated by the quotes above, Reithian broadcasting was based on a heavy dose of paternalism, with the public broadcaster providing programmes that people ought to watch rather than simply those they wanted to watch. Today, the idea that a public broadcaster or government agency knows better than viewers themselves what is good for them, and should exert control over what they watch, gains less acceptance. Moreover, a centrally controlled broadcasting system is open to the risk of bias towards material that the government wants people to see rather than that which it is in their best interests to watch.

Nonetheless, paternalism remains evident in controls on the broadcasting of harmful and offensive material, such as violent or sexually explicit scenes, even now that encryption can be used to prevent unintentional viewing of such material and thus restrict it to those who have chosen to watch.[58] A significant degree of paternalism quite naturally exists in relation to children's viewing. Many parents express concern about the programming that their children are exposed to, as well as the total time spent viewing, and wish to exert some control over this. Wider public concerns have also been raised (e.g. by the UK government and various agencies) over areas such as food advertising to children. This debate presumes that children (in particular) are not capable of making wise choices about what is good for them and that there is a public, as well as parental, obligation to protect them.

Wider impacts of television viewing

A number of arguments for intervention in broadcasting arise from externalities associated with television viewing. That is to say, if large numbers of people watch certain kinds of programmes, this affects the wider population in some way that the viewers themselves do not take into account. An externality may be either positive, generating external benefits, or negative, causing detriment elsewhere. In the presence of positive externalities the market level of consumption is too low from the social perspective; with negative externalities consumption is too high. In either case measures which induce something closer to the socially optimal outcome are justified, as long as this benefit outweighs the cost of intervention.

In this section we examine various external effects of television viewing that have been cited by commentators, starting with positive externalities before then turning to negative ones.

Positive externalities

A number of positive externalities have been claimed for television broadcasting:

- educational benefits;
- network externalities (the 'water cooler' effect); and
- social or 'citizenship' benefits.

That there may be educational effects from television viewing, and external benefits generated by education, is uncontroversial. As well as offering directly educational material (such as schools programming), television can be a powerful medium for providing information about, and stimulating interest in, a variety of topics – ranging from science and technology to history and languages – that can be broadly defined as educational. As with formal types of education this benefits the economy through the creation of a more educated and productive workforce. There may also be direct benefits to particular individuals – for example, if information gathered from watching a medical drama is used to administer life-saving first aid. Since these benefits are quite diffused, they are unlikely to be internalised by market participants and there is a serious prospect that educational programming will be underprovided.

The role of television viewing as a common experience that people discuss 'around the water cooler' might be regarded as a form of network externality. To the extent that these discussions raise enjoyment of viewing commonly watched programmes, there may be a positive externality between the viewing behaviour of different individuals. But the creation of widely known brands through 'water cooler' discussions is commonplace for market-driven products such as pop music, sports teams, novels and Hollywood movies; it is unclear why the existence of such an effect justifies intervention in broadcasting. Mechanisms exist to internalise such externalities: viewers themselves may coordinate their viewing as benefits flow in both directions; meanwhile broadcasters, as beneficiaries of greater uptake, have an incentive to create popular and distinctive programmes that stimulate discussion. Although difficult to quantify, it is unlikely that (uninternalised) effects of this kind are of great importance.

The 'water cooler' effect has also been mentioned as a forum for shared experiences that in turn generate other social benefits. In this view it is not the effect itself but rather its wider behavioural implications that are an externality. For example, Brookes (2004) highlights the role of television in building 'social capital' by improving understanding and building trust between people through shared experiences. However, as noted above, there is little reason to suppose that the mechanism itself will break down under market provision of television. Moreover, there is some irony in highlighting as a mechanism for promoting social cohesion a medium that is also much criticised for contributing to greater isolation and reducing participation in community activities.[59] (Negative effects of television viewing are examined further below.)

There is also the currently popular notion that television is an important medium for building 'citizenship'. The most obvious aspect of this is that accurate reporting of news and current affairs can help create a well-informed citizenry who can adequately discipline government and other powerful interests, to the benefit of all. The role of the media, especially television, in the political process is the focus of current research.[60] However, empirical evidence concerning the impact of television on political involvement is mixed. Prat and Strömberg (2006) find that the introduction of commercial television in Sweden in 1990 raised voter turnout. Gentzkow (2006), however, finds the growth of television to have had a negative impact on voter turnout in the USA, perhaps by inducing substitution away from other media (such as newspapers) which carry more political coverage.

Moving beyond political involvement, it is sometimes argued that people become more community-oriented, or more tolerant, as a result of watching certain behaviour on television. However, a direct link between the messages and representations in television programmes and viewers' behaviour is highly contentious, with little clear evidence. Moreover, even if such a link exists, this must be placed alongside the isolating effect of television noted above. All in all, it is highly unclear that television should be promoted as a means of inducing people to be more community-spirited.

Negative externalities

There are a number of negative externalities associated with television viewing. Quite apart from the possibility of undesirable behavioural responses to particular broadcast content – just as for positive attributes, the link between violence portrayed on television and violent behaviour is controversial – there are a number of reasons to discourage heavy television viewing.

It is sometimes argued that many people spend too much time watching television, from both an individual and a social perspective. On average, each individual in the industrialised world watches television for about three hours every day. Among concerns regarding the sedentary nature of modern life, television viewing is a significant contributing factor. Children's viewing habits in particular are a cause for concern: watching television has been found to lower a child's metabolic rate, reduce physical exercise and invite over-eating (especially when combined with tempting adverts for junk food). Spitzer (2005) argues that television impairs a child's ability to learn and to concentrate. He also estimates that viewing habits and resulting obesity lead to the premature death of around 20,000 Germans each year.

Putnam (2000) summarises various studies about viewing habits and factors that are correlated with them. For instance, he documents a strong correlation between heavy viewing and various indicators of anti-social behaviour (such as the number of letters written to friends, 'giving the finger' to another driver, and so on). Although one would hesitate before inferring any direction of causality – socially isolated individuals might turn to television to fill their time – Putnam also reports the findings of a number of 'natural experiments' where local communities were suddenly able to receive television signals. Field observations indicated a causal link between the introduction of television and the subsequent reduction in community activities.

In its early years, it was hoped that (radio) broadcasting might enliven national life by stimulating other activities. William Haley, then Director General of the BBC, wrote in 1947:[61]

[The public service broadcaster] does not want people to be listening all the time ... For broadcasting will not be a social asset if it produces a nation of listeners ... If it cannot give to literature more readers than it withholds, it will have failed in what should be its true purpose. Its aim must be to make people active, not passive, both in the fields of recreation and public affairs.

Viewed from today, this ambition would appear to have been over-optimistic.

Intervention to mitigate externalities

While there may be disagreements about the source and scale of externalities, there is a coherent rationale for intervention in the broadcasting market to promote those programmes generating positive externalities and to diminish those with negative externalities.

To diminish the negative aspects, broadcasting standards could be imposed to restrict the broadcasting of harmful or inappropriate programming.[62] In relation to children, measures might be adopted to facilitate parents' efforts to control their children's viewing, such as clear programme labelling and time-of-day controls (e.g. the UK's 'nine o'clock watershed', before which the broadcasting of programmes unsuitable for children is not permitted).

Regarding positive externalities, intervention may be desirable to increase the provision of socially beneficial programming. For example, subsidies for educational material may be justified. Provision may be increased by means of obligations imposed on designated public service broadcasters or by giving inducements to all broadcasters to show such programmes. However, in order to generate their desired effects it is crucial that these programmes are actually watched, not just that they are broadcast. We turn to this issue next.

Will people watch what we want them to watch?

In principle, consumption of a product can be increased by reducing its price. In broadcasting, however, individual programmes are typically viewed as part of a channel and once a subscription has been taken out, or in any case if it is broadcast free-to-air, the incremental price for watching any programme is zero. With many attractive programmes available for free at the margin, a negative price (i.e. a payment to the viewer) might be required to increase consumption of socially beneficial content to the optimal level, especially if it does not directly appeal to the viewer's tastes. It is difficult, however, to come up with an effective system to make payments for watching.[63] The price mechanism therefore seems inadequate as a means of inducing people to watch what we want them to watch.

Broadcasters have strategies which exploit viewer behaviour to increase the audience for less popular programmes. If viewers tend to remain tuned to the same channel at the end of a programme, it may be possible to retain their attention for less gripping material by scheduling this between more popular shows (a practice known within the industry as 'hammocking'). However, as viewers increasingly switch around between an ever-expanding range of channels, this strategy becomes less effective.[64]

Ultimately, a more effective approach might be to include PSB messages *within* popular programmes, analogously to the 'product placement' strategy of advertisers. This might include, for example, first-aid techniques demonstrated during medical dramas or instances of racial tolerance occurring within the story lines of popular soaps. The view that by tackling difficult social issues in a responsible manner, soaps are 'providing an important public service' might be interpreted as advocating something similar to this.[65] An historical instance of the strategy of conveying public information messages through popular entertainment is the long-running Radio 4 drama series *The Archers*, originally conceived as a way of keeping farmers informed on best practice.[66] As a means of catching viewers' attention in a multi-channel environment this strategy could become the most, even the only, effective technique to stimulate viewing of PSB material, although care must be taken not to undermine the popularity of a show by overloading it with 'worthy' messages and losing its original appeal.

4.5 Provision of public service broadcasting

Supposing that some form of intervention in broadcasting content is desirable, say to increase the provision of programmes generating educational benefits, how is this to be achieved? The term 'public service broadcasting' encompasses a range of systems and institutions. This section describes and assesses the main options available to policymakers.

To be effective, public service broadcasting needs to achieve two purposes. First, the relevant types of programmes (say, those with educational content) need to be produced and made available to viewers through broadcasting. Second, as explained in Section 4.4, people must be induced to watch them. Since the aim is to satisfy social purposes beyond the viewer's preferences, it cannot simply be presumed that uptake will be sufficiently high to achieve the social optimum.

Two broadly defined systems for providing PSB may be distinguished; in each case the broadcasters may be commercial companies or public bodies (or a combination of the two):

- *licensing*: public service broadcasters are obliged to meet certain programme requirements as conditions of their licence to operate; or
- *commissioning*: public service programmes are commissioned from producers and broadcasters using contestable funding.[67]

We examine the two types of system in turn.

Licensing of public service broadcasters

Under a licensing system, public service obligations are imposed on broadcasters as conditions of their licence. An easily specified and limited obligation would be to require a certain amount of airtime to be devoted to news coverage during peak hours. A more wide-ranging intervention might be to require certain minimum amounts of specified types of programming (e.g. of different genres or with certain educational content). Quality requirements might be stated, although what is meant by quality is subjective and difficult to specify, making this intrinsically harder to regulate. A similar problem applies to innovation.

Programme obligations (beyond what the commercial market would anyway provide) are costly to broadcasters, either directly (by increasing production costs) or as an opportunity cost (by requiring less popular, and hence less profitable, programmes to be shown). Their sustainability depends on two factors: the method of revenue generation used and whether or not the number of channels is constrained. If licence fee funding is used then, in principle at least, its level can be set to match the cost of the obligations. With advertising funding or pay-TV, obligations are sustainable as long as broadcasters can generate sufficient revenues to cover the costs incurred. While the number of channels is tightly constrained due to spectrum scarcity, the high rents that accrue to commercial broadcasters[68] can be used as an implicit form of funding, cross-subsidising public service obligations. Without spectrum constraints, competition between channels eliminates scarcity rents. Public service obligations must then either be reduced so as not to undermine these broadcasters' viability or imposed on all broadcasters so that even with entry (which will then be more limited) costs can still be covered. Alternatively, direct funding of public service obligations, from a licence fee or general taxation, could be used.

A regulator must specify licence obligations, monitor compliance and determine the renewal or reallocation of licences. The burden of regulation increases with the complexity of licence terms and the number of licensees. If licences are granted for a lengthy period (e.g. for several years at a time), the incentive for compliance is weak: the ultimate penalty for failure to meet programming obligations is licence withdrawal, but this is a distant (and sometimes implausible) threat.

Commissioning of public service programmes

In a commissioning system, funds from a licence fee or taxation are used to finance programme commissions. In principle, programmes may be sourced from any producer (including independent production units) and broadcast on any channel, either purchasing the programme and the broadcasting slot separately or procuring them together from a vertically integrated broadcaster. Competitive tendering mechanisms provide incentives for efficient production and minimise acquisition costs: competitive bidding will drive subsidies down to the difference between production cost and revenues gained from elsewhere (e.g. from advertisers), not the full programme cost. Moreover, with frequent commissions, repeated interactions stimulate producers to build and sustain a reputation for delivering high quality.

Although the focus of recent attention, the idea that broadcasters might compete for public funds is not a new one.[69] In 1936 *The Economist*, quoted in Coase (1950), asked: 'Is it really necessary to choose [between the American and British systems]? Could not the merits of both systems be combined? ... Let the State continue to collect the licence, let it, if you will, own the actual transmitting stations. But let the programmes be provided by two corporations, say the ABC and the BBC, competing with each other. They should share the licence revenue and the listener might even be permitted to distribute some very small fraction of his ten shillings as a mark of favour to the corporation which he considers the better.'

A commissioning body or 'Arts Council of the Air' would be needed, to call for tenders or specify areas within which programmes are invited, assess competing bids and award contracts. Multiple commissioning bodies might be used:[70] this could introduce competition (or at least benchmarking) into the commissioning activity itself and help prevent good projects from falling through the net. Alternatively there could be specialisation in the commissioning process, with separate bodies for music, the sciences and so on. Moreover, a system with multiple commissioning bodies would be less susceptible to capture by a particular broadcaster or interest group.

In either a licensing or commissioning system, requirements must be determined with a view to the ability to attract viewers, both when devising commissions or licence obligations and in selecting broadcasters. Innovative formats and non-traditional broadcasters may be effective in reaching new audiences, especially those that are traditionally harder to reach.[71]

4.6 Public service broadcasting in the analogue era

We now draw on the analysis set out above to examine the rationale for, and provision of, public service broadcasting. First, in this section, we consider the traditional analogue environment; then, in Section 4.7, we turn to the digital world. Technological developments are a crucial part of this, so each section starts by briefly describing the relevant features. We examine the applicability of market failure and 'citizenship' arguments for intervention given those characteristics, drawing out implications for the nature and scope of PSB. Finally, we consider the means by which public service broadcasting might be provided in each setting and its relative effectiveness.

Analogue terrestrial broadcasting is characterised by two key features:

- *spectrum constraints* limit the number of channels and broadcasters earn scarcity rents since returns cannot be driven down by free entry; and
- *non-excludability* of viewing requires programmes to be broadcast free-to-air, eliminating subscription as a means of generating revenue.[72]

Since commercial broadcasters are unlikely to have access to licence fee funding,[73] in practice the second feature implies that advertising is their sole source of funds. Thus, under analogue broadcasting a market system would consist of just a small number of advertising-funded broadcasters. Drawing on the analysis in Section 4.3 it can be seen that the outcome of such a market would fail to meet the demands of television viewers in a number of respects; clearly, a 'market failure' rationale for PSB exists in analogue broadcasting:

- *diversity* of programming is insufficient, with broadcasters duplicating popular genres rather than serving niche tastes;
- *quality* of programming is too low;
- *innovation* incentives are poor; and
- *airtime devoted to advertising* tends to be excessive, especially if its nuisance cost to viewers is high.

Added to this, there are wider concerns beyond the viewer's preferences that may justify some form of intervention. Although arguments that viewers fail to make the best choices for themselves do not seem sufficiently strong to merit intervention in the generality of cases, a more paternalistic approach towards children may be justified. With all channels broadcast free-to-air, it may be necessary to prohibit certain types of unpleasant material to prevent unintentional viewing. While disagreements exist over the precise sources and magnitude of externalities, wider social and educational effects of television provide a coherent rationale for intervention to increase provision of programmes generating positive externalities and diminish those with negative externalities.

To summarise, in the analogue context an appropriate system of PSB would be designed to:

- provide programmes catering for interests which would otherwise be left unserved;
- stimulate higher quality and innovation in programming;
- limit the amount of airtime given over to advertising (if this can be done without further weakening broadcasters' incentives for quality provision);
- restrict the broadcasting of harmful material and protect children; and
- promote the provision and viewing of socially beneficial programmes, such as those containing educational material.

Most of these purposes can be seen in existing systems of public service broadcasting, including the UK's. A case study of this system is given in Section 4.8.

Turning to provision, rents resulting from spectrum constraints can be used as an implicit source of funding for costly public service obligations (via a licensing system), reducing the need for direct government subsidy or a (higher) licence fee. A further implication of spectrum constraints is that the viewer faces a limited choice of channels. If public service broadcasters account for a high proportion (perhaps even all) of these channels, they can largely determine what people watch. Historically, in the face of limited competition, socially desirable but less popular programmes have nonetheless been able to gain a reasonable audience.

4.7 Public service broadcasting in the digital world

The adoption of digital technology, with related developments, fundamentally alters the characteristics of television broadcasting. Specifically the following technological changes, often referred to under the umbrella term of 'digitisation', are taking place:

- *digital compression techniques* allow many more channels to be broadcast for a given spectrum allocation, greatly relaxing the constraint on the number of channels;[74]
- *conditional access systems* facilitate the exclusion of unauthorised viewing,[75] making subscription funding feasible; and
- *personal video recorders* give the viewer far greater control over the timing and content of television viewing.

Moving to pay-TV, especially when combined with a huge expansion in the number of channels, greatly mitigates the market failures arising under advertising-funded broadcasting. Since viewer surplus can be extracted, commercial broadcasters have an incentive to deliver a diverse range of programmes, with quality appropriate to viewers' willingness to pay.[76] Fewer adverts are shown in pay-TV;[77] moreover, if the use of PVRs becomes widespread this will undermine advertising as a source of funding and further reduce the number of adverts shown, perhaps to a level that is too low from a social (and viewers') perspective, as shown in Appendix 4.1. Viewer charging can be implemented in ways that minimise exclusion of desired viewing, using pricing techniques such as bundling and windowing.

The move to pay-TV might raise certain access issues. Charging may mean that some viewers watch a more limited number of channels than if all were broadcast free-to-air. Although this is largely a matter of individual choice, and some of the programming would not have been produced anyway without the ability to charge viewers, distributional concerns might be raised. For example, with its ability to capture viewer surplus, pay-TV can outbid free-to-air broadcasters for popular sports rights (although this may be mitigated by other benefits to football clubs from retaining some amount of free-to-air coverage). For this reason, in the UK certain sports events deemed to be of national importance are 'listed' to restrict the acquisition of exclusive pay-TV rights and ensure wide public access to them.[78]

In the digital world, viewer sovereignty in the market place largely removes the 'market failure' basis for PSB, as the unregulated market will give people broadly what they want to watch. This does not necessarily imply that there is no basis for intervention, however. We saw in Section 4.6, for the case of analogue broadcasting, that there are arguments for controls on the broadcasting of certain types of harmful material and for increasing the provision of programmes which generate wider social benefits. These arguments do not disappear with digitisation, although some changes might be possible.

Enhanced viewer control, resulting from encryption and PVR use, allow individuals to avoid seeing unwanted material. These technologies can also assist parents in controlling what children view. If these protections are deemed adequate it might be possible to relax existing prohibitions on the broadcasting of certain material, as long as this is shown only on encrypted channels (perhaps with PIN protection) and clearly labelled as to its nature.[79] Where significant negative externalities arise, however, an outright ban would probably still be justified.

There is little reason to suppose that the magnitude of positive externalities alters significantly with digitisation. It is possible that market provision of some types of socially beneficial programmes will increase, to the extent that these are favoured by minority tastes that will now be served. Even so, market underprovision of socially beneficial programmes remains very likely and some form of intervention to increase supply may be desirable.

However, following digitisation the question of whether people will actually watch socially beneficial programmes becomes a critical one. In its early, monopoly days the BBC could effectively force viewers to watch the programmes it thought they should, since the only alternative was to switch off. The introduction of competition from commercial television reduced the BBC's control, but while the number of channels remained limited the audience for public service material held up fairly well. In the digital world the availability of a huge range of competing channels with electronic programme guides to assist selection, together with the introduction of PVRs, increases enormously the ease with which the viewer can switch channel or skip some part of it as soon as less appealing content comes on. When presented with so much attractive material, viewers may exercise this option by choosing entertainment over more challenging and educational material.[80] In this environment socially beneficial programmes may struggle to gain attention: even if we think it is desirable for people to watch more, or higher-quality, news than they would do if left to themselves, there may be little that can be done about this. As Richard Eyre, then Chief Executive of ITV, put it succinctly:[81]

Free school milk doesn't work when the kids go and buy Coca-Cola because it's available and they prefer it and they can afford it. So public service broadcasting will soon be dead.

Unlike the Reithian era, the idea that competition should be held back – if this were even possible – so that viewing can be directed towards public service programming would not gain acceptance today. With no realistic scope for reducing commercial competition, alternative means of promoting the uptake of public service content must be found if the system is to continue. As described in Section 4.4, this might utilise methods akin to 'product placement', but there are limits to how far this can be taken without undermining a programme's appeal. Whatever their desirability, if positive externalities cannot, in fact, be realised then these constitute a weak basis for public intervention. With the 'market failure' rationale largely removed and growing difficulties in getting people to watch 'what we want them to watch', the likely outcome is that (aside from controls on harmful material) public service broadcasting will indeed soon be dead.

Provision of public service broadcasting in the digital world
On the assumption that some level of intervention to increase the provision of certain types of programming is nonetheless desired, we next examine the implications of digitisation for the funding and delivery of PSB.

Following digitisation and the relaxation of spectrum constraints, channel entry intensifies competition and eliminates the scarcity rents of incumbents. Whatever the source of revenue, commercial broadcasters' profits fall as audiences fragment.[82] Advertising revenue is additionally threatened by the use of PVRs to avoid adverts. Unless spectrum availability is artificially constrained, gifted spectrum can no

longer confer sufficient value to fund expensive programming requirements. Onerous PSB obligations imposed on commercial broadcasters
become unsustainable, threatening the survival of a broad system of
provision that includes commercial as well as public broadcasters.
If commercial broadcasters are to participate, direct subsidies will
be required and these must be funded out of general taxation or by
'top-slicing' the licence fee revenues currently granted to public
broadcasters.

The licence fee, unlike advertising revenue, is immune to commercial
pressure. However, as a compulsory charge on all TV viewers, it is
subject to popular acceptability. This is likely to be threatened in the
digital world, for two main reasons. First, the growing use of broadband, and even mobile phones, for video streaming blurs the distinction
between the television set and other devices, rendering a licence fee that
applies to one but not the rest increasingly arbitrary. Extending the
licence fee to these areas, however, is likely to be politically unpalatable
and difficult to enforce, making its abolition the more likely outcome.
Second, while the licence fee is acceptable to most people when the
programmes it funds constitute the major part of their viewing,[83] this
support is likely to fall in line with the viewing share of the public
broadcaster (and as increasing numbers also subscribe to pay-TV).
Ofcom reports that '[t]he TV licence fee is already questioned by viewers whose use of the BBC's services is declining',[84] while survey evidence suggests that the majority of viewers regard the licence fee as no
longer justified in a multi-channel environment.[85] As Gavyn Davies
predicted some years ago:[86]

> The digital age will increasingly be one in which many or most consumers of
> television pay for packages closely tailored to their needs. As they become
> more accustomed to choice, to subscription and to pay-per-view, it could be
> that the licence fee will come to seem an anachronism.

If correct, this analysis implies that the licence fee as well as commercial
funding of PSB is undermined in the digital world. Funds might instead
be provided out of general taxation, although this too requires political
support and in practice the amount involved is likely to be much more
limited. If multiple providers are to be retained, public funds must be
made available to commercial as well as public broadcasters, perhaps
through a competitive commissioning system.

The scope of public broadcasters

A further problem arises from the blurring of the boundary between the activities of public broadcasters and those of commercial operators. In an analogue setting where purely commercial broadcasters would fail to generate the kinds of programmes that viewers desire, the role of public broadcasters in fulfilling viewer demands was uncontroversial. But now that the commercial sector is capable of meeting these demands, the activities of public broadcasters are increasingly in conflict with this. With licence fee funding given to public broadcasters alone, commercial broadcasters complain of unfair competition and crowding out. Whether this is detrimental to welfare depends on the relative efficiencies of the broadcasters and the attractiveness to viewers of their respective services, but the distortion of competition is likely to generate some inefficiency.

To tackle this problem, a tighter definition of the role of public service broadcasters, limiting this to areas that the commercial sector would not otherwise provide, is advisable. Licence fee funds (if the licence fee is retained) would also need to be ring-fenced and potentially made available to other broadcasters if they produce programmes to fulfil public purposes.

4.8 Public service broadcasting in the UK

As a case study, we describe the system of public service broadcasting in the UK. This regime was developed in the analogue era, with its origins dating back to the 1920s (initially for radio broadcasting). It now faces pressure from digitisation: many households have already adopted digital television and digital switchover (i.e. turning off the analogue signal) is due to be completed by the end of 2012.

The section has two main parts. First, we describe in detail the purposes stated for PSB in the UK and its current system of provision, relating these features to the analysis of Section 4.6. Second, we discuss threats to the future sustainability of this system with the onset of digital broadcasting.

The UK's public service broadcasting system

The purposes of the UK's brand of public service broadcasting are defined under the Communications Act 2003 (hereafter 'the Act').

Section 264(4) of the Act provides general statements of purpose, while detailed elements are specified in Section 264(6). The full text of the latter is set out in Box 4.4. In addition to the kinds of public service obligations described in this chapter, the remit includes an element of national and regional industrial policy; see Section 264(6)(j).[87]

Examining the stated purposes of PSB in the light of the analysis presented in Section 4.6, the following features can be noted. A diverse range of programme types is specified, including comedy and drama, news and current affairs, religion, the arts, sports and other leisure interests. Moreover, 'matters of specialist interest' are explicitly mentioned. These can be interpreted as a response to the traditional market failure resulting in insufficient programme diversity: some of these genres would most likely be underprovided by advertising-funded broadcasters in the analogue era, although many others seem sufficiently popular to survive without intervention.[88]

The breadth of this remit – explicitly stating 'entertainment' as a purpose of PSB – allows the BBC (the licence fee-funded public broadcaster) to show considerable amounts of popular entertainment, especially during peak hours on its flagship channel, BBC1. It has also been used to justify the authorisation as PSB of new BBC channels covering general entertainment (BBC3) and rolling news (BBC News 24), to the dismay of commercial broadcasters.

Public service broadcasting also aims to mitigate traditional market failures regarding quality and innovation. Section 264(4) of the Act requires the maintenance of 'high general standards' in respect of programme content, production quality and editorial integrity. Specifying what 'quality' means precisely and monitoring this are difficult however; see relevant parts of Ofcom (2004a, 2004b, 2005). Innovation is encouraged, most notably in relation to Channel 4 which is required under the Act to demonstrate 'innovation, experiment and creativity in the form and content of programmes'; as for quality, this is difficult to regulate.

The UK's historic PSB system, consisting of monopoly provision by a single public broadcaster (the BBC), provided poor incentives for innovation. The main spur to innovation has tended to come from competition, not always from desirable or legal sources.[89] The recognition that competition could be beneficial led to the licensing of ITV (Channel 3) in 1955 and subsequently Channels 4 and 5. This has stimulated innovation somewhat, although both the BBC and ITV have been criticised for lack of originality and use of derivative formats.[90]

Box 4.4: PSB under the Communications Act 2003

264(6) A manner of fulfilling the purposes of public service television broadcasting in the United Kingdom is compatible with this subsection if it ensures –

a) that the relevant television services (taken together) comprise a public service for the dissemination of information and for the provision of education and entertainment;

b) that cultural activity in the United Kingdom, and its diversity, are reflected, supported and stimulated by the representation in those services (taken together) of drama, comedy and music, by the inclusion of feature films in those services and by the treatment of other visual and performing arts;

c) that those services (taken together) provide, to the extent that is appropriate for facilitating civic understanding and fair and well-informed debate on news and current affairs, a comprehensive and authoritative coverage of news and current affairs in, and in the different parts of, the United Kingdom and from around the world;

d) that those services (taken together) satisfy a wide range of different sporting and other leisure interests;

e) that those services (taken together) include what appears to OFCOM to be a suitable quantity and range of programmes on educational matters, of programmes of an educational nature and of other programmes of educative value;

f) that those services (taken together) include what appears to OFCOM to be a suitable quantity and range of programmes dealing with each of the following, science, religion and other beliefs, social issues, matters of international significance or interest and matters of specialist interest;

g) that the programmes included in those services that deal with religion and other beliefs include –

  i) programmes providing news and other information about different religions and other beliefs;

  ii) programmes about the history of different religions and other beliefs; and

  iii) programmes showing acts of worship and other ceremonies and practices (including some showing acts of worship and other ceremonies in their entirety);

h) that those services (taken together) include what appears to OFCOM to be a suitable quantity and range of high quality and original programmes for children and young people;

Box 4.4 (cont.)

i) that those services (taken together) include what appears to OFCOM to be a sufficient quantity of programmes that reflect the lives and concerns of different communities and cultural interests and traditions within the United Kingdom, and locally in different parts of the United Kingdom;

j) that those services (taken together), so far as they include programmes made in the United Kingdom, include what appears to OFCOM to be an appropriate range and proportion of programmes made outside the M25 area.

Educational programmes and those 'of educative value' are included among the purposes of PSB under the Act. Coverage of news and current affairs must be comprehensive and authoritative, 'facilitating civic understanding and fair and well-informed debate'. Programmes dealing with social issues are mentioned, as are those 'that reflect the lives and concerns of different communities' in the UK. These specifications would seem to reflect various positive externalities associated with television: education, social concerns and the building of community understanding.

Certain exclusionary controls apply to television broadcasting. Advertising ceilings are placed on broadcasters to counter the bias towards excessive advertising in a free-to-air system.[91] The BBC provides its channels advertising-free, motivated in part by the threat posed to editorial freedom from reliance on advertising revenue, though it should be noted that this may result in underprovision compared with the welfare (as opposed to viewer) optimum. Controls also exist on the broadcasting of potentially harmful material, in the form of broadcasting codes.

Turning now to provision, the UK's is a licensing system. Licences are awarded to a number of broadcasters,[92] including both statutory (i.e. public) corporations (the BBC, Channel 4 and S4C) and commercial companies (the Channel 3 licensees, known collectively as 'ITV', Five and Teletext). Licences specify programme obligations (which vary between broadcasters) and are awarded for a number of years (the BBC's charter is typically renewed for ten years). Key facts about each public service broadcaster are summarised in

Table 4.1: UK public service broadcasters

Broadcaster	PSB channels	Structure	Funding
British Broadcasting Corporation (BBC)	BBC1, BBC2 plus six digital-only	Statutory corporation	TV licence fee
Channel 3 licensees	ITV1	5 commercial companies	Advertising
Channel 4 Corporation	Channel 4 (not in Wales)	Statutory corporation	Advertising
S4C	S4C (Wales only)	Statutory corporation	Government grant, advertising and BBC programming
Five	Five	Commercial	Advertising
Teletext	Text service	Commercial	Advertising

Table 4.1; further details and historical background are contained in Appendix 4.2.

In return for programme obligations public service broadcasters are granted funding concessions, either a guaranteed revenue stream (the licence fee or government grant) or gifted spectrum from which advertising revenues are earned. Revenue from the licence fee, set at £131.50 per annum for a household in 2006–2007, goes entirely to the BBC. All public service broadcasters hold gifted spectrum, for which the commercial licensees (the ITV franchisees and Five) pay annual licence fees to the government, though lower amounts than would be paid in a purely commercial system.[93] As public bodies Channel 4 and S4C pay no licence fees; S4C also receives a grant from the government and some programming from the BBC.

The public service broadcasters operate the only analogue channels, while on digital platforms they compete with other, fully commercial broadcasters.[94] The BBC offers six digital-only channels in addition to its two analogue ones. All PSB channels are shown on the cable and satellite platforms under must-carry/must-provide regulations.

The impact of digital broadcasting

With the growth of digital broadcasting the UK's system of PSB is facing a number of distinct but related threats to its long-term sustainability:

- public acceptance of the licence fee is in decline as more households adopt multi-channel TV;
- spectrum rents used to provide implicit subsidies to advertising-funded public service broadcasters are diminishing; and
- for commercial broadcasters, acceptance of programme obligations in return for gifted spectrum may prove unattractive close to digital switchover (even if some spectrum rents remain).

As discussed in Section 4.7, acceptance of a compulsory licence fee appears to fall as households adopt multi-channel (especially pay-) TV and their viewing of BBC channels declines. The BBC has recently been criticised by some for 'dumbing down' its output and engaging in ratings wars with ITV in an attempt to maintain its popularity. Now, faced with renewal of its charter in 2007, the BBC has changed tack with a campaign to define its role as the promoter of 'public value'.[95] If the current level of licence fee funding cannot be defended and its public service role is to be maintained, the BBC may eventually need to raise revenue by alternative means (e.g. subscription) or be given funds from general taxation.

The licence obligations of the other public service broadcasters are funded by means of analogue spectrum concessions. ITV plc, the largest of the commercial public service broadcasters, has estimated its additional programming costs at around £250 million per annum.[96] As digitisation relaxes spectrum constraints and competitive entry takes place, the rents used to fund PSB obligations are being eroded.[97] Ultimately, as these rents disappear, programme obligations must either be removed (and hence public service broadcasting largely abandoned, except by the BBC)[98] or subsidised out of public funds.

A further issue arises for the commercial public service broadcasters (the Channel 3 licensees and Five). As shareholder-controlled firms looking to maximise returns, their willingness to participate in PSB cannot be taken for granted (as it can for the BBC, Channel 4 and S4C). These companies have the option of abandoning (or not seeking to renew) their PSB licences and instead undertaking purely commercial broadcasting on digital terrestrial and other platforms (although not on analogue terrestrial, for which spectrum is available only through the PSB licences). The relative return to the two modes of broadcasting is crucial to this decision. With costly PSB obligations, they will participate only if the benefits of PSB, relative to the commercial alternative, exceed this cost.

As noted above, digitisation undermines the value of spectrum concessions granted to public service broadcasters. Another possible benefit of participation in PSB is 'due prominence' on electronic programme guides (EPGs) given to PSB channels. But although EPG positioning is important to broadcasters since this allows their channels to be found more easily,[99] prominence might be obtained in other ways.[100] In any case, this value is unlikely to be sufficient to sustain a lot of costly PSB obligations. A further incentive for continued participation over the next few years is that, until digital switchover, PSB licences retain a value from linkages between analogue and digital viewing. As well as carrying their existing analogue audiences over to the digital platform, giving these channels an inherited advantage in the digital world, broadcasters can (and do) use airtime on their analogue channels to cross-promote their digital services and thus increase viewing shares for all their digital channels. Until digital switchover becomes imminent, commercial broadcasters are unlikely to want to abandon their PSB licences.

Although it is unclear precisely how these calculations stack up, serious threats to the long-term sustainability of ITV1, Channel 4 and Five as PSB channels must be recognised. Under the worst-case scenario the BBC will be left as the only significant provider of PSB. Moreover, with support for the television licence fee in decline, even the BBC's position cannot be seen as unassailable.

Although it may be possible to prop up the PSB system, perhaps by increasing direct public funding and spreading this between a wider range of providers, it must be questioned whether this is actually worthwhile. Market provision in the digital world is far less prone to traditional market failures and will supply broadly the programmes that viewers wish to watch. Although remaining externality and 'citizenship' concerns provide a rationale for ongoing, but much more limited, public intervention, the weakening of broadcasters' ability to ensure that public service material is actually watched undermines the effectiveness of such intervention. It would not be unreasonable to conclude that, given the declining benefits and major costs of intervening in this market, including the distortion to competition due to the presence of a state-funded broadcaster, the time has come when large-scale intervention is no longer appropriate.

4.9 Conclusion

To conclude, we put forward key messages from our analysis for students, researchers and policymakers.

Lessons for students: what have we learned?

For the student, the following conclusions may be drawn from this chapter.

- Advertising-funded broadcasting is prone to a number of market failures. In particular:
  - an insufficiently diverse range of programme genres is produced;
  - programme quality is too low;
  - innovation incentives are weak; and
  - the airtime devoted to advertising tends to be excessive, especially if its nuisance cost to viewers is high. This is a form of allocative inefficiency.
- When broadcasters can charge viewers (i.e. in pay-TV) these biases are largely mitigated. Compared with advertising-funded broadcasting:
  - a diverse range of programme genres is produced, satisfying the breadth of viewers' tastes;
  - quality is higher and broadly appropriate to viewers' willingness to pay;
  - incentives to invest in innovative programming are higher;
  - fewer adverts are shown, benefiting viewers but harming advertisers; and
  - price discrimination through channel bundling can mitigate inefficient exclusion of viewers.
- Spectrum scarcity in analogue broadcasting creates a barrier to entry, limiting competition and generating scarcity rents. Digital technologies relax spectrum constraints and facilitate competitive entry, eliminating rents.
- A number of externalities are cited for television broadcasting, both positive and negative.

Lessons for researchers: what do we still need to know?

There is a long literature on the economics of broadcasting, stretching back almost sixty years. We have drawn on many of these papers in this chapter. Even so, a number of important questions call out for further research, especially empirical investigation.

- To what extent is excess entry a significant issue in digital broadcasting?
- How can the 'quality' of television programmes (in the sense defined in Section 4.3) be measured? What underlying factors does it depend on?
- As the ownership and use of the personal video recorder becomes widespread, to what extent do people use its enhanced capabilities to avoid advertising in television? What is the impact on advertising revenue? Can we infer from such behaviour the disutility of advertising for viewers?
- Can robust evidence be gathered about the relationship between television viewing and individual behaviour? What are the behavioural effects of television viewing in general? What are the behavioural effects of viewing specific types of programming?
- Can the various externalities cited for broadcasting be quantified?

Lessons for policymakers: what are the priorities for policy in this area?

The future of public service broadcasting has been the focus of recent policy debate in the UK. The UK is in a period of transition between analogue and digital broadcasting: the number of homes that have adopted digital television is increasing steadily[101] and digital switchover is due to be completed by 2012. Thus, the impact of digitisation on public service broadcasting needs to be recognised and addressed in the near future. As a contribution to this debate, both in the UK and elsewhere, we put forward the following recommendations for policymakers:

- Public service broadcasting systems in countries such as the UK were coherent responses to the market failures inherent in advertising-funded broadcasting and thus were relevant in the analogue era. Digital broadcasting is less prone to traditional market failures and will supply the programmes that viewers broadly wish to watch. With this development, the 'market failure' rationale for PSB largely falls away.

- The remaining rationale for public intervention is linked to externality and 'citizenship' concerns. There is a case for continued intervention, but of more limited form and at a scale appropriate to the magnitude of these externalities.
- Although wider benefits of public service content may merit intervention, the ability to ensure actual viewing of programmes that do not appeal directly to the viewer's preferences is increasingly constrained in the digital world. If public service messages are to gain viewer attention, methods similar to 'product placement' may be required. If significant audiences cannot be captured, policymakers should reconsider whether continued intervention is appropriate.
- Relaxation of spectrum constraints will eliminate the rents currently used as an implicit source of funding for part of the UK's public service output. One possibility is to replace this amount with public funds. But raising the level of public funding at a time when the rationale for, and effectiveness of, PSB is declining would be highly questionable.

Appendix 4.1: A duopoly model of programme quality

This appendix presents the formal model discussed in Section 4.3. There are two broadcasters, A and B, each supplying a single channel.[102] Suppose that over the relevant period each viewer watches a single channel. There is an exogenous level of horizontal product differentiation between the two channels: if broadcaster i supplies viewers with utility u_i it will obtain a market share of viewers given by the Hotelling formula

$$s_i = \frac{1}{2} + \frac{u_i - u_j}{2t}$$

where $t > 0$ measures the exogenous degree of channel differentiation and u_j is utility provided by the rival broadcaster. Utility u_i is made up of three ingredients:

$$u_i = v_i - \delta n_i - p_i,$$

where v_i is the endogenous quality of the broadcaster's output, n_i is the number of adverts shown on the channel and p_i is the subscription charge (if any). The parameter δ represents the perceived nuisance of each advert to viewers. Suppose that a broadcaster's advertising revenue is proportional to its audience. More precisely, suppose that if a broadcaster chooses a quantity of advertising n it receives advertising revenue $R(n)$ per viewer. Assume that there are decreasing returns to the number of adverts shown, in the sense that $R(.)$ is a concave function. A broadcaster can choose its quality v_i by incurring the quadratic fixed cost $\gamma v_i^2 / 2$. There are no other costs involved in delivering programmes to viewers. In sum, the profit of broadcaster i is

$$\pi_i = \left(\frac{1}{2} + \frac{v_i - \delta n_i - p_i - (v_j - \delta n_j - p_j)}{2t}\right)(p_i + R(n_i)) - \frac{1}{2}\gamma v_i^2. \quad (1)$$

We next analyse the outcomes of this model, first in the case where broadcasters can charge directly for viewing and then when broadcasters must rely on advertising revenue alone to fund their operations.

Pay-TV regime
One can show that broadcaster i's profit in (1) is concave in (p_i, v_i) if and only if

$$4t\gamma > 1 \quad (2)$$

and this is assumed henceforth. (If this condition does not hold, then there is no market-sharing equilibrium and a channel wishes to corner the market for viewers by setting a high-quality level.)

Since $p_i = v_i - u_i - \delta n_i$, broadcaster i's profit in expression (1) can be written as

$$\pi_i = \left(\frac{1}{2} + \frac{u_i - u_j}{2t}\right)(v_i - u_i + R(n_i) - \delta n_i) - \frac{1}{2}\gamma v_i^2.$$

Therefore, it is a dominant strategy (i.e. regardless of the broadcaster's chosen level of utility u_i) for each broadcaster to choose the advertising intensity n_1, where

$$n_1 \text{ maximises } R(n) - \delta n. \quad (3)$$

Given market share s_i, which is determined by the two broadcasters' choices of utilities u_i and u_j, firm i's most profitable choice of quality is given by $v_i = s_i / \gamma$. Thus, when subscription charges are used, private and social incentives to supply quality coincide and broadcasters supply the socially optimal level of programme quality given the size of their audience. (This result is an artefact of the assumption that all viewers have the same preferences about programme quality.)

One can calculate that the symmetric equilibrium subscription price and quality are respectively given by

$$p_1 = t - R(n_1); \ v_1 = \frac{1}{2\gamma}. \tag{4}$$

Note from (4) that if $R(n_1) > t$ then firms would like to charge a *negative* price for viewing: the revenue from advertising is so great that firms wish to pay viewers to watch. Since this outcome is not likely to be feasible in practice, we impose a non-negativity constraint on subscription prices. With this assumption, if parameters are such that $R(n_1) > t$ then the regime of 'pay-TV' collapses to the free-to-air advertising-funding regime, since firms do not charge viewers (even though they could). Therefore, differences between the two regimes exist only when

$$R(n_1) < t, \tag{5}$$

and this is assumed henceforth.

Broadcasters break even if and only if the concavity condition (2) is satisfied, in which case the industry profit is $t - 1/(4\gamma)$. Notice that this equilibrium profit is *increasing* in γ, the cost of making better programmes. (Of course, keeping a rival broadcaster's actions fixed, one broadcaster's profits will decrease if its cost γ rises. However, when each firm's cost rises, there is a strategic effect that softens competition and the net effect in this model is for equilibrium profits to rise.)

One policy intervention that would increase viewer surplus (but not overall welfare) is to require channels to raise the quality of their programmes above the equilibrium level of $v = 1/(2\gamma)$. As long as this does not cause the channels to go bankrupt, it has no effect on the prices offered to viewers. Of course, however, programme quality is something that is intrinsically hard to regulate.

Finally, consider the effect of advertising becoming impossible (say, due to the widespread adoption of PVRs). In this model, the only effect is to increase the price to viewers; programme quality is not affected. Viewers are strictly worse off: the increase in price outweighs a viewer's benefit of not having to watch adverts. The equilibrium level of advertising in expression (3) describes a viewer's ideal amount of advertising, given that the revenue from advertising is passed on to the viewer in the form of a reduced subscription charge. A similar point is that, in the pay-TV regime, there is no argument (even from the perspective of viewers alone) for regulation that places a ceiling on the amount of advertising that broadcasters show.

Advertising-funded TV

Turning next to the advertising-only framework, a broadcaster's profit is

$$\pi_i = \left(\frac{1}{2} + \frac{v_i - \delta n_i - \left(v_j - \delta n_j\right)}{2t}\right) R(n_i) - \tfrac{1}{2}\gamma v_i^2$$

(This is just expression (1) with the subscription prices set equal to zero.) The first-order conditions for symmetric equilibrium in advertising intensity and programme quality are

$$\frac{R'(n_2)}{R(n_2)} = \frac{\delta}{t} \tag{6}$$

and

$$v_2 = \frac{R(n_2)}{2t\gamma} \tag{7}$$

From (3), (5) and (6) we have

$$\frac{R'(n_1)}{R(n_1)} = \frac{\delta}{R(n_1)} > \frac{\delta}{t} = \frac{R'(n_2)}{R(n_2)}$$

By concavity, the function R'/R is decreasing in n and so we deduce that there is *less* advertising in the pay-TV regime than in the advertising-funded regime.

Since $n_2 > n_1$ it follows by concavity that $R'(n_2) < R'(n_1) = \delta$, and so expression (6) demonstrates that $R(n_2) < t$. This inequality implies that quality v_2 in (7) is *lower* than in the pay-TV regime, when quality was given by $v_1 = 1/(2\gamma)$. Of course, in the case of advertising-funded television, the widespread adoption of PVRs would most likely prove fatal.

We must check that broadcasters break even in this model with advertising funding. Industry profits are

$$R(n_2) - \gamma v_2^2 = R(n_2)\left(1 - \frac{R(n_2)}{4\gamma t^2}\right)$$

where the equality follows from (7). Notice that these profits are 'inverse-U' shaped in advertising revenue: too little advertising revenue obviously leads to low profits, but too much revenue causes firms to compete very hard for viewers by offering high-quality programmes and this also drives down profits. As in the pay-TV regime, the broadcasters' profits are increasing with γ. The above expression shows that profits are positive provided that $R(n_2) < 4\gamma t^2$. However, we have just shown that $R(n_2) < t$ and so a sufficient condition for this is that $4\gamma t > 1$, which is exactly the condition (2) that ensures that the broadcasters break even in the pay-TV regime. Therefore, whenever broadcasters break even in the pay-TV regime they will also break even when they must rely on advertising alone. (Note that we are not suggesting that profits are higher with free-to-air broadcasting; in many cases they will not be.)

Comparison of viewer surplus

Finally, we can compare viewer surplus in the two funding regimes. First, consider the case of exogenously fixed programme quality v (or, equivalently, the case of very large γ). In this case, viewers in the pay-TV regime have utility

$$u_1 = v + R(n_1) - t - \delta n_1 \tag{8}$$

whereas in the free-to-air regime, viewer utility is

$$u_2 = v - \delta n_2 \tag{9}$$

When $t < R(n_1)$ the two regimes coincide if negative prices are not feasible. When $t = R(n_1)$ one can check that $n_1 = n_2$ and so expressions (8) and (9) are equal. Next, consider the effect on the two utilities of raising t above $R(n_1)$. Clearly, from expression (8) we have $du_1/dt = -1$. However, by differentiating expression (6) it follows from

(9) that $du_2/dt \geq -1$. We deduce that for $t > R(n_1)$, i.e. in all situations where the two funding regimes are different, viewers are worse off in the pay-TV regime when programme quality is fixed. The benefit that viewers obtain from seeing fewer adverts is outweighed by the extra price they must pay to subscribe.

The effect of making programme quality endogenous, however, can reverse viewer preferences over the two regimes. Take the linear example where $R(n) = \alpha n$ and where $\alpha < \delta$. In this case, a pay-TV channel (which chooses n_1 to maximise $R(n) - \delta n$) will not offer any adverts and so from (4)

$$u_1 = \frac{1}{2\gamma} - t$$

A free-to-air channel will, from (6) and (7), choose

$$n_2 = \frac{t}{\delta}; \ v_2 = \frac{\alpha}{2\delta\gamma}$$

which yields a lower viewer utility: $u_2 < u_1$. Thus, in this case, the higher-quality programmes in the pay-TV regime more than compensate viewers for the higher price they pay to watch programmes.

To summarise the main results derived in this duopoly model:
- compared with the pay-TV regime, advertising-funded broadcasting involves lower-quality programmes and more adverts; and
- viewers are better off in a free-to-air regime if there is little scope for affecting programme quality, while they are better off in a pay-TV regime otherwise.

Appendix 4.2: Public service broadcasters in the UK

The UK has five public service television broadcasters: the British Broadcasting Corporation (BBC), the ITV network (properly known as Channel 3), Channel 4 (except in Wales), S4C (in Wales only) and Five. A TV-based information service, Teletext, is also licensed as a public service broadcaster. These broadcasters are subject to explicit programming and production obligations in relation to their PSB channels, in return for either a guaranteed funding stream or gifted spectrum from which advertising and sponsorship revenues may be earned. They must also meet basic standards of taste and decency, accuracy and impartiality required of all broadcasters.

There are several important differences in the nature and funding of the various public service broadcasters. These are detailed as follows.

The BBC

The BBC is a statutory corporation. It was founded as the British Broadcasting Company in 1922 by a group of wireless manufacturers to transmit radio (rather than television) broadcasts. In 1927 it received its first Royal Charter and became the British Broadcasting Corporation. It began television broadcasts in 1936 and its Charter was renewed in 2006. The BBC is largely self-governing, with various regulatory functions being in the hands of its own governors.

The BBC's PSB channels and services are funded from a licence fee of £126.50 per annum (in 2005–2006) paid by every TV household (with concessions for those aged over 75 and the blind). This raises annual revenues for the BBC of £2.94 billion (in 2004–2005). In addition, the BBC's income from its commercial businesses totalled £151 million in 2004–2005. The BBC operates two analogue channels, BBC1 and BBC2. It has a further six digital PSB channels, shown free-to-air: BBC3, BBC4, BBC News 24, BBC Parliament and the children's channels CBeebies and CBBC. It also has a text information service, Ceefax, which started transmission in 1974.

Channel 3 (ITV)

Channel 3, generally known as ITV, was established in 1955. It is a network of fifteen distinct regional licences, each with its own set of public service obligations designed to reflect the particular character of the region. ITV plc, formed by the merger of Carlton and Granada in February 2004, owns the eleven Channel 3 licences in England and Wales. Scottish Media Group (SMG plc) holds the two licences for Scotland, while Ulster Television plc and Channel Television Ltd hold one licence each, for Northern Ireland and the Channel Islands respectively. There is also a national licence for breakfast-time TV, held by GMTV Ltd.

The Channel 3 licensees are shareholder-controlled companies. They benefit from gifted spectrum and pay licence fees to the government. The Channel 3 network's PSB channel, ITV1, is advertising funded. It is licensed under Section 216 of the Communications Act 2003, which sets out its PSB obligations and provides for both analogue and digital transmission and is regulated by Ofcom (formerly by the Independent Television Commission, ITC). Over 90 per cent of the programmes shown on ITV1 are common across the regional licence areas: these are coordinated through the ITV Network Centre, which commissions and schedules programmes for broadcast over the network as a whole. There is a small element of regional programming in each area, as required under the licences.

In addition to ITV1, there are three further ITV channels: ITV2 and ITV3, which are wholly owned by ITV plc, and ITV News. These channels are available on digital platforms only and are outside the public service broadcasting system.

Channel 4

Channel 4, along with S4C in Wales (see below), was created by Act of Parliament in 1982. C4C (the Channel 4 Corporation) is a statutory corporation, headed by a board appointed by Ofcom in agreement with the Secretary of State for Culture, Media and Sport. It receives no public funds, being funded from its own advertising revenue and other commercial activities.

Channel 4 is required under the Communications Act 2003 to provide a broad range of high-quality and diverse programming which demonstrates innovation, experimentation and creativity, appeals to the tastes and interests of a culturally diverse society, includes programmes of an educational nature and exhibits a distinctive character. It is a commissioning broadcaster, not a producer, purchasing its programming from over 300 independent production companies across the UK.

In addition to its PSB channel, the Channel Four Group operates two pay-TV channels: E4, a general entertainment channel, and FilmFour, a specialist film channel. The FilmFour division produces and coproduces feature films for the UK and global markets.

S4C

S4C (Sianel Pedwar Cymru, or 'Channel Four Wales') is a statutory corporation established in 1982 (alongside Channel 4) to broadcast in Wales. It is regulated by the Welsh Authority, whose chair and members are appointed by the Secretary of State for Culture, Media and Sport in consultation with the National Assembly for Wales. It has the distinctive role as public service broadcaster to the bilingual community in Wales, with Welsh language broadcasts an important part of its remit. It is supported by a government grant (£85.7 million in 2004) in addition to its own advertising revenues, and receives some programming from the BBC provided using licence fee funding.

Like Channel 4, S4C is a commissioning broadcaster, not a producer. During peak hours (18:00–22:00) the majority of its output must be in the Welsh language; in total it carries an average of thirty-two hours of Welsh language programming each week. Of this, ten hours is provided by the BBC while the rest is commissioned from independent producers including the local ITV franchise, HTV (part of ITV plc). The rest of S4C's output is English language programming from Channel 4, over 70 per cent of whose output is shown on S4C, usually rescheduled.

Five

Channel 5 (now rebranded as 'Five') was launched in March 1997. It has restricted coverage (its analogue signal reaches around 82 per cent of UK homes, though this is being expanded by digital coverage) and inferior picture quality in some areas due to low transmission power. It is a shareholder-controlled company, majority owned by RTL/Bertelsmann, and is funded from sales of advertising airtime. It has very little in-house production, relying mainly on original commissions and acquired programming.

Teletext

Teletext provides the analogue text services on ITV1, Channel 4 and Five. Teletext is also available on digital TV, the internet and mobile phones. The first full text services, BBC Ceefax and Oracle (operated by ITV), began transmission in 1974. Teletext, an independent franchise, took over from Oracle at the start of 1993. Teletext Ltd is a commercial organisation owned by Harmsworth Media (a subsidiary of the Daily Mail and General Trust) and Media Ventures International.

References

Adams, William, and Janet Yellen (1976) 'Commodity bundling and the burden of monopoly', *Quarterly Journal of Economics*, 90, 475–498.
Anderson, Simon, and Stephen Coate (2005) 'Market provision of broadcasting: a welfare analysis', *Review of Economic Studies*, 72(4), 947–972.

Armstrong, Mark (2005) 'Public service broadcasting', *Fiscal Studies*, 26, 281–300.

Armstrong, Mark (1999) 'Price discrimination by a many-product firm', *Review of Economic Studies*, 66, 151–168.

Armstrong, Mark, and John Vickers (2006) 'Competitive nonlinear pricing and bundling', mimeo.

Bakos, Yannis, and Erik Brynjolfsson (1999) 'Bundling information goods: pricing, profits and efficiency', *Management Science*, 45, 1613–1630.

BBC (2004) *Building Public Value: Renewing the BBC for a Digital World*, available at www.bbc.co.uk

Beebe, Jack H. (1977) 'Institutional structure and program choices in television markets', *Quarterly Journal of Economics*, 91, 15–37.

Besley, Timothy, and Andrea Prat (2006) 'Handcuffs for the grabbing hand? Media capture and government accountability', *American Economic Review*, 96, 720–736.

Brookes, Martin (2004) *Watching Alone: Social Capital and Public Service Broadcasting*, BBC and The Work Foundation.

Camerer, Colin, Samuel Issacharoff, George Loewenstein, Ted O'Donoghue and Matthew Rabin (2003) 'Regulation for conservatives: behavioural economics and the case for "asymmetric paternalism"', *University of Pennsylvania Law Review*, 151, 1210–1254.

Coase, Ronald H. (1946) 'The marginal cost controversy', *Economica*, 13, 169–182.

Coase, Ronald H. (1948) 'Wire broadcasting in Great Britain', *Economica*, 15, 194–220.

Coase, Ronald H. (1950) *British Broadcasting: A Study in Monopoly*, Longmans, Green and Co.

Coase, Ronald H. (1966) 'The economics of broadcasting and government policy', *American Economic Review*, 56, 440–447.

Crampes, Claudes, Carole Haritchabalet and Bruno Jullien (2006) 'Competing with advertising resources', CESifo Working Paper no. 1591.

Davies, Gavyn (1999) *The Future Funding of the BBC*, report of the Independent Review Panel to Department for Culture, Media and Sport.

DCMS (2005) *Review of the BBC's Royal Charter: A strong BBC, independent of government*, Department for Culture, Media and Sport Green Paper, March.

Elstein, David (2004) *Beyond the Charter: The BBC after 2006*, Broadcasting Policy Group.

Gentzkow, Matthew (2006) 'Television and voter turnout', *Quarterly Journal of Economics*.

Hansen, Claus Thustrup, and Søren Kyhl (2001) 'Pay-per-view broadcasting of outstanding events: consequences of a ban', *International Journal of Industrial Organization*, 19, 589–609.

Matutes, Carmen, and Pierre Regibeau (1992) 'Compatibility and bundling of complementary goods in a duopoly', *Journal of Industrial Economics*, 40, 37–54.

McAfee, Preston, John McMillan and Michael Whinston (1989) 'Multiproduct monopoly, commodity bundling, and correlation of values', *Quarterly Journal of Economics*, 104, 371–384.

Nalebuff, Barry (2003) *Bundling, Tying and Portfolio Effects. Part 1: Conceptual Issues*, DTI Economics Paper 1.

Ofcom (2004a) *Ofcom Review of Public Service Television Broadcasting. Phase 1 – Is Television Special?*, April.

Ofcom (2004b) *Ofcom Review of Public Service Television Broadcasting. Phase 2 – Meeting the Digital Challenge*, September.

Ofcom (2005) *Ofcom Review of Public Service Television Broadcasting. Phase 3 – Competition for Quality*, February.

Oliver, Mark (2005) 'The UK's public service broadcasting ecology', in *Can the Market Deliver? Funding Public Service Television in the Digital Age*, John Libby Publishing.

Peacock, Alan (2004) 'Public service broadcasting without the BBC?', in *Public Service Broadcasting Without the BBC?*, Institute of Economic Affairs.

Peitz, Martin and Tommaso Valletti (2005) 'Content and advertising in the media: pay-TV versus free-to-air', mimeo.

Prat, Andrea and David Strömberg (2006) 'Commercial television and voter information', mimeo.

Putnam, Robert D. (2000) *Bowling Alone: The Collapse and Revival of American Community*, Simon and Schuster.

Spence, Michael (1975) 'Monopoly, quality and regulation', *Bell Journal of Economics*, 6, 417–429.

Spence, Michael, and Bruce Owen (1977) 'Television programming, monopolistic competition, and welfare', *Quarterly Journal of Economics*, 91, 103–126.

Spitzer, Manfred (2005) *Vorsicht Bildschirm!*, Klett Ernst Verlag GmbH.

Steiner, Peter O. (1952) 'Program patterns and preferences, and the workability of competition in broadcasting', *Quarterly Journal of Economics*, 66, 194–223.

Strömberg, David (2004a) 'Mass media competition, political competition, and public policy', *Review of Economic Studies*, 71(1), 265–284.

Strömberg, David (2004b) 'Radio's impact on public spending', *Quarterly Journal of Economics*, 119(1), 189–221.

Terrington, Simon and Caroline Dollar (2005) 'Measuring the value created by the BBC', in *Can the Market Deliver? Funding Public Service Television in the Digital Age*, John Libby Publishing.

Whinston, Michael (1990) 'Tying, foreclosure and exclusion', *American Economic Review*, 80, 837–859.

Wilbur, Kenneth (2004) 'Modeling the effects of advertisement-avoidance technology on advertisement-supported media: the case of digital video recorders', mimeo, University of Virginia.

Notes

* The authors would like to thank Chris Giles, Robin Mason, Paul Seabright, Jon Stern, John Vickers and Mark Williams for helpful comments and discussion. The views expressed and any errors are those of the authors. Many of the ideas in this chapter appeared in brief form in Armstrong (2005).

1. The UK government has suggested expanding the BBC's mission statement with five distinctive purposes: 'sustaining citizenship and civil society; promoting education and learning; stimulating creativity and cultural excellence; representing the UK, its nations, regions and communities; and bringing the UK to the world and the world to the UK'. See DCMS (2005), p. 5.

2. Similar social purposes are found in PSB systems of other countries. The PSB Charter for Ireland's Radio Telefis Éireann (RTÉ) includes among its guiding principles 'the democratic, social and cultural values of Irish society'. NZ On Air, the funding body for PSB in New Zealand, states as its mission, 'to reflect and foster the development of New Zealand culture and identity through broadcasting'.

3. This chapter discusses television rather than radio. Some of the arguments we present do not apply to the latter medium: since subscription is rarely used for radio, the practical choice is between public and advertising funding and the latter gives rise to a number of market failures (see Section 4.3).

4. See Ofcom (2004a), p. 9.

5. In particular, the presence in the market of a large, publicly funded broadcaster creates distortions to competition, arguably reducing the market's effectiveness in meeting viewer demands.

6. See, for example, Ofcom (2004a), p. 48.

7. See Davies (1999), p. 10.

8. The UK is unusual in having separated terrestrial transmission from broadcasting.

9. The cost per hour of BBC-originated programmes is highest (and by a large margin) for drama (£526,300), followed by entertainment (£199,300), sport (£150,400), music and arts (£133,600) and current affairs (£130,600). Relatively cheapest programme genres are news and weather (£43,300),

followed by children's programmes (£80,200). From BBC, *Annual Report and Accounts 2005/2006*, Broadcasting facts and figures, Table 16.

10. This phenomenon can already be seen for music, with the growth of websites such as iTunes and Napster.

11. Though for a period in the UK wire broadcasting was also used for radio; see Coase (1948).

12. Terrestrial transmission requires a network of transmission sites, with masts and antenna systems, and the viewer must install an aerial. Satellite transmission uses transponders to broadcast the signal, while viewers need a dish and set-top box to pick this up and convert it for viewing. Cable transmission requires a cable to be laid to each viewer's premises. In each case the viewer must also purchase a television set.

13. Spectrum is the relevant resource for terrestrial transmission. In satellite transmission transponder capacity may become constrained, while cable capacity is the relevant factor in cable transmission. We refer to spectrum scarcity throughout, although it should be borne in mind that other resources may be the limiting factor for alternative transmission methods.

14. In the UK this is a flat-rate charge per household levied for possession of television-receiving equipment, and is set at £131.50 per annum in 2006–2007 (for a colour TV).

15. In the UK the BBC's collection costs amounted to £152 million in 2004–2005; additional court costs are not quantified. Its success is mixed, with evasion estimated at 5.0 per cent at March 2005, resulting in a total cost to the BBC of 10.2 per cent of revenue. From TV Licensing Annual Review.

16. As well as facilitating charging, encryption can prevent the inadvertent viewing of unwanted channels and (perhaps with the addition of a PIN mechanism) provides parents with a reliable mechanism to prevent children having access to unsuitable material.

17. Programmes are recorded onto a hard disk rather than a tape, allowing the viewer to record many more programmes and to move between them easily as with a CD or DVD. The PVR also has flexible viewing capabilities, allowing the viewer to pause and then resume viewing from the same point even while the programme is being broadcast.

18. See Wilbur (2004) for an analysis of PVR use on advertising revenue and broadcasting.

19. The same is also true for subscription channels, though not for pay-per-view. The difference between the licence fee and subscription is the size of the bundle of channels – with the licence fee covering all television (even if its revenues are given to a single broadcaster) – and the compulsory nature of the licence fee.

20. A similar analysis can be applied to an advertising-funded broadcaster, where the 'price' of its service is the time spent watching adverts on its channels.
21. As an analogy, consider the case of free newspapers on trains. Knowing that this is freely available, a traveller is less likely to buy another newspaper even if they actually prefer it.
22. The level of the licence fee may also be different in the two scenarios. Terrington and Dollar (2005) argue that if the licence fee were voluntary, it would have to be increased to offset the fall in uptake. This is a pessimistic counter-factual, however, since the public broadcaster would have an incentive to price its services efficiently, implying that not all viewers pay more, and might operate more efficiently if it had to compete for subscribers, reducing the costs it needed to cover.
23. If the commercial broadcaster were instead advertising funded, a similar analysis would imply that viewing time devoted to its channels, and hence the broadcaster's revenue, is inefficiently low.
24. This may explain why the pay-TV sector so far has failed (in the view of some) to provide more diverse, high-quality programmes.
25. Advertising may be enjoyable to some viewers; if so, this should be taken into account in calculating the net cost of advertising.
26. This model involves informative advertising and assumes that each viewer watches a single channel over the relevant time horizon.
27. If advertising is overprovided by commercial broadcasters this could be restricted by imposing a ceiling on the amount of airtime that may be devoted to advertising (as occurs in the EU under the Television Without Frontiers Directive) or by providing advertising-free channels (such as those of a publicly funded broadcaster).
28. Coase (1946) advocates multi-part tariffs – a form of price discrimination – as a solution to the marginal cost controversy.
29. In a sense, the TV licence fee could be regarded as the price of a pure bundle covering all television viewing.
30. For literature on the use of price discrimination to reduce allocative inefficiency, see Adams and Yellen (1976), McAfee, McMillan and Whinston (1989), Armstrong (1999) and Bakos and Brynjolfsson (1999).
31. Such as for the licence fee when there are no other broadcasters; see earlier in this section.
32. At worst, the pure bundling outcome can be replicated in a mixed bundling scheme by setting very high component prices.
33. Adams and Yellen (1976) raise this possibility, noting that the 'exclusion' of such inefficient consumption is a desirable property of a mixed bundling scheme.

34. If channel production costs are very high, however, mixed bundling may be necessary to generate sufficient revenue to ensure provision.

35. Although this tends to be disliked by viewers who feel that they are forced to pay for programmes that they do not watch. Although understandable, this perception is based on the incorrect assumption that the sum of individual component prices (were these to be offered) would equal the price of the bundle, while economic principles tell us that bundles offer a discount on the sum of stand-alone prices.

36. See Whinston (1990). For a survey of the literature on bundling, see Nalebuff (2003).

37. In 2002 the UK Office of Fair Trading investigated BSkyB's mixed bundling of its premium channels (among other concerns); for the conclusions of this investigation see *BSkyB: The Outcome of the OFT's Competition Act Investigation*, Office of Fair Trading, December 2002.

38. This result is found in the model in Appendix 4.1.

39. Pay-per-view gives a direct measure of viewers' willingness to pay for individual programmes. Bundling, both of programmes into channels and of channels into packages, may obscure the valuations of particular programmes. However, in pay-TV a channel typically focuses on a single genre, implying that valuations of programmes within that channel do not differ greatly from that of the channel as a whole. Moreover, experimentation with channel and package contents allows the values of various programme genres to be estimated.

40. Coase (1946) notes this problem in the absence of a pricing system.

41. This is relevant to the BBC, which levies no viewer charges (leaving aside the licence fee). DCMS (2005) proposes that the BBC Trust should measure audience opinion by means of quantitative and qualitative research, viewer consultation through, for example, elected regional broadcasting councils, open meetings, e-forums and research among 'representative groups' of viewers and listeners.

42. With a limited number of channels, plurality of opinions can be sustained only if several viewpoints are put forward within each channel. This is reflected in the PSB obligation in the UK and elsewhere to provide comprehensive and balanced coverage of news and current affairs. No requirement of this nature is imposed on printed media, where the multiplicity of newspapers can represent a variety of views (although people's tendency to read a single newspaper implies that a given individual will not necessarily receive diverse opinions).

43. We ignore the choices of a licence fee-funded broadcaster, both here and in Section 4.3. Apart from the (very weak) constraint of ensuring that viewers do not switch off entirely, this mechanism provides no specific

incentives towards diversity or quality provision (although a licence fee-funded broadcaster which gains revenues from secondary rights, foreign sales and related merchandise may thereby have greater incentives). Incentives arise in relation to the continuation of licence fee funding, where this may be made subject to certain programming commitments. Popularity of programming may also play a role, but for political rather than economic reasons: wide popular appeal might be necessary for the political acceptability of the licence fee.

44. Even if viewers were heterogeneous in their value to advertisers, e.g. due to their socio-economic characteristics or having particular interests related to the advertiser's product, these values would need to be closely correlated with the individual's own valuation of programming for advertising funding to achieve the welfare-maximising outcome.

45. See Oliver (2005), Figure 7.

46. Ofcom (2004b, 2005) defines high quality as 'well funded and well produced'. 'Well produced' would concur with the descriptions given here. 'Well funded' reflects the fact that raising quality tends to increase production costs, thus higher-quality programmes typically require greater funding.

47. Ofcom (2004a, pp. 34–36) examines programming expenditure by genre (in total and per hour) and the change in these amounts over time, and it also considers that the amount of original UK production (as opposed to overseas acquisitions or repeats) is a useful indicator of quality. None of these is a robust measure of quality, however: expenditure may be higher, or may increase, for several reasons without raising programme quality and it is unclear why overseas output should be regarded as being of low quality.

48. An interesting question concerns the relationship between programme quality and the amount of advertising that commercial free-to-air broadcasters are permitted to show. In many countries, regulation constrains the amount of advertising airtime. However, it is plausible that if broadcasters were allowed to show more adverts, they might then choose to provide higher-quality programmes. The reason for this is that having more adverts generates higher advertising revenues per viewer, giving broadcasters an incentive to compete harder for viewers, which they do by offering higher-quality programmes. Against this must be set the disutility of more frequent or longer interruption by adverts, thus the net effect on viewer welfare is ambiguous.

49. Spence (1975) shows that when consumers differ in their preference for quality, a monopoly firm might choose too high or too low a level of quality, as the ranking of marginal and average value of quality is ambiguous.

50. For example, while discussing 'competition for quality' Ofcom (2004a) states, 'The BBC kept ITV honest; ITV kept the BBC on its toes.'

51. This principle applies to many creative activities. Successful innovators, such as pop stars and best-selling authors, generate very high returns. Commercial backers are willing to take the risk of promoting new artists, and to underwrite the costs involved, because they share in the revenues gained by the successful ones.
52. These quotes are from 1924 and 1925. See Coase (1950), p. 47.
53. Coase (1950), p. 177.
54. The BBC used this argument to protect its position when it was threatened with competition from wire broadcasting (a relay exchange system) in the 1930s, stating, 'The system ... contains within it forces which uncontrolled might be disruptive of the spirit and intention of the BBC charter'; see Coase (1948). The BBC view gained support from elsewhere: a *Times* leader article published from around that time, quoted in Coase (1950), argued, 'What is certain about the relay system is that, under present conditions, it will spread both widely and rapidly among the poorer classes of the population; and this country will not for long be able to congratulate itself on a broadcasting system under which, while broadcasting is controlled with enlightenment and impartiality by a responsible public corporation, the listening is controlled by Tom, Dick and Harry.'
55. Note that the last two mechanisms can be used for a single programme that is not part of a series, as for movies.
56. Coase (1966) expresses scepticism about the ability of a public broadcasting authority to determine which programmes should be broadcast in the best interests of viewers. Referring to the UK's 1962 *Pilkington Report on Broadcasting*, he states, 'The committee avoids the question of how it should be decided which programmes to transmit and for the phrase "what the public wants," they substitute another and better, "what the public authority wants." What the public authority should want, how it would get the information which would enable it to do what it should, and how in practice it would be likely to act are questions which all disappear in a cloud of pious platitudes.'
57. See Coase (1966) for quotes from early public reports and Ofcom (2005) for a recent example.
58. See Camerer et al. (2003) for an economic argument in favour of certain forms of paternalism.
59. Putnam (2000, p. 217) provides an apt quote from T. S. Eliot, who in 1963 wrote that television 'is a medium of entertainment which permits millions of people to listen to the same joke at the same time, and yet remain lonesome'.
60. In these models, media affect political outcomes through a variety of routes: by building (or destroying) a politician's reputation, through monitoring of politicians' actions and by enhancing the salience of particular issues at the ballot box. For example, based on the premise that

politicians deliver policies that favour informed voters, Strömberg (2004a, 2004b) examines the media's role in this process as the provider of information. Besley and Prat (2006) examine the role of press freedom; in this analysis, features of the media industry determine the government's ability to capture the media and to control political outcomes.

61. See Coase (1950), pp. 175–176.

62. Note that, to be effective, these measures must apply to all broadcasters, not just public service channels. In a multimedia world it might seem desirable to extend similar standards to other media, such as the internet, but such controls would be wide-ranging and difficult to enforce.

63. In particular, whether someone has watched, and done so attentively, is unverifiable.

64. Ofcom (2004a) reports that even in analogue terrestrial homes, viewers typically watch at least three of the five channels over the course of an evening (supporting documents, Vol. 1 Part 4).

65. From an interview with Tessa Jowell, the UK Secretary of State for Culture, Media and Sport. See *The Independent*, 'Watching with Tessa', 2 March 2004.

66. When *The Archers* was first broadcast in 1950 it was hoped that, although farmers would listen for the stories, they would along the way pick up messages to help them increase production at a time when Britain was still subject to food rationing. In fact its educational purpose far outlived rationing, continuing until 1972.

67. Programme commissioning is used in New Zealand and Singapore.

68. Indeed, the phrase 'a licence to print money' was coined when the licences for ITV, the first commercial television channel in the UK, were awarded in 1955. Funding from spectrum rents has been a major building block of PSB in the UK over the past fifty years; see Section 4.8.

69. A competitive commissioning system has been advocated in the UK by Elstein (2004) and Peacock (2004). In January 2005 the government-appointed Burns panel recommended the creation of an independent Public Service Broadcasting Commission (PSBC) with among its powers the ability to award some licence fee funds to broadcasters other than the BBC. The government did not follow this recommendation in its subsequent Green Paper, DCMS (2005).

70. Funding of medical research would be a good analogy for this, with (in the UK) the Medical Research Council, Wellcome Trust, European Union and numerous charities each offering funds.

71. Prat and Strömberg (2006) found that commercial television was more effective than the public broadcaster in raising viewers' knowledge of political matters and raising voter turnout, especially among (harder-to-reach) younger and less informed viewers.

72. Cable connection can be denied to non-payers and satellite services can use encryption for analogue as well as digital services. These platforms are excluded from our analysis as they have been developed in the UK only recently.

73. A group of equipment manufacturers could perhaps add a surcharge to sales of television sets to fund broadcasting services, as was initially the case for radio in the UK, but competition between suppliers would undermine this. In practice government support is necessary for enforcement of a licence fee.

74. Depending on spectrum allocation, digital terrestrial transmission allows several dozen channels to be broadcast, while digital satellite and cable platforms can support a few hundred. Although demand growth might eventually alter this conclusion if technological improvements do not keep pace, spectrum availability is no longer a binding constraint on channel numbers.

75. Although pay-TV piracy through copying of smart cards may sometimes be a problem, this can be overcome by periodically issuing new smart cards to subscribers and improving encryption software.

76. A sceptic might argue that the current state of pay-TV in the UK is evidence against this claim. However, caution should be exercised in forming judgements about the output of a fully commercial broadcasting market based on the existing pay-TV sector, as the presence of a state-funded, sometimes high-quality broadcaster – namely, the BBC – greatly diminishes a commercial broadcaster's incentive to supply high-quality programming.

77. Interestingly, digital television is witnessing the emergence of shopping channels such as QVC whose primary purpose is advertising and that are watched for this reason. Like advertising-only newspapers, the use of such formats may increase as these become a more effective means of reaching potential viewers than traditional advertising methods.

78. See Hansen and Kyhl (2001) for an analysis of the effects of this system.

79. Although in its 2005 Broadcasting Code, Ofcom decided that such measures would be inadequate to protect children and maintained the prohibition on R18-rated (i.e. pornographic) material.

80. Ofcom (2004a) reports that more serious and challenging programmes are most affected by multi-channel competition, with their share of viewing more than 50 per cent lower in multi-channel homes compared with those having analogue terrestrial channels only (see Ofcom 2004a, Figure 28). However, being a contemporaneous comparison between self-selected groups these data suffer from selection bias and are likely to overstate the magnitude of any change in behaviour by individual households when faced with a greater choice of channels. The fact that as multi-channel TV has grown (entertainment-focused) BBC1 and ITV1

have experienced large falls in viewing share while (more factual and culture-based) BBC2 and Channel 4 have held up relatively well, indicates a significant selection effect. See Ofcom (2004a), Figure 22; BARB data for a longer period show trends stretching back to the launch of pay-TV in 1991.

81. MacTaggart lecture at the Edinburgh International Television Festival, 27 August 1999.

82. Ofcom (2004a) reports that the most popular programmes on analogue terrestrial in the UK could expect audiences of 16–17 million viewers in the late 1990s, but by 2003 14 million was a typical ceiling. Data provided by the British Broadcasters Audience Research Board for October 2006 indicate that audiences for the most popular programmes had declined further to around 11 million viewers.

83. Although the need to retain public support by giving them entertaining programmes creates some tension with PSB objectives.

84. See Ofcom (2004a), p. 8; also Figure 44.

85. A YouGov poll conducted for the *Telegraph* in October 2002 showed that 58 per cent of those surveyed believed the current system to be no longer justified in a multi-channel world (*Daily Telegraph*, 'Unwanted licence fee', 28 October 2002).

86. Davies (1999), Section 5, p. 144.

87. 'The M25 area' refers to the area within London's major ring road, i.e. the Greater London region.

88. Surveys conducted for the Ofcom review of public service television broadcasting indicate that several elements of PSB output are popular, with viewers placing a high value on their own consumption of news, serious factual programmes and drama, as well as entertainment; see Ofcom (2004a), Figure 33.

89. For example, in the early days of the Second World War some UK radio listeners found the Nazi propagandist Lord Haw Haw more entertaining than the BBC's austere diet of organ recitals and public announcements. This prompted the BBC to lighten its tone with a new emphasis on entertainment. In the 1960s, the BBC's failure to respond to changing music tastes led to the growth of pirate radio stations, culminating in harsh enforcement action – and also the launch of a new BBC station, Radio 1.

90. See, for example, the findings presented in Ofcom (2004a).

91. Advertising ceilings are specified under the EU Television Without Frontiers Directive.

92. The BBC has a Royal Charter rather than a licence. The remaining public service broadcasters are licensed under the Communications Act 2003.

93. Channel 3 ('ITV') licences were auctioned following the 1990 Broadcasting Act. Renewal fees for these and the Channel 5 licence

(held by Five) are determined by Ofcom. In 2004 the licensees collectively paid £230 million. This was estimated to have dropped to around £90 million in 2005, reflecting the falling scarcity value of analogue spectrum resulting from the growth of digital households.

94. Digital satellite, operated by BSkyB, has near-universal coverage. There are two regional cable companies, NTL and Telewest, passing approximately 50 per cent of homes. Digital terrestrial television has less than universal coverage but this is increasing, with a view towards digital switchover around 2012. Following the demise of ITV Digital in March 2002, Freeview, an umbrella platform for various free-to-air channels, was launched in October 2002. A limited pay-TV service, Top Up TV, was launched in March 2004.

95. See BBC (2004).

96. From *The Times*, 'ITV unveils strategy for digital fightback', 24 June 2004.

97. In practical terms, the audiences and advertising revenues of advertising-funded public service channels are coming under pressure. Concern has already been raised over the future viability of Channel 4 (see 'Preserving C4's provision', *Financial Times*, 19 April 2004, written by Mark Thompson, then Chief Executive of Channel 4). Although S4C also sells advertising, the major part of its funding comes from a government grant and it is therefore largely protected from this threat.

98. The concern that public service output on advertising-funded channels will eventually disappear underlies Ofcom's proposal to create a 'public service publisher' (PSP) to compete with the BBC. A public funding source would be needed for this body, however, with the practical options being limited to top-slicing licence fee revenue (assuming that the licence fee itself can be defended) or a grant out of taxation.

99. EPG positioning has been the subject of several disputes between broadcasters, including the positioning of BBC channels on the satellite EPG and of Top Up TV's channels on the digital terrestrial EPG.

100. For example, EPG rankings by viewing shares would place the existing analogue channels at or close to the top of the list due to their inherited base of viewers.

101. 'Digital television penetration surpassed 70 per cent of UK households in early 2006' (Ofcom, *The Communications Market 2006*, Section 4.2.2).

102. The following model is similar to Anderson and Coate (2005) except that here the quality of programmes is chosen by the broadcasters. For related theoretical models of competition between broadcasters, see Crampes et al. (2006) and Peitz and Valletti (2005). The former paper,

which has exogenous programme quality, examines a free-entry model of broadcasting (or media more generally) and also allows the advertising revenue function to be non-linear (unlike the model described in this appendix). The second paper models (duopoly) broadcasters as choosing the degree of horizontal differentiation, i.e. the degree of programme diversity, rather than (vertical) programme quality.

5 | Regulation for pluralism in media markets

MICHELE POLO

5.1 Introduction

Pluralism – the fair, balanced and unbiased representation of a wide range of political opinions and views – is a fundamental component in the working of modern democracies. Assuring pluralism in modern economies, characterised by a well-developed set of media markets, requires political and social actors from across the spectrum to have proper access to the different media.

The last two decades have seen an impressive development in the number and range of media that today contribute to form public opinion, with technological innovations and new policies leading the process. Cable and satellite transmission during the 1980s relaxed the constraint of limited frequencies over the hertzian spectrum that had previously restricted the number of TV channels. Moreover, these technologies, together with encrypted signals over the air, enabled exclusion of non-payers and thereby contributed to the development of pay-TV services, adding a new source of revenues for private operators. At the same time, public policies more favourable to private companies promoted wide reforms of broadcasting markets in Europe, where commercial channels financed with advertising started to erode the audience of the incumbent public channels. Today there are many more channels available to the public than two decades ago. The current phase of development of digital broadcasting will further increase the number and nature of TV services offered to the public, with a convergence between media and telecommunication industries. Finally, the internet has offered a new and potentially cheap channel of diffusion of ideas and contents that adds to the other processes. Considering these developments, therefore, we might argue that the realisation of pluralism is today in much better shape than two decades ago, with an incomparably larger number of media available for the diffusion of ideas.

Table 5.1: Concentration ratio (C3) in the media markets 2002–2003

	Media			
	National press	*Regional press*	*Free-to-air TV*	*Radio*
France	70.0	46.7	80.7	59.1
Germany	87.4	27.9	90.9	56.8
Italy	44.8	–	88.7	58.7
Spain	–	47.3	71.4	76.6
UK	70.6	51.6	69.9	72.3

Source: Ward (2004)

If we look at these media markets in the main European countries, however, we observe in most cases very high levels of concentration. In Table 5.1 we present the C3 concentration ratio[1] by media company in the main markets, calculated according to the distribution of viewers, readers or listeners.

Free-to-air television is the most concentrated segment while the regional press ranks relatively low, although it should be considered that the national data do not fully portray concentration in an industry that is characterised by a large set of very concentrated local markets. It is difficult to interpret these data, and the implicit problems for pluralism that they might imply, given that the process of development of new media markets is far from concluded. Innovations in telecommunications and the media, moreover, suggest that the picture might change even more. Hence, in order to establish how the objective of pluralism should be pursued we cannot refer simply to the status quo; we need to rely also on some theoretical considerations that allow us to identify the leading forces of the process in the early future.

Although pluralism is a political more than an economic objective, its realisation today (and in the near future) will depend first of all on the outcome of market forces. Since today most of the suppliers in media markets are private companies, and these markets are characterised by persistent concentration and risks of foreclosure, we need an economic analysis of the functioning of the media markets in order to evaluate whether the new technological opportunities will lead to the realisation of pluralism. This chapter analyses whether private incentives in the media markets are sufficient to realise pluralism or whether it needs to be an explicit objective of regulation.

The chapter is organised as follows. In Section 5.2 we introduce a double definition of pluralism, distinguishing between external pluralism (which characterises the range of content in a given media market) and internal pluralism (which characterises the range of content supplied by a single media company). In Section 5.3 we ask whether the market can be expected to provide enough external pluralism, pointing out some key reasons for caution. The more analytical features are treated in subsections, marked with *, that can be skipped by less technically minded readers. Section 5.4 then considers whether private incentives are sufficient to provide internal pluralism, identifying further reasons for market failures in this case. Section 5.5 reviews the main regulatory tools that are used in European countries, evaluating whether they can remedy the kinds of market failures that have been identified and discussing a set of open issues. Section 5.6 concludes the chapter.

5.2 Pluralism: a double definition

When we define pluralism as the objective of ensuring a balanced, fair and unbiased access of all political opinions and views to the media we leave unspecified an important part of the question: do we want citizens to find a full range of political views expressed among the existing media outlets in an overall media market or do we want individual media outlets to host a variety of opinions across the ideological spectrum? The former characteristic is usually called external pluralism (EP). The latter is called internal pluralism (IP).

The distinction between external and internal pluralism suggests looking separately at how whole markets provide for the expression of political opinions and views and how such provision is made by individual media companies. In both cases we need to clarify further how pluralism should be measured. It might simply refer to the availability of all political views, with no reference as to how (and when) they are made available; or we might desire to check that the general public can have access to them on equal terms (for instance, at similar viewing times or within the same programmes). In other words, the realisation of pluralism can be assessed by looking at the mere availability of different views or instead by focusing on the public's actual choices among the available contents.

If we refer to availability, we look at the media companies' supply of political views and information; we might assess, for instance, whether newspaper shops carry the full range of publications and do not refuse to sell some of them or whether there exists the full range of TV channels received by the whole population during prime time, when the largest audience is reached. Under this approach, the central quantitative measure for external pluralism would be the number of media (TV channels, newspapers, radio stations) and the number of media companies (TV broadcasters, publishers, communication groups).

When instead viewers' and readers' actual choices are the central issue for pluralism, the simple availability of access may not be enough if most of the public patronises a limited subset of the available media. In this case some measure of concentration applied to audience or readership, such as for instance the Herfindahl Index, might be used to assess market concentration and the lack of external pluralism.

If we think that the general public is in the position to make informed and independent choices on the media or programme/article to patronise, availability of different views should be all that matters; if we presume that the public always chooses its preferred political contents, the *ex post* observation of actual choices should simply reflect the distribution of preferences, over which we should be neutral.

If, however, there are frictions and lock-in effects in the way the different media are chosen, actual choices will not necessarily reflect preferences over political information. Lock-in effects can occur, for instance, in TV since programmes on different channels do not start exactly at the same time. Suppose, for instance, that a TV channel has a very popular programme during prime time just before the news, so that a large portion of the public watches the programme and goes on to watch the news on the same channel.[2] Even when the news programmes are announced at the same time (say, at 8pm) on two rival channels, there is usually some slight difference in the starting time of newsflashes, or previews may be offered some minutes before the official time. This creates a lock-in of the viewers. The high audience of a news channel, therefore, may derive from the popularity of the previous scheduling rather than from an appreciation of the news itself.

Lock-in effects may occur for different reasons in newspapers. Since local news gathering requires a dedicated staff of journalists and a local editorial office, national newspapers cannot usually offer coverage in the same way as local newspapers. But given the limited dimension of the market, only a few local newspapers, and quite often only one or two, can survive in a given area, a tendency that we observe in many countries including the USA. Since most newspapers must be purchased, most readers buy just one. The concentration of local readership will be due to the nature of local news gathering rather than to the political positioning of these media.

Lock-in effects, as described above, are likely to be relevant when we look at external pluralism, since the choice of a reader's preferred political content might require switching from one media outlet to another (incurring some costs). If there is internal pluralism, with a variety of opinions expressed within the same media outlet, readers may be much less affected by such lock-in effects. Therefore, our discussion of the measurement of pluralism with respect to the available contents or to the actual choices of the public refers mainly to the implementation of an EP objective.

While the choice between internal and external pluralism objectives is beyond the scope of economic analysis, we think that the implementation of either policy objective, and therefore the success in pursuing the general goal of pluralism, requires a careful analysis of what can be expected from the private incentives of media companies. If we are pursuing an EP goal, the relevant issues are the degree of differentiation among media companies and the features of the media market structure under free entry. If instead we follow an internal notion of pluralism, we need to understand whether a media company finds it profitable to offer multiple policy positions, an issue related to the choices of firms in other industries between single and multiple product lines.

The next sections will therefore address three main questions, drawing on the existing literature on media markets:

1. Do media companies tend to offer in equilibrium a differentiated supply of contents (including policy positions)?
2. What are the possible long-run equilibrium market structures (in terms of the number of firms and the distribution of their audience or readership) and their determinants in the media industries?
3. What are the incentives of a single media company to offer a variety of contents (including different policy positions)?

While the first two issues are relevant for the assessment of EP market provision, the last one focuses on the private incentives for IP.

5.3 Does the market provide enough external pluralism?

Before looking at the equilibrium degree of differentiation and at the equilibrium market structure, it is useful briefly to review some modelling issues in media markets. The media today include a very diversified set of industries, including the written press, television and radio broadcasting, and electronic communications over the internet. It is hard to analyse the main features of equilibrium in these markets in general, as industry specificities may play a role in driving the results. In this section, therefore, we will focus mainly on the features of the television broadcasting industry and, to a certain extent, of the press industry, which are arguably the most influential today in forming public opinion.

Modelling media (broadcasting and press) markets

The economic literature on the television industry is relatively small. Early works[3] focused on the choice of programme variety between competing broadcasters, using a horizontal differentiation or monopolistic competition framework. More recently, the interplay between the broadcasting market and that for advertising has been modelled, addressing issues like the over- or underprovision of advertising (Anderson and Coate (2000)) or the degree of differentiation among channels (Gabszewicz et al. (1999), Gabszewicz et al. (2001) and Gal-Or and Dukes (2001)). The links between product market rivalry, as influenced by advertising, and equilibria in broadcasting markets is further explored in Nilssen and Sørgard (2001) and, again, Gal-Or and Dukes (2001)). Finally, long-run equilibria under free entry are analysed in Motta and Polo (2001). We can summarise the main features of these models as follows:

- Media industries, including TV and radio broadcasting and the press, in which advertising is an important source of revenue, are *two-sided markets*:[4] media outlets can be considered as platforms linking the market for audience (viewers, listeners, readers) and the market for advertising.
- Audience exerts a positive externality on advertising, as the larger the audience, the more effective are expected to be the commercials. However, in most cases advertising creates a negative externality on the audience, by interrupting and fragmenting the content of the

media. This negative effect is usually recognised and empirically documented in the marketing literature for TV and radio broadcasting, since the viewer cannot exclude the commercial breaks by turning immediately back to the programme he or she was watching or listening. The externality of advertising on the readers of the press is more debated:[5] press advertising is often more informative, providing a service to the reader;[6] moreover, the reader is not constrained to read the messages and can simply skip the pages of advertising and move to the articles of interest. For these reasons, we might have some readers who like and others who suffer from advertising in the press. In any case, these effects create *inter-market network externalities*, as the larger is one market, the stronger is the externality on the other market.

• Both markets are characterised by *heterogeneity of the agents*: viewers/ readers have different preferences over the varieties and the quality of the contents and advertisers have different willingness to pay for advertising space or time. We can therefore obtain from these preferences a demand for audience and a demand for advertising. The specification of preferences of the two groups of agents (viewers/ readers and advertisers) draws heavily from the literature on product differentiation. The specific features, and their important consequences for market equilibria, lead to two main approaches, which we discuss in the following paragraphs, highlighting their implications for market equilibria.

Do media companies offer differentiated contents?

Our first question on the supply of differentiated contents can be addressed within the so-called monopolistic competition (MC) approach to media markets. It assumes that viewer/reader preferences are characterised by a taste for variety or by heterogeneous tastes for specific varieties, which is usually defined as horizontal product differentiation: that is, either every viewer likes a mixture of entertainment, sport, movies, information, or there are audience niches each patronising a particular variety.[7] There is no variety that is always preferred by all viewers, although there might be a concentration of tastes over the more popular varieties (e.g. movies or sports). As a result, offering a mixture of different contents is the best way to reach a significant fraction of the audience. In this setting, the media company's main decision is to select the (mixture of) varieties of contents it is willing to offer to its potential public. Political views, information and opinions are an additional dimension on which the media company has to choose its positioning.[8]

Turning back to preferences, all viewers (but not necessarily all readers) dislike advertising, which therefore plays a role similar to an implicit price for watching the programme. Finally, advertisers' willingness to pay depends on the audience reached by the media (and by their profit expectations from advertisements).[9]

In this framework, media companies choose their varieties in order to attract viewers or readers, exploiting a larger audience in the advertising market through larger quantities of advertising and/or higher prices for the commercials. The key point in this setting is that if two media companies offer relatively similar programmes, the viewers/readers are relatively willing to switch from one channel/newspaper to the other if the former increases its advertising time/space. Hence, a low degree of differentiation constrains adversely the sales of advertising and the profits of the media company.

Our discussion leads to the main result of this approach: the media companies facing a public of viewers/readers characterised by different preferred varieties of programmes and disliking advertising messages will choose maximally differentiated programme schedules (Gabszewicz et al. (1999)).

The maximum differentiation outcome might suggest that the media companies will choose to differentiate their contents also over the political dimension, in order to attract different political niches of the public. Before jumping to this conclusion, however, it is worth noting that a media company usually offers a wide range of varieties in a bundle (entertainment, movies, sport, news, etc.), calibrating them to reach its targeted public. If, for instance, a TV channel is focused mainly to a public of teenagers, it will choose the distribution of programming time among movies, music, sports, entertainment, news, etc. and for each of these types the programmes that better match the tastes of the public of young people. Not all the varieties included will be equally important to the public of viewers. This affects the choice of whether or not to differentiate from the offerings of competing media.

In particular, by differentiating their contents over the more relevant varieties the media companies create loyalty and reduce audience mobility, while by offering more similar (popular) contents on less important varieties they further increase the audience and the value of their advertising space. In our previous example, differentiation might occur on some dimensions that are more relevant for the targeted viewers/readers (for instance, the kind of music or movies in the case of teenagers) while convergence occurs on other dimensions that are less important for teenagers, such as the news. That is to say that the result of maximum differentiation does not necessarily imply that media companies will differentiate over all the varieties, and in particular over the political views they express, since these might be a relatively unimportant component of the overall contents offered.

Putting the point another way, if the public is highly concerned with politics, we might expect maximum differentiation to occur in political positioning, as arguably in the broadsheet press. If, however, most viewers of commercial TV or popular newspapers are much less interested in politics than in entertainment or sport, then we might expect differentiation in the latter dimensions but not in political views, which might converge to a 'median' political position.

So, to answer our first question, competition among media companies financed by advertising revenues induces them to offer diversified contents, as long as advertising exerts a negative externality on the audience and increases the gross profits of the advertising firms in the product market (as seems to be true for commercial TV channels and at least in part for the written press). Whether maximum differentiation extends also to the political views expressed by the media companies is, however, an open question; this may be so only for those media whose audience is strongly interested in politics. We can therefore conclude that the market provides sufficient incentives for media companies to offer a diversified range of contents along some dimensions, but this feature does not necessarily extend to political viewpoints.

The MC approach: analytical results (*)

The typical representation of preferences in the MC approach is:

$$U(x_i, a_i, p_i, t) = v^* - \lambda a_i - p_i - \psi(x_i - t)^2$$

where v^* is the willingness to pay for the media, that is decreased by the amount[10] of advertising a_i (with weight λ), the price (subscription fee) paid p_i (if any) and the mismatching of actual (x_i) vs preferred (t) variety.

In the MC approach the equilibrium degree of differentiation, our first question, can be properly addressed within a multi-stage game framework where programme (political) variety x_i is chosen first and then advertising quantity a_i (or rates) is chosen taking into account the viewers'/readers' and the advertisers' demand.

In the simpler case the media companies obtain revenues only by selling advertising time/space, while giving for free the contents to the viewers/readers.

In this setting we obtain:

Proposition 1

The media companies facing a public of viewers/readers characterised by different preferred varieties of programmes and disliking advertising messages will choose maximally differentiated programme schedules (Gabszewicz et al. (1999)).

Hence, the Principle of Maximum Differentiation established in d'Aspremont et al. (1979) within the simpler Hotelling model still holds true in the more complex two-sided markets framework that takes into account the specific features of the media industry. It is important to contrast this result with alternative outcomes that suggest a lower degree of differentiation, in order to evaluate the robustness of our conclusion.

A minimum differentiation result can be obtained if we ignore the negative externality of advertising on viewers and readers: in this case the inter-market externalities work in one direction only, with a larger audience increasing the willingness to pay of advertisers. The design of programme variety in this case is driven by the pursuit of a large audience, that is better accomplished once more 'central' or popular varieties are selected: since the viewers are not negatively affected by the number of ads, moving to the centre has only the positive effect of eroding the rival media audience. This set-up, and the resulting conclusion that very similar contents will be offered in the media market, can be found in the pioneering works of Steiner (1952) on radio broadcasting.

More recently, Gabszewicz et al. (2001) find similar conclusions regarding the press industry: they consider press editors who raise revenues from both the sale of newspapers and of advertising space. Readers are interested in the policy position of the newspaper but not in the amount of advertising. The revenues coming from newspaper sales provide an incentive to follow the ideological position of the readers, pushing towards a strong differentiation of the media companies. Conversely, advertising revenues depend on total audience, which can be reached by locating more centrally. When the readers are not heavily concerned about the political positions taken by the newspaper while the advertising market is large, the latter effect dominates and minimum differentiation emerges.[11] On the contrary, when the readers pay more attention to the policy position taken by the newspapers and the advertising market is a less important source of revenues, the usual maximum differentiation result occurs.[12]

We think that the negative effect of advertising on the audience is a fundamental (empirical) fact of the TV industry and it seems to be relevant in many submarkets of the press industry as well. Hence, the outcome of minimum differentiation obtained by ignoring the negative impact of advertising on the audience cannot be considered a general result in media markets.

A second case in which minimum differentiation occurs is shown in the Gal-Or and Dukes (2001) paper. In this case the link between advertising and product market competition plays a central role: since the authors consider only informative advertising, a larger quantity of advertising makes customers in the product market more informed and mobile, with an increase in competition and a fall in the advertisers' gross profits. In this case media companies, by selecting more similar contents, reduce the amount of advertising in equilibrium (as in Proposition 1 above), making the product market less competitive. The higher gross profits resulting in the product market allow media companies to increase their profits as well when selling advertising time.[13] Hence, minimum differentiation occurs. Although the paper by Gal-Or and Dukes is interesting, highlighting a further link between the advertising market and the product market, it seems that the overall result is driven by the assumption of informative advertising. If ads increased consumer loyalty, reducing (instead of increasing) product market elasticity,[14] the result would be reversed, since more differentiation, inducing more advertising, allows an increase in product market gross profits and the advertising revenues of the media companies.

While the nature of advertising (informative, loyalty enhancing or both) is first of all an empirical matter, experience suggests that, in particular for TV commercials, advertising messages are more focused on loyalty enhancement or information about product characteristics than on prices, in contrast to the assumptions of Gal-Or and Dukes (2001). We argue, therefore, that in this case too the minimum differentiation outcome cannot be considered a general result for the media markets.

However, a final remark on equilibrium differentiation seems important. Proposition 2 summarises the result.

Proposition 2

If firms have to differentiate their products over several dimensions (characteristics), in equilibrium the firms will maximally differentiate on the characteristics more important for the consumers, while converging to minimum differentiation on the other (less important) characteristics (Irmen and Thisse (1998)).

With multiple characteristics, product differentiation can be realised with more degrees of freedom. By diverging on the key characteristics (those with a higher ψ) the firms relax advertising competition, while convergence on the other dimensions is driven by the desire to maximise total demand (once Bertrand competition is avoided).

Do media industries tend towards concentration or fragmentation?

Our second relevant question regarding media market concentration has not been properly addressed so far in the MC approach. Moreover, although the MC approach to the media industry has the important merit of highlighting the forces that lead to differentiation in the supply of contents among market operators, it leaves aside an important element of the picture. The supply of contents requires firms not only to choose a particular variety (or mix of varieties) but also to invest in the scarce inputs that make a programme (within a given variety) attractive for viewers/readers, something that we can in general describe as talent. For instance, a TV channel has not only to choose whether to focus more on sport events or movies – a typical horizontal differentiation decision. Once it has chosen to focus on sports, for instance, it has to decide between the major sporting events, as the Champions League or the Olympic Games, or a less attractive programme based on minor sports or less important international matches. In the same vein, a channel more specialised in movies might decide to collect and broadcast the seasonal blockbusters or less popular movies.

This observation leads us to recognise that viewers/readers have a taste for both variety and the attractiveness ('quality') of the contents transmitted or published: going back to the product differentiation literature, the audience demand reacts to both the horizontal (variety) and vertical (attractiveness) decisions of the media companies.

Targeting contents according to both variety and attractiveness has dramatic effects not only on the revenue side (more attractive programmes, more audience, more advertising revenues) but also on the cost side, as the more popular programmes tend to be more expensive, reflecting their larger revenue potential.[15] The fixed costs therefore increase with the attractiveness of the contents provided.

We define as the natural oligopoly (NO) approach to the analysis of the media market one that stresses the double role of investing in the attractiveness of contents: increasing the revenues (from advertising, through a larger audience, or from subscriptions) and the (fixed) costs of the operators. The NO approach offers a richer description of the interaction among media companies, which can compete for audience not only by moderating their advertising space but also by investing in programming.

In this framework the long-run equilibria under free entry, our second key question, are described in the following statement: when viewers/readers have a taste for both the variety and the attractiveness of the contents, and more attractive contents imply higher fixed costs, the maximum number of firms sustainable in a free entry equilibrium, N, is bounded above for any dimension of the advertising market. Moreover, the market in the limit is more fragmented the more horizontally differentiated are the contents across media companies (Motta and Polo (2001)).

The intuition of this result should be straightforward once the basic mechanisms of the NO model have been understood: N is determined by the free entry condition once the fixed costs of programming are strictly covered by advertising revenues. A larger advertising market increases the revenue potential from advertising, boosting the incentives to compete for the audience through a higher level of attractiveness of the contents. This pushes up both advertising revenues and fixed programming costs, with no room, at some point, for further entry.[16] If there is scope, given the viewers'/readers' preferences, for more horizontal differentiation of contents, competition for audience is realised by targeting different contents and is therefore relaxed, and the mechanism that pushes up the fixed costs of programming slows down, with lower fixed costs in equilibrium. This is consistent, for given dimension of the advertising market, with a higher number of firms.

Summing up, the NO approach identifies some elements that govern the equilibrium market structure under free entry. Suppose the tastes of the viewers/readers are concentrated on a limited number of varieties (say sport, movies and entertainment) and, within them, on the more popular versions of the different types (say soccer, comedies and quiz shows) – what we might label as the case of the *popular viewer/reader*. Then the media companies have limited scope for horizontal differentiation. Competition for audience then forces them to target the same attractive contents, which pushes up the costs of programmes, creating endogenously high fixed costs and resulting in a concentrated industry, even with large advertising markets. An alternative scenario, that we might label as that of the *sophisticated viewer/reader*, corresponds to an audience with very diversified tastes or one that likes to mix and match programmes from different schedules and channels. In this case media companies can easily differentiate their contents and competition for attractiveness (and the fixed costs of the best programmes) is reduced.

A similar case can be found looking at an important segment of readership that is interested in local news and is ready to patronise the local press even if it has a more limited coverage of national and international events. In this case the prevalent dimension that influences the reader's choice is the coverage of local news rather than coverage of international events. The 'attractiveness' dimension loses importance in favour of the 'variety' dimension. The local press segment therefore will be fragmented, with many small newspapers selling in different areas. When the importance of variety is strong, therefore, many small-size media companies (e.g. small thematic TV channels or local newspapers) can coexist in a fragmented market.

The popular and the sophisticated viewer/reader examples represent two polar cases that induce very different market structures. Intermediate situations, in which we might have a core market with few large operators covering the more popular varieties and a fringe of small ones focused on diversified market niches, can also be imagined and seem to fit well with the case of the press market. While the evolution of TV broadcasting seems so far closer to the popular viewer case, it seems plausible that the drift in the future will be towards the sophisticated viewer scenario. However, the speed of the process and whether it will completely replace the popular tastes are very difficult to predict.[17]

What we can conclude according to the NO approach is that the real challenge to EP comes from the persistent concentration of many media markets, in particular in the free-to-air TV broadcasting industry, dominated by the public's relatively undifferentiated tastes for a limited number of content varieties. This concentrated situation creates a strong limit to the possibility of offering a diversified range of political views in the TV industry supply. Hence, once we consider the escalation of fixed costs that characterises these markets, our trust in the market provision of external pluralism is much weakened.

The NO approach: analytical results (*)

We define the natural oligopoly approach to the media market with reference to two distinctive modelling choices: first, viewers/readers have a taste for both the variety and the attractiveness of the contents; second, more attractive contents, while increasing the audience, require higher fixed costs. The NO approach has been proposed in Motta and Polo (2001), who analyse the free entry equilibrium structure of the media markets, in Nilssen and Sørgard (2001), who study the effects of product market competition on the broadcasting market equilibrium, and in Armstrong (2004), focusing on the choice of programme quality of pay-TV vs. advertising financed TV.

A typical linear specification of the share of viewers that can be found in these models is:

$$s_i = \alpha(N) + \beta(N)(\nu_i - \lambda a_i - p_i) - \sum_{\substack{j=1 \\ j \neq i}}^{N} \gamma_j(N)(\nu_j - \lambda a_j - p_j)$$

where s_i is the share of audience, N is the number of media, ν_i is the quality of media i's contents, a_i is the amount of advertising and p_i the subscription fee (if any). The parameters $\alpha(N)$, $\beta(N)$ and $\gamma_j(N)$ can be obtained once the underlying preferences have been specified.[18] Improving the attractiveness of the contents boosts the fixed (programming) costs of the media company, a mechanism reminiscent of the endogenous sunk cost case proposed in Sutton (1991) and (1998).

In all these models the choice of the variety is not addressed, assuming an exogenous degree of product differentiation among media companies.[19] Hence, the models that have followed the NO approach cannot help to answer the first question about EP, that is whether in equilibrium there will be sufficient differentiation of contents among media companies. However, the NO paradigm seems particularly suited to consider the second relevant issue, namely the equilibrium market structure, which is not adequately considered in the MC approach.

The basic effects that work in equilibrium can be described as follows. First, when media companies set their advertising space given advertising demand, they compete in strategic complements, as already observed for the MC models: increasing the amount of advertising space shifts some audience to the rival company and increases its demand for advertising, inducing the other company to increase its advertising space as well. Second, a company offering more attractive contents exploits its advantage in the audience by selling more advertising time (and collecting higher prices). Hence, more attractive contents pay off in terms of higher advertising revenues. Third, the marginal effect of an increase in attractiveness on advertising revenues is more pronounced the more similar are the contents in terms of varieties: with very similar programming, offering more attractive contents leads to a sharp increase in audience and the advertising revenues.[20] Hence, the incentive to invest in attractive programmes is higher the more similar are the varieties chosen by the media companies. Horizontal contents differentiation, meanwhile, reduces the incentive to invest in attractive programmes.

For a given degree of substitutability among media contents, the optimal level of attractiveness is determined by equating the marginal benefit (as described above) and the marginal cost of programme quality. Overall, the less horizontally differentiated the programme schedules, the more intense the competition for attractive programmes and the higher the level of fixed (programming) costs in equilibrium.

Proposition 3 describes the equilibrium market structures.

Proposition 3

When viewers/readers have a taste for variety and for the attractiveness of contents, and more attractive contents imply higher fixed costs, the maximum number of firms sustainable in a free entry equilibrium, N, is bounded above for any dimension of the advertising market. N is larger the more horizontally differentiated are the contents across media companies (Motta and Polo (2001)).

Vertical integration and foreclosure

So far we have focused our analysis on the segment of the media industries corresponding to the packaging of contents and the sale of advertising space. Some media segments, and in particular TV broadcasting, have a relatively rich vertical structure in which the production of contents can be separated from that of packaging, followed by other phases such as the packaging of channels and the delivery of them (in particular for the pay-TV segment).

Vertical integration upstream can create serious foreclosure concerns when a TV broadcaster cumulates the production of several key varieties. Exclusive rights of transmission may have a similar effect even without formal integration. Pay-TV broadcasting is a good example. The more popular channels in a bundle are usually sport and movie channels, and competition for the most attractive contents is very intense in this segment. Movies can be diversified by type (comedies, adventures, thrillers, etc.) and can be exploited on a multiple-window programming schedule. We might therefore expect more than one thematic channel specialised in movies to survive in equilibrium. Sporting events seem more problematic: they usually display far more concentrated tastes (the public is usually interested in no more than a few sporting disciplines and a few international events, though these may differ by country) and require direct transmission, while multiple windowing has almost no value. So what matters in sports broadcasting is to obtain the transmission rights of a few major sporting events. This process is self-reinforcing, as a channel that already owns some major sports and a large base of subscribers is often able to offer more for the transmission rights of other disciplines and events. The emergence of the BSkyB position in the UK market, thanks to the rights of transmission of the Premier League, or the consolidation of the two pay-TV Italian channels under the umbrella of the Murdoch group and the progressive migration of all the soccer teams within its programming, are extremely telling stories.

If a single operator were able to obtain most of these contents on an exclusive basis, a real possibility of market foreclosure would emerge. The mixture of competition for the more attractive contents and the vertical links between producers and distributors creates a market position that is very hard for new entrants to contest.

A second ground of foreclosure can arise downstream, in the distribution of the signals. Both cable and satellite distribution entail proprietary issues and a problem of access. Cable TV operators usually own (or have a long-term concession over) the broadband wires used for distributing the signals. If the cable TV operators are integrated in the distribution segment, standard problems of access can arise for competitors. Satellite distribution requires the customers to use a set-top box to decode the signal, whose standard can be proprietary. Compatibility among satellite TV operators can avoid the doubling of the investment, but compatibility might be strategically denied by an incumbent operator to foreclose new rivals.

Consideration of vertical integration and foreclosure therefore suggests even more reasons to be sceptical of a market solution to EP.

We now turn to the complementary question of whether there are adequate private incentives for internal pluralism.

5.4 Are private incentives sufficient to provide internal pluralism?

When the number of independent media companies is not sufficient to provide a full range of varieties and policy positions, or when we observe strong concentration in audience or readership among a few channels or newspapers, the objective of IP becomes fundamental, as it may be the only way to ensure pluralism in access to information. Internal pluralism requires that each media company chooses a bundle or mixture of political views to satisfy the demand of a wide range of citizens. We have argued in the previous section that models of the media industry consistent with the Hotelling approach are rather flexible in describing the editorial choices of the media companies, which usually select a particular mixture of the main types of contents. Hence, the analysis of market equilibria summarised in the previous section is compatible with even a few media companies offering contents that, in different proportions, cover the main types appreciated by the public.

In fact, we observe in most media markets a key role for such operators: commercial TV channels offer a programme schedule that includes (several types of) movies, news, entertainment, sport, cultural events, etc.; the same holds true for general public newspapers and magazines; even thematic pay-TV channels are usually offered in bundles, giving access through subscription to a full range of varieties.

Content differentiation is therefore mostly realised by mixing in different proportions the main types of contents, rather than through specialising in a single variety. This is probably due to the fact that viewers/readers are very often interested in more than one variety and appreciate a mixture of them. The more obvious exceptions to this stylised fact – sporting newspapers – are in a sense an indirect confirmation of this claim, as sport fans are probably one of the few single-variety constituencies for media content.[21]

So far we have treated the choice of contents in general and of political views in particular as equivalent, considering the latter as one additional variety in information and entertainment supply. And we have discussed how far the tendency to differentiation extends from contents to political views. At this point it is important to look more carefully at the specific choice of the political position of a media firm on the part of its owners. Two points are fundamental, one on the demand side and one on the supply side.

First, while we have stressed that most of the viewing or reading public tends to have a taste for a variety of content, the same does not seem to be true for political information. While those members of the public who are not strongly interested in politics simply do not care for political discussion, those who actively participate and require political information seem to prefer to patronise media outlets close to their own views rather than to range over a variety of political opinions. In other words, the demand for political information seems to be naturally partisan and not to exhibit any comparable taste for variety. Hence, media companies are much less likely to mix over different political opinions than when mixing their programming among different varieties or types of movies, sports, etc. While some sports fans like to watch football and basketball matches, and motorbike and Formula 1 races, there are few politics fans who derive the same satisfaction when listening to both left-wing and right-wing politicians.[22]

On the supply side, if a single channel or newspaper tends to patronise one political position, we might still have a range of views represented if there are multi-channel or multi-media companies active in the market. If the objective of the media company is simply to maximise its profits in the market, it would be optimal to differentiate its political positions (and more generally its mix of varieties) among the channels or newspapers of the group. Thus even in a situation with a limited number of operators, we might observe significant variety in political views if there were multi-product rather than single-product operators, provided they aimed at maximising (media market) profits.

However, before drawing this conclusion we have to look in more detail at the media companies' motivations. So far we have considered their choices as driven by the profits that can be obtained in the media market through advertising, sales, subscriptions, etc. However, there are considerations that may cast doubt on this assumption.

The first is that some companies have a partisan identification, due to the opinions of their owners. In such case, sponsoring the owners' preferred political views is the natural choice, even if this leads to a sacrifice of profits. Should we expect, in this case, a bias in favour of a particular segment of the political spectrum?[23] In other words, will the selection mechanism among partisan media companies determine in equilibrium the survival of operators over the entire range of political views or will entry benefit only a part of the range (such as the right-wing positions)? This is a hard question that cannot be addressed in general terms without observation of real markets. It is important to remember, however, that in those segments where concentration is more likely, due to high costs of content, a media company has to raise a large amount of capital to operate and therefore entry requires considerable access to financial markets.

The second consideration is that firms often have a wider interest in communication than simply the maximisation of profit in the relevant market. Media markets are often heavily regulated and the hertzian spectrum is considered a public good that is licensed by the state to private companies. Hence media companies have a strong interest in public policies governing their markets. But they also control something in which political parties and the government have a strong interest, namely the supply of political information. Hence the decision to support one political party or another not only has an impact on the choices of viewers and readers, and on advertising revenues, but it implies also a (much less transparent) basis for negotiation with public institutions over policies for media markets and for the companies involved. These effects are even more important when the media companies belong to diversified conglomerate groups active (and influenced by public policies) in many markets. In these cases, the choice of political positioning depends heavily on such factors. And a bias in favour of the government and of the major political parties can be expected.

Notice that when a media company determines its political views according to these latter (partisan or lobbying) motivations, having multi-channel broadcasters or press groups makes the problem of pluralism even worse, since we should expect homogeneous political positioning of all the media of the group and not, as imagined above for a profit-maximising conglomerate, a differentiation of views within the group.

Our general conclusions about private incentives for the provision of pluralism in the media market are rather negative. Looking at market equilibria (EP) we have stressed that although differentiation in contents can be expected, with a diversified supply of the main types of content, this effect can be severely limited by the persistent concentration of many media markets, driven by competition for the more attractive contents. If the number of key players remains limited, we have to rely on a sufficient differentiation of content on the part of each individual company (IP). We have argued that although there are private incentives for differentiation with respect to many types of content and entertainment, the representation of political views and opinions tends to be more partisan, both with respect to the (ideological) demand of viewers and readers and with respect to the pro-government bias that tends to characterise media companies. IP is therefore poorly provided by private incentives. It is now time, therefore, to consider regulation for pluralism.

5.5 Regulation for pluralism

In this section we first review the main regulatory tools used in advanced economies to preserve pluralism, with a main focus on the EU.[24] We offer an evaluation of their merits and limits in the light of the analysis of private incentives developed above.

The main regulatory tools

We can distinguish the main tools used in actual regulation by type of instrument: as will be clear in the discussion, similar instruments find a justification with a reference to different pieces of the picture or, put another way, they are designed mostly with an objective of IP or EP in mind. Although we do not present a complete review of the actual policies of the European countries, we shall offer several examples of the different regulatory regimes. We can distinguish:

1. *Constraints on ownership*: in several countries regulation sets limits on the ownership of media companies. We can further distinguish among:

    1.1 *Ownership of single media companies*: these limits are usually set for TV broadcasting operators and define an upper bound to the share of a single owner in the company, in order to induce a more fragmented ownership structure. For instance, in France and Spain no single investor can own more than 49 per cent of the shares and the voting rights of a TV broadcasting company.[25]

    1.2 *Ownership of different media*: the regulation limits the participation of a single investor in companies belonging to different media segments. Since operating in TV and radio broadcasting markets implies holding public licences while operating in the press segment can be defined in terms of ownership of newspapers, inter-industry limits are usually designed as limits to cumulating ownership in the press and licences in radio or TV broadcasting. For instance, in France[26] and the UK[27] participations in TV and radio broadcasting, or broadcasting and the press, are severely limited. Ownership constraints between media and telecommunication companies, which were frequent both in Europe and in the USA before the liberalisation of telecoms, have now mostly been lifted.

    1.3 *Foreign ownership*: foreign investors not belonging to the European economic area are usually restricted from ownership of broadcasting companies: the limits, as before, are expressed in terms of prohibition of holding broadcasting licences. These constraints are set in Italy, France (maximum of 20 per cent of shares), Germany and the UK. Foreign investors, however, can hold licences if their country of residence or establishment applies rules of reciprocity with European countries.

    1.4 *Absolute prohibitions*: in Germany and the UK an absolute ban is set on the ownership of TV broadcasting companies (holding of TV broadcasting licences) for public (central or local) institutions, for central or local governments and for political parties.

2. *Limits on the number of licences*: in this group we include constraints that try to influence, by setting a maximum number of licences, the concentration of single media segments, namely TV

broadcasting. In France a single national or regional licence can be held in TV (terrestrial or satellite) broadcasting. In the UK no company can hold more than one national (Channel 3 or Channel 5) licence, or more than two Channel 3 regional licences in the same area; moreover, Channel 4 and the BBC cannot hold Channel 3 or Channel 5 national or regional licences. In Spain only one national or local licence can be held by private companies.

3. *Limits on market shares*: in some countries, such as Germany and Italy, limits to concentration are set not in terms of the number of licences that a single company can hold but in terms of market shares that can be computed in terms of audience or turnover. In Germany an upper bound of 30 per cent of the audience for television services is set: in case a group, considering all its channels, breaks this limit, no further licence can be assigned nor any acquisition of TV channels allowed. In Italy a recent regulation sets a limit of 20 per cent of total resources, defined over a very wide and diversified market (the so-called 'integrated communication system') that includes TV and radio broadcasting, the press, advertising and commercial promotions, movies, journals and book publishing.

4. *Limits on advertising*: in most countries some limits on advertising messages on TV and radio broadcasting are set, on an hourly and daily basis, and distinguishing between private and public channels. Although this regulation is not usually explained directly with reference to pluralism, indirectly these rules constrain market equilibria in the TV broadcasting markets and the allocation of advertising expenditures between broadcasting and the press. Hence, their indirect impact on the resources of the different media segments (and, in this way, on pluralism) is very strong.

5. *Limits on content*: specific rules are applied in many countries during electoral campaigns, constraining information programmes and news in TV and radio broadcasting. The rules require balancing the presence of parties and candidates in the programmes and in the news, regulating the free and paid direct access of political parties, and offering a timely right of reply. These rules are monitored during electoral campaigns not only quantitatively (for total time) but also qualitatively (for tone and completeness), although this latter crucial feature is very hard to implement.[28]

6. *Public media (TV channels)*: the presence of the state in media markets is today almost everywhere limited to TV and radio

broadcasting. In Europe public TV channels still play a crucial role. During the Fifties public channels allowed TV broadcasting to develop in continental Europe and until the Eighties they represented the only broadcasting supply. Public channels have to follow a set of public obligations that rely on the notion of public TV service and include information and culture, granting access to a variety of cultural, social, political and religious interest groups within a country. Hence, ensuring (IP) pluralism is certainly among the goals of public TV channels, which in this sense can be considered as a further tool for public policies on this issue.

This short review allows us to appreciate some general regularities in the norms that regulate media markets and some country specificities as well. First, it is immediately evident that TV (and radio) broadcasting are much more heavily regulated than the press. This is due in part to the fact that in these markets a public licence is needed to operate, since a scarce public good, the hertzian spectrum, must be allocated: hence, the licensing policy offers a powerful and general instrument to regulate the structure of the market. The other, complementary reason derives from the presumption that TV and radio broadcasting are much more widely diffused and therefore more powerful in influencing public opinion than are newspapers.

Second, looking at the specific tools, some of them, such as the limits to the number of licences in a single market, or the market share ceilings in terms of audience or turnover, are clearly inspired by the goal of external pluralism, aimed at preserving a deconcentrated market. Constraints to ownership, referring to a single company's ownership structure or to its participation in several segments of the media market, can instead be rationalised in terms of an IP objective. In particular, they are justified if it is very likely that the owner in control of the company will condition the political positioning of its media according to partisan or lobbying motivations. To balance this effect, dispersed ownership and limited inter-market links are pursued.

Third, it is not always clear whether regulation has shaped the features of the media market or instead the existing and powerful interests of media companies have been able to impose regulation corresponding to their own interests. In Germany, for instance, no limits are set on the ownership of broadcasting companies or on the number of licences, with a single constraint on the overall audience of the group: multi-channel TV broadcasting has been one of the distinctive features of the

German market since the Eighties. Is it the result of a gap in regulation or did regulation adapt to multi-channel operators that from the beginning characterised the market?

The answer is easier when we look at the Italian case. The opening of private broadcasting markets occurred in the mid-Eighties within a sort of regulatory vacuum, while the consolidation of the Mediaset group was allowed by the norms approved by the parliament, which set limits in terms of licences that always fitted the actual market positions of the strong private group. The recent reform approved by the Italian parliament sets market share limits defined over so large and composite an aggregate that no real constraint binds. Unfortunately, Italy offers a new and dramatic swing to the old theme of regulatory capture, with the prime minister owning the first private communication group and controlling the public TV channels, giving what amounts to around 90 per cent of the audience and 85 per cent of total advertising revenues.

Regulation for pluralism: open issues

We try in this section to evaluate the regulatory tools most frequently used, and to propose a possible set of interventions. We start from some general issues and then move to a discussion of the EP and IP objectives.

General issues

Our first point refers to *measuring pluralism*, a hard but necessary step when public policies must be designed. In the discussion on the objectives of public policy for pluralism we have proposed a double definition, external and internal pluralism, pointing out that the EP objective can be implemented looking at the mere availability of different views or alternatively by considering the actual choices of the public.

In the case of EP, for instance, availability can be evaluated by considering the number of media in a market (the number of channels, of newspapers, of radio stations), together with a check of the effective differentiation of contents and political views. In the case of IP, availability would require guaranteed access to all political views on an equal basis, for instance with equal exposure and time given to each position.

If actual choices are the concern, EP should be ascertained through some measure of concentration of the audience or the readership. What really matters, in this case, is whether the actual choices reflect the policy preferences of the public or instead are driven by some lock-in effect. In a country with an electorate with concentrated political views, for instance, we should not be surprised to observe a polarised distribution of the public's viewing or reading choices across the media. Hence, what really matters should be the difference in concentration between the audience and the votes for political parties or coalitions, where a higher concentration of the former measure with respect to the latter might signal problems with EP.[29] This approach is not immune from serious implementation problems, but seems close to how the problem of EP is perceived. The main difficulty is to evaluate the political positioning of the different media; a second relevant issue is how to treat a media outlet that presents several political views and not a single one (should we treat NBC news differently from Fox news?).[30]

We think that when media markets are more concentrated than the distribution of political views (votes), EP should be evaluated according to the actual choices of the public (concentration) and not simply looking at the number of media in a market.

The second general point is the *relation between regulation for pluralism and competition policies*. Although regulatory limits on market shares in the media market are often labelled as antitrust restrictions, it is important to stress that competition policy is inspired by public goals (welfare and efficiency) and applied in practice in ways that are not necessarily consistent with regulation for pluralism. Hence, competition policy cannot be considered as a complete substitute for the public policies for pluralism, although in some areas pluralism benefits from antitrust interventions.[31]

The clearest example of the difference in approaches is given by the relevance of efficiency arguments for multi-product firms. It is hard to deny that a media group can benefit from relevant synergies: some inputs and contents can be used on different media and their contents can be better differentiated, covering several market niches; compatibility in standards, as for instance in the use of the same set-top box to receive satellite transmissions, benefits viewers and calls for agreements among firms or the concentration of many channels in the supply of a pay-TV broadcaster. Hence, efficiency arguments should play a relevant role when discussing, for instance, a concentration project and the creation of a communication group. Antitrust policies should take these synergies into account.

Regulation for pluralism, meanwhile, having as an objective the preservation of independent operators and access for political views, has no reason to consider these efficiencies in its evaluation: from the point of view of pluralism, the only relevant effect of such concentration would be that of extending the control of a company over more media, something dangerous if partisan or lobbying motivations condition the editorial choices of the company in political information.

Once we have acknowledged the differences, it must be recognised that competition policy can be of great help for pluralism, by monitoring and preventing practices that would further reduce competition in media markets. Consider, for instance, the foreclosure issues that we have discussed in the previous sections and that seem particularly serious in the pay-TV segment. If exclusive contracts or vertical integration upstream and the use of proprietary distribution infrastructures and technologies downstream are used by a TV operator to consolidate its position, standard antitrust analysis and intervention are required. Opening the market to newcomers, however, creates a more favourable environment not only for competition but also for external pluralism.

External pluralism

As we argued above, EP should be assessed first of all by looking at concentration in media markets. *Market definition* should be very strict in this context, distinguishing different media (free-to-air TV, pay-TV, newspapers, radio stations), because we want to assess market by market whether EP is provided, establishing whether the additional objective of internal pluralism should come into the picture. Geographic markets should be carefully addressed as well, in order to assess the set of media that the public effectively receives in different regions. From this point of view, the press market is particularly important because the key role of local news makes local newspapers an important actor in small geographical markets, although we may overlook this effect if we consider only national circulation figures: in many countries, local newspapers (or even national newspapers with a traditional entrenchment in a given town or region) reach a very high share of the readers in a given area, although their individual position in the national market is negligible.

Once the relevant markets have been defined, a comparison should be made between a *concentration index* (say, the Herfindahl Index) of the audience/readership and an analogous measure applied to the votes for political parties. When we observe the former measure to be significantly higher than the latter, EP becomes problematic and remedies should be considered.

Our general approach is to design public policies in order to prevent the creation of companies that are very strong in a specific market, while allowing the creation of a diversified communication group active (but not dominant) in many media markets. Hence, a media market dominated by a multi-channel TV operator or by a publishing group with many newspapers is not desirable, while a set of media markets with communication groups active (but not dominant) in TV, the press or the radio would be welcome.

We can distinguish *regulatory limits to concentration* and remedies that come into play when a merger project is scrutinised. The former includes a limitation in the number of licences for broadcasting or radio transmission, limits to ownership of media companies or divestiture of specific activities. For instance, when market concentration becomes very high, the largest companies might be forced to sell a licence; alternatively, a ceiling to the number of individual licences might be set when the overall audience of the group exceeds a certain threshold. Analogous measures on the number of licences might be triggered by an expansion of a media group in other segments such as the press market, once a given market share is reached. These measures can be easily introduced when the broadcasting and radio segments, where a licence is needed to operate, are involved. We are in a weaker position when market concentration is truly internal to other segments, such as the press market, where creating a new media outlet does not require public authorisation. Still, requiring a publishing group to divest a newspaper is not very different from other deconcentration measures that can be applied to lines of business of a dominant firm in non-media markets.

The second basis for dealing with concentration refers to *merger control*. A merger project should be reviewed not only by the antitrust authority but also by the institution in charge of the regulation of pluralism. And the project should obtain the double approval of the two institutions or be revised according to the remedies required. Among potential remedies, the divestiture of specific media outlets (single TV channels, or newspapers or magazines, or radio stations) should be the preferred commitment,[32] since it is immediately effective and does not require a long-lasting monitoring activity on the part of the regulator.

How, then, should mergers be evaluated? Borrowing from antitrust jargon, we may say that we should prohibit mergers that 'substantially lessen pluralism'. While we can establish a direct link between pluralism and market fragmentation, the economic analysis of free entry equilibria has suggested (under the NO approach) that in some cases concentration cannot be avoided, being the outcome of competition on the merits; in other cases (under the MC approach), small local press markets cannot sustain more than very few operators. In the move towards a (concentrated) free entry equilibrium, the emergence of a few winners can take the form of mergers and acquisitions of the losers, or their bankruptcy. Merger control, in this case, has to seriously consider the *failing firm defence argument*: if in a long-run equilibrium some operators have to exit, merger with the failing competitors should be acceptable not only from a competition policy perspective but also under regulation for pluralism.[33]

While the tendency to a reduction in the number of media operators in a market can be driven by competitive forces and in some cases cannot be avoided by merger regulation, the *creation of a multi-media operator in the same market* (a communication group with many TV channels or many newspapers, etc.) should be constrained not only through *ex ante* regulatory limits, as discussed above, but also at the stage of merger control. Here the analysis under competition policy and that under regulation for pluralism diverge, and the efficiency defence arguments can be used in an antitrust case but should not be considered when pluralism is involved.

Advertising limits can indirectly influence market concentration if they reduce broadcasters' advertising revenues,[34] softening the rise in the fixed costs of programming (according to the NO approach). From the point of view of pluralism, however, these measures are usually justified mainly for their effect of shifting advertising investments from the TV to the press segments. The point here is that advertising messages are considered to be more effective on video than in the press and this creates a bias of advertisers in favour of TV. From the point of view of pluralism, however, such a bias has no justification since news is equally important whether transmitted through broadcasting or in the press. Regulation for pluralism should therefore correct this distortion. Further research is needed to evaluate whether it is preferable to intervene through advertising limits or using transfers to newspapers drawn from the licence revenues collected from the TVs.

Internal pluralism

In our view as set out above, the main danger to IP comes from the partisan and lobbying motivations of the media owners, while in the absence of these distortions some degree of internal differentiation would be provided. Regulation should therefore intervene primarily on these grounds.

Restrictions on company ownership are not particularly effective: a 49 per cent ceiling on individual shares does not really limit in practice the control of a single owner. Creating a more fragmented ownership structure in order to prevent the interference of shareholders in the editorial choices of the media seems a rather naive approach. If the control group has partisan or lobbying motivations, it is not this kind of measure that can solve the problem, as it would seem rather easy to find other investors with similar interests or political views, while formally respecting the constraints. What should be considered is setting *limits to ownership by investors who have strong interests in other heavily regulated activities* and who for this reason might try to use the media as a lobbying device.[35] Moreover, the constraints would be upon horizontal *cross-participations* by the same investors in different media companies: interlocking directorates have a well-established treatment in antitrust interventions against collusion; an additional effect, relevant for pluralism, of these links might be that of homogenising the political positioning of different media companies.

With the future development of digital transmission, which will allow broadcasting of a very large number of TV channels, the absolute ban on broadcasting licences for political parties or religious movements has no motivation and should be lifted.

Internal pluralism should be reinforced during *electoral campaigns* through stricter *rules on news, policy debates and programming in TV broadcasting*: the rules to be followed should require balance and fair access to all parties, candidates and policy positions. Moreover, a quick *right of reply* should be granted not only on TV programmes but also in the press. Such rules are often difficult to implement, however, because it is easier to define them in terms of quantity (space/time) than in terms of the quality and fairness of political information. Moreover, enforcement of such rules during the short deadlines of electoral campaigns is problematic, since often the fines, if any, are set after the elections.

For this reason we think that while private operators should follow such regulations, a *public TV channel* might be a complementary tool for ensuring internal pluralism. In a sense, the public service obligation of fair political information is realised in different ways according to the nature of the TV companies: for private operators regulation is imposed by setting rules to be followed; in addition to them, a public TV channel can also be controlled more directly by a parliamentary committee or an independent authority that monitors its programmes and requires changes and amendments if political information is unfair: the distortions that are more difficult to avoid through direct regulation[36] can still be controlled under the direct intervention of the committee/authority. This role of a public TV channel does not call for maintaining the extremely large role that public TV still has in Europe, often offering programming that hardly differs from that of commercial rivals. Hence, when we recognise the important role of public TV for internal pluralism we can also support at the same time proposals to reduce the number of public channels and strongly limit the dimensions of public TV, which should not be competing for resources from the advertising market.

All our examples refer to broadcasting markets, where there is very high concentration in all countries. However, there is a parallel concentration process in many segments of the written press, where local markets are often dominated by a single newspaper. Hence, an issue of IP is potentially relevant also for press markets. This is a very delicate point, as traditionally newspapers have not been regulated; nevertheless the issue is worth debating.

Finally, with all these measures forming the framework of regulation for pluralism, an *independent authority* should be in charge of its enforcement. Supervising the licensing policy of free-to-air broadcasting and cross-participation in different media segments, controlling the ownership structure of media companies and authorising new shareholders, running merger control and implementing the rules for fair and balanced information during electoral campaigns would be among the main tasks of such an institution. Its appointment and governance structure should avoid direct influence by government and political parties.

5.6 Conclusion

In this chapter we have analysed whether and how the market mechanism and private incentives can provide pluralism in media markets, from the point of view both of a diversified supply of different political positions in each market (external pluralism) and of a fair and complete representation of the political spectrum within each media outlet (internal pluralism).

Lessons for students: what have we learned?

First, what are the main insights that the economic analysis of the media market offers today? We argue that recent research and, more broadly, the literature on modern industrial organisation offer several contributions to an understanding of media markets and the private provision of pluralism. Relying on this body of literature, we argue that the market mechanism tends to create differentiation in the contents of the media companies, but this heterogeneity does not necessarily extend to the representation of political opinions and points of view. Moreover, in many segments of media markets, competition for the more attractive content tends to push up the fixed costs of the operators, creating and preserving concentrated structures. For these reasons, we expect that the market will not adequately satisfy the need for external pluralism.

Moving to internal pluralism, while media companies usually offer a mixture of different contents that matches the taste for variety on the part of the public, as far as political information is concerned, viewers and readers tend to have much more partisan tastes and do not demand a diversified presentation of many political views. Moreover, partisan or lobbying motivations of the media company owners can create a strong bias in favour of the government and the major political parties. For these reasons we do not expect that the general tendency to offer differentiated contents would extend to the political views expressed by each media company. Private incentives to provide internal pluralism seem quite poor.

Lessons for researchers: what do we still need to know?

Although recent research offers important contributions to our understanding of media markets and pluralism, we find many open issues that make the research agenda quite rich in this area. A full application of the insights of two-sided markets to the choices of quality and variety differentiation of media contents, the choice of contents within a single media outlet, the political economy analysis of media positioning when political lobbying is relevant, and the links between media markets and political processes are among the most fascinating open issues that research in the field should address.

Lessons for policymakers: what are the priorities
for policy in this area?

Having argued that market processes will not provide adequate incentives for pluralism, we considered regulation, describing the main tools used in the European countries and proposing a possible list of interventions, reflecting our view of the priorities for policy in this area. We think that external pluralism should be assessed by looking at market concentration (compared with concentration of votes in elections) and not simply by checking the availability of different contents. Competition policy can be of great help for pluralism, for instance in avoiding the foreclosure that may arise from vertical integration, but it cannot be considered a complete substitute for proper regulation, since in some areas the two approaches diverge. Regarding the implementation of EP, public policies should try to prevent through regulatory limits and merger control the creation of multimedia groups dominant in a single market, although allowing for cross-market activities. IP should be implemented by limiting the role of investors active in heavily regulated industries, by regulating content during electoral campaigns and by maintaining a public TV channel. Finally, all these interventions will require an independent authority that enforces regulation for pluralism out of the control of the government and of the political parties.

References

Anderson, S. and S. Coate (2000) Market Provision of Public Goods: the Case of Broadcasting, working paper, National Bureau of Economic Research no. 7513.

Armstrong, M. (2004) Subscription versus Advertising-Funded Television: the Case of Programme Quality, *mimeo*.

Beasley, T. and S. Coate (1997) 'An economic mode of representative democracy', *Quarterly Journal of Economics*, 108, 85–114.

Benabou, R. and J. Tirole (2002) 'Self-confidence and personal motivation', *Quarterly Journal of Economics*, 117, 871–915.

d'Aspremont, C., J. Gabszewicz and J.F. Thisse (1979) 'On Hotelling's "Stability in Competition"', *Econometrica*, 47, 1145–1150.

Dixit, A. and J. Stiglitz (1977) 'Monopolistic competition and optimum product diversity', *American Economic Review*, 67, 297–308.

Gabszewicz, J., D. Laussel and N. Sonnac (1999) TV-Broadcasting Competition and Advertising, *mimeo*.

Gabszewicz, J., D. Laussel and N. Sonnac (2001) Press Advertising and the Political Differentiation of Newspapers, *mimeo*.

Gal-Or, E. and A. Dukes (2001), 'Minimum differentiation in commercial media markets', *Journal of Economics and Management Strategy*, 12, 291–325.

Gustafsson, K. (1978) 'The circulation spiral and the principle of household coverage', *Scandinavian Economic History Review*, 1–14.

Hotelling, H. (1929) 'Stability in competition', *Economic Journal*, 39, 41–57.

Ireland, N. (1987) *Product Differentiation and Non Price Competition*, Basil Blackwell.

Irmen, A. and J. F. Thisse (1998) 'Competition in multi-characteristics spaces: Hotelling was almost right', *Journal of Economic Theory*, 78, 76–102.

Motta, M. and M. Polo (1997) 'Concentration and public policies in the broadcasting industry: the future of television', *Economic Policy*, 25, 294–334.

Motta, M. and M. Polo (2001) 'Beyond the spectrum constraint: concentration and entry in the broadcasting industry', *Rivista di Politica Economica*.

Motta, M., M. Polo and H. Vasconcelos (2003) 'Merger remedies in the EU: an overview', in F. Leveque and H. Shelanski (eds.) *Merger Remedies in American and European Competition Law*, Edward Elgar.

Neven, D. and J. F. Thisse (1988) On Quality and Variety Competition, *mimeo*.

Nilssen, T. and L. Sørgard (2001) The TV Industry: Advertising and Programming, *mimeo*.

Osservatorio di Pavia (2003) 'Guidelines for media monitoring of elections'.

Polo, M. (1991) 'Hotelling duopoly with uninformed consumers', *Journal of Industrial Economics*, 39, 701–716.

Rochet, J. C. and J. Tirole (2003) 'Competition in two-sided markets', *Journal of the European Economic Association*, 1, 990–1029.

Rochet, J. C. and J. Tirole (2004) Two-Sided Markets: an Overview, *mimeo*.

Sonnac, N. (2000) 'Readers' attitudes towards press advertising: are they ad-lovers or ad-averse?', *Journal of Media Economics*, 13, 249–259.

Spence, M. and B. Owen (1977) 'Television programming, monopolistic competition and welfare', *Quarterly Journal of Economics*, 91, 103–126.

Steiner, P. (1952) 'Programme patterns and preferences, and the workability of competition in radio broadcasting', *Quarterly Journal of Economics*, 66, 194–223.

Sutton, J. (1991) *Sunk Costs and Market Structure*, MIT Press.

Sutton, J. (1998) *Technology and Market Structure*, MIT Press.

Ward, D. (2004) *A Mapping Study of Media Concentration and Ownership in Ten European Countries*, Commissariaat voor de Media, The Netherlands.

Notes

1. The C3 concentration ratio computes the sum of the market shares of the largest three firms. In the table the market shares are computed according to the distribution of the viewers (TV), readers (press) or listeners (radio).
2. This effect may be quite important. In 2005, the main Italian public TV channel, Rai1, decided to insert an advertising break between a very popular quiz show and the prime-time news at 8pm. Since the break interrupted the sequence of programming, viewers had time to switch to other channels for the news. The leading commercial channel, Canale 5, broacasts its news at the same time; due to the commercial break on the rival channel, Canale 5 improved its audience share by around 5 per cent.
3. See Steiner (1952) on programme differentiation in radio broadcasting and Spence and Owen (1977), who use a monopolistic competition set-up to analyse programme diversity in TV broadcasting.
4. See, for a review, Rochet and Tirole (2003) and (2004).
5. See, for instance, Gabszewicz, Laussel and Sonnac (2001) and Sonnac (2000).
6. Consider, for instance, the submarket of magazines focused on a female public, in which huge amounts of advertising come from the dress and fashion industry. It seems natural to consider that the images of the advertising messages convey a substantial amount of information to the public of readers.
7. The general case of tastes for variety is treated, for instance, in Dixit and Stiglitz (1977), while the preference for (heterogeneous) single varieties was introduced by Hotelling (1929).
8. It is important to stress that when dealing with political information a variety might be the presentation of a single political opinion (for instance on a fact or on an issue), but also a particular mixture of views that gives a certain weight to some (or all) the political views. In this latter case, moreover, some positions might be presented in a positive light while others might be presented critically. Hence, when we refer to the notion of varieties in political information we have a very wide range of different opportunities. A fair and balanced representation of political views should correspond to messages that convey the key positions of political parties without judgements and embellishments.
9. This element creates a further link with product market competition, as a more competitive market, implying lower profits, will reduce the firms' willingness to pay for advertising. See on this point Gal-Or and Dukes (2001) and Nilssen and Sørgard (2001).
10. It is worth noticing that advertising *quantities* play the same role as product *prices* in the standard Hotelling model, i.e. the two media companies play in strategic complements when setting the amount of

advertising space. The reason is that when media 1 sells more ads, it creates a shift in the audience towards media 2, that will sell more ads as well.

11. Notice that the usual problem of non-existence of equilibrium that arises in the standard Hotelling model does not occur here, where firms have a double source of revenue: locating at the centre, in fact, will force media companies to give the newspapers for free to the readers, but will maximise the revenues from advertising.

12. This paper can shed some light also on the pay-TV market, in which media companies collect revenues both from advertising and from subscription fees.

13. Gal-Or and Dukes (2001) obtain this result by assuming that media companies and advertisers bargain over advertising prices, using a Nash Bargaining solution. It seems, however, that a similar result could be obtained by assuming the media companies set a price along the advertisers' demand function for commercials.

14. Moreover, informative advertising can focus on particular elements of firms' supply, as prices or varieties. In a Hotelling duopoly with a fraction of consumers uninformed, the equilibrium prices fall below the full information price when consumers observe prices but not variety, while the price increases above the full information benchmark when varieties but not prices are observed. Hence, even within informative advertising the content of the messages can have opposite effects on firms' gross profts. See Polo (1991).

15. For instance, the transmission rights of the major sporting events and of the more popular movies are priced according to the number of TV sets and the value of the advertising investments in the country.

16. This process has been described at a qualitative level according to the paradigm of *circulation spiral* in Gustafsson (1978). In his description the effects come through readers who like advertising rather than through more attractive contents. However, the argument works quite consistently with our story: 'The larger of two competing newspapers is favoured by a process of mutual reinforcement between circulation and advertising, as a larger circulation attracts advertisement, which in turn attracts ... more readers.'

17. We may notice that in the US market, after more than twenty years of harsh competition from a large number of small pay-TV channels, the four main commercial networks still obtain around half of the audience in the prime time.

18. Different approaches can be chosen: a Hotelling-type specification giving localised effects among adjacent varieties (Armstrong (2004), i.e. $\gamma_j \neq 0$ only for $j = i - 1$, $i + 1$; a quadratic utility specification that admits generalised substitution patterns, i.e. $\gamma_j > 0$, $\forall_j \neq i$; and a discrete

choice approach. For this latter case, see Motta and Polo (2001), Appendix.

19. This might be rationalised by referring to the results of maximum differentiation of the MC approach, in the sense that the supply of contents exploits the maximum differentiation allowed by viewers'/readers' tastes. This is obviously not an analytical result, but simply an educated guess that the results obtained in the MC approach extend to a more complex horizontal + vertical model of viewers' behaviour. See also Neven and Thisse (1988) and Ireland (1987).

20. This effect holds when preferences are characterised by a generalised substitution pattern: in this case, increasing attractiveness steals viewers from all the rival channels. When substitution is localised, as in the Hotelling-type specification, closer varieties reduce the equilibrium advertising revenues since the channel cannot steal viewers from 'distant' channels. See Armstrong (2004).

21. Not surprisingly, in fact, pay-TV channels have always used sport and movie channels as the tools to open and create markets for pay-TV services.

22. This attitude on the part of voters is reminiscent of the 'self-serving' beliefs analysed in Benabou and Tirole (2002). Their approach may represent a foundation based on intrapersonal behaviour of such attitude in politics.

23. See Beasley and Coate (1997).

24. We focus on the European countries since the market dimensions, the important role of public TV channels and the vertical articulation of the industries are relatively similar. The USA offers important insights on the future development of the European markets, but the problems involved, in particular for what concerns external pluralism, are rather different (see Chapter 8 in this volume). On the European and US broadcasting markets see Motta and Polo (1997).

25. The limits are further refined in France by setting a constraint of 15 per cent of shares if a single investor has participations in two TV companies and a ceiling of 5 per cent in case of shares in three TV companies. An upper bound of 50 per cent of the shares is set also to individual participations in satellite TV.

26. The rules are particularly articulated in France. For *national broadcasting*: no company can have a TV or radio licence if two conditions in the following list are met: it has already a radio licence reaching a basin of at least 30 million people; it has already TV or radio licences for cable broadcasting reaching a population of at least 6 million people; it offers TV services reaching more than 4 million people; it owns newspapers covering at least 20 per cent of the total readers. For *local broadcasting*: no company can operate in local broadcasting markets if it already has

licences for national over the air or cable TV broadcasting, and if it owns national or local newspapers.

27. In the UK there are limits to multiple licences at both the national and the local level. At the *national* level, no company can have a licence for national TV broadcasting (Channel 3 or Channel 5) and a national radio broadcasting licence or ownership of national newspapers with a share of at least 20 per cent of the national readership. At the *local* level, no double licences are permitted between regional Channel 3 TV broadcasting and regional radio or digital TV broadcasting; a Channel 3 regional TV broadcasting licence cannot be held if the company owns a local newspaper with more than 20 per cent of the local readership.

28. On media monitoring and the associated methodological and practical implementation issues, see the report Osservatorio di Pavia (2003).

29. For instance, in Italy the centre-right coalition obtained around 50 per cent of votes in the 2001 elections and controls directly (through ownership) three commercial TV channels and indirectly (through the appointment of the management) at least two of the three public channels, with a cumulative audience of around 80 per cent.

30. In a recent paper S. Mullainathan and A. Shleifer have used the classification of the Americans for Democratic Action (ADA), based on votes in committees and at the Senate of the USA, on how close are 100 senators to the positions of the Democratic party. Then, given this ranking, they have studied the frequency of citations of different think tanks and policy organisations (Brookings Institution, Rand Corporation, Amnesty International, etc.) by the senators, identifying a pair (policy positioning, frequency of citations). Finally, they have studied the frequency of citations of the same organisations in the news of the leading newspapers. By comparing the frequency of citations of a newspaper and of a senator, they are able to identify indirectly the policy positioning of the newspaper as well. Apart from *Fox News* and the *Washington Times*, all the other national newspapers obtain an ADA ranking above 60, that can be interpreted as being close to Democratic positions.

31. We think that antitrust policies should become the main policy tool for the development of the media markets, substituting in many cases for industry-specific regulations. The defence of pluralism, however, should maintain an independent status, specific tools and institutions. On public policies for broadcasting markets, see Motta and Polo (1997).

32. These divestitures are in line with the approach followed by the European Commission for merger remedies under competition policy. The aim of the divestiture is to create a new and viable competitor in the market. Hence, divesting entire lines of business (single media) is

preferred to selling a miscellaneous set of assets. On the logic of merger remedies see Motta, Polo and Vasconcelos (2003).

33. The 2001 merger Stream/Tele + in the Italian pay-TV market approved under commitments by the European Commission can be interpreted in this way.

34. We may expect that in a non-cooperative equilibrium with no advertising limits, media companies sell too little advertising space with respect to a monopolist. A company, by increasing its advertising space, in fact exerts a positive externality on the rivals, which observe an increase in their customers. Since in a non-cooperative equilibrium this externality is not taken into account, the companies sell less space than a monopolist. Then, if the advertising limits are binding, they induce even less space sold, with a fall in advertising revenues.

35. For instance, banning participation in media markets by operators in the energy or transport industries can be a straightforward application of this approach. More problematic is the extension of this ban to telecoms, which have genuine industrial reasons due to technological convergence for entering media markets.

36. There is a full range of examples of how formal rules can be circumvented if a TV broadcaster has strong political biases: the opinions of the rival party can be described using a critical or sceptical tone, or reviewed in such a way that the viewer hardly understands the relevant points; when different coalitions compete in an electoral campaign, only the more extremist politicians of the rival coalition are invited into the debate, producing a distorted representation of the coalition as a whole, etc.

6 | Regulation of television advertising

SIMON P. ANDERSON*

6.1 Introduction

Most nations restrict the advertisements that are broadcast on television. There are restrictions on both the length of commercial breaks and the content of the advertisements themselves. This chapter is concerned with the economic rationale underlying such regulations. Examples of the types of regulatory constraints on advertising broadcast on television are drawn from Europe, the United States and, most prominently, Australia. The Australian case is particularly useful because the regulations are clearly set forth in official publications. Many of the regulations in Australia have counterparts in other nations.

Length restrictions are widespread in developed nations, with the conspicuous exception of the USA (the USA does not restrict the broadcasting of commercials, except during children's programming). Understanding the economic rationale for length restrictions requires first understanding the complex interactions in the market for television advertisements. The main players in the market are the advertisers, the television viewers and the broadcasters who coordinate the two sides of the market. Advertisers want to communicate with viewers, who are the prospective consumers of the products touted in the ads. Viewers want to enjoy the programme content and 'pay' for it through being exposed to the advertisements. Broadcasters must balance the revenues earned from delivering eyeballs to advertisers with the distaste to ads that viewers express by switching off or switching over. A broadcaster's calculus does not fully internalise the net social costs of ads (viewer distaste minus advertiser surplus) and broadcasters are also able to exploit market power in delivering viewers to advertisers. Furthermore, the private demand for advertisements may exceed or fall short of the social demand, depending on the type and role of advertising (or, indeed, one's view thereof). This means that the unregulated broadcast market can involve too much or too little advertising. The case for advertising caps revolves around there being excessive advertising in a market system.

Length restrictions are socially harmful if there is underadvertising, where the term underadvertising is used to denote less advertising than would be socially optimal. Underadvertising may arise if nuisance costs to viewers are relatively low and if the social benefits (from informing viewers of socially valuable transaction opportunities, for example) are high. Nevertheless, length restrictions may be beneficial if it can be argued that the market system leads to excessive advertising. Such over-advertising is likely if the nuisance to viewers is large relative to the benefits to advertisers. The benefits to advertisers may in turn overstate the social benefits from advertising (although the converse is also possible). However, a simple study of whether there is too much or too little advertising, taking as given the existing market parameters, may seriously misread the full economic effects of advertising length caps. Indeed, advertising caps may reduce programme quality, the breadth of programming and overall choice diversity by reducing the profitability to broadcasters of producing programming. These factors need to be incorporated too into the evaluation of the desirability of regulations.

Advertising content restrictions are also widespread in developed nations. Many countries ban or restrict the advertising of certain products. These can mostly be understood as being demerit goods (like tobacco, liquor and gambling). The argument for banning advertising of such goods reflects paternalistic concerns about the consumption of these goods. The goods themselves are frequently heavily taxed. One question here is why the ads themselves could not be taxed instead or perhaps the products might be taxed even more heavily. In response, one might argue that it might seem to be rather hypocritical (or a counter-productive effect at any rate) if a cigarette advert were followed by an antismoking ad financed by the revenues from the previous ad or the advertised product. So it is that several commodities cannot be legally advertised and consumers are protected from harmful products that advertising might otherwise glamorise or indeed make consumers more aware of consumption possibilities.

This type of consumer protection is taken further when it comes to children's advertising. Regulations in this area are even stricter and some countries completely ban advertisements during programming aimed at children or even ads using characters from children's programming. Here, presumably, the view is that children are not able to

make fully rational consumption decisions themselves, either through
limited information or through limited decision-making capacity.
Advertisements may put undue pressure on parents to purchase products the parents might otherwise deem not in the best interests of
their offspring (rather like the signs in some supermarkets that indicate
certain check-out lanes where confectionery is not on display). Knowing that children are not subverted by advertising messages may reas-
sure parents to allow television-watching privileges. One might view
the paternalism inherent in banning cigarette advertising to adults as
rather similar, with some manipulable consumers being (somewhat)
protected from making bad consumption decisions.

The converse case to demerit goods is illustrated by the fact that many
countries require stations to carry certain public service announcements
(PSAs) as well as party political broadcasts in election season. One might
view these as merit commodities that are encouraged by the government
with an implicit subsidy to their promotion. Another related type of
regulation in the television context is local content – for example, some
European countries restrict the amount of material broadcast of foreign
origin.

There may be perverse economic effects in the industry sectors that
are affected by restrictions or banning (although it seems unlikely that
such effects in practice do underlie actual restrictions). For example,
drawing on the economics of advertising, it is conceivable that an
advertising ban might even raise industry profits. This outcome might
transpire if an unrestricted outcome would involve much advertising
that served mainly to shuffle demand among producers. An interesting
and controversial case in its own right is that of direct-to-consumer
advertising of prescription drugs. Only two nations allow such advertising and it is arguable that it leads to overprescribing of drugs. A
counter-argument is that consumers are better informed and may be
better induced to get treatment once they know of potential cures.

The rest of the chapter is organised in the following way. The next
section describes the regulations for Australia in more detail and also
gives details on EU regulations and selected European countries.
Section 6.3 sets out a model of advertising caps and discusses the
market interaction in television markets between viewers and advertisers, intermediated by broadcast 'platforms'. The discussion of the
basic market form is extended to allow for quality choice and format
competition. Section 6.4 addresses why certain goods are barred from

being advertised in some countries and also discusses some possible implications for the product markets concerned. Section 6.5 concludes.

6.2 Regulations and restrictions

In what follows, the Australian case is treated in some detail, followed by short remarks for salient features from other nations. There is a detailed set of guidelines to draw on for Australian television.[1] Many of the regulations in Australia have counterparts in other nations. Australian television is governed by the Australian Broadcasting Authority (ABA). One of its objectives is to promote the development and reflection of Australian identity, character and cultural diversity through what is broadcast. While the ABA leaves the primary responsibility for ensuring that broadcasts meet community standards with the television stations themselves, it also has developed a code of practice that suggests guidelines as well as some compulsory standards. These include Australian content and children's programme content.[2] They also include restrictions on both the length of advertisements (advertising caps) and the content of advertisements and the types of goods that may be advertised.

The Australian Broadcasting Authority's Code of Practice

The ABA Code of Practice is intended to regulate the content of commercial television according to current community standards and ensure that viewers are helped to make firm choices about their viewing and that of their children. There is quite a complex layer of regulations and publications that describes the guidelines. The code operates alongside three overlapping authorities. These are ABA standards that regulate programmes for children and sustain Australian content; advertising codes from the Australian Competition and Consumer Commission (ACCC) governing the content of television commercials and advertising generally; and the commercial television advisory notes which respond to cultural diversity, people with disabilities, etc.

There are several requirements in the code concerning television commercials. First, television advertisers are expected to make sure that their ads comply with both the Advertisers' Code of Ethics[3] and the code for advertising for children. The code sets up restrictions on the amount of advertising and other programme matter that stations may air during the day. There are also placement restrictions on certain types of 'sensitive' advertising. Moreover, commercials must not be too noisy or strident or even sound louder than adjacent programming, and transmission should not be higher in advertising breaks.[4] In addition, commercials and other promotions[5] must be easily distinguished by viewers from programme material. This is especially important where children are concerned. There are also guidelines for disclosure of commercial arrangements, for example, if products or services are endorsed or featured in the programme and such endorsements have been paid for by the sponsoring firm. The ABA requires that at least 80 per cent of advertising time broadcast each year between 6am and midnight be used for Australian-produced advertisements.[6]

Rules on commercials and promotions intend there to be 'a reasonable balance between programme and non-programme matter broadcast by a licensee'.[7] Non-program matter includes several subcategories. The most important are spot commercials, which are defined as advertising for a product, service or belief that is scheduled within a programme break or between programmes. The second subcategory comprises advertising that takes the form of superimposed text occupying all of the screen during the programme. The third type is a programme promotion (known as a 'tune-in' in the United States) or station promotion. The code exempts several categories from being non-programme matter. These include a prize, a competition or an information segment. Another exempted category includes community service announcements that promote a charitable cause or activity and are broadcast free by licensees. Likewise exempted are announcements for an election authority and sponsorship announcements.[8] Interestingly, infomercials are also excluded. Another way to get an exemption is to use a voice-over or promotion over the closing credits of another programme or superimposed text over only part of the screen during the programme. Various other announcements and restricted 'tune-ins' are exempted. As long as they contain no more than ten seconds of programme content, these announcements include those that indicate that a programme will not be shown when advertised, a list of programmes to be broadcast that day, a short announcement of the next programme and a movie opener (a brief introductory sequence to a feature film). Also permitted are station identification, a plot summary at the beginning of an episode of a series and a programme trailer for a future episode if this is broadcast before the closing credits.[9]

Having described what counts as advertising, we now consider the Australian Rules for Limitations to the number of adverts that may be aired. There are both average limitations and limitations for particular hours. These are quite close together in terms of number of minutes (as opposed to the European context, in which the numbers are quite different). In Australia, an average of thirteen minutes of non-programme matter may be broadcast between 6pm and midnight and fifteen minutes at other times (excepting in P and C periods as discussed below). In any particular hour, between 6pm and midnight up to fifteen minutes may be broadcast, but no more than fourteen minutes (average) in any four hours. During election periods, stations can add one minute of political matter. At all other times, the maximum hourly limit is sixteen minutes. The two categories of programming that concern children are P and C periods. No commercials may be broadcast during P periods. In the C period, each half hour may contain no more than five minutes of commercials and one minute of other promotions. Further restrictions on advertising to children are described below.

Placement of commercials for certain types of goods and services is also restricted. Alcoholic drinks (including beer, wine and spirits) may be advertised only in mature and adult time periods. Exceptionally, they may accompany live broadcasts of sporting events on public holidays and weekends. Commercials for betting and gambling must only be shown during mature audience periods although government lotteries, etc. are accepted. Commercials for X-rated films may not be broadcast and commercials for R-rated films only after 8.30pm.

Additional regulations concern children. The AANA code for advertising to children concerns advertising self-regulation towards children of fourteen years or less. Notably, adverts for food and drink should not encourage an inactive lifestyle nor promote unhealthy eating habits. Also, the host or the character in the programme must not promote products or services. Finally, children's television standards must not demean people or groups on the basis of ethnicity etc., nor must they distress or frighten children or display unsafe situations. Advertisements to children must not mislead or deceive them and must be clearly understood by them. Advertising must not cause children to put undue pressure on their parents to buy goods. They also must not undermine parental authority, nor must they imply that a product makes children who own it superior to their peers or that people who buy what is advertised are more generous than those who do not buy such products.

Any claims made in advertising must be clear and truthful. If prices are mentioned, they must be accurate. The presentation should not then play down prices by using such qualifying adjectives as 'only' or 'just'.

Regulations in European countries

In Europe, broadcast advertising has been legally controlled via the Television Without Frontiers Directive enacted by the Council of the European Community in 1989. The purpose of the TWF Directive is to secure access for viewers and listeners in all Member States to broadcasting signals emanating from any other Member State, and the harmonisation of European Union broadcast advertising standards. The directive contains chapters devoted to promotion of television programme production and distribution, protection of minors, television advertising and sponsorship, and right of reply.

The TWF Directive (89/552/EEC, as amended by Directive 97/36/EC) allows nine minutes of commercials on average, with a maximum of twelve minutes in any given hour. Some Member States have stricter limits. For example, in France, all broadcast channels must carry at most six minutes of commercials on average, with a maximum of twelve minutes in any given hour. The exception is the Franco-German venture ARTE, which is restricted to four minutes of commercials on average and a maximum of nine minutes in any given hour. Cable television is governed only by the EU standard.

In the UK, no advertising is allowed on public television (the BBC). The average viewer time in Great Britain is 225 minutes per day and 41 per cent of the viewers of broadcast television and 28 per cent of satellite viewers watch the BBC. Commercial broadcasting is allowed no more than nine minutes per hour average per day, with a maximum of twelve minutes in any given hour, in accord with European laws. However, there can be no more than seven and a half minutes on average in prime-time viewing. Cable television is also regulated by the EU standard. Ads must fall in natural breaks in programming and be at least twenty minutes apart. Ads are not allowed to interrupt certain types of programmes such as religious ceremonies, royal ceremonies or programmes including members of the Royal Family, parliamentary broadcast, and scholastic and children's programmes. Excluded sectors are political ads, tobacco, betting, private detective agencies, weapons, pornography, prescription medicine and products that mask the effects of alcohol. Some restrictions are applied to religious messages, those soliciting donations, marital agencies, alcohol, financial messages, food products, betting and medicines. It is understood that spirits should not be advertised. There are also specific rules that forbid subliminal ads and comparative ads are authorised only under reservations. The volume of ads should not be louder than the surrounding programming.

In the Netherlands, the overall law for time limits conforms with the EU directive of 20 per cent per hour, but in practice the Dutch minister sets a much tighter limit of 6.5 per cent of daily programming for the public television stations. Advertisement spots are in blocks of at least two minutes and must occur only in natural breaks. Excluded sectors include tobacco, prescription drugs and ideological messages. Alcohol is allowed to be advertised, but with a three-second educational slogan such as 'Drink but moderately', 'Stay sociable. Drink moderately', 'Let's stay sociable and drink with moderation'. The Dutch also have several regulations designed for the protection of children: there should be no pressure for under-twelves to buy products and children's inexperience and credulity should not be abused; for confectionery ads, a pictogram of toothbrush and toothpaste is featured prominently.

Sweden has one of the highest percentages of TV household ownership at 97 per cent, with an average daily viewing time of 140 minutes per person. Half of the viewers of broadcast television are equally split between two public stations, SVT1 and SVT2. These are not allowed to advertise. For other stations, the time allowed for advertisements is eight minutes maximum in any given hour, rising to ten minutes between 7pm and midnight. However, ads may take up only an average of six minutes per hour over the whole day and six minutes per hour from 6pm to midnight. Ads must fall in natural breaks in programming (such as halftime in football matches) and they must be at least twenty minutes apart. Advertising spots must be clearly identified in terms of beginning and end points. Products which are excluded from advertising are alcohol, tobacco and prescription medicine. Sweden has the strictest regulations concerning children.[10] Indeed, no advertisement may be directed primarily at children under twelve years old, there can be no advertising before and after children's programmes and presenters of children's programmes must not feature in any adverts.

Outside the EU, in Norway, a broadcaster is now allowed to interrupt a programme with advertising breaks to a larger extent than previously.[11] The rules are quite complicated. For example, a fictional series like

Friends could not be interrupted under the old rules. It may now be interrupted once, with a commercial break lasting at most sixty seconds.

6.3 A model of advertising caps

Commercial (or free-to-air) television exists because of advertising revenues. Advertising caps might therefore substantially alter the performance of the industry. As well as having a direct effect on reducing nuisance to viewers and curtailing information flows from firms to prospective purchasers, caps may change both the types of programmes, the quality of programming and the variety of programmes offered. To understand how advertising caps may affect broadcast firms' incentives (and the ensuing equilibrium), we need to carefully describe the structure of competition within the industry. The broadcast industry has a very interesting economic structure quite different from the industrial organisation of most markets for consumer goods. The basic business model is that broadcasts are used as entertainment for viewers and these broadcasts also carry advertisements. Viewers are then exposed to advertisements as a side product of their consumption of the entertainment content. The entertainment content is paid for by advertisers who use the intermediary of the broadcast company to deliver messages to the advertising firms' prospective customers. This set-up may be described as a two-sided market with network externalities.[12] In this vein, we may view the intermediary, the broadcast company, as a 'platform' that needs to get both sides on board in order to generate revenues. That is, the broadcaster must deliver viewers to advertisers and does so by judicious choice of the level (and perhaps the type) of advertising it proposes along with a vehicle attractive enough to entice the prospective buyers to watch. Competition with other broadcasters (other platforms) is also an important feature of the competitive landscape. A broadcaster needs to take into account the extent to which increasing the number of advertisements shown will cause viewers to switch off or switch channels and this decision also impacts the amount of revenue raised per viewer from the advertisers.

A careful description and construction of a model of platform competition in two-sided markets therefore requires that we describe the behaviour of the three types of agent who interact on the platform. We first describe advertisers, then viewers, then the broadcasters that bring the two together.

Advertisers

Advertisers wish to communicate with viewers who are the prospective consumers of the wares they advertise. We describe the advertiser side of the market by their willingness to pay to communicate. We shall abstract from various well-established features of advertising. First, marketers recognise that a viewer typically needs to see an advertisement at least two or three times before there is any marked change in his or her awareness of the good being advertised. Thereafter the benefit from 'hitting' a particular consumer with an ad falls off quite rapidly after several exposures in a short time frame. Instead, it is assumed here that a single 'hit' suffices to reach a viewer. Second, we also abstract from the time dimension. In particular, by assuming that there is a single viewing period, we circumvent the issue that a broadcaster may be able to deliver to an advertiser in one time slot a viewer who was delivered by a different broadcaster in another time slot. Third, we shall furthermore assume that all viewers are homogeneous to advertisers so that there is no matching of advertisements to programmes (golf clubs in a golfing programme). Fourth, we shall assume also that the demand for advertising time by a particular advertiser is a simple linear function of the number of viewers delivered. This means that if an ad delivers twice as many viewers as another, then the advertiser is willing to pay twice as much in order to air the ad before the higher group size.

Let the demand price per viewer when a adverts are aired be given by $p(a)$. Thus if a broadcaster delivers N_i viewers and airs a_i advertisements, the broadcaster's advertising revenue is $N_i p(a_i) a_i$. It will be convenient in what follows to write $R(a_i) = p(a_i) a_i$, as the revenue earned on a per-viewer basis when a_i advertisements are screened. We shall assume that $R(.)$ is log-concave, meaning that $\ln R$ is concave. This in turn implies that the ratio R'/R is a decreasing function. This means that the revenue function has the standard hump shape, although it does not necessarily have to be strictly concave.

Viewers

We assume that viewers react to the full price, f_i, associated to viewing option i. This full price may be decomposed into advertising nuisance, which we assume to be a linear function of the number of adverts watched, and any direct monetary subscription price for watching television, if applicable. That is,

$$f_i = \gamma a_i + s_i,$$

where γ is the nuisance cost imposed per ad, a_i is the number of ads screened on channel i and s_i is its subscription price. Viewers choose which channel to watch according to a discrete choice model: viewers choose to watch the programme that yields the highest utility. The conditional utility to a viewer from watching channel i depends on the match value of the option minus the full price paid:

$$u_i = \varepsilon_i - [s_i + \gamma a_i],$$

where the term in square brackets is the full price, f_i, and ε_i is the idiosyncratic evaluation of the consumer for the particular viewing option. Viewers all dislike ads to the same degree.[13] In the sequel, this idiosyncratic benefit may be visualised as a distance function (as in models based in spatial economics) or else a random draw from a taste distribution (as in standard discrete choice models).

Denote by $N_i(f_i, f_{-i})$ the number of viewers in the population who choose to watch channel i where f_{-i} denotes the vector of full prices of other stations. We shall frequently invoke the assumption of fully covered markets, which means that each viewer selects one of the n available stations to watch. Let $N_i' < 0$ denote the derivative of the own viewer share with respect to own full price and we will use the notation N' to describe the derivative under a symmetric market situation. Thus, for example, the derivative $\frac{\partial N_i}{\partial a_i}$, when evaluated at a symmetric solution, will be written as simply $\gamma N'$.

Broadcasters

There are n broadcasters in the market and they are each individually assumed to maximise profits. These profits are given by the product of the number of viewers and the total revenues earned per viewer. The revenues per viewer potentially comprise two terms, the subscription price and the advertising revenues. Thus

$$\pi_i = N_i(f_i, f_{-i})[s_i + R(a_i)].$$

First consider the case of a monopolist which chooses only its advertising level (we refrain from considering subscription prices for the moment). The monopolist's first-order condition for its choice of advertising level is

$$\frac{\partial \pi_i}{\partial a_i} = \gamma N_i'(f_i) R(a_i) + N_i(f_i) R'(a_i) = 0.$$

Since N_i' is negative then marginal revenue, $R'(a_i)$, is necessarily positive at any interior solution. This means that the monopolist reins back advertising levels so as to not lose too many viewers. This condition can usefully be written as

$$\frac{R'(a_i)}{R(a_i)} = \frac{-\gamma N_i'(f_i)}{N_i(f_i)}.$$

The left-hand side is strictly decreasing under the assumption that R is log-concave and the right-hand side is increasing in the advertising level under a similar assumption on the demand function, $N_i(f_i)$. The optimal choice is then visualised as a familiar-looking intersection (with the quantity of ads on the horizontal axis) of a downward-sloping curve with an upward-sloping one. The effect of an increase in γ is then seen to be that the upward-sloping curve shifts up and so the chosen advertising level must fall. This is because a higher γ corresponds to a higher nuisance value from advertising and so a higher loss rate from raising the number of ads. Put another way, individual viewer demand becomes more elastic in advertising and so the advertising 'price' paid by viewers falls.

For the welfare analysis that follows, we must consider the surpluses accruing to three types of agent in the model.[14] We therefore sum the broadcasters' profits, the advertisers' surplus and the viewers' entertainment benefits. Note that the advertising revenue component of the broadcasters' profit is simply the revenue under the advertising demand curve, so that the total surplus from advertising is measured simply as the full area below the advertising demand curve. In the case of a fully covered market (i.e. if all viewers watch), the analysis is also simplified because subscription prices are simply a transfer from viewers to broadcast firms and the subscription price level is therefore revenue neutral and plays no role in the overall welfare analysis. It is, however, crucial in determining the distributional effects of any policy change.

Now consider the optimal level of advertising when there is a single broadcast channel. If the market is fully covered, the optimal level of advertising stipulates simply that the marginal cost of advertising equals the marginal benefit of advertising. With fully covered markets, the marginal cost is just the nuisance to viewers, γ (this insight carries over to the analysis of several broadcast channels which follows). The marginal social benefit is the per-advertisement per-viewer demand price, p, and so the social optimum stipulates the equality of advertising nuisance and demand price per viewer. In the case of markets that are not fully covered (so that there is some leakage to the non-viewing option at the margin), the marginal social cost of advertising must be augmented by the lost surplus caused by inducing another viewer to switch off. This lost surplus consists of the advertiser benefits that no longer accrue on account of that viewer.

We can now compare the optimal level of advertising with the equilibrium level for the monopoly as described above. From this comparison we can determine whether (binding) advertising caps have beneficial or detrimental social consequences. Notice first that if the advertising nuisance, γ, is very low then the monopolist's optimal choice of advertising will be where marginal revenue is practically zero. This is because the monopolist holds back advertising levels in order to extract the maximum revenue per viewer from the advertising market. However, the social optimum, in the case of negligible nuisance costs to viewers, stipulates that all advertisers with positive demand prices ought to be allowed access to the viewers (who anyway do not view the adverts as an intrusion in this particular benchmark case). This clearly implies that the market equilibrium level of advertising is below the optimal level – in the same manner that a monopolist's output is below the competitive output. Any advertising cap in such a situation would just exacerbate the market failure because a binding cap must be less than the monopolist's advertising choice and therefore even further from the socially optimal level of advertising.

Consider now the opposite scenario where the advertising nuisance per advertisement is high. Indeed, this nuisance can be higher than the demand price of the advertiser with the highest willingness to pay to reach viewers (prospective consumers). In this case the socially optimal level of advertisements is zero because no consumer ought to be disturbed by an ad that returns to its sender less benefit than it inflicts on the unfortunate viewer whose entertainment is disturbed by it. However, the market equilibrium must always involve a positive level of advertising. Even though this level of advertising falls with the nuisance cost to viewers (because the higher the advertising cost, the larger the propensity for viewers to turn off, a situation the monopolist guards against), this level of advertising must always be positive. This is because, in the absence of the ability (or the technology) to use subscription pricing, the only source of revenue for a free-to-air broadcaster is revenue from advertising. In this scenario the market level of advertising is necessarily too high. Any ad cap will then improve social welfare by drawing down the level of advertising by the monopolist to closer to the socially optimal level. Notice that there are strong distributional consequences to such an advertising cap. The broadcaster's profits fall (because marginal revenue is positive in the neighbourhood of its choice); viewers' utility rises since they suffer less nuisance from ads; and advertisers' surplus necessarily falls as the reduced level of advertising implies a higher price per ad per viewer and correspondingly fewer producer surpluses for the advertisers. Some care is needed with the provisional conclusion that welfare rises from such an ad level restriction. The fact that broadcast profits have fallen will mean, in the broader context of several firms, that some firms may no longer find it profitable to enter and serve the market. Viewers would then suffer an additional loss from reduced variety of television offerings. Second, even with a fixed number of broadcast firms in the market, the change in profit incentives induced by the advertising cap may in turn change the quality and the type of programming offered. We turn to these themes below.

Quality

We now address how the presence of advertising caps may affect the quality provision of television programming in the market place. The presence of binding advertising caps affects the revenue earned per consumer reached and so affects the incentive to provide quality. For simplicity, we consider a monopoly.

Let the utility of a consumer be given by

$$u = q - \gamma a - tx,$$

if the consumer watches television and zero otherwise. Here q denotes quality of the programme and the firm may be viewed as locating at zero; t is the disutility cost faced by viewers per unit distance away from the ideal type, x.[15] Hence, the market length served by the monopolist is proportional to

$$\hat{x} = \frac{q - \gamma a}{t},$$

and the monopolist viewership is given by

$$N = 2\phi\hat{x},$$

where ϕ is the consumer density and the 2 simply represents the fact that the monopoly serves consumers in both directions away from its own location. The monopolist's profit is therefore given by

$$\pi = 2\phi\hat{x}R(a) - C(q).$$

First consider the monopoly solution in the absence of any restriction on advertising levels. The advertising first-order condition is

$$\frac{\partial \pi}{\partial a} = 2\phi\left[\hat{x}R'(a) - \frac{\gamma}{t}R(a)\right]$$

and the quality first-order condition is

$$\frac{\partial \pi}{\partial q} = 2\phi\frac{R(a)}{t} - C'(q).$$

These first-order conditions show how advertising levels and quality are related. In particular, a higher consumer density ϕ will entail a higher-quality provision because of economies to scale in providing quality that the television programme is effectively a public good.

The advertising first-order condition above gives the following relation:[16]

$$\frac{R'}{R} = \frac{\gamma}{t\hat{x}} = \frac{\gamma}{q - \gamma a},$$

and the conditions may be combined to give $2\phi\hat{x}R'(a) = \gamma C'(q)$.

Now consider the effects of an advertising cap set at level $\bar{a}$. Then the firm's profit is

$$\pi = 2\phi\hat{x}R(\bar{a}) - C(q),$$

meaning that the quality choice is determined, as above, by

$$\frac{\partial \pi}{\partial q} = 2\phi\frac{R(\bar{a})}{t} - C'(q).$$

This shows that a lower advertising cap will cause the monopolist's quality choice to be smaller. The social effects of this cap depend both on whether advertising was previously overprovided and whether quality was overprovided or underprovided. In particular, the monopolist's quality choice depends upon the extra revenue that may be extracted from the marginal viewer, while the socially optimal level of quality depends upon the improvement in average total surplus from further quality.

The social welfare function for this problem comprises three component parts, for viewers, broadcasters and advertisers. The viewer surplus is the average surplus of $(q - \gamma a - t\hat{x}/2)$ over the $2\phi\hat{x}$ viewers served. The profit is $2\phi\hat{x}R(a) - C(q)$ and advertiser surplus is $2\phi\hat{x}\left\{\int_0^a p(\tilde{a})d\tilde{a} - R(a)\right\}$. The last term represents the number of viewers reached times the advertisers' surplus per viewer. Note that the revenue per viewer is simply a transfer from advertisers to the broadcaster. We can then write the welfare function as

$$W = 2\phi\hat{x}\left\{q - \gamma a - t\hat{x}/2 + \int_0^a p(\tilde{a})d\tilde{a}\right\} - C(q),$$

where $\hat{x} = \frac{q-\gamma a}{t}$. Denote the term in brackets by Ω, which is therefore the surplus per consumer.

It is a useful point of reference to derive the full optimum for this model. First of all, the optimal quality choice is determined by

$$2\phi\hat{x} + \frac{2\phi}{t}\Omega - C'(q) = 0.$$

This indicates that, like the equilibrium, the optimum quality choice is increasing in the consumer density. The fixed cost of quality is then spread over a larger consumer base and so the quality will be higher. Such a result also underscores the empirical findings of Berry and Waldfogel (2001) for newspapers and is in turn based on insights in Sutton (1991) and Shaked and Sutton (1987).

The socially optimal advertising choice (again, when interior) is determined by

$$-2\phi\hat{x}\gamma - \frac{2\phi\gamma}{t}\Omega + 2\phi\hat{x}p(a) = 0,$$

and so reduces to

$$\hat{x}[p(a) - \gamma] = \frac{\gamma}{t}\Omega.$$

The left-hand side of this expression represents the positive divergence between demand price and nuisance cost, which is caused by the rate of viewer turn-off and the consequent surplus lost on that account, as represented on the right side. An alternative interpretation (Anderson and Coate, 2004) is to view $\frac{\gamma}{tx}\Omega$ as an additional term (on top of the direct nuisance term, γ) in the marginal cost of advertising: this term is the lost surplus per consumer (Ω) times the turn-off rate $\left(\frac{\gamma}{t}\right)$.

The next issue to consider is the effect of a cap on advertising levels. Clearly, the monopolist is worse off through being constrained. Moreover, the monopolist provides a lower programme quality because the cap reduces its incentives to attract viewers. A priori, it is unclear whether viewers are better off (because they suffer less nuisance from commercials) or worse off from the lower programme quality. The next example gives a case where viewers are always worse off with a tighter cap.

Suppose that advertisers' demand for ads per viewer is perfectly elastic at rate β per ad per viewer. This implies that the revenue function is $R(a) = \beta a$. The monopolist's choice of advertising for a given quality is from the advertising first-order condition above as

$$a = q/2\gamma. \tag{1}$$

Suppose further that the cost of quality provision is given by $C(q) = q^3/3$. Then the profit derivative with respect to quality, q, is $\frac{2\phi\beta a}{t} - q^2$. This implies that the monopolist's quality choice, as a function of the advertising level, is given by

$$q = \sqrt{\frac{2\phi\beta a}{t}}. \tag{2}$$

Combining these last two equations indicates that the unconstrained monopoly solution is to set quality at $q^m = \frac{\phi\beta}{t\gamma}$ and to set advertising at $a^m = \frac{1}{2\gamma}$.[17] It is useful for what follows to further note that the marginal profit from increasing the advertising level, given a starting level of advertising $\bar{a}$, given that the firm is choosing its quality to maximise profits, is proportional to $\sqrt{\frac{2\phi\beta\bar{a}}{t}} - 2\gamma\bar{a}$. The consumer surplus for this problem is given by

$$CS = 2\phi\frac{(q - \gamma a)^2}{2t},$$

and, given from (2) that the quality chosen varies with an advertising cap, $\bar{a}$, according to

$$\frac{dq}{d\bar{a}} = \sqrt{\frac{2\phi\beta}{t\bar{a}}},$$

the consumer surplus varies with the advertising cap, $\bar{a}$, according to

$$\frac{dCS}{d\bar{a}} = 2(q - \gamma a)\left[\sqrt{\frac{2\phi\beta}{t\bar{a}}} - \gamma\right].$$

Now, as long as the cap is binding, that is, $\sqrt{\frac{2\phi\beta\bar{a}}{t}} > 2\gamma\bar{a}$, as noted above, this expression is necessarily positive. Hence, consumer surplus necessarily rises with a cap. Put differently, a more binding cap necessarily hurts consumers because the downgrading the broadcaster makes to quality more than offsets the direct benefit to reduced nuisance from advertisements themselves. Since the monopolist itself is worse off with a more binding cap, a cap is welfare deteriorating for all involved. Thus tighter advertising caps make all market players worse off.

We now address the generality of these properties. Let $N(\gamma a - q)$ denote the demand (number of viewers) for the monopolist's programme, as a function of the full price, $\gamma a - q$. Assume that the monopoly problem

$$\max_{\{a,q\}} R(a)N(\gamma a - q) - C(q)$$

has an interior solution. If there is an advertising cap at some level, $\bar{a}$, below the monopoly's preferred choice, then it satisfies

$$R'(\bar{a})N(\gamma\bar{a} - q) + \gamma R(\bar{a})N'(\gamma\bar{a} - q) > 0. \tag{3}$$

The first-order condition for quality choice at level q^* is

$$-R(\bar{a})N'(\gamma\bar{a} - q^*) - C'(q^*) = 0$$

(where the first term is positive since $N'(\gamma\bar{a} - q^*) < 0$).

Applying the implicit function theorem, this tells us that the quality choice varies with the cap according to the relation

$$\frac{\partial q^*}{\partial \bar{a}} = \frac{R'(\bar{a})N'(\gamma\bar{a} - q^*) + \gamma R(\bar{a})N''(\gamma\bar{a} - q^*)}{(R(\bar{a})N''(\gamma\bar{a} - q^*) - C''(q^*))}, \tag{4}$$

where we assume the denominator is negative from the second-order condition for a maximum to the quality-choice problem. If $N'' \leq 0$, then the numerator is necessarily negative, so that a concave demand function implies that quality falls as the cap gets tighter. Otherwise, consider the following argument. From the binding ad cap condition, (3), we have that

$$\gamma R(\bar{a}) < -R'(\bar{a}) \frac{N(\gamma \bar{a} - q)}{N'(\gamma \bar{a} - q)},$$

and hence (considering the numerator of (4)) that

$$R'(\bar{a})N'(.) + \gamma R(\bar{a})N''(.) < R'(\bar{a})N'(.) - R'(\bar{a}) \frac{N(.)}{N'(.)} N''(.)$$

for $N''(\gamma \bar{a} - q^*) > 0$. Now, since $R'(\bar{a}) > 0$, the RHS of this expression is necessarily negative if $N(.)$ is strictly log-concave $((N')^2 - N'N \geq 0)$. Hence the LHS is also negative and so $\frac{\partial q^*}{\partial a} > 0$. The intuition for this condition is that an ad cap reduces the revenue yield per viewer delivered to advertisers and so the broadcaster's marginal benefit is lower than without an ad cap. This leads to lower provision of quality. It is also straightforward to find conditions under which $\frac{\partial q^*}{\partial a} < 0$. For example, if unconstrained, the monopoly advertising first-order condition (3) holds with equality. This implies that, for a binding cap in the neighbourhood of the unconstrained monopoly optimum, quality is unchanged for a log-linear demand and it actually rises with a tighter cap if the viewer demand is more 'convex' than log-linear (i.e. strict log-convexity, but not more than (-1)-concavity since otherwise the second-order conditions may be violated). In such cases, viewer surplus necessarily rises as the cap tightens (locally).

This latter case of log-convex demand and a cap in the neighbourhood of the unconstrained solution is also interesting because quality rises with a (slightly) tighter cap, so viewer surplus does too. Indeed, from the demand function, $N(\gamma \bar{a} - q^*)$, a lower full price, $\gamma \bar{a} - q^*$, will mean higher surplus per viewer (and also a higher equilibrium number of viewers) so that viewer surplus rises with the level of the ad cap (equivalently, the tighter the cap, the lower the viewer surplus). Moreover, a tighter cap also is a tighter constraint on the broadcaster's actions and so decreases profit, but in the neighbourhood of a non-binding cap, this effect is second-order small. The total welfare effect is therefore that welfare rises with a slightly tighter cap.

In summary, if demand is 'convex' enough, both viewer surplus and total welfare may rise with a tighter ad cap. Otherwise, the quality reduction resulting from a cap offsets the direct viewer gain. If the quality reduction outweighs the direct effect (as was shown in the linear demand example), then tighter caps reduce the surplus of all market participants.

Product selection and advertising caps

Advertising caps may also affect the breadth of products offered in an equilibrium. The basic insight follows from Gabszewicz, Laussel and Sonnac (2004). To see this, consider a simple sketch of duopoly product selection along the lines of the well-trodden framework pioneered by Hotelling (1929). In the simplest version of the model (see Lerner and Singer, 1937, and Eaton and Lipsey, 1975), firms simply compete by choosing locations (programme formats in the current context) in order to maximise the number of viewers. Such would be the relevant behavioural assumption when firms are constrained by an advertising cap, or indeed if viewers face no nuisance cost from the presence cost of the advertising and advertising was fixed from the demand side. This set-up is then the classic 'ice-cream sellers' problem' with two firms striving to sell to the most consumers. The (unique) equilibrium is that both firms choose the central location in the market, a situation described by Boulding (1955) as the 'Principle of Minimum Differentiation'. Any location of one firm away from the centre would induce the other to locate right next to it on the longer side of the market. Notice for the later development that as long as firms are constrained by ad caps, each wants to move in closer to its rival. This is because the market served by a firm is determined by the midpoint between its own location and that of its rival and so is increasing as the firm moves closer to its rival (leaving aside for the moment the possibility of jumping over its rival's location).

Now consider the ingredient to this model, namely the version of the Hotelling model written down by d'Aspremont, Gabszewicz and Thisse (1979). This model, as did Hotelling's, considers a subgame perfect equilibrium in which two competing firms are to choose locations on the unit segment, following which they both rationally anticipate the subgame equilibrium choice of prices that ensues from the location chosen in the first stage of the game. The difference introduced by these authors over the original Hotelling specification was to define transportation as a quadratic function of distance, as opposed to Hotelling's original linear specification. D'Aspremont, Gabszewicz and Thisse (1979) show that the unique subgame perfect equilibrium involves the firms locating at the extreme points of the unit interval.[18] This outcome results from the balance of two opposing forces that apply to the pricing subgame. First, *ceteris paribus*, moving closer to one's rival triggers a more acute level of price competition, in particular a lower rival's price, which a firm strives to avoid by locating far away. However, as we argued above in the fixed-price version of the model, locating closer to the rival also gives the firm a higher market share. In the version of the model with quadratic transportation costs, the former effect dominates throughout the location on the unit integral leading to the maximal differentiation result.

We now show how to translate this location result into the context of the advertising framework. Suppose that the demand for ads is perfectly elastic and each advertiser is willing to pay β in order for their advertisement to be seen by a prospective consumer (television viewer). Assume, too, that the number of viewers attracted to the station depends linearly on the nuisance caused by the advertising and indeed that we may write the utility of a viewer at location $x \in [0,1]$ is

$$u_i = y - \gamma a_i - t|x - x_i|^2, \quad i = 1, 2$$

where y is consumer income (for simplicity the same for all consumers), x_i is the location of product i and t is the transportation rate per unit distance. The demand addressed to firm i, N_i, is then determined by the measure of consumers for whom u_i exceeds u_j, $i \neq j$. This is exactly the same viewer demand equation as in the standard spatial formulation. The profit to firm i can then be written as

$$\pi_i = \beta a_i N_i,$$

which is exactly the same (up to a multiplicative constant) as the formulation of d'Aspremont, Gabszewicz and Thisse (1979), with a_i replacing the standard price p_i. Therefore, the maximum differentiation result holds under this specification, that is, firms avoid intensive advertising competition by locating as far apart as possible. They still would like to come closer to increase unilateral market share, but refrain from doing so to keep advertising levels, and hence advertising revenues, as high as is possible under Bertrand-Nash advertising competition.

We now allow for advertising caps in the framework sketched out above. First note that, as a function of symmetric locations, the sub-game equilibrium advertising levels are greatest the further apart are the firms. This means that an advertising cap, if set below the level that attains at maximally differentiated locations, will necessarily be locally binding on both firms. Consequently, under such a binding cap firms will find their profits locally increasing as long as the cap is binding, as they move in towards each other, following the logic of the fixed-price model. However, at some point the cap must necessarily be reached since the equilibrium advertising level falls continuously to zero at the point of minimal differentiation (when firms locate together then they are indistinguishable and there is not product differentiation so that competition à la Bertrand with homogeneous products and price goes to the competitive level, namely zero). As soon as the cap is reached, the firms clearly wish to go no further together from the logic of the model with endogenous advertising levels expounded above.

The lesson from this simple sketch is first of all that advertising caps may have an impact on product selection and the existence of caps may increase the proclivity of firms to produce similar programming. Indeed, the seminal analysis of Steiner (1952) suggests that duplication may be a prevalent problem in television broadcast selection.[19] His analysis, however, relies on the assumption that broadcasters aim to maximise the number of viewers, an assumption that is effectively tenable only if advertising levels are capped (or indeed if viewers do not care about the level of advertising they consume). Nevertheless, some care ought to be exercised in taking literally the result from the quadratic cost model. In particular, this model always predicts that the free market equilibrium product selection is socially excessive (the optimal format choices being at the quartiles). Other transportation cost functions, and hence the possibilities of other outcomes, prove remarkably difficult to analyse in a tractable fashion but there is no a priori presumption that the equilibrium format choices would neces-sarily lie outside the optimal ones as they do for the quadratic model.

Notice that the equilibrium in the presence of the advertising caps is at the location at which the cap is binding. This means that the cap could be judiciously set so as to induce equilibrium format choices at exactly the socially optimal level.[20]

6.4 Content restrictions

The restrictions on the products that are not allowed to be advertised can be understood by reference to the economics of externalities and government paternalism. Perhaps surprisingly, banning or restricting advertising may also increase industry profits under some circumstances. This section explores these themes along with the particular case of prescription drug advertising to consumers.

Paternalistic altruism and merit goods

Cigarette advertising is widely banned – even cigarette firms' sponsorship of motor racing was recently made illegal in Belgium. Goods that impart negative externalities on others (e.g. second-hand smoke effects) can traditionally be treated with Pigouvian taxes on their consumption and/or direct quantity regulations (banning smoking in bars, banning smoking by those under age). Alcohol also may be associated with negative externalities (drunk-driving and violent behaviour towards others). Consumption of these goods is also often viewed as addictive. Economists usually prefer taxation to outright bans in cases of negative externalities: individuals' preferences are respected, albeit under the modification that the full price paid reflects all harm done to others.

However, it may be that a consumer who is deterred from consumption may not become addicted or may give up or reduce the habit and may later be thankful for having been induced to moderation. If people care about other individuals' consumption levels of such 'dangerous' goods, they may support regulations or taxes. In the earlier literature, the concept of 'merit goods' (such as education) corresponded to goods that were to be encouraged according to an implicit governmental welfare function. Cigarettes, alcohol, gambling, etc. fall in the opposite category of demerit goods that are to be discouraged. The encouragement or discouragement reflects paternalism by the government or, indeed, the individuals who elect the government to act on their behalf. Why, then, are bans used instead of further taxes? Rather than banning cigarette advertising, taxes could be levied on advertising tobacco products and/or the product could itself be taxed still more. Perhaps the authorities make their decision without full consideration of the range of available options for reducing consumption and the symbolism may be more significant with a ban than with a higher tax (where, after all, one might suspect the government of wanting higher consumption to raise more revenue). It may be viewed as inherently rather contradictory for the product's makers to be persuading people to smoke on the one hand (and the government collecting revenues from that activity) and the government on the other hand spending money persuading them not to smoke.

The effects of an advertising ban on industry profits

Banning advertising of some products also has direct economic consequences in the industries affected. The economics of advertising traditionally separates informative advertising from forms of persuasion. If the prime role of the advertising is informative (telling people where and how to buy the product and informing them of new products), then a ban in advertising through some channels (cigarettes may still be advertised in magazines in the USA, for example) may be analysed rather like an increase in the costs of advertising. Then, some surprising results by Grossman and Shapiro (1984) suggest that oligopolists might actually see their profits rise as costs rise.[21] This is because prices rise substantially after the reduced level of information transmitted in equilibrium decreases the overlap of informed consumers and so reduces competition. Another form of informative advertising, sometimes attributed to many television advertisements, is quality signalling (see, for example, Nelson, 1974, and Milgrom and Roberts, 1986). Eliminating this role for advertising could either cause firms to switch to other forms of signalling (product price reductions or sponsorship of sporting events, perhaps) or shut down signalling completely. In the latter case, one would expect it to be very difficult to launch new products: in such industries one might expect only mature brands without new ones being contemplated.

Some advertising is sometimes proffered as an example of a zero-sum game. Insofar as cigarette advertising serves only to reshuffle consumers without corresponding new consumers being drawn in, all advertising expenditures are 'wasted' and firms' profits would be higher if the government would do them all a favour by eliminating what they cannot avoid competing over and ban advertising completely. The welfare economics of persuasive advertising are already quite controversial (even before we get to demerit goods!) because, aside from the informative context where it is clear how to proceed with evaluating the effects of more information (through advertising), there is not much agreement of whether or how advertising affects tastes. For economists in the Chicago tradition (Stigler and Becker, 1977, and Becker and Murphy, 1993), tastes are fundamental and advertising can be viewed as contributing a complementary consumption enjoyment. Banning advertising would close this down – although it is still a reasonable question to ask whether closing down a device that promotes 'smoking is cool' could possibly be viewed as a cause for concern! Lastly, Dixit and Norman (1978) take an agnostic stand on whether the right welfare measure to evaluate quantity changes induced by advertising is to be based on the demand before or after the advertising. Insofar as they claim that advertising is already excessive without social preferences over goods, then, in the context of demerit goods, reducing advertising (by banning TV advertising, say) must presumably be beneficial.

Direct-to-consumer (DTC) prescription drug advertising

Advertising of prescription drugs directly to consumers is prohibited all over the world except for the United States and New Zealand. In the USA, the Wheeler-Lea Act 1938 granted the Federal Trade Commission (FTC) jurisdiction over all drug advertising.[22] However, in 1962, authority over prescription drug advertising was transferred to the Federal Drug Administration (FDA) while the FTC retained regulatory authority over over-the-counter (OTC) drug advertising. According to the FDA regulations on prescription drug advertising, the advertisement must comply with two major requirements. First, the ad must include a 'brief summary', which includes providing the drug's side effects, contra-indications, warnings and precautions and the indications for use. Second, the ad must comply with the 'fair balance doctrine', meaning that the ad must provide a balanced account of all clinically relevant information, the risks and the benefits.

The FDA recognises three different types of prescription drug advertisements, which are regulated differently. The first category is 'reminder advertisements', which call attention to the name of the drug product but do not include the specification of the drug product. Second, help-seeking ads (or disease-oriented advertisements), which are generally broadcast with the heading 'see your doctor', describe the symptoms of a disease or condition and encourage consumers to consult their physician to discuss treatment options, but do not mention the drug's name. Finally, 'product claim' (or 'indication' advertisements) reveal both the drug's name and the indication. While product claim ads are subject to brief summary requirement and the fair balance doctrine, reminder advertisements and help-seeking advertisements are exempt from the brief summary and fair balance requirements, as they do not reveal information about the effectiveness of a drug.

Although the brief summary requirement can be easily met by print advertisements, it can be impractical for a broadcast advertisement (which normally lasts for only about thirty seconds). In August 1997, the FDA issued the 'Draft guidance for industry, consumer-directed broadcast advertisements', allowing sponsors of broadcast advertisements to make 'adequate provision' of approved product labelling (known as a major statement) instead of the brief summary. After receiving the comments on the draft guidance, the final guidance was issued by the FDA in August 1999. The FDA requires that an ad broadcast through media such as television, radio or telephone communications systems must disclose the product's major risks in either the audio or visual parts of the ad. This disclosure of risks is known as the 'major statement'.[23]

This change in the FDA guidance on DTC advertising of prescription drugs, introduced in 1997 and finalised in 1999, opened the door to a flood of TV advertisements in the USA. There are, of course, proponents on both sides of the debate over whether the effective legalisation of TV advertising of prescription drugs is socially desirable.

On one side, patients may be induced to clamour for drugs that are inappropriate for their conditions. At the same time, patients may be 'persuaded' by an advertisement that they have some condition that can be alleviated, which in turn would increase the number of visits to the doctor, allowing for discussions on the drug they are exposed to. This may be seen as undermining doctors' authority in prescription and wasting their time on unnecessary discussions. Some argue that due to these patient demands, doctors may overprescribe or prescribe something costly or inappropriate, which in turn would bring negative effects on the patient.

On the other hand, DTC ads may be seen as informing the consumer about new drugs and treatments for various conditions, hence increasing the number of visits to the doctor. If the consumer was diagnosed with a condition and was prescribed a medically justified treatment, it could be welfare improving as many diseases are underdiagnosed. DTC ads can also increase the awareness of certain conditions and the available treatments for these conditions among the consumers. This may help improve the communication between the doctor and the patient, which in turn could help the doctor to make the best treatment choice for the patient.

Empirical results from the study conducted by Iizuka and Jin (2002) on patient and doctor behaviour suggest that DTC advertising leads to a large increase in outpatient visits but no impact on doctors' choice of drug within a therapeutic class.[24] However, the study by Wosinska (2002) on the role of DTC advertising and the demand for the cholesterol-reducing drug suggests that DTC advertising has a significant positive effect on the demand for an individual brand for the drugs that have preferential status with the insurer (are listed on the formulary). The debate on what ought to be (not) advertised on TV will remain an active one.

6.5 Conclusion

The regulations on commercial length are broadly as follows. The EU directive allows for nine minutes of commercials on average, with a maximum of twelve minutes in any given hour. In Australia, broadcast channels must carry at most thirteen minutes of commercials on average, with a maximum of fifteen minutes in any given hour. As a matter of comparison, some programmes on the major networks in the United States have recorded advertising levels in excess of twenty minutes. The only length restrictions in the United States concern advertisements during children's programmes, where the rules allow ten and a half minutes an hour, which rises to twelve minutes during weekdays.

The economic analysis of commercial length restrictions (advertising caps) should be sited in a fully fledged two-sided market model of the broadcasting sector. If the quality, number and types of programmes are all treated as constant, the market equilibrium delivers too little advertising for low nuisance costs. Conversely, it delivers too many advertising messages for high nuisance costs to viewers. This constitutes the economic efficiency argument for regulatory length restrictions. Careful structural empirical study of the two-sided market structure in TV broadcasting can determine the crucial parameter values of nuisance cost and advertiser benefits.[25] These values can then be used to see whether ad caps are desirable, and the appropriate level. However, because ad caps reduce profits, they may cause a reduction in the variety (number) of programmes provided. They may also decrease differentiation among existing programme types and decrease the quality of programmes (at least, if viewer demand is not 'too' convex). This means that empirical work needs to account for these other performance dimensions too.

Turning to commercial content regulations, EU, US and Australian regulations are quite similar in the broader scheme of things. All prohibit cigarette advertising, for example. There are typically restrictions ensuring ads are not indecent (relative to current community standards), subliminal or broadcast at higher volume than surrounding programming. The general codes regarding advertising are also applicable to TV advertising – for example, restrictions that ads must not be misleading are covered by FTC rules in the USA. There are some interesting anomalies in certain countries. France prohibits ads for tobacco, weapons, employment, prescription medicines, alcohol, literary print, press and movies (with some exceptions). In the UK, ads must not interrupt religious ceremonies or programmes in which members of the Royal Family appear. In Sweden, no ads are allowed before children's programmes. In the USA and New Zealand, direct-to-consumer advertising of prescription drugs is allowed, but this is not permissible elsewhere.

The advertising content restrictions observed in practice might be ascribed in most cases to paternalistic altruism and the goods so restricted could be described as demerit goods. One issue is why such goods are not taxed more directly. The answer lies perhaps in the limited horizons of the policymakers.

Banning TV commercials for certain products increases the cost of advertising (or indeed eliminates it). When the product industry equilibrium involves too much advertising (from the standpoint of the welfare accruing directly in the industry), raising advertising costs may reduce overadvertising. For demerit goods, this must be socially beneficial. In the ('money-burning') theory of advertising to signal product quality, eliminating the possibility of signalling might be expected to make it difficult to successfully launch new brands. It might then be expected that only mature brands survive (in the cigarette industry, for example). Finally, prescription drugs advertising remains controversial. On the one hand, it may be helpful in getting patients to go to doctors to have their conditions properly diagnosed. On the other hand, doctors might be deluged with hypochondriacs and respond by overprescribing inappropriate medicines.

Lessons for students: what have we learned?

There are several messages here for students of industrial organisation and students of media economics. First, the economics of television requires a separate analysis that specifically embodies its two-sided structure. Namely, advertisers want to contact prospective customers and do so by accessing a 'platform' (the broadcaster), which bundles together advertising that viewers dislike with entertainment content that they do like. In this context, advertising caps may have a direct beneficial effect on viewers, but they may have indirect effects given the business model: it may be that less variety is supported and perhaps lower quality of broadcasts. Second, understanding the other types of advertising regulation means looking at categories of goods such as merit and demerit goods.

Lessons for researchers: what do we still need to know?

There are many important future research directions for this subject. One big gap in the theoretical literature is that public television is not modelled and most systems have a mixture of public and private broadcasting. Indeed, there are frequently other ingredients in the mixture of broadcast offerings, such as pay-television, that survive alongside the commercial broadcasters. While it is reasonably straightforward to model a market environment with both pay-television and commercial television (see Anderson, 2003, for a mixed-market model and Peitz and Valletti, 2005, for a model comparing the two 'pure' systems), a major challenge is to convincingly model the objectives of public broadcasters. Only with a reasonable description of their objectives can we proceed to determine the performance of the overall industry and only then will we get closer to the full economics of the desirability of advertising caps. Careful empirical work will also be most useful in evaluating proper policy. For example, some measure of the nuisance cost of ads to viewers is crucial. Work by Wilbur (2005) gives some estimates from a structural empirical model of the industry, taking full account of its two-sided nature. Wilbur is also able to address the effects on industry equilibria of devices (such as TiVo) that allow viewers to bypass ads.

Another area for further research is the economics of advertising itself. Themes and empirical regularities already described in the marketing literature could be usefully brought into the mainstream of economics of the product. While the welfare economics of informative advertising is quite well understood conceptually (at least in terms of how to perform welfare analysis, although perhaps not in terms of what information is contained in ads), other forms of advertising (e.g. 'persuasive' advertising) pose a greater challenge in describing benefits and how they accrue. Since ads are crowded out by caps, it is especially important to determine the welfare costs and benefits from advertising. Structural empirical work again can provide estimates for some important magnitudes.

Lessons for policymakers: what are the priorities for policy in this area?

The message for policymakers follows from the two above. Specifically, media markets are different because of their two-sided structure: the basic business model is unlike that in traditional markets because advertising finances programming content. There is no presumption that market forces should deliver excessive advertising and careful empirical work is needed in evaluating nuisance costs to viewers and the social desirability of ads. It should be recognised that advertising finances the media and curtailing it may reduce both programme quality and programme variety by reducing the incentive to compete for advertisers and reducing revenues overall. The surplus accruing to advertisers is another part of the total benefits created and this is typically not included in discussions of television regulation (or indeed, other policy aspects, such as merger analysis), but ought to be. To do so properly means also taking into account the possible divergence between the private and the social demand for advertising. Structural empirical work can be helpful in measuring various costs and benefits.

References

Anderson, Simon P. (1988) 'Equilibrium existence in the linear model of spatial competition', *Economica*, 55, 479–491.

Anderson, Simon P. (2003) 'Broadcast competition: commercial and pay TV', mimeo, University of Virginia.

Anderson, Simon P. and Stephen Coate (2004) 'Market provision of broadcasting: a welfare analysis', *Review of Economic Studies*, 72(4), 947–972.

Anderson, Simon P., André de Palma and Jacques-François Thisse (1992) *Discrete Choice Theory of Product Differentiation*, MIT Press.

Armstrong, Mark (2004) 'Competition in two-sided markets', mimeo, University College, London.

Bagwell, Kyle (2002) 'The economic analysis of advertising', mimeo, Columbia University.

Becker, Gary and Kevin Murphy (1993) 'A simple theory of advertising as a good or bad', *Quarterly Journal of Economics*, 107, 942–964.

Beebe, Jack (1977) 'Institutional structure and programme choices in television markets', *Quarterly Journal of Economics*, 91, 15–37.

Berry, Steven and Joel Waldfogel (2001) 'Product quality and market size', NBER working paper #9675.

Boulding, Kenneth (1955) *Economic Analysis. Volume I: Microeconomics*, 3rd edition, Harper & Row.

Caillaud, Bernard and Bruno Jullien (2001) 'Competing cybermediaries', *European Economic Review*, 45, 797–808.

Caillaud, Bernard and Bruno Jullien (2003) 'Chicken and egg: competition among intermediation service providers', *RAND Journal of Economics*, 34(2), 309–328.

Commercial Television Industry Code of Practice (2004) Free TV Australia, Mosman, NSW 2088, July, www.freevaust.com.au

Crampes, Claude, Carole Haritchabalet and Bruno Jullien (2004) 'Competing with advertising resources', mimeo, IDEI, Université de Toulouse.

d'Aspremont Claude, Jean J. Gabszewicz and Jacques-François Thisse (1979) 'On Hotelling's "Stability in competition"', *Econometrica*, 47(5), 1145–1150.

Dixit, Avinash and Victor Norman (1978) 'Advertising and welfare', *Bell Journal of Economics*, 9, 1–17.

Dukes, Anthony J. (2004) 'The advertising market in a product oligopoly', *Journal of Industrial Economics*, 52, 3.

Eaton, B. Curtis and Richard G. Lipsey (1975) 'The Principle of Minimum Differentiation reconsidered: some new developments in the Theory of Spatial Competition', *Review of Economic Studies*, 42, 27–49.

Gabszewicz, Jean J., Didier Laussel and Nathalie Sonnac (2004) 'Programming and advertising competition in the broadcasting industry', *Journal of Economics and Management Strategy*, 13(4), Winter, 657–669.

Gabszewicz Jean J. and Jacques-François Thisse (1979) 'Price competition, quality and incomes disparities', *Journal of Economic Theory*, 20(3), 340–359.

Grossman, Gene and Carl Shapiro (1984) 'Informative advertising with differentiated products', *Review of Economic Studies*, 51, 63–81.

Hansen, Claus and Soren Kyhl (2001) 'Pay-per-view broadcasting of outstanding events: consequences of a ban', *International Journal of Industrial Organization*, 19, 589–609.

Hotelling, Harold (1929) 'Stability in competition', *Economic Journal*, 39, 41–57.

Iizuka, Toshiaki (2004) 'What explains the use of direct to consumer advertising of prescription drugs?', *Journal of Industrial Economics*, 52(3), 349–379.

Iizuka, Toshiaki and Ginger Zhe Jin (2002) 'The effects of direct-to-consumer advertising in the prescription drug market', mimeo, University of Maryland.

Kind, Hans J., Tore Nilssen and Lars Sørgard (2004) 'Advertising on TV: over- or underprovision?', mimeo, Bergen.

Lerner, Abba Ptachya and Hans Werner Singer (1937) 'Some notes on duopoly and spatial competition', *Journal of Political Economy*, 45, 145–186.

Milgrom, Paul and John Roberts (1986) 'Prices and advertising signals of product quality', *Journal of Political Economy*, 94, 796–821.

Mussa, Michael and Sherwin Rosen (1978) 'Monopoly and product quality', *Journal of Economic Theory*, 18, 301–317.

Nelson, Phillip (1974) 'Advertising as information', *Journal of Political Economy*, 82, 729–754.

Olsen, Edgar O. (1979) 'The simple analytics of external effects', *Southern Economic Journal*, 45, 847–854.

Peitz, Martin and Tommaso Valletti (2005) 'Content and advertising in the media: pay-tv versus free-to-air', mimeo, Imperial College, London, CEPR working paper #4771.

Rochet, Jean-Charles and Jean Tirole (2003) 'Platform competition in two-sided markets', *Journal of the European Economics Association*, 1(4), June, 990–1029.

Rochet, Jean-Charles and Jean Tirole (2004) 'Two-sided markets: an overview', mimeo, IDEI, Université de Toulouse.

Rysman, Marc (2004) 'Competition between networks: a study of the market for yellow pages', *Review of Economic Studies*, 71(2), 483–512.

Shaked, Avner and John Sutton (1987) 'Product differentiation and industrial structure', *Journal of Industrial Economics*, 36(2), 131–146.

Shapiro, Carl (1980) 'Advertising and welfare: comment', *Bell Journal of Economics*, 11, 749–752.

Spence, Michael and Bruce Owen (1977) 'Television programming, monopolistic competition and welfare', *Quarterly Journal of Economics*, 91, 103–126.

Stegeman, Mark (2004) 'A model of internet advertising', mimeo, Virginia Polytechnic Institute.

Steiner, Peter O. (1952) 'Program patterns and preferences, and workability of competition in radio broadcasting', *Quarterly Journal of Economics*, 66, 194–223.

Stigler, George J. and Gary S. Becker (1977) 'De gustibus non est disputandum', *American Economic Review*, 67, 76–90.

Sutton, John (1991) *Sunk Costs and Market Structure*, MIT Press.

Tirole, Jean (1988) *The Theory of Industrial Organisation*, MIT Press.

Wilbur, Kenneth C. (2005) 'Modeling the effects of advertisement-avoidance technology on advertisement-supported media: the case of digital video recorders', mimeo, University of Virginia.

Wosinska, Marta (2002) 'Just what the patient ordered? Direct-to-consumer advertising and the demand for pharmaceutical products', mimeo, Harvard Business School.

Wright, Julian (2003) 'One-sided logic in two-sided markets', Brookings Working Paper 03–10.

Notes

* I gratefully acknowledge research funding from the NSF under grant SES-0137001. I thank Juan Carlos Bisso for research assistance and Ed Olsen for discussion. Special thanks are due to Cat Tyler, Rachel Mocny, Paul Seabright and Ken Wilbur for their comments on earlier drafts.
1. The July 2004 draft of the Australian 'Commercial Television Industry Code of Practice' is available online at www.freevaust.com.au and from Free TV Australia, Mosman, NSW 2088, Australia.
2. The ABA also has specific regulations aimed at sports content. They include an 'antisiphoning' list that prevents certain sports events from being siphoned off by pay-television – this would prevent free-to-air viewers from being able to watch the event. Conversely, the ABA also enforces free-to-air broadcasters via an antihoarding provision that is intended to discourage them from holding back the live coverage of certain events. Concerns similar to those that underscored the Australian regulation were also a worry in the European Union. Hansen and Kyhl (2001) give some background details to the European case, as well as providing an analysis of the positive and normative economics of pay-per-view broadcasts.
3. The Australian Association of National Advertisers (AANA) was adopted for advertising self-regulation. The intention is to ensure that ads are legal, decent, honest and truthful with a 'fair sense of responsibility to competitors'. In particular, ads should not be misleading or deceptive, nor likely to be so, and 'shall not contain a misrepresentation which is likely to cause

damage to the business or goodwill of a competitor'. Neither should ads portray people in a discriminatory way (disability, age, sex, ethnicity, etc.). Ads should not present violence, sex or obscene language unless justified by context. There is a separate Automotive Code of Practice that relates to advertising for motor vehicles.

4. Casual empiricism regarding radio advertisements for used cars in the USA suggests such standards are not applied in America! Likewise, television commerical breaks in the USA are often noticeably louder than the surrounding programming.

5. These include programme promotions ('tune-ins'), station promotions and community service announcements.

6. Since 1981, New Zealand commercials have fully qualified as Australian.

7. The code uses as a reference point the amount of non-programme matter on the final schedules. These are the last schedules prepared before the broadcast and indicate when breaks are to be aired and what is aired within the breaks. The idea here is to give flexibility and not oblige licensees to force breaks in live programmes because of unpredicted segment lengths.

8. Sponsorship announcements must make no reference to prices, nor last more than ten seconds per sponsor (with a maximum of thirty seconds).

9. Since the types of advertisement exempted (such as tune-ins) are primarily informative, the economic question is whether informative advertisements can be excessive in equilibrium. Few economic analyses suggest that information provision may be excessive in a market equilibrium. Grossman and Shapiro (1984) find such a result for oligopolists providing information about their competing products. Dixit and Norman (1978) also find that oligopolists may overadvertise in the context of persuasive advertising. These issues are discussed in more detail below.

10. Sweden voted against the regulations promoted by the European Community because it felt that they were not strict enough.

11. I thank Tore Nilssen for this information. The Norwegian regulations were last amended in July 2004. The 'old' Norwegian regulations (the English version has not been updated since 1998) on broadcasting, including advertising, can be found at http://www.odin.dep.no/kkd/engelsk/acts_regulations/018001-990111/index-dok000-b

12. For more on such two-sided markets, see Armstrong (2004), Caillaud and Jullien (2001 and 2003), Rochet and Tirole (2003 and 2004) and Wright (2003).

13. We might also deduct from the full price any expected surplus the consumer expects from buying products showcased in the ads seen. Such surplus (loosely) reduces the effective γ and may even make it negative. Infomercials may constitute an example of negative γ insofar as some consumers actively watch to garner information about such

goods as exercise bikes. Such advertising provides a positive net benefit rather than a loss.

14. The following draws on Anderson and Coate (2004). Other authors who have addressed welfare issues include Crampes, Haritchabalet and Jullien (2004), Dukes (2004), Hansen and Kyhl (2001), Kind, Nilssen and Sørgard (2004) and Stegeman (2004).

15. The term 'quality' is meant in the sense of a positive shift in demand for viewing. This may not necessarily be synonymous with a higher art form. 'Higher quality' could well be Howard Stern or *Friends* over a BBC documentary or a Shakespearean drama!

16. If the advertising demand is linear, $p(a) = \alpha - ba$, and the cost of providing quality is quadratic, $C(q) = \frac{q^2}{2}$, then the problem is not concave. Care must be exercised in such problems with quality fixed costs if there is insufficient curvature to marginal quality.

17. The second-order conditions hold at this solution.

18. This maximal differentiation result relies on the restriction that the locations are constrained to lie within the unit interval. There does not seem any technological reason why indeed the support of the product specification must necessarily be the same as the support of the consumer taste distribution. Relaxing this restriction and instead allowing the firms to locate anywhere on the real line gives instead the equilibrium locations as $-1/4$ and $5/4$, which means that firms do locate far apart but not as far apart as might be physically possible. See Anderson (1988) for further details.

19. See, though, Beebe (1977) for a contrary appraisal.

20. However, the advertising level itself may be suboptimal. Under the current specification, in which consumers always watch one of the two channels and advertisers are willing to pay a constant amount per viewer reached, the optimal level of advertising is zero if $\gamma > \beta$ and is infinite if $\gamma < \beta$.

21. See also the discussion in Tirole (1988) for a simple exposition of their model. Bagwell (2002) provides a fine survey of the overall economics of advertising.

22. I thank Jayani Jayawardhana for this material.

23. The adequate provision requirements include 1) disclosure in the advertisement of an operating toll-free telephone number, through which the consumer can choose to have the labelling information mailed or have the labelling information read over the phone; 2) reference in the advertisement to an alternative mechanism, such as to a print advertisement, to provide package labelling to consumers with restricted access to the internet or those who are uncomfortable actively requesting additional information; 3) disclosure in the advertisement of an internet web page

address that provides access to the package labelling; 4) disclosure in the advertisement that pharmacists, or healthcare providers, may provide additional information.
24. Iizuka (2004) finds higher advertising for drugs that are new, of high quality, for undertreated diseases and in more concentrated industries. He argues that DTC advertising expands markets but involves little business stealing.
25. See Rysman (2004) and Wilbur (2005).

7 Market definition in printed media industries: theory, practice and lessons for broadcasting

ELENA ARGENTESI AND MARC IVALDI*

7.1 Introduction

Rapid technological change in media markets has highlighted the importance of delineating relevant markets in this industry. Indeed, the degree of substitutability among different newspapers, but also between newspapers and internet sites, or between different kinds of television or cable channels, is a key element in competition analysis.

Recent theoretical advances[1] stress the two-sided character of this industry, which has repercussions for market definition. Media outlets compete not only for readership or audience but also for advertisers, who in turn are attracted by the possibility of reaching potential consumers. The advent of new media and recent technological advances in information transmission have an impact on the degree of substitutability between different media and also on the ways in which advertising messages are conveyed to the public. Therefore the evolution of media markets creates closer interconnections between different media services with regard to both the circulation side and the advertising side. Antitrust agencies and regulators should take into account the changing features of these markets when addressing issues of market definition and assessing the degree of substitutability between different media outlets.

At least three notions then should drive the definition of relevant markets in the press industry. The first one, just mentioned, is two-sidedness. The markets for news and advertising are closely linked by inter-market network externalities. Our conjecture is that failing to consider this link may lead to a biased estimation of own- and cross-price elasticities. Second, product differentiation (both horizontal and vertical) is a crucial factor in readers' choice and must be properly accounted for in order to obtain accurate cross-price elasticities. Finally, in part as a result of the application of the first two notions, a correct estimation of the potential market size is required. Indeed, the competitive constraint imposed by the substitutability between printed media and other media like television or the internet, which do not belong to the same relevant submarket of printed media, might have significant effects on the levels of elasticities.

Note that the delineation of relevant markets is a competition policy notion aimed at identifying the competitive constraints faced by a firm or a group of firms. It is not a concept developed or employed by microeconomic theory. The objective of market definition is to search for the smallest set of products that is subject to a sufficiently high degree of mutual substitution to be treated as a single product for the purposes of an antitrust investigation. In the search process, three competitive constraints can play a role: demand substitution, supply substitution and potential competition.[2]

Here we focus mainly on demand substitution. The usual criterion adopted by antitrust agencies to evaluate the strength of this competitive constraint is by means of the so-called SSNIP (Small but Significant Non-transitory Increase in Prices) test. According to this test, a set of products (or geographical areas) is considered as belonging to the same product (or geographic) market if a hypothetical monopolist on this market could profitably raise prices above the current level by a given amount (usually 5–10 per cent) in a non-transitory way.[3] If this is the case, the set of products considered constitutes a separate market because consumers do not substitute away sufficiently after a price increase to constitute a check on the power of a firm that might (perhaps hypothetically) control these products. If instead the price increase would not be profitable, there are other products that are substitutes to the ones considered and demand would be partly conveyed to these products if prices increased. In this case, the set of products considered for market definition should be enlarged to include closer substitutes of the previous set of products. The SSNIP test should be performed on this wider market and the exercise should continue with further enlargements of the market until the SSNIP test gives a positive answer, i.e. a price increase by a hypothetical monopolist would be profitable.

The type of reasoning that is behind the SSNIP test should drive the analysis of the assessment of market definition. In practice, however, the SSNIP test is not implemented. It serves as a guide to obtain indirect evidence on the effects of a price increase. Two of the main pieces of information that are clearly involved in the mechanism of the SSNIP test and can be used to draw inferences about the effect of a price increase on demand are own- and cross-price elasticities. Indeed, own-price elasticity allows us to evaluate the profitability of a price increase because it measures the decrease in demand due to a price increase. Cross-price elasticity is obviously important to evaluate the competitive constraints provided by other products. It is particularly useful in the case where the magnitude of own elasticity would suggest that a price increase by a hypothetical monopolist would not be profitable and then it is necessary to find the closer substitutes to proceed with further steps of the SSNIP test.

Own- and cross-price elasticities can be estimated on the basis of a correctly built and estimated econometric model. Therefore econometric models are an important tool for the implementation of the SSNIP test. As we further discuss, the peculiar features of the media markets that we previously pointed out call for special considerations when formulating an econometric model for this industry.

The objective of this chapter is fourfold. First, we discuss the approach adopted to delineate markets in some recent antitrust cases and evaluate the extent to which two-sidedness and the other above-mentioned elements have been incorporated into the antitrust analysis. We argue that an econometric analysis that does not incorporate both sides of a media market can lead to biased estimates of elasticities. We then propose a simple econometric model that encompasses the three distinctive features of this industry outlined above. Third, we review some empirical papers that analyse the issue of demand estimation in printed media. Finally, we perform a statistical estimation on a dataset of magazines in order to show the possible bias that could arise in the estimation of elasticities when one does not use the proper model.

The chapter is organised as follows. In the next section we review the approaches to market definition adopted in some recent decisions by competition agencies. In Section 7.3 we sketch an econometric model that would allow estimating the demand on both the readers' and the advertising sides. In Section 7.4 we discuss the growing empirical literature on printed media. In Section 7.5 we show results from the estimation exercise and we conclude in Section 7.6.

7.2 Case review

Here we present the arguments that antitrust authorities have considered in practice for defining media markets in recent cases, both in Europe and in the United States. In particular we focus on the extent to which the peculiar characteristics of the printed media industry have been incorporated into the antitrust investigation. The objective is to evaluate whether the actual practice introduces a bias in the analysis in the light of the recent theoretical developments. For instance, as we argue below with reference to a specific case, this is a crucial issue particularly when the assessment of relevant markets relies on econometric tools. We show that the econometric analysis might be biased if the specific characteristics of the industry (particularly two-sidedness) are not accounted for.

The definition of relevant markets in printed media industries should take into account the distinctive features of competition in this industry. First of all, there is competition between newspapers belonging to the same product group. A first task consists therefore of assessing the strength of substitution between different types of product in terms of content (titles of general information versus specialised titles, for instance), quality (tabloids or quality press) and frequency.

Another important dimension of printed media is their geographic and spatial location. The majority of titles have a local scope and therefore the extent to which there are overlaps between different titles affects the strength of competition in the local markets.

Finally, the boundaries of the relevant market depend also on the competitive constraint provided by other, non-newspaper media, namely other printed media, television or the internet. The assessment of these boundaries should also account for the rapid growth of new forms of information transmission that are provided by technological change.

The analysis of these elements constitutes the core of the analysis of relevant markets in most antitrust decisions in the EU. For some recent merger cases in the written press industry, the European Commission analyses relevant markets according to the criteria mentioned above. In the *Recoletos/Unedisa* case,[4] for example, product categories are defined according to frequency (daily and non-daily publications), content (general information, sport and financial papers) and quality of the publication (tabloids or quality press). In the case of magazines, further divisions are made according to content. The same criteria for product market definition are used in other decisions of the Commission, for example in the cases *Gruner + Jahr/Financial Times/JV* and *Newspaper Publishing*.[5]

The same approach is adopted by the Italian antitrust authority in the *Ballarino/Grandi quotidiani* decision. In subsequent decisions,[6] the market of daily newspapers of general information is considered as separate from the market of daily business or sport newspapers.[7]

The geographic dimension applies to cases involving local newspapers. In some recent cases in the UK, the Competition Commission devotes an important part of the relevant market analysis to the assessment of competition in local markets. In the decision *Regional Independent Media Ltd and Gannett UK Ltd/Johnston Press plc/ Guardian Media Group*,[8] the competition assessment focuses on the local area analysis, as the titles involved compete primarily for a local readership. In particular, the decision identifies 'overlap areas', i.e. areas in which at least one newspaper of each of the publishers involved achieves a household penetration rate of 10 per cent or more. The analysis is conducted by looking at the likely competitive impact of the proposed transfers in any given overlap area, also taking into account 'core areas', which represent 'that part of a newspaper's circulation or distribution area in which the bulk of its copies are circulated or distributed'.

In the above-mentioned *Ballarino/Grandi quotidiani* decision (as well as in subsequent decisions), the Italian antitrust authority defines local and national publications as belonging to two separate (albeit adjacent) markets. This is motivated by the observation that the information provided in local papers has mostly a local scope and therefore their readership is different from that of national titles. However, it should also be taken into account that national newspapers have progressively increased the coverage of local events by introducing dedicated sections in the newspaper or, more recently, by bundling the national paper with a local one. Moreover, many of the newspapers with a national circulation have 'core areas' (as defined above) that coincide with local areas such as regions or big cities. Therefore the overlapping between national and local papers seems to have increased over the last decade and this should be taken into account in future antitrust decisions.

Therefore, at least from a demand-side perspective, printed media markets are usually segmented in relatively tiny submarkets according to their frequency, content and local characterisation.

Both the European Commission and national antitrust agencies have considered the substitutability of printed media with other media services in determining the competitive constraints faced by the firms under consideration. The written press is usually regarded as distinct from other media products. In the *Recoletos/Unedisa* case, the Commission argues that the written press offers a product that is not substitutable with TV and radio services in terms of the range and depth of information provided. Similarly, the UK Competition Commission, in the *Newsquest Ltd/Independent News and Media plc* case,[9] explains that, albeit there is some competition to local newspapers coming from other forms of printed media (advertising-only publications, niche titles, directories and direct mail), non-printed media cannot generally be regarded by readers as realistic substitutes. Note, however, that these considerations are based on qualitative analyses. No empirical analysis is performed to evaluate precisely the competitive impact of other media on the press industry.

So far we have dealt with aspects of the printed media market that are related to the demand side. However, as pointed out in the *Candover/ Cinven/Bertelsmann-Springer* decision, a strict demand approach 'would lead to the definition of a multitude of relevant markets of imprecise boundaries and small dimensions' because 'from a demand-side point of view, it is rare that two publications be viewed as perfect substitutes'. Therefore, another dimension of market definition that has been considered in antitrust cases is the supply side. In the *Recoletos/Unedisa* case, supply-side considerations are used to evaluate the substitutability between different titles and in particular to assess the profitability for a publisher of launching a new title. Supply-side considerations are particularly relevant in cases that concern specialised publications, as in the *Candover/Cinven/Bertelsmann-Springer* case, where elements such as image and reputation of a title, its expertise in a given area and 'an image of accuracy, reliability and comprehensiveness in the information supplied'[10] are identified as the elements required to launch a publication. Supply-side substitution is also considered in some UK cases, as for example in the *Johnston Press/Trinity Mirror* case.[11]

Finally, another important dimension along which newspapers compete is advertising revenues. The recognition of the two-sidedness feature is present in most antitrust decisions on the written press. In the *Recoletos/Unedisa* decision, it is stated that 'newspapers' editors operate in two broad markets: the market for written press, in which the consumers are the buyers of the newspaper as a source of information, and the market for advertising space, in which the consumers are the advertisers who buy space in order to promote sales'.

For this reason, the analysis of competition between newspapers in the advertising market often proceeds in parallel with the analysis of the readers' market. The substitutability between newspapers from the point of view of advertisers is closely linked to the proximity of titles from the point of view of readership. In other words, as it is made clear in the *Newspaper Publishing* decision, different categories of news-papers 'provide different channels through which to reach different socioeconomic groupings of readers' and cannot therefore be consi-dered substitutes from the point of view of buyers of advertising space. Therefore in many European Commission decisions the markets for advertising space are defined according to the type of readers to which each publication is addressed.

Similarly, the Italian antitrust authority has identified advertising in printed media as a separate market to advertising on television media, on the basis of the differences in the advertising message and the targeted audience between the two types of media.[12] In particular, television is described as more effective to convey 'persuasive' advertis-ing messages, whereas printed media would be more suitable for 'informative' advertising. A further distinction has been made between advertising on daily and non-daily publications, which are considered as two separate (albeit adjacent) markets from the point of view of the audience (more targeted for periodical publications, wider for daily titles). The advertising market has been segmented even further in the *Class Editori/Il Sole 24 Ore* case,[13] where advertising on daily papers specialised in business and financial information has been considered as a separate market to advertising on newspapers of general informa-tion. In the opinion of the Italian antitrust authority, complemen-tarities seem to outweigh substitutabilities because of the different characteristics of readerships between the two types of publications.

An alternative definition of advertising markets is proposed by the European Commission in the decision *Recoletos/Unedisa*, where it is suggested that the sale of advertising space in the written press could be considered as a single market.[14] This approach is motivated by the consideration that the written press as a whole generally attracts the most educated segments of society and therefore it is already a specific public. The second reason adduced to justify this approach is the fact that advertising space is often bought by large agencies which resell it to single customers and are therefore more likely to purchase space in different media outlets rather than in specialised publications only.

However, some qualifications of this issue are needed. First, even if it is true that daily newspapers of general information on average attract a more highly educated public than television, this is unlikely to be true for other types of publications such as specialised magazines (think of the tabloid kind of magazines, for instance). Second, the fact that there are large-scale buyers of advertising space does not imply that different outlets are substitutable from the point of view of advertisers. These points therefore stand against considering the entire printed media as a single market from the point of view of advertising demand.

A narrower market definition is adopted in many US cases, for example in the decision *US vs Donrey Media Group* (C.n. 95-5048), where local daily papers are considered as a separate market both on the readers' market and on the advertising market. From the point of view of readers' demand, even if it is true that some services provided by newspapers compete with radio, TV or other publications, the decision says that this does not mean that these other media can be considered as belonging to the same market. The same definition is applied also to the advertising market: the court considered that a small price increase in the local daily newspaper market would not be constrained by other media. In particular, an expert testified that most print advertisers would not switch to television or radio for a price increase of less than 20 per cent, which suggests a limited substitutability from the side of advertising demand.

The UK Competition Commission performs very detailed analyses of competition in local advertising markets. It conducts surveys in order to assess the substitutability between different titles from the point of view of buyers of advertising space. In the case *Newsquest Ltd/Independent News and Media plc*, a regression analysis is also performed. The exercise aims at understanding the price mechanisms implemented by newspapers with respect to advertisers and in particular at explaining the large variability in advertising rates across advertisers. An OLS (ordinary least squares) regression of realised advertising rates on circulation (measured by copy volume) shows that for the titles considered, higher market shares are associated with higher advertising rates. This finding is consistent with the direction of the inter-market network externality that links the readers' market to the advertising market.

The Competition Commission performs an analysis of market definition on the advertising market also in the recent case *Archant Limited/Independent News and Media Limited* (22/9/2004). An SSNIP test is invoked and quantitative survey data are used in order to assess whether a price increase by the merged entity could be profitable. Even considering the possibility of price discrimination, the Commission concludes that a price increase would not be profitable and consequently defines the relevant market as the local one, even if a wider range of titles than the local ones is taken into account.

Apart from limited regression analysis, market definition in printed media does not seem to have relied much on econometric analysis. The assessment of competition and substitutability between titles is conducted through qualitative considerations and survey methods rather than through the estimation of own- and cross-price elasticities.

One recent exception is a case involving *SOCPRESSE/Groupe Express-Expansion*,[15] two publishers of magazines and newspapers in France. On this occasion, the French competition authority sought to define the boundaries of the market for weekly magazines of general information and conducted an econometric analysis to ascertain whether this definition should include a larger number of titles than the definition used in previous decisions. The objective was to estimate the cross-price elasticities between different titles in order to decide which ones were to be included in the market definition.

The econometric methodology consisted in estimating a regression based on a panel of the time series of market shares of circulation and cover prices with magazine fixed effects. More formally, the estimating equation is:

$$s_{jt} = \alpha_j - \beta p_{jt} + \varepsilon_{jt}$$

where s_{jt} represents the market share of circulation for magazine j at time t, α_j is a time-invariant fixed effect for each magazine, p_{jt} is the magazine's cover price and ε_{jt} is the error term. The estimated price coefficient of this regression, and the price coefficient of an aggregate demand function, are then used to compute cross-price elasticities.

The estimation results are not reported in the decision, but it is said that the estimated elasticities are small. The Conseil de la Concurrence concludes that since the different titles appear to be differentiated and imperfect substitutes, it is difficult to delimit the exact boundaries of the market.

These very low estimates of elasticities could be the outcome of an inadequate econometric specification. First, the specification does not control for other variables that might have an impact on readers' demand. Some observable magazine characteristics, such as the number of pages, the presence of dedicated sections and the age of the title, should be regarded as important explanatory factors of readers' demand.[16] In other words, it seems that a missing variable problem is not correctly addressed.

Second, the estimation may be biased due to identification problems. Since there is no particular reason to think that prices are exogenous or predetermined, the estimation methodology described in the decision may lead to a biased estimation of the price coefficient due to endogeneity. One solution to the endogeneity problem would be to instrument the prices, possibly with some cost-related variables.

Finally, the two-sided nature of the market for printed media requires considering both sides of the market in the estimation model. A model that does not take into account the link between readers' demand and advertising demand is potentially mis-specified and may lead to biased estimations of price coefficients and related elasticities. Therefore, a structural model for the printed media industry (and for media industries in general) should include two demand systems, one for each side of the market, and link them with appropriate parameters. We propose and illustrate such a model in the next section.

7.3 An econometric framework

The aim of an empirical model for market definition is to provide estimates of demand parameters and in particular of the price sensitivity parameters which are crucial to determine the substitution pattern between titles. As we have already discussed, an econometric model for the printed media industry should be based on three main elements: two-sidedness, product differentiation (both vertical and horizontal) and definition of the total market size (using the notion of an outside good).

Some further qualifications of the latter issue are needed. The logit model of demand, which is one of the most widely used econometric models for antitrust purposes, requires the specification of an outside option reflecting the possibility that the consumer may choose none of the products considered (the 'inside' products). The existence of an outside good allows for the possibility that a homogeneous price increase of all the products considered decreases the aggregate quantity demanded. However, the introduction of an outside good imposes a measure of the market share for this good, which usually is not directly observed. Since the share of the outside good is the difference between the total (potential) size of the market and the combined shares of the inside goods, the potential market must be large enough to allow for a positive share of the outside good. The definition adopted for the total potential market size can have a significant impact on the estimation results. Therefore, one should test the robustness of the results using different specifications of the total market (and therefore of the outside option). One way to do that is to start with the largest possible definition and then restrict it on the basis of the estimated cross-price elasticities.

In the printed media industry, the potential market on the readers' side is commonly defined as the total population above the age of fourteen (an alternative being the number of households above the age of fourteen). On the advertising market, the largest possible market size would include all the media, i.e. TV, radio, the internet, the press. As we discussed in the previous section, narrower definitions might be more appropriate given the limited substitutability between different media services.

The model proposed below generalises a framework introduced by Argentesi and Filistrucchi (2005). Market definition on both the newspaper market and the advertising market requires an estimation of own- and cross-price elasticities of demand which should be derived from the parameters of two distinct (but interconnected) demand models. It is therefore necessary to estimate both the demand for the newspaper by readers and the demand for advertising space by advertisers. We propose to estimate a system of logit demands (or nested logit if this is more appropriate to the market characteristics) where the two demand systems are linked by an inter-market network externality (which may be positive or negative).

More specifically, readers' demand for magazine j is assumed to depend on some observable characteristics of the magazine, on cover price and on advertising quantity in the following way (the superscript R indicates Readers as opposed to advertising, which is indicated with A later on):

$$\ln(s_j^R) - \ln(s_0^R) = \mathbf{x}_j^R \beta^R - \alpha^R p_j^R + \gamma^R y_j^A + \xi_j^R$$

where $\mathbf{x}_j^R$ is a vector of characteristics that can include age (the longevity of a publication can explain the loyalty of readers), number of content pages (i.e. non-advertising pages), special sections, promotions, inserts, changes of editors; p_j^R is the cover price of the magazine (in real terms); y_j^A is the quantity of advertising contained in magazine j; and ξ_j^R is an unobservable component that can be interpreted as a fixed effect.

Similarly, advertising demand can be written as:

$$\ln(s_j^A) - \ln(s_0^A) = \mathbf{x}_j^A \beta^A - \alpha^A p_j^A + \gamma^A y_j^R + \xi_j^A$$

Here the vector of product characteristics can include variables related to the composition of audience (income, education, etc.), variables about the quantity of content pages of the publication or other characteristics such as the format, colour pages and so on. Similar to readers' demand, here y_j^R is magazine j's circulation, which may impact on advertising demand.

The parameters γ^R and γ^A capture the link between the two markets. Readers' demand is affected (either negatively or positively) by the amount of advertising and advertising space demand is affected by the circulation of the magazine. Therefore there is a problem of endogeneity when estimating either demand system. Failing to consider the link with the other market (through the corresponding parameter γ) leads to biased estimates of elasticities. Estimating a model like the one proposed here should overcome this problem and lead to a correct identification of the price sensitivity parameters which are the basis of any analysis of market definition.

Still the identification issues due to the potential endogeneity of prices and quantities in both equations might remain. The usual way to overcome this problem is by applying an instrumental-variables procedure. The possibility of finding suitable instruments for the variables of interest is often constrained by data availability. In the next section we further discuss this issue in the context of some recent empirical applications.

7.4 A review of the literature

Despite the growing body of theoretical literature on competition and pricing in two-sided markets, initiated by the work of Rochet and Tirole (2003, 2006) and Armstrong (2004), there is still little work on the empirical implications of these theories and few empirical tests of two-sidedness.

To our knowledge, the issue of market definition has not been explicitly considered in any recent paper. There are, however, a few recent empirical papers which analyse the printed media industry taking into account its peculiar features. Some of them, in order to explain the price structure in this market, focus in particular on the estimation of the two-sided demand faced by printed media publishers. This is the case of the paper by Kaiser and Wright (2004), whose objective it is to conduct an empirical examination of the structure of price–cost margins between the two sides of the market. They estimate an adapted version of Armstrong's (2004) model of competition in a two-sided market where magazines are horizontally differentiated. The model is then tested on a dataset of German magazines. The model rests on the assumption that there are only two media outlets, which limits the applicability of the model to real-world situations where there are often more than two titles competing. The theoretical model gives rise to a system of two demand equations, one for the advertising market and one for the readers' market. The latter is assumed to depend on the quantity of the magazine's content pages (as opposed to advertising pages), on its cover price, on the quantity of advertising and on a transportation cost, which depends on the location of consumers in the characteristics space. Advertising demand similarly depends on the size of the readership, on advertising rates and on the intrinsic preference of advertisers for either of the two magazines.

The model is completed with the conditions for profit maximisation for the magazine firm. The methodology consists of estimating the two demand systems and plugging the parameters obtained into the first-order conditions for profit maximisation, under the assumption that the two firms are symmetric.[17] Solving the system of first-order conditions gives the mark-up equations that are the expressions of central interest.

The central result of the theoretical model concerns the structure of these margins. The model holds that 'equilibrium cover prices are marked up above marginal cost to the extent of product differentiation on the readership side, but discounted to reflect the externality generated on the advertising side of the market from a magazine attracting more readers' (Kaiser and Wright, 2004, p. 6). Therefore if advertisers value readership a lot, a magazine may prefer to set a low cover price to attract readers. The same reasoning holds for the mark-up on advertising rates. If readers have a high valuation for advertising, the mark-up might be lower than the standard one.

The estimation results for readers' demand suggest that the relative number of content pages is an important factor in determining the size of the readership. The effect of advertising quantity is much weaker, but is weakly positive. The coefficient of cover prices is not significantly different from zero, which might suggest that cover prices are not an important determinant in the readers' choice. As to advertising demand, circulation seems to have an important effect on the share of advertising of one magazine versus the other. Again, the price coefficient is not statistically different from zero.

The parameter estimates of the two demand systems allow inferring the implied price–cost structure in this two-sided market. In particular, it is useful to decompose the margins in the standard mark-up coming from horizontal differentiation and the additional term which represents the network effect. Estimates of the two network effects suggest that the network externality on the equilibrium cover price is much bigger than the externality on the equilibrium advertising price. In other words, the readers' side is subsidised by the advertising side. However, the authors recognise that since the estimates of the price sensitivity of demand are not precise, the results obtained should be interpreted only as illustrative of the role that the network effect can play in determining the price–cost structure in two-sided markets.

There are two more observations about the methodology used in this paper that are worth mentioning. The first one concerns the specification of the model, and in particular the issue of identification. In both demand equations, there is an issue of endogeneity with respect to both prices and quantity, which is reinforced by the two-way causation between advertising and readership. This problem is solved by using variables about other titles published by the same firm as instruments. For example, the size of the readership in the advertising demand equation is instrumented with the average readership of other magazines from the same publisher. This choice rests on the assumption that cost factors are common across titles in the same publishing house. This identification strategy seems to be justified in this context by the high correlation that instruments show with the explanatory variables and by the fact that orthogonality of instruments with the residuals of the equation of interest cannot be rejected. However, this choice of instruments might not be appropriate in other contexts where the publishers do not have many comparable publications. Other possible instruments that have been proposed in the literature are input cost or the (exogenous) characteristics of other firms.[18] In any case, the choice of the appropriate instruments should depend on data availability and on the specific characteristics of each market.

The other observation regards the limitations implied by the assumptions of the theoretical model. As we have already mentioned, the applicability of the model is limited to cases where there are only two newspapers competing in the same market. Furthermore, the model assumes that the total number of readers and the total number of advertisers are fixed. This assumption does not allow for an outside option: all readers buy one magazine and all advertisers buy space in one magazine. This implies that there is no scope for market expansion or market reduction and therefore implicitly that demand is globally inelastic to prices. In this respect, recall that in the above-mentioned case *SOCPRESSE/Groupe Express-Expansion* in France, the authority performed an estimation of global price elasticity, which shows that the average price of magazines would have a strong impact on the demand for magazines, which seems to contrast with the assumption of Kaiser and Wright (2004).[19]

A related paper, Kaiser (2004), builds a model of profit maximisation in the German magazine market. The theoretical model is composed of an equation for readers' demand, a behavioural equation for advertising rates and a first-order condition for profit maximisation. Readers' demand is estimated with a nested logit model, assuming that demand depends on content and the share of advertising pages as in Kaiser and Wright (2004). This specification takes into account the link between the readers' market and the advertising market. Moreover, it overcomes the two problems of that paper mentioned above. First, it considers the existence of an outside good because the nested logit model explicitly allows for the possibility that consumers do not buy anything. Second, it can be applied to markets with more than two competitors.

However, compared with Kaiser and Wright (2004), Kaiser (2004) puts much more structure on the formulation of the advertising side. Advertising prices are assumed to be a function of previous period circulation and a vector of observed and unobserved characteristics of the magazine and of the readership. Advertising quantity is instead assumed to be fixed.

The model is closed by a first-order condition for profit maximisation. The only choice variable of the magazine firm is the cover price because advertising rates are assumed to adjust in the way described above and advertising quantity is fixed. The first-order condition leads to a mark-up formula for cover prices which has similar characteristics to the one of Kaiser and Wright (2004), with the difference that here there is only one mark-up instead of two. Cover price deviates from the usual mark-up formula by a term that depends on the circulation elasticity of advertising demand: the more elastic advertising demand is to circulation, the more cover price deviates from the standard mark-up formula.

An interesting result that comes from readers' demand estimation is that consumers seem to have a taste for advertising. This would confirm the importance of considering advertising content in order to avoid possible biases in the estimation of readers' demand, at least for magazines. This would also confirm the theory of the 'circulation spiral' of Gabszewicz, Laussel and Sonnac (2002), whereby the circumstance that readers like advertising and advertisers look for readers leads to equilibria where both the readers' market and the advertising market are fully monopolised by a single firm. However, Kaiser (2004) seems to draw opposite conclusions from his results. Given the structure of the price–cost margin, an increase in cover price by a merging firm would have a negative impact on advertising and would not be always profitable. This conclusion, however, does not seem to take into account that if the externalities linking the two markets are both positive, the circulation spiral effect might lead to an increase of market power *on both markets*, leading in the extreme case to monopolisation.

Estimating market power is the objective of the paper by Argentesi and Filistrucchi (2005), who perform an empirical analysis on the Italian newspaper market. As in the previous two papers, the model consists of three main elements: a demand equation for readership, a demand equation for advertising and a profit-maximising condition. The paper is aimed at estimating the strength of competition in the market by comparing the estimated price–cost margins under the alternative hypotheses of oligopolistic competition and collusion with some measure of observed costs in order to assess which is the true structure of the market.

The specification of the two demand systems is similar to the one proposed in this paper, except that in the basic version advertising is not included as an explanatory variable in readers' demand. This assumption is made for simplicity but it is also justified by the fact that the publications considered are national newspapers of general information, where the role of advertising quantity in determining demand does not seem to be as crucial as for magazines. Newspapers' demand is estimated with a logit model, which captures the feature of product differentiation that characterises this market.

The link between the two markets is due to the fact that advertising demand is a function of circulation. Advertising demand is not assumed to follow a specific behavioural function as in the Kaiser (2004) model but is estimated with a logit model. This requires a definition of total market size, which raises the issue, already mentioned, of the definition of boundaries of the advertising market. In particular, it should be assessed to what extent other media provide a substitute to the newspapers considered from the point of view of advertisers, which is an important issue for market definition analysis.

The profit maximisation condition on cover prices gives an expression for mark-up similar to the ones derived in the papers previously discussed. The implication is that the optimal cover price is lower than the standard mark-up because of the impact of the advertising market, which reduces the incentive to increase price because this would reduce the readership and as a consequence advertising demand.

All three models discussed above constitute attempts to incorporate the two-sidedness of the market into the econometric analysis of printed media markets. Gronnevet and Steen (2004) consider another possible source of bias that can arise in the estimation of demand in these industries. The source of endogeneity stems from the choice of a newspaper's political line. Choosing whether to adopt a political profile or not is considered a strategic decision for the newspaper. Given that the political line is a potential determinant of newspaper demand, one would be tempted to include a political dummy in the demand estimation. However, since the choice of the political profile is endogenous, this would raise problems of identification. The authors propose therefore a two-step estimation procedure which helps to solve this endogeneity problem.

All the models presented in this section provide different ways to estimate demand taking into account the distinguishing features of printed media markets. Correct demand estimation is the basis for a sensible analysis for market definition because the latter relies on elasticity estimates to draw conclusions on the degree of substitutability between media outlets. As we have seen, the biases in the demand estimation can have different sources and market definition analysis should rely more and more on econometric analyses that encompass the complexity of these interacting factors.

7.5 An econometric illustration

We use a dataset of French magazines and construct a demand system based on a nested logit model of readers' demand.[20] The nested logit model assumes that there are two levels in the choice of consumers: a consumer first chooses among the available magazines, then has to decide between buying a one-year subscription and buying the magazine each week at the newsstand. The first decision includes the option to choose an 'outside' magazine or another type of printed media. The model is motivated by evidence suggesting that there are relevant differences among the publications considered in terms of the ratio of subscriptions to unit sales. In particular, the magazines could be broadly grouped in three classes according to the proportion of subscriptions with respect to newsstand sales. Figure 7.1 displays these three groups. Clearly the three magazines – *La Vie*, *Pèlerin* and *Valeurs Actuelles* – are mainly distributed through subscription. In contrast, *Marianne*, *Paris Match*, *VSD* and *Figaro Magazine* are bought each week at newsstands. In between there are magazines having more balanced distribution schemes. These three groups correspond to different types of magazines. Those distributed by subscription have a

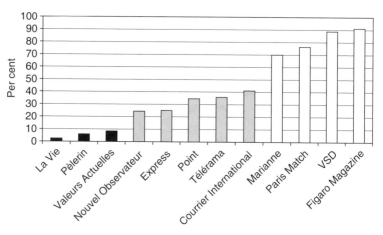

Figure 7.1. Share of unit purchases in total sales (average 1996–2001)

smaller and more specific audience, while those usually sold per unit have a much broader audience and have a reputation for building their image around scoops or strongly emotional events.[21]

After estimating the model without considering the advertising market, we estimate the same system by using a measure of advertising revenues as an instrument and show how elasticity estimates change due to the above-mentioned endogeneity problem.

The dataset consists of a panel of eight French magazines from 1996 to 2001.[22] For each magazine, the dataset contains information on circulation, subscriptions, sales at newsstand, free distribution, cover prices, subscription fees and revenues (both total and from sales only). The difference between the total turnover and the total sales from subscriptions and unit purchases is roughly a measure of revenues from advertising. By dividing this measure by the number of free copies, we derive a proxy for the price of advertising per free distribution.

The demand model is specified as:

$$\ln(s_j) - \ln(s_0) = x_j\beta - \alpha p_j + \sigma \ln(s_{j|m}) + \xi_j$$

where s_j is the market share of magazine j in the whole market, s_0 is the market share of all alternative magazines (namely, the outside alternative measured by the total number of magazines sold in France), $s_{j|m}$ is the market share of magazine j in the group of magazines sold under subscription or unit purchase, x_j is a set of exogenous variables to measure the specific reputation of each magazine by means of a dummy variable for the magazine, a dummy to signal the distribution mode, the number of issues per year and a time trend, and p_j is the unit price or the subscription price (per issue) according to the chosen mode of purchase. The parameter α measures the sensitivity of the representative customer's utility to prices, while the parameter vector β provides a measure of the sensitivity of the representative customer's utility to quality. The parameter σ indicates how demand is affected by the differentiation in terms of distribution systems. Finally, ξ_j is a random term measuring the effect of unobservable variables that enter the mean value of each magazine.[23]

We build a system of two equations, one for the demand of magazine j sold under subscription and one for the demand of magazine j sold under unit purchase. We estimate the model using three-stage non-linear least squares under two alternative sets of instruments. In the first case, the set of instruments includes all exogenous variables and the previous year's circulation. Given the paucity of this dataset, this is basically the only way to take care of the endogeneity problem. In the second set of instruments, we replace the previous year's circulation by our proxy for the price of advertising revenues, its lagged value and the number of free and complimentary copies.

We have selected this last set of instruments in order to minimise the objective function and to increase the identification of parameters of interest. In both cases, the parameter σ is significant and well identified. Its estimated value (0.52 with a t-ratio of 1.95 under the second set of instruments) shows that the differentiation in terms of purchase or distribution mode matters. However, the parameter α which is not significantly different from zero under the first set of instruments becomes significant under the second set of instruments. Moreover, the first-stage R-squared which is a measure of the goodness and relevance of instruments increases with the estimation made with the second set of instruments.[24]

The results for the estimated own- and cross-price elasticities provided in Tables 7.1 and 7.2 are striking. Note in particular that when advertising is used as an instrument, the range of values taken by the own-price elasticities increases. In the first case, i.e. when advertising is not used as an instrument, the range of absolute values for elasticities is between 0.20 and 0.36 while elasticities take absolute values between 0.67 and 1.22 when advertising is an instrument. Not only the average value of own-price elasticities increases but also the spread of values. Note also that the demand for some magazines becomes elastic. Estimated values for all cross-price elasticities increase drastically, providing much more room for substitution between magazines. The values of cross-price elasticities are three to four times higher when advertising is included as an instrument than when it is not.

These results are just illustrative of the bias that can arise in the estimation of elasticities if the feedback effect between the two sides of the market is neglected. It would be better to specify a full econometric model which encompasses both sides of the market simultaneously, in the spirit of the framework advanced in Section 7.3. Nonetheless, the estimation exercise proposed in this section gives some support to our argument that two-sidedness has an important effect on the nature of the market and implies that models taking this feature into account should be used for market definition wherever possible.

Table 7.1: Own-price elasticities for some French magazines

	Estimation without advertising as an instrument	Estimation with advertising as an instrument
La Vie	−0.24	−0.81
	(0.000)	(0.000)
Le Figaro Magazine	−0.36	−1.22
	(0.001)	(0.003)
Le Nouvel Observateur	−0.31	−1.06
	(0.000)	(0.001)
Le Point	−0.28	−0.95
	(0.000)	(0.001)
L'Express	−0.28	−0.95
	(0.001)	(0.002)
Paris Match	−0.20	−0.67
	(0.002)	(0.005)
Valeurs Actuelles	−0.36	−1.22
	(0.044)	(0.148)
VSD	−0.20	−0.67
	(0.018)	(0.060)

Note: Each cell provides the average estimated value of the elasticity and, in parentheses and italics, the empirical standard deviations.

The set of instruments used in the estimation can make an important difference to the policy conclusions that could be drawn from the analysis. If demand for magazines appeared to be inelastic and if magazines were not substitutes, the relevant market defined in the traditional way could shrink to the magazine itself. In terms of the antitrust policy, a merger in this industry would not be investigated and its impact would not be perceived in the same way. Recall that mergers between complements are not usually harmful. This suggests that attention to correct estimation may be important for directing the attention of the competition authorities to situations in which there may be genuine competition between media firms that are threatened by mergers and other potential abuses.

Though the example we have investigated here is from the printed media, the general lessons apply also to broadcasting, at least to those broadcasting services that are financed by advertising. However, the

Table 7.2: Cross-price elasticities for some French magazines

	Estimation without advertising as an instrument	Estimation with advertising as an instrument
La Vie	0.000	0.001
	(0.000)	*(0.000)*
Le Figaro Magazine	0.041	0.137
	(0.001)	*(0.003)*
Le Nouvel Observateur	0.008	0.025
	(0.000)	*(0.001)*
Le Point	0.006	0.020
	(0.000)	*(0.001)*
L'Express	0.008	0.027
	(0.001)	*(0.002)*
Paris Match	0.026	0.087
	(0.002)	*(0.005)*
Valeurs Actuelles	0.001	0.002
	(0.000)	*(0.001)*
VSD	0.009	0.031
	(0.001)	*(0.002)*

Note: Each cell provides the average estimated value of the elasticity and, in parentheses and italics, the empirical standard deviations. Each row j provides, for any magazine i different from j, the average elasticity of the demand for magazine i with respect to the price of magazine j, i.e. the average cross-price elasticity of magazine i with respect to magazine j. This is a well-known property of the logit model.

specific lessons in broadcasting may be somewhat different. In particular, printed magazines typically (though not always) sell for a positive cover price, but advertising-financed broadcasting services are typically free to the viewer or listener. However, for such services the crucial questions of market definition often arise on the advertiser side – regardless of whether two viewers would view the services as close substitutes, channels might be regarded as being in the same relevant market if a rise in the price of advertising on one would lead advertisers to switch to advertising on the other. What the model here reminds us is that we need to take into account the influence of viewer figures on the demand for advertising if we are to calculate the relevant demand elasticities correctly. For instance, if a rise in the price of advertising means that a channel can increase its supply of premium content such as popular movies or sports broadcasts, this may (by increasing viewer figures) make advertisers appear to be unwilling to switch away to rival channels, thereby giving the impression that the channels are less close substitutes than in fact they are. No less than in the printed media, then, neglect of the two-sided character of the market may lead to excessively narrow market definitions and a consequent distortion of competition and regulatory policy.

7.6 Conclusion

This chapter discusses the issue of market definition in the context of printed media markets. The issue is crucial for two reasons. First, technological progress is rapidly changing the boundaries of media markets, making the exercise more complex and sensitive. Second, media markets are characterised by peculiar features that should be taken into account in the analysis of market definition and market power. In particular, the econometric models that are increasingly used to implement the SSNIP test should incorporate the elements of two-sidedness that are intrinsic to these markets.

We review some recent antitrust cases and show to what extent these characteristics of printed media markets have been taken into account. The importance of considering these peculiar features increases with the use of econometric models in antitrust analysis. Failing to consider them may lead to biased estimates of own- and cross-price elasticities. We illustrate the bias that can arise in the estimation of elasticities with an econometric exercise on a dataset of French magazines. We compare two alternative specifications of readers' demand for magazines, one without advertising and one where advertising is used as an instrument, and show that neglecting the effect of advertising may have a relevant impact on the estimated elasticities.

A proper econometric model for the estimation of elasticities remains to be built. We propose a framework to model the two-sided demand that characterises printed media markets. Alternative methodologies are also conceivable and we discuss some approaches that have recently been proposed in the literature. Given the topicality of the issue of market definition in media industries and the need to find appropriate econometric models to implement it, further research is needed to capture the complexity of these industries.

Lessons for students: what have we learned?

- We show the importance of analysing media markets in the light of the recent theory of two-sided markets.
- Failing to take into account the two-sided nature of these markets may lead to biased estimates of elasticities and therefore vitiate the analysis of relevant markets in antitrust cases.

Lessons for researchers: what do we still need to know?

- Our discussion highlights the importance of developing appropriate econometric models for the analysis of media markets (and of two-sided markets in general).

Lessons for policymakers: what are the priorities for policy in this area?

- Standard SSNIP tests tend to underestimate the substitutability of products, so market definitions err on the narrow side and policy-makers should be particularly aware of the possible presence of substitute products to those they are considering as in the relevant market.
- Economic research has shown that market definition in this industry is not a simple task, but it does not yet go far enough to provide precise guidance. Therefore policymakers have to be cautious in evaluating merger cases in these industries.

References

Argentesi, E. (2004) 'Demand estimation for Italian newspapers: the impact of weekly supplements', *Working Paper of the European University Institute ECO*, 2004/28.

Argentesi, E. and L. Filistrucchi (2005) 'Estimating market power in a two-sided market: the case of newspapers', *Working Paper of the European University Institute ECO*, 2005/7.

Armstrong, M. (2004) 'Competition in two-sided markets', mimeo, University College London.

Berry, S. T. (1994) 'Estimating discrete-choice models of product differentiation', *Rand Journal of Economics*, 25(2), 242–262.

European Commission (1997) 'Commission Notice on the Definition of Relevant Market for the Purpose of Community Competition Law', *Official Journal*, C372, 9 December.

Gabszewicz, J.-J., D. Laussel and N. Sonnac (2002) 'Concentration in the press industry and the theory of the "circulation spiral"', *CORE Discussion Paper*, (64).

Gronnevet, G. and F. Steen (2004) 'Branding news with political opinion', mimeo, Norwegian School of Economics and Business Administration.

Ivaldi, M. and S. Lörincz (2005) 'A full equilibrium relevant market test: application to computer servers', *IDEI working paper*.

Ivaldi, M. and F. Verboven (2005) 'Quantifying the effects from horizontal mergers in European competition policy', *International Journal of Industrial Organisation*, 23(9), December, 669–691.

Kaiser, U. (2003) 'The effect of website provision on the demand for German women's magazines', mimeo, revised version of NBER Working Paper No. w8806.

Kaiser, U. (2004) 'An estimated model of the German magazine market', Centre for Economic and Business Research, Discussion Paper 2004–09, Copenhagen.

Kaiser, U. and J. Wright (2004) 'Price structure in two-sided markets: evidence from the magazine industry', Centre for Economic and Business Research, Discussion Paper 2004–08, Copenhagen.

Motta, M. (2004) *Competition Policy. Theory and Practice*, Cambridge University Press.

Nevo, A. (2001) 'Measuring market power in the ready-to-eat cereal industry', *Econometrica*, 69(2), 307–342.

Rochet, J.-C. and J. Tirole (2003) 'Platform competition in two-sided markets', *Journal of the European Economic Association*, 1(4), 990–1029.

Rochet, J.-C. and J. Tirole (2006) 'Two-sided markets: a progress report', *Rand Journal of Economics*.

Notes

* We are grateful to Massimo Motta and Paul Seabright for comments on a previous draft and to participants at the IDEI-ZEI Conference on 'Regulation of media markets', Toulouse, October 2004 for discussions and suggestions.
1. See Rochet and Tirole (2003, 2006) and Armstrong (2004).
2. See European Commission (1997).
3. For a discussion on the SSNIP test and its implementation, see Motta (2004), Chapter 3. See also, for an econometric application, Ivaldi and Lörincz (2005).

4. Case No. IV/M.1041 – *Recoletos/Unedisa*, 01/02/1999.
5. Cases No. IV/M.1455 – *Gruner + Jahr/Financial Times/JV*, 20/04/1999 and No. IV/M.423 – *Newspaper Publishing*, 14/03/1994 respectively.
6. See Provv. n. 3354 *Ballarino/Grandi quotidiani* (26/10/1996), Provv. n. 4822 *Italia Oggi Editori/Il Sole 24 Ore* (20/3/1997) and following decisions.
7. In Italy, there is no such thing as tabloids: daily newspapers are differentiated on the basis of their geographic circulation (local or national) and political orientation, but not so much on a 'vertical' dimension.
8. 2000, www.competition-commission.org.uk
9. 2003, www.competition-commission.org.uk
10. Quoted from Case No. COMP/M.3197 – *Candover/Cinven/Bertelsmann-Springer*, 27/07/2003.
11. 2002, www.competition-commission.org.uk
12. This distinction can be found in the case *Publitalia 80/S.P.E./S.P.I.* (Provv. n. 2517, 1/12/1994).
13. Provv. n. 3336, *Class Editori/Il Sole 24 Ore*, 19/10/1995.
14. It should be noted, however, that the Commission did not conclude on the definition of these markets because under either market definition the concentration considered did not give rise to antitrust concerns.
15. 2005, www.conseil-concurrence.fr
16. These are some of the explanatory variables that Kaiser (2003) included in the demand equation for women magazines in Germany, together with the launch of online versions. In addition, Argentesi (2004) includes the presence of inserts, the changes in the editorial line and exogenous events like sport events or elections that might have an impact on newspapers' circulation as explanatory variables in the estimation of demand for Italian newspapers.
17. This assumption is a necessary simplification due to the impossibility of identifying all the parameters of the general model with a limited dataset.
18. As motivated in Berry (1994) and Nevo (2001), the characteristics of products produced by other firms are appropriate instruments because they are correlated with price through the condition for profit maximisation, but are assumed to be exogenous to the model.
19. To estimate cross-price elasticities in the *SOCPRESSE/Groupe Express-Expansion* case, the methodology adopted by the Conseil de la Concurrence requires estimating the price elasticity of the aggregate demand in this market. This estimation is based on a time-series regression which explains the consumption of magazines by global consumption and by the evolution of relative cover prices of magazines with respect to some consumer price index.
20. See Ivaldi and Verboven (2005) for further details of this model.

21. This is not true for *Figaro Magazine* which is sold as a supplement with the weekend edition of the daily newspaper *Le Figaro*.
22. Four magazines – *Courrier International, Marianne, Pèlerin* and *Télérama* – have been excluded from the dataset used for estimation either because of lack of data or because they are not strictly comparable to the included magazines. For instance, *Télérama* is considered as a TV magazine rather than a news magazine.
23. This model is discussed in detail by Ivaldi and Verboven (2005).
24. The estimated value of α is equal to 0.36 (with a t-ratio of 2.01) under the second set of instruments and 0.11 (with a t-ratio of 0.34) under the first set of instruments. Detailed results are available from the authors.

PART III

Institutional approaches in various jurisdictions

8 Policymaking and policy trade-offs: broadcast media regulation in the United States

PETER J. ALEXANDER AND
KEITH BROWN*

8.1 Introduction

The Federal Communications Commission (FCC) has a statutory obligation to pursue the 'public interest' through its regulation of broadcast media. The FCC's interpretation of the public interest has led it to pursue three policy objectives: competition, localism and diversity. This policy triad reflects both efficiency and antitrust considerations and concerns about the social, political and cultural effects of media. Therefore, in addition to pursuing competition in broadcast markets through (quasi)-antitrust analysis, the FCC considers the additional elements of diversity and localism – elements that can add considerable nuance and complexity for policymakers.[1]

The FCC employs two broad classes of regulatory tools: structural (ownership) rules and behavioural (content) regulation. The FCC's structural rules often take the form of ownership limits on the number of broadcast stations a single entity may own within and across local markets. The FCC has changed these caps periodically over the last fifty years, but since the 1990s there has been the most substantial change in broadcast ownership policies.

The FCC first permitted the ownership of multiple radio stations within the same market in 1992, allowing entities to own up to two FM and two AM stations within a market with at least fifteen stations, provided that the combined audience share of the stations did not exceed 25 per cent. For stations in markets with fewer than fifteen radio stations, a single licensee was permitted to own up to three stations, of which no more than two could be AM or FM stations, provided that the owned stations represented less than 50 per cent of the total number of radio stations in the market. The 1996 Telecommunications Act directed the FCC to change ownership limits once again: in radio markets with forty-five or more radio stations, a company could own up to eight stations, only five of which could be in

255

one class, AM or FM. In markets with between thirty and forty-four radio stations, a company could own seven stations, only four of which could be in one class. In markets with between fifteen and twenty-nine radio stations, a company could own six stations, only four of which could be in one class. In markets with fourteen or fewer radio stations, a company could own five stations, only three of which could be in one class and an owner could not control more than 50 per cent of the stations within these markets.[2]

The FCC also limits the number of national viewers that a single television broadcaster can reach via station ownership.[3] From 1954 to 1984, the FCC limited national ownership to seven stations, where each station was in a separate geographic market. In 1984, the FCC expanded ownership limits to twelve stations, provided that the total number of stations owned did not reach over 25 per cent of the national market. The 1996 Telecommunications Act raised the broadcast television ownership limit to 35 per cent of the national market and eliminated the station ownership limit. Subsequently, the FCC's decision in 2000 to retain a national broadcast television ownership limit was challenged by Fox Television Stations in the US Court of Appeals, DC Circuit, and the Court reversed the FCC's decision, sending the rule back to the FCC for further consideration. In 2003, the FCC increased the ownership limit to 45 per cent of the national market. This decision proved controversial and the United States Congress set a statutory limit of 39 per cent in 2004.

As a result of these various regulatory decisions, ownership concentration in broadcast media has increased, most markedly since the Telecommunications Act of 1996. For example, the ratio of unique owners to full-power commercial broadcast television stations has gone from approximately 2/5 in 1996 to approximately 1/4 in 2004.[4] While broadcast networks have generally argued that ownership consolidation generates efficiencies that rationalise increased ownership concentration from a purely economic standpoint, the Federal Appeals Court for the District of Columbia noted, *inter alia*, in 2002 that:

Congress may, in the regulation of broadcasting, constitutionally pursue values other than efficiency – including in particular diversity in programming, for which diversity of ownership is perhaps an aspirational but surely not irrational proxy. Simply put, it is not unreasonable – and therefore not unconstitutional – for the Congress to prefer having in the aggregate more voices heard.

Thus, the Court concluded that Congress (and by proxy the FCC) might reasonably prefer and pursue ownership goals other than those presumed to promote simple economic efficiency, in this case diversity.[5]

Others aver that media substitutability and digital convergence diminish the importance of broadcast media ownership concentration. These observers argue that substitutability and convergence decrease the effects of concentration within any given medium by increasing the overall size of the relevant market. By this argument, if radio substitutes for television which substitutes for newspapers which substitutes for internet content, then concentration within radio, television, newspapers or internet content does not necessarily confer any market power or diminish the diversity of viewpoints. In short, any potential welfare losses due to intra-modal concentration will be offset by gains from inter-modal competition. Clearly, the extent of the market and degree of substitutability are important issues, which may render moot many of the arguments against broadcast media ownership concentration.

Perhaps surprisingly, empirical evidence regarding substitutability between various media (e.g. television, radio, the internet, newspapers) for media consumers is scant. Waldfogel (2002) undertakes a comprehensive public study of media substitutability. Using a variety of detailed datasets exploring a wide range of media, Waldfogel performs six different regressions and reports four different tables of correlations, then details variables that are significant in any of these ten sets of results.

The significant (5 per cent level) coefficients from Waldfogel's (2002) six regressions of media substitutability yield the following results: (1) one hour of internet use subtracts, on average, approximately four minutes of broadcast television viewing; (2) for each instance of internet news use, broadcast television news use is reduced by approximately two and a half minutes; (3) for every 1 per cent increase in the cable penetration rate, the rate of increase in daily newspaper circulation per capita decreased by 18 per cent; and (4) if daily newspapers increase in number by one, weekly newspapers decrease in number by eight.

The clearest results of Waldfogel's (2002) effort suggest that consumers may substitute between broadcast television and internet use, although the magnitudes of substitution seem to be modest. Importantly, there appears to be little other significant substitutability among other media.[6] Instead of various media readily substituting for one another and forming a single large media market place (a large and growing pond, to paraphrase some observers), each medium's small pond may be completely unconnected to other media ponds or connected only by very narrow tributaries. Ownership concentration within any individual media may therefore warrant careful regulatory attention.

In what follows, we detail the evolution of FCC policymaking on competition, diversity and localism, summarise some extant economic literature relating to these objectives, highlight possible policy conflicts and make suggestions for future research. Defining competition, diversity and localism is difficult and inherently subjective; we can, however, bring some precision that should help policymakers address these issues, in particular by constructing more precise definitions of competition, diversity and localism.

8.2 The public interest: competition, diversity and localism

Competition, diversity and localism are deeply entangled and not readily harmonised – as we suggest later in the chapter, the early history of broadcast licence allocation suggests implicit trade-offs among these three policy goals. In short, enhancing one element of the competition–diversity–localism policy triad may diminish another. The initial allocation of broadcast television and radio licences by the FCC, for example, had some intent of promoting 'localism' by allocating channels to local communities. This assignment of broadcast frequency to local communities precluded six national VHF channels in favour of (for most communities) fewer VHF channels. These fewer channels, however, were locally based. In effect, this allocation traded off competition and diversity in favour of localism. Regulators and researchers therefore may benefit from a deeper understanding of each policy objective and its interactions with the other objectives.

The nature of media has changed significantly since the FCC began licensing broadcasters: the emergence of cable and satellite television has given consumers myriad viewing choices; national satellite radio has begun to penetrate radio markets; high-speed internet, via cable and telephony, offers consumers a broad array of information choices; moreover, the transition from analogue to digital broadcasting, already under way in the United States, will provide additional capacity and options. This broad and growing array of potential substitutes may ultimately blunt some of the possible trade-offs in media policy. However, while the increase in media options expands the total capacity of existing services, it does not necessarily change the fundamental policy trade-offs. Surprisingly, convergence and attendant expansion of the spectrum of media may imply stricter, and not looser, limits on broadcast media concentration. As we illustrate later, as channel capacity increases, the gains to consumers from concentration-induced diversity may decrease.

We divide the broadcast media economics literature into three broad yet often inter-related strands. The first strand focuses on market structure and differentiated products and is historically the best developed. The second strand explores what we call the 'strategic' approach and examines the strategic interaction between broadcast media firms and its effect on broadcasters' choice of programming content and advertising levels, for example. The third strand focuses on the political-economy aspects of broadcast media, e.g. their relationship to voting outcomes. The political-economic elements of broadcast media have recently received greater attention from economists and this literature helps us understand localism and diversity. We view the first and third strands as particularly relevant to the competition, diversity and localism objectives of any thoughtful media policymaker.

Competition

Competition can be defined as a setting in which intense rivalry forces prices to the level of production costs. As a policy matter, competition is relatively easy to benchmark (e.g. the Justice Department's use of an 1800 HHI to indicate potential structural concerns)[7] and this provides a useful foundation for policymakers. Of course, the use of structural metrics such as the HHI is not foolproof, but they can yield useful initial guidance.[8]

Broadcasters typically compete for advertising revenue by bundling programming with advertising and selling the advertising time. In this sense, the broadcaster mediates between advertisers and consumers in a two-sided market. Two-sided markets are markets where a platform facilitates the market interaction of two different groups or end-users (Rochet and Tirole, 2004). Two-sided markets have attracted increasing attention from economists.[9]

Early literature relating to broadcast media competition (and product diversity) includes Steiner (1952), Beebe (1977) and Spence and
Owen (1977). This literature, however, provides only modest guidance
to regulators. As Anderson and Coate (2003) rightly note, this early
literature's treatment of advertising is unsatisfactory:

> First, advertising levels and prices are assumed fixed ... and each program
> is assumed to carry an exogenously fixed number of advertisements. Second,
> the social benefits and costs created by advertisers' consumption of broad-
> casts are not considered. These features preclude analysis of the basic issue of
> whether market-provided broadcasts will carry too few or too many adver-
> tisements. More fundamentally, since advertising revenues determine the
> profitability of broadcasts, one cannot understand the nature of program-
> ming the market will provide without understanding the source of advertis-
> ing revenues. Since these revenues depend on both the prices and levels of
> advertising, [this] literature offers an incomplete explanation of advertising
> revenues and hence its conclusions concerning programming choices are
> suspect.

Competition in two-sided markets does not necessarily carry
straightforward welfare implications (Cunningham and Alexander,
2004; Anderson and Coate, 2003). First, there are two relevant groups
of consumers: viewers[10] and advertisers. Should advertisers' welfare be
counted in the social welfare calculation? In their most recent media
ownership rulemaking, the FCC eschewed consideration of advertisers'
welfare. This approach may significantly understate welfare losses by
failing to also consider the effects of advertising on consumer welfare in
goods markets (Cunningham and Alexander, 2004; Gal-Or and Dukes,
2003). Moreover, even if the regulatory authority counts only viewers
in its consumer welfare calculations, there is still the question of
whether the regulatory authority computes and counts the informative
value of advertising to viewers in their welfare calculation or just the
viewer's welfare from non-advertising media content (Anderson and
Coate, 2003; Gal-Or and Dukes, 2003). Once the regulatory authority
addresses these questions, it needs models of two-sided media markets
and, ideally, empirical estimation of these models' parameters to assess
relevant competition issues.

A thoughtful regulator might also examine the implications of competition (or, more broadly, market structure) on media quality, as
media quality may form an important part of consumers' preferences.
Theoretically, this would require a (possibly stochastic) relationship

between investment by media producers and media quality in a vertical product differentiation model. Empirical examination of competition's effect on programme quality would likely require a metric of broadcast quality or data on media producers' programming costs.

Finally, a thoughtful regulator might examine the effects of competition on news accuracy. Does increased competition imply greater accuracy or is accuracy unaffected by structure? This question is important as news accuracy may affect voter behaviour and the quality of political decision making. Coase (1974), Besley and Burgess (2002) and Besley and Prat (2001) suggest that a competitive market structure induces greater accuracy in the reporting of news. Alternatively, Mullainathan and Schleifer (2002) suggest that media competition does not by itself produce greater accuracy in reporting – rather, competition produces accuracy only if consumers prefer content heterogeneity and consume news from multiple sources. This environment produces a convergence to some 'average accuracy'.

Diversity: product, source and viewpoint

Diversity can refer to one of three somewhat elastic concepts: product, source and viewpoint. Product diversity refers to the number of different programme types; source diversity refers to the number of firms, ownership structure and the availability of substitutes; while viewpoint diversity refers to the variety of perspectives on important issues.

How, then, should a thoughtful regulator approach the diversity issue? First, the regulator needs to examine product diversity using product differentiation models and evaluate consumers' preferences for different types of programming. Because the economic approach to product diversity is rooted in the actual preferences of media consumers, the regulator might weight this type of product diversity heavily when evaluating diversity under the public interest standard. In short, empirical estimation of a two-sided media market model with product differentiation would inform the regulator about concentration's effect on product diversity. The regulator could then construct structural rules that reflect the social welfare-maximising or the consumer welfare-maximising market structure.

Generic product differentiation models demonstrate a trade-off between price competition (e.g. advertising levels for media consumers) and product diversity (e.g. greater product diversity implies softer price competition). Therefore, the regulator might trade off possible consumer benefits from lower advertising (i.e. price) levels and the consumer benefits from media product diversity. Because product differentiation models examine welfare effects of both price competition and product diversity, empirical estimation of these models would enable the regulator to approximate the market structure that maximises welfare while accounting for both price competition and product diversity.

The thoughtful regulator could therefore use these two-sided market models to combine its economic analysis of competition and diversity. This analysis could be used to maximise the welfare of consumers or the combined welfare of consumers, media producers and advertisers within media markets. Wilbur (2004) outlines an empirical strategy for estimating such models. While Berry and Waldfogel (2001) present evidence that mergers in the radio industry increased music diversity and listenership, Wilbur's analysis might allow the regulatory authority to examine the actual effect of different media market structures on product diversity, advertising levels and consumer and advertiser welfare. Even within this framework, the regulator would have to make some important choices, since different types of product differentiation models generate different welfare effects from product diversity. The representative consumer model, for instance, generates much greater welfare increases from increases in product variety than does the Salop (1979) model.[11]

The regulator would still face yet more work on diversity. In addition to programme diversity, the regulator considers other 'types' of diversity, which include source (i.e. the number of firms, ownership structure, availability of substitutes) and viewpoint (i.e. a variety of perspectives on important issues) diversity. Source and viewpoint diversity have their roots in political-economic concerns about limiting the power of any single media owner to influence voters' beliefs, and consideration of source and viewpoint diversity could substantially affect the regulator's evaluation of overall diversity in media markets.[12] For example, the debates between different political factions about talk radio and media bias clearly illustrate the importance of viewpoint diversity to political discourse.

One might initially assume that the regulator can completely observe the welfare effects of the availability of substitutes within the framework of two-sided markets with product differentiation. However, if the availability of substitutes also affects citizens' abilities to make informed votes within the political market place, then consideration of these effects should also factor into the regulator's calculation of the optimal media market structure.[13] The additional consideration of viewpoint diversity could mitigate either for or against concentration. If, for example, firms treat viewpoint as a product characteristic and concentration increases product differentiation, then the extra political-economic benefits of increased viewpoint diversity actually favour greater concentration.

Note that, by definition, increasing concentration reduces source diversity. Thus, viewpoint diversity and source diversity might be complements or substitutes, depending on the relationship between concentration and viewpoint diversity: if concentration increases viewpoint diversity, then viewpoint diversity and source diversity are substitutes; however, if concentration decreases viewpoint diversity, then viewpoint diversity and source diversity are complements.

Moreover, if 'viewpoint' is an important product characteristic in a broadcaster's product differentiation decision, then product diversity *is* viewpoint diversity. The thoughtful regulator then might consider a product differentiation model that heavily weights product diversity because increased viewpoint diversity may generate more voter-relevant information. For example, the regulator could employ a Hotelling model of viewpoint differentiation and assume a strongly convex consumer 'transportation cost' to reflect the public good of viewpoint diversity.[14]

Along these lines, Djankov et al. (2003) suggest that government ownership of media sources correlates with less political and economic freedom for citizens, a finding that does not contradict the idea that viewpoint diversity allows the citizenry to more effectively exert control over their government. Moreover, Mullainathan and Schleifer (2002) contend that competition generates a distribution of viewpoints that roughly mirrors the viewpoint distribution among media consumers.

Because source diversity does not necessarily imply more product or viewpoint diversity, the concept of source diversity suffers serious problems. If one defines source diversity as simply the number of media firms, then one confronts the following tautology: more owners increase source diversity because source diversity is defined as the number of owners. This line of reasoning does not prove particularly helpful. However, we may be able to rescue the idea of source diversity with a more nuanced definition. Source diversity could refer to media owners with additional political-economic interests that lead them to cover (or not cover) news events in a particular way. For example, a media owner with extra-media business interests bidding for a contract with a municipality may face incentives to avoid negative coverage of that municipality's officials. If media owners have extra-media interests that may affect their news coverage, then regulatory authorities may have an interest in guaranteeing sufficient competition from other sources. This would be an instance where viewpoint and source diversity would have a complementary relationship. This possibility may loom larger at the local level than at the national level as consumers may tend to access fewer sources for their local news coverage.

Localism

Localism may be the feature of the FCC's media regulation that most differentiates the FCC from a conventional antitrust authority. Localism is not well defined but appears to be political in origin. The policy goal of localism likely flows from three unique institutional features of the United States' version of democracy. First, the locally representative United States Congress is separate from the executive branch. Unlike most European parliamentary democracies where the representative branch and executive branch are the same, the locally elected US congressional representatives serve in a different body than the nationally elected US executive. Second, the United States is large and extremely diverse and the locally elected representatives therefore serve far more divergent interests than locally elected representatives in many other representative democracies. These interests can also diverge heavily from those of the nationally elected executive, even if the representative and executive belong to the same political party. Finally, the United States Congress is bicameral, with two equally powerful legislative bodies, the House of Representatives and the Senate. One of those legislative bodies, the Senate, gives equal representation to each of the fifty states, regardless of their size. California, with a population of 35.5 million, has two senators, as does Wyoming, with a population of 0.5 million.

When radio, the first mass medium, began achieving significant penetration in the late 1920s and early 1930s, the United States

Congress and the newly created FCC created a regulatory framework that gave each representative and senator the capacity to reach their constituents through radio. This new regulatory framework also tried to (1) meet the representatives' and senators' goal that their constituents receive radio services that reflected their unique (and undefined) local needs and (2) meet representatives' and senators' desire that virtually all of their constituents receive at least one relatively clear radio signal. Given the locally based radio requirement, this framework eliminated a BBC-type model, where one dominant government-subsidised firm provided mass media services to the entire population. In addition, this framework eliminated the competition-maximising model of additional competing national networks because radio had to be locally licensed. By allowing only a small number of nationally available radio networks, this framework also insulated the National Broadcasting Company from strong competition from other potential national radio broadcasters.

We have suggested that the pursuit of localism has flowed from specific institutional features in the United States' political structure and this pursuit led to specific regulatory features. Still, no one has clearly defined localism itself. We therefore face the following two options. First, localism receives the tautological status of being whatever the FCC (with congressional approval) decides it is because the FCC, by definition, makes decisions that promote localism. Second, the FCC and/or Congress define localism in a way that makes it measurable, which then creates benchmarks for evaluating the efficacy of regulatory decisions.[15]

Recently, the FCC announced the launch of a 'Localism Task Force' to evaluate the performance of broadcasters in local markets. As FCC Chairperson Michael Powell stated:

Broadcasters must serve the public interest, and the Commission has consistently interpreted this to require broadcast licensees to air programming that is responsive to the interests and needs of their communities.[16]

Thus, the definition of localism employed by the FCC appears rooted in the idea of communities.[17] The concept of a community is particularly useful when the objectives of policymakers are political-economic, since measures of state- and county-level localism have the benefit of clear, well-defined boundaries. One could therefore construct a definition of localism based on political coverage that is specifically relevant to voters in a locality. This could include coverage of a state's US senatorial delegation, coverage of a US representative within the representative's district, coverage of the state legislature, coverage of a state representative within their district and coverage of local politics.

One reason why political boundaries might matter is that the information consumed within these boundaries may affect voters' ability to attract government funds. Stromberg (2004a), through a study of disbursements under a 'New Deal' programme during the 1930s, demonstrates that the availability of media can have a very strong effect on political outcomes and income transfers. Under the particular programme Stromberg explores, the federal government made cash grants to state governments, which then disbursed the money to various counties. According to Stromberg, radio penetration within a county increased that county's aid disbursement – the funds allocated to a county increased by approximately 5 per cent for every 10 per cent increase in radio penetration. Stromberg also finds that radio penetration increased voter turnout by 1.2 per cent for every 10 per cent increase in radio penetration.

Moreover, George and Waldfogel (2002) find evidence that locally based media increase turnout in local elections. They suggest that an increase in local penetration by the *New York Times* decreases local penetration by the local newspaper, reducing local news content and participation in local elections. They contend that consumption of local media may therefore confer a consumption externality. This contention may, perhaps heroically, assume that somebody's choice to vote somehow confers benefits on others. Meanwhile, voter participation may proxy for other forms of socially valuable civic engagement (e.g. attending school board meetings). This difference raises an important issue: if voting itself confers positive externalities, then political boundaries are the relevant boundaries for analysing the public goods flowing from local content. However, if voting simply proxies for civic engagement, then the relevant local boundaries may not be political but rather reflective of the social, demographic and geographic characteristics that define a community.

Practically speaking, one can construct necessary and sufficient conditions for defining localism using market-generated systems that define local communities. For example, one might define communities in the United States using the delineation of designated market areas (DMA) as determined by Nielsen Media Research (an independent audience measurement system). According to Nielsen, 'In designing the DMA regions, Nielsen Media Research uses proprietary criteria, testing methodologies and data to partition regions of the United States into geographically distinct television viewing areas, and then expresses them in unique, carefully defined regions that are meaningful to the specific business we conduct.'[18] The 'specific business' referred to is the sale of advertising time and space to advertisers. According to the California Newspaper Publishers Association:

DMA is a term used by advertising agencies to define specific geographical areas where groups of people tend to live, work and conduct their normal day-to-day activities similar to others in the same general region. DMA boundaries are often defined by significant geographical changes in a region's landscape such as mountain ranges, deserts, or sparsely populated areas. These 'natural barriers' often tend to create different and unique lifestyles among entire populations of people, creating unique and identifiable designated market areas. Each DMA generally has its own unique market characteristics and measurable consumer media usage patterns used by media buyers to help identify the newspapers, TV and radio stations most likely to reach the audience targeted by the client.[19]

Thus, the 'necessary' part of the necessary and sufficient conditions for market-based localism is that media coverage takes place within the DMA.

A second element of localism, the 'sufficient' condition, concerns the broadcast output, i.e. when is output reported by a station within the DMA 'local' output? One decision rule might be that the output is local if it is of at least marginally greater importance to the mean individual residing within the DMA than to the mean individual not residing within the DMA, and if one believes the mean individual within the DMA would identify the output as local.[20] Thus, it is the value of the output to the individual within a DMA, and that individual's perception of the output as local relative to individuals in other DMAs, that gives the output its 'sufficient' local context.[21]

Using this definition of localism, researchers would then need to observe a sample of media output across a variety of locales and assess which output is local under the necessary and sufficient conditions. This output would then have the product characteristic called 'local'. Researchers could then study various measures of consumer appeal (such as ratings) in these locales to assess which market structures in different locales deliver the level of localism that viewers most prefer.

This method would ideally be part of a structural analysis of two-sided media markets. In addition, researchers could use this definition of localism to examine whether localism has an effect on outcomes such as election turnouts or government disbursements like George and Waldfogel (2002) and Stromberg (2004b). One might also want to focus on coverage of local politics or of an area's representative and their ability to bring state or federal government largesse to their locality.

Finally, unlike the policy goal of diversity, where the FCC adopted a purely structural index, the FCC appears to vacillate between embracing and eschewing structural mechanisms for achieving the policy goal of localism. Consider the comments of Commission Chairperson Michael Powell:

> We again affirm the goal of promoting localism through limits on ownership of broadcast outlets. We sought to promote localism to the greatest extent possible through broadcast ownership limits.[22]

Despite this comment, one month later Powell stated:

> It is important to understand that ownership rules have always been, at best, imprecise tools for achieving policy goals like localism. That is why the FCC has historically sought more direct ways of promoting localism in broadcasting. These include things such as public interest obligations, license renewals, and protecting the rights of local stations to make programming decisions for their communities.[23]

Thus, it may be unclear whether the FCC wishes to employ structural measures, behavioural mechanisms or perhaps both. Importantly, besides the obvious conceptual reasons for employing structural measures, there are practical motivations that might warrant employing a structural approach. For example, if content regulation is found to impinge on a broadcaster's First Amendment rights, then the FCC, absent structural regulation, would have no means of addressing an important policy variable. Importantly, if researchers could measure localism using political and/or market-based metrics, they could test Powell's proposition and evaluate the efficacy of both structural and behavioural mechanisms in promoting localism.

8.3 Policy trade-offs: an illustration

We have articulated the policy rubrics of competition, diversity and localism that the FCC pursues under its statutory obligation to serve the public interest and we have shown that economic analysis illuminates each of these policy goals, even those that appear difficult to define. In addition, we have discussed some of the trade-offs and tensions between competition, diversity and localism. Before exploring the potential effects of a generalised transition to digital delivery platforms, a brief historical discussion regarding broadcast licence allocation helps illuminate these trade-offs in the context of a concrete FCC policy.

The FCC's initial allocation of broadcast licences reflects some of the policy tensions and contradictions that we have just explored. The initial allocation of broadcast television and radio licences by the FCC had some intent of promoting localism. This localism objective, and the assignment of broadcast frequency to local communities, had at least one important opportunity cost: a greater number of national networks and hence a greater number of VHF channels for residents of most locales. Given the constraints imposed by available spectrum and power, most residents in the USA could have accessed six national VHF channels; instead the available frequencies were assigned to local channels, precluding additional national networks and limiting residents of many localities to far less than six VHF channels.[24]

Adopted on 11 April 1952, the FCC's Sixth Report and Order, in Docket 8736 and 8975, assigned television spectrum using 'five priorities'.[25] The five priorities were:

1. Provide at least one television station to all parts of the United States.
2. Provide each community with at least one television broadcast station.
3. Provide a choice of at least two television services to all parts of the United States.
4. Provide each community with at least two television broadcast stations.
5. Assign any channels which remained under the foregoing priorities to the various communities depending on the size of the population of each community, the geographical location of such community and the number of television services available to such community from television stations located in other communities.

The five priorities were originally expounded in the 22 March 1951 Third Notice of Proposed Rule Making. Interestingly, these principles may be based on a facially innocuous misquoting of the 1934 Act. Section 307(b) of the 1934 Federal Communications Act states that 'the Commission shall make such distribution of licenses, frequencies, hours of operation, and of power among the several States and communities as to provide a fair, efficient, and equitable distribution of radio *service* to each of the same' (emphasis added). However, the Third Notice said that it had 'endeavored to meet the twofold objective set forth in Sections 1 and 307(b) of the Communications Act of 1934, to provide television service, as far as possible to all people of the United States and to provide a fair, efficient, and equitable distribution of television broadcast *stations* to the several states and communities' (emphasis added).

This apparently small distinction between *stations* and *service* may have important implications. For example, had the FCC licensed the television spectrum nationally, all viewers in all localities could have received six VHF channels, which could have carried six national television networks. By licensing *stations* locally, the FCC may have created a less equitable distribution of *service* for viewers: due to spectrum scarcities, viewers in smaller localities received fewer VHF channels. Aside from legal issues, in pursuing priority two to guarantee at least one channel to each locality and priority four to guarantee at least two channels to each locality (in combination with rules capping ownership at five VHF stations), the FCC traded channel space, which would have provided more competition and diversity, for locally licensed and locally owned channels. In fact, due to the increasing returns nature of media distribution, the FCC's decision may have promoted localism at the expense of diversity as well as competition.

8.4 Digital transition and convergence

Spence and Owen (1977) first noted that media firms faced large up-front fixed costs and constant (and often low) marginal costs. Any given programme or content therefore required an audience large enough to cover these up-front fixed costs. George and Waldfogel (2002) introduced the notion of preference externalities, which stem from media's distinctive cost structure. Because any content requires a large enough audience to cover its up-front fixed costs, each consumer's utility depends on the preferences of other consumers. If, for example, only one radio listener in Smallville likes jazz, then no radio station will air jazz because no radio station could cover its fixed costs with only one listener. Stromberg (2004b) points out the political-economic implications of these preference externalities resulting from scale effects, observing that 'minority' groups might be politically underrepresented, which could then bias public policy.[26] However, at least some of these policy concerns may be offset by media 'convergence'.

Generalised digital platforms (e.g. cable, satellite, digital television) are expanding the set of delivery systems and content for consumers and potentially diminishing the separation between radio, television, cable, telephony and newspapers. As we noted in the introduction, this increase in overall capacity may have surprising and counter-intuitive implications for media policy. In particular, the increase in capacity may lessen both the diversity gains from concentration and the diversity loss from localism. There are two related facets to this argument.

Steiner (1952) suggests that concentration increases product diversity.[27] Expanding channel capacity, however, diminishes the marginal gain in diversity from any marginal increase in concentration. Following Steiner, we can illustrate this point with an example. Assume there are three available programmes – a baseball game, an opera and a play – and three types of viewers. Further assume that 1,000 viewers like the baseball game, 200 viewers like the opera and 100 viewers like the play. Finally, assume there are three channels.

As Steiner (1952) points out, three competitors would all duplicate the baseball game because it would attract 333 viewers for each of the three channels, which is more than the 200 viewers who would watch an opera or the 100 viewers who would watch a play. If a monopolist owned all three channels, however, they would choose to air the baseball game on one channel, the opera on another channel and the play on the final channel, thereby capturing all of the viewers. Quite simply, because the monopolist internalises the business-stealing externality, they have no incentive to duplicate programming. Therefore, in our three-channel world, the monopolist delivers programming that appeals to 1,300 viewers, while a competitive market structure would only deliver programming that appeals to 1,000 viewers (after rounding). In the three-channel world, the monopolist would serve 300 more viewers than the competitive market structure.

Now imagine that a technological change expands the capacity to six available channels. A monopolist would still air a baseball game, an opera and a play. Under a competitive market structure with six independently owned channels, however, five competitors would air the baseball game, each attracting 200 viewers, and one competitor would air the opera, also attracting 200 viewers. Thus, a monopolist delivers programming that appeals to 1,300 viewers, while a competitive market structure would deliver programming that appeals to 1,200 viewers. In the six-channel world, the monopolist now would serve only 100 more viewers than the competitive market structure.

Finally, if technological change expanded the number of channels to thirteen, a competitive market structure would serve as many viewers as the monopolist. Baseball would air on ten channels, opera would air on two channels and one channel would air the play. As we suggested above, as capacity expands, the relative gains to consumers from concentration-induced product diversity fall.[28]

In addition, nationally distributed media may solve another challenge to diversity. Many media products incur up-front fixed costs and constant (and often low) marginal costs. Consequently, media firms will produce only content that appeals to enough people to cover their fixed costs. Locally based media may not produce adequate diversity because not enough consumers with a particular preference live in the same locality. Nationally available media like satellite radio help resolve this problem because they can aggregate the preferences of consumers across the nation, which means they can cover the fixed costs of producing content that appeals to small (locally vanishing) groups of consumers.

Assume that a radio station requires 150 listeners to be viable. In city A 100 listeners like jazz and 100 listeners in city B like jazz. Local radio stations in cities A and B will therefore not air jazz because no station in A or B could attract enough listeners to be viable. A national radio service that reaches listeners in both cities, however, will produce jazz because the national radio service reaches 200 jazz listeners, which more than covers the fixed costs of its jazz service.

Increased capacity can thus increase diversity without increasing concentration. In addition, changes in platform technology promote new national media platforms that produce more diverse content by aggregating preferences across localities. Therefore, local over-the-air broadcasting could focus on localism without trading off as much competition or diversity and a regulator could promote localism without incurring as large a social cost.

8.5 Conclusion

Lessons for students: what have we learned?

The policy goals of competition, diversity and localism are sometimes at odds and economists may find it difficult to represent them all in a single framework. For example, a model of two-sided markets with product differentiation may be able to address competition, product diversity and perhaps one aspect of localism in a single framework; however, this framework would not address the political-economic issues in viewpoint diversity, source diversity and localism (i.e. localism that embodies externalities). As we have noted, the FCC has interpreted its public interest obligation through the lens of competition, diversity and localism. While competition policy may be tractable, the additional elements of diversity and localism lend considerable complexity and nuance for policymakers – in fact, as we have suggested, accounting for diversity and localism changes the nature of the competition analysis. We clarified diversity and offered definitions of localism that might help researchers and policymakers to more precisely measure both diversity and localism – this might enable policymakers to clearly observe trade-offs between competition, diversity and localism.

Lessons for researchers: what do we still need to know?

This chapter raises some possibly useful questions about media policy that researchers can probably help to answer. Researchers, such as Wilbur (2004), are currently estimating empirical models of two-sided media markets with product differentiation in broadcast television, which should help media policymakers address the issues of competition and product diversity in media markets. Further extensions in this area could prove helpful, e.g. empirically estimating two-sided models with both direct-pay and advertiser-supported television. Researchers could examine two-sided product differentiation models in national televisions news (both broadcast and cable) to determine how much news channels differentiate on content and viewpoint, and the implications of different policies on that differentiation. It is possible that researchers could tie these product differentiation models in two-sided markets with work on news accuracy and competition to analyse the effects of media policies on news accuracy.

With respect to localism, researchers might analyse the effects of different market structures on the diversity and content of local television news.

Finally, researchers might consider the effects of changing technology and convergence of technology on media content. For example, new technologies may enable consumers to choose their preferred programming and preferred advertising – advertisers may even compensate media consumers for watching their advertising. Researchers could then model two-sided media markets where consumers also choose the advertising they watch.

Lessons for policymakers: what are the priorities for policy in this area?

Obviously, policy weights of the three objectives are vital to any analysis. Thus, for example, political-economic considerations may imply policies that diminish the competition-diversity objective, e.g. mandated content might crowd out programming or other higher private-value advertising. Policymakers should trade away privately valued content for public interest content *only* when the public interest content confers sufficient external public benefits.

How can the FCC or any other regulator calculate this seemingly incalculable trade-off? Moreover, even if the FCC could calculate this trade-off, the FCC depends on congressional appropriations and is sensitive to interest group activism. Do these political incentives lead to FCC policies that enhance the social welfare or do they lead to FCC policies that diminish social welfare? The answer to this question may determine whether the FCC should regulate media content at all.

References

Anderson, Simon and Coate, Stephen (2003) 'Market Provision of Public Goods: The Case of Broadcasting', NBER Working Paper 7513.
Armstrong, Mark (2002) 'Competition in Two-Sided Markets', mimeo, Oxford University.

Beebe, Jack (1977) 'Institutional Structure and Program Choices in Television Markets', *Quarterly Journal of Economics*, 91(1), 15–37.

Berry, Steven and Waldfogel, Joel (2001) 'Do Mergers Increase Product Variety? Evidence From Radio Broadcasting', *Quarterly Journal of Economics*, 116(3), 1009–1025.

Besley, Timothy and Burgess, Robin (2002) 'The Political Economy of Government Responsiveness: Theory and Evidence from India', *Quarterly Journal of Economics*, 117(4), 1415–1451.

Besley, Timothy and Prat, Andrea (2001) 'Handcuffs for the Grabbing Hand? Media Capture and Government Accountability', Working Paper, London School of Economics.

Coase, Ronald (1974) 'The Market for Goods and the Market for Ideas', *American Economic Review*, 64(2), Papers and Proceedings, May, 384–391.

Cunningham, Brendan M. and Alexander, Peter J. (2004) 'A Model of Broadcast Media and Commercial Advertising', *Journal of Public Economic Theory*, 6(4), 557–575.

Djankov, Simeon, McLiesh, Caralee, Nenova, Tatiana and Schleifer, Andrei (2003) 'Who Owns the Media?', *The Journal of Law and Economics*, 46, 341–382.

Gabszewicz, J.J., Laussel, D. and Sonnac, N. (2000), 'TV-Broadcasting Competition and Advertising', Working Paper, Catholique de Louvain – Center for Operations Research and Economics.

Gal-Or, Esther and Dukes, Anthony (2003) 'Minimum Differentiation in Commercial Media Markets', *Journal of Economics and Management Strategy*, 12(3), 291–326.

George, Lisa and Waldfogel, Joel (2002) 'Does the New York Times Spread Ignorance and Apathy?', Working Paper.

Mullainathan, Sendhil and Schleifer, Andrei (2002) 'Media Bias', Working Paper.

Nilssen, Tore and Sørgard, Lars (2000) 'TV Advertising, Programme Quality, and Product-Market Oligopoly', Working Paper Series CPC00-012, Competition Policy Center, Institute for Business and Economic Research, UC Berkeley.

Rochet, Jean-Charles and Tirole, Jean (2004) 'Platform Competition with Two-Sided Markets', Working Paper.

Salop, Steven (1979) 'Monopolistic Competition with Outside Goods', *Bell Journal of Economics*, 10(1), 141–156.

Spence, Michael and Owen, Bruce (1977) 'Television Programming, Monopolistic Competition, and Welfare', *Quarterly Journal of Economics*, 91(1), 103–126.

Steiner, Peter (1952) 'Program Patterns and Preferences, and the Workability of Competition in Radio Broadcasting', *Quarterly Journal of Economics*, 66(2), 194–223.

Stromberg, David (2004a) 'Radio's Impact on Public Spending', *Quarterly Journal of Economics*, 119(1), 189–221.

Stromberg, David (2004b) 'Mass Media Competition, Political Competition, and Public Policy', *Review of Economic Studies*, 71(1), 265–284.

Waldfogel, Joel (2002) 'Consumer Substitution among Media', Washington, DC: FCC Media Ownership Working Group, October.

Wilbur, Kenneth (2004) 'Not All Eyeballs Are Created Equal: A Structural Equilibrium Model of Television Advertisers, Networks, and Viewers', Working Paper.

Notes

* The views and opinions expressed in this chapter are strictly our own and do not necessarily reflect those of the Federal Communications Commission, any of the Commissioners or any other staff. We thank Paul Seabright, David Sappington and Adam Candeub for their many useful comments.

1. One important thread throughout this work, often implicit in the analysis of media industries, is whether diversity in civic discourse is fundamentally distinct from entertainment diversity in commercial media markets.

2. In its June 2003 media ownership rulemaking, the FCC changed the methodology by which it calculated relevant local radio markets, replacing its signal contour methodology with a geographic market methodology. The FCC permitted those owners that had been within the ownership limits under the old signal contour methodology but which now exceeded the limits under the new geographic market methodology to retain ownership of their stations.

3. Affiliate agreements with independent stations provide networks with national reach.

4. In 1996 (2004) there were approximately 1,132 (1,275) full-power commercial broadcast television stations and 450 (331) unique owners.

5. As we explore later in this chapter, the argument for diversity in ownership has been linked to the robustness of broader democratic processes and some recent research suggests that ownership diversity in broadcast media may be a necessary (although not sufficient) condition for a healthy democratic process.

6. The state-contingent nature of media consumption (e.g. one cannot watch television or read the newspaper while driving but can listen to the radio)

may be an important element regarding substitutability not accounted for in current research. Moreover, changes in the number of commuters and overall commuting time is an important as yet unexplored factor in determining consumption patterns. In addition, one-way substitution patterns may drive many of the important results (e.g. one cannot watch television while driving but can listen to the radio while cooking).

7. The HHI (Hirschman–Herfindahl Index) is the sum of the squared market shares of the firms within a market.

8. Although arbitrary, an HHI of 1800 has become focal for policymakers. This metric, however, is only half the issue. As we note, there may be a trade-off between competition and diversity, such that increasing concentration within broadcast media may actually promote greater diversity of output.

9. Armstrong (2002) offers a summary of recent work. Cunningham and Alexander (2004), Gabszewicz, Laussel, and Sonnac (2000), Gal-Or and Dukes (2003) and Nilssen and Sørgard (2000), and Anderson and Coate (2003) model advertiser-supported media markets in explicit two-sided frameworks.

10. These would be listeners in the context of radio markets.

11. The Salop model, for example, finds parameters where introducing a tax increases economic welfare within the market because the scale effects from having fewer firms outweigh the lost welfare from decreased product variety.

12. In 2003, the FCC completed a review of media ownership rules and proposed new media ownership guidelines (which were subsequently remanded by the United States Third Circuit Court in 2004). As part of the proposed guidelines, the Commission developed a structural measure, designed to mimic the HHI, for source diversity (i.e. the number of firms, ownership structure, availability of substitutes). In essence, the FCC proposed that one could add up the various 'voices' in a market and then sum them into one discrete metric that would serve much the same function as the HHI does for the Justice Department. However, the Third Circuit Court concluded that the Diversity Index, as presented, was 'arbitrary and capricious', stating that a 'diversity index that requires us to accept that a community college television station makes a greater contribution to viewpoint diversity than a conglomerate that includes the third-largest newspaper in America (the *New York Times*) requires us to abandon both logic and reality'. It appears therefore that a simple counting measure will not suffice as a metric for viewpoint diversity.

13. One may want to consider the relative size of this effect if voters choose some degree of rational ignorance.

14. In the Hotelling and other location-type models, the consumer transportation cost reflects the disutility that consumers suffer from moving away from their preferred product type. A high transportation cost therefore creates a strong social benefit from product diversity.
15. We leave the question open as to which option Congressional representatives and the FCC prefer.
16. http://www.fcc.gov/localism/ Last accessed 27 October 2004.
17. We recognise but abstract from the notion of communities that are connected via cyberspace. Instead, we opt for definitions that have a purely physical proximity component. Without this component, we suggest that the definition of localism as related to communities becomes far too elastic to be useful to policymakers.
18. Federal Communications Commission document, letter from Nielsen Media Research to the Commission, 3 April 2003, 98–206. Geographic continuity is a standard feature of all 210 DMAs except three.
19. California Newspaper Publishers Association, http://www.cnpa.com/snap/dma_map.htm
20. For example, news about a bake sale in Phoenix is likely to be more important to a resident of Phoenix than to a resident of Boston. In addition, the resident of Phoenix would probably identify news about a bake sale in Phoenix as local. Meanwhile, news regarding federal budget issues would likely be non-local even to residents of Washington DC even though the negotiations take place in Washington, since the average resident of Washington would probably not classify the story as local.
21. DMA is specific to the medium of television as Nielsen developed this measure for the purpose of measuring television audiences in different locales. In order to perform a similar analysis with radio, one could use Arbitron Metro Survey Areas, which classify radio stations by community and correspond to the United States Census Bureau's Metropolitan Statistical Areas. In fact, in its most recent media ownership rulemaking, the FCC proposed using Arbitron Metro Survey Areas to define local radio markets.
22. Statement of Chairman Michael K. Powell, re: 2002 Biennial Regulatory Review – Review of the Commission's Ownership Rules and Other Rules Adopted Pursuant to Section 202 of the Telecommunications Act of 1996; July 2003 – http://hraunfoss.fcc.gov/edocs_public/attachmatch/FCC-03-127A3.doc
23. FCC press release, 'FCC Chairman Powell Launches Localism in Broadcasting Initiative', 20 August 2003.
24. Some may contend that the modern MVPD universe (i.e. cable and satellite) makes irrelevant the concern over an additional one-to-six VHF channels. However, because a single VHF channel can be subdivided

into several digital channels, the upcoming transition to digital signals multiplies the opportunity cost of each lost VHF channel.

25. Paragraph 63.

26. This possible bias may be more likely in a European-style parliamentary system than that of a federal system as found in the United States.

27. Steiner's model has been roundly and rightly criticised for its restrictive assumptions. Anderson and Coate (2003) demonstrate, however, that Steiner's 'monopoly increases welfare' result can occur in a much richer, more flexible model.

28. Monopoly may still dominate from a social welfare perspective if the monopolist serves as many viewers while incurring fewer costs.

9 | *The European Union*

PIERRE BUIGUES AND VALÉRIE
RABASSA*

9.1 Introduction

An overview of media markets shows that rapid growth and the integration of some of the most dynamic market segments are characteristics of this fast-moving industry. The main players are the established incumbents upstream and the delivery segments of media downstream. The presence of incumbents, inheritors of previous public monopolies, has led Member States to use regulation in a complementary role with competition.

In these markets, strategies to deliver new products and services and to serve new geographic markets focus less on organic growth than on alliances and mergers in order to create multi-media offshoots, bid for control of content rights, increase the diffusion of products and services, and develop technologies for conditional access and transmission standards to capture advantages through proprietary technology. As a result, vertically integrated dominant positions either upstream or downstream have tended to emerge. There is nothing wrong with vertical integration except when there is market power at one stage of the vertical chain.

Indeed, as far as the media industry is concerned, there are some specific challenges at the European level. The new EU regulatory framework grants some specific competition principles which can be integrated into *ex ante* regulation. EU merger control may also prevent potential distortion of competition resulting from the creation or the strengthening of a single or collective dominant position in the media sector at a horizontal level, or from foreclosure effects at a vertical level. EU antitrust control may also ensure that media firms do not engage in restrictive agreements with competitors or abuse their market power to the detriment of competitors and consumers. Last, the application of the EU state aid rules should guarantee that competition issues in the media sector are properly addressed.[1]

9.2 Overview of the media industry

Market players, market size and the value-added chain

Many players interact along the media vertical chain (see Figure 9.1). The classical typology of activities in media markets is the following:[2]

- *The rights holders* (sports, books, music labels, events, etc.) usually include rights owners and rights dealers. Rights owners are the primary source of content rights. They usually grant rights to content

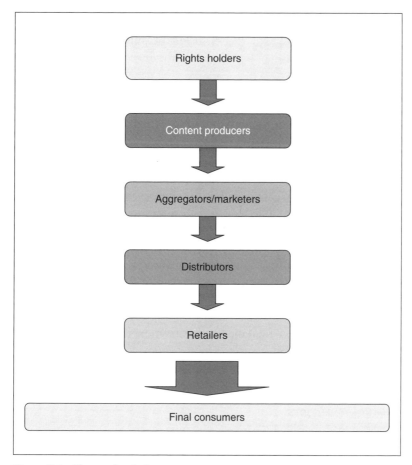

Figure 9.1. The media chain

producers. Rights dealers are intermediary players who may exploit the rights directly from the rights owners or may intervene in the selling of content productions.

- *The content producers* (film producers, TV producers, publishers, etc.) are responsible for the production of content by combining know-how and the exploitation of rights.[3]
- *The aggregators/marketers* are responsible for the aggregation of different contents. In the TV business, typical aggregators are public service or free commercial broadcasters as well as pay-TV operators. The growing importance of the internet has prompted internet service providers (ISPs) to become also aggregators of content and content suppliers are offering their services more and more via the internet. In the book industry, marketers are also called diffusors and are responsible for the diffusion of publishing houses. The aggregators are often associated with distributors, though not always.
- *The distributors* are responsible for the transport and the distribution of content products to end-users – either *retailers* or *final customers* – via all forms of distribution technologies or *networks*: satellite, cable, terrestrial ADSL, mobile network or via traditional transports of books, CDs, etc. The cable industry dominated the pay-television landscape with a mostly one-way analogue system capable of delivering forty channels, but the direct broadcast satellite now competes with the cable industry's former monopoly position. The competition from satellite in the pay-TV market has had the effect that now cable operators hugely invest in upgrading their old infrastructure into a two-way digital broadband system. Distributors also may be considered as access providers whose role is to manage end-users and are responsible for the billing process and customer relationship.
- *The retailers* are the final media players in the value chain. Retailers sell the content products to the final customers either directly or via end-user equipment such as set-top boxes, etc.

Business strategies

Increasing competition and the importance of technological investment have brought about a change in the industry structure leading to the creation of large integrated and international audio-visual groups.[4] In particular, the industry evolution has been characterised by various trends in the past years:

- the diversification of access providers and networks into content production and the packaging industry, these companies wanting to move up the value-added chain of industry and to capture a larger share of consumer spending;[5]
- the investment of paper-press firms in the audio-visual industry, since audio-visual operators are competing for the same advertising budgets;[6]
- the diversification of companies not previously active in the media industry into the audio-visual industry, expecting that media would generate higher returns than traditional industries;[7]
- the diversification of the customer equipment industry into content production to be able to impose their standards when launching new services.[8]

Indeed, these different strategies on the part of the media players have led to a large change in the media industry structure. Key forces in the media environment may also have an effect on the market structure. Increasing costs for premium rights content may increase competition between broadcasters and may favour *de novo* a strategy of vertical integration. In other segments like the content production, barriers to entry may decrease as a result of the digitalisation of the industry. The proliferation of new formats may also lead to new entrants. The increasing number of network technologies may raise competition between access providers and between aggregators/marketers for audience and advertising. Market consolidation by large pan-European groups may limit the access to distribution channels for small or regional content producers or aggregators/marketers.

Finally, the media industry is characterised by a clear dynamic trend. As a result of emerging technologies and innovation, new formats and products are constantly appearing, thus creating new markets with new rights attached. The strategies of the different media players have also led to (i) a higher degree of media convergence and (ii) in order to protect or extend market power to another segment of the media chain, strong vertical relationships – either through exclusive contracts or ownership linkages. Indeed, the key questions for competition authorities and regulators are as follows:

- Within the EU, both at national and European level, should these market changes result in changes in the regulatory framework?

- Should antitrust and merger control apply to the media industry as in other sectors?
- In particular, how does competition policy apply to premium rights like sports or film rights?

9.3 Regulation versus competition in the communication services and media sector

Are competition rules sufficient to ensure consumer welfare in sectors that have been recently liberalised, such as television, telecommunications or the media more generally?

It is widely accepted that in the media industry 'relying mainly on competition policy to regulate the industry may not be the best approach, not only because ... competition policy does not safeguard specific objectives attached to the broadcasting industry (e.g. maintaining a pluralism of views) but also precisely because of the particular nature of the competition in this industry' (Rey, 1997).

Moreover, these sectors are still dominated by incumbents who are the inheritors of previous public monopolies. This has led Member States to use regulation and competition in a complementary role in the process of liberalisation. In some EU countries, competition and regulatory authorities are even merged or they combine the regulators of related sectors. In the UK, Ofcom[9] combines regulatory and competition competences and has supervisory functions such as overseeing media plurality, control of use and regulated use of common facilities.

On the regulatory side, the European Union has developed a framework in which national regulatory authorities (NRAs) implement European-wide directives in close cooperation with the Directorate General of the Commission in charge of the specific regulation (DG INFSO, DG EAC) and EC competition law (DG COMP) applies in parallel. That implies close cooperation between regulators and competition authorities in the liberalised sectors (telecommunications, television, radio).

In the old regulatory framework for electronic communications, different rules applied for basically the same services depending on the use of different technical infrastructures. The new regulatory framework for electronic communication services and networks (which has been in place since July 2003) is a response to the convergence challenge with the possibilities offered by new technology (in particular digital technology) that enable data to be transmitted to a very large number of users through different networks. Applications and services are decoupled from the mechanisms of transmission, and radio and television programmes may be delivered by mobile networks, cable, satellite, the internet, etc. At the same time, traditionally separate media may be put together (sound, video, voice, text) in a single multi-media production using digital technology. In the new regulatory framework, the same regulation applies for the same service independently of the technical infrastructure used.

If different services such as television, telephony and internet access can now be provided by different infrastructures (cable, television, telephone network or satellite), consumers are not interested in the network infrastructure itself but in what the new networks make possible in terms of media and content. At the same time, there is the question of whether the best approach to help consumers in terms of prices and range of services is through *ex ante* regulation or the application of competition rules. In principle, as competition becomes more effective with the process of liberalisation, much of the sector-specific regulation will be replaced by the application of general competition rules. *Ex ante* obligations should be imposed only where competition law remedies are not sufficient to address the problem. From that point of view the general objective of the new regulatory framework was to find the appropriate balance between an *ex ante* regulatory approach and an *ex post* competition approach (see Appendix 9.2 on the new regulatory framework).

Ex ante regulation focuses on the conditions of access to common facilities (pricing, non-discrimination) but also on other aspects, in particular in the media sector. In the USA, the Federal Communications Commission has long had regulations limiting media concentration and cross-ownership between different kinds of media such as newspapers or television. Competition policy instruments are used in the cases of abuse of dominant position or cartels to find structural or behavioural remedies. In the EU, regulatory and competition authorities are both trying to push the process of liberalisation of telecom and media sectors, opening the way to new entrants. As far as the media and communication sectors are concerned, there are challenges in areas where new technology developments and business strategies have required a response at a European level: recent challenges have arisen for both institutions with the promotion of competition in the last link with the final consumers via the cable or the local loop.

Cable

In June 1999, the Commission adopted a directive under Article 86(3)[10] on competition in telecommunication and media services. Pursuant to this directive, Member States must ensure that telecommunication operators in dominant positions pursue their cable television activities in structurally separate companies. A telecom operator active in cable and telephone networks is faced with the conflict of interests that exists between the operation of the two networks: investment and upgrading of the cable network that competes with its own telephone network or investment and upgrading of the telephone network which also allows broadband transmission and television services. Structurally, legal separation was the minimum regulatory requirement needed to deal with this problem but several operators took the decision to go one step further with the divestment of their cable network.

The directives also require Member States to allow cable television networks to provide telecommunication services under the same regulatory conditions as any pure telecommunication operators.

In the case of France, the provision of telecommunication services by the cable operators required the prior consultation of all the municipalities concerned and a number refused to allow cable operators to provide telephone services. Moreover, cable operators do not enjoy the same conditions for using public facilities as the telecommunication operators. For example, the charges for the use of public facilities are much higher for cable operators than for telecommunication operators. The Commission started an investigation in response to a complaint from the French Association of Multi-Service Network Operators and on 8 April 2003 sent France a reasoned opinion for having failed to comply with the 'Cable Directive' and the 'full competition' directive concerning the abolition of the restriction on the use of cable television networks for the provision of already liberalised telecommunication services.

Local 'loop unbundling'

In July 2000, the Commission proposed a new regulation requiring local loop unbundling which came into force on 2 January 2001. This regulation imposes mandatory access by new entrants to the incumbent telecommunication operator's local network in order to introduce competition in the last segment of the telecom networks. The local loop was considered to be the most appropriate means of delivering broadband services relatively cheaply, rapidly and efficiently to a widespread customer base. In many EU countries a very limited proportion of households is connected to a cable network and in other Member States cable networks still need costly upgrades to be appropriate for two-way broadband communication.

The main point of discussion was not so much the principle of the unbundling but the pricing of the local loop. In a report for the Commission, J. Gual and P. Seabright presented the two economic considerations to take into account: 'The first is that, given the networks are in place, access to these networks should be available to the operator that would make the most efficient use of them. The second issue is that investment in future networks should be encouraged by the promise of prices that enable a proper rate of return, including a return to risk taking.'

On 21 May 2003, the Commission adopted an Article 82 decision regarding the pricing strategy of Deutsche Telekom AG (DT).[11] The Commission found that DT was charging new entrants for wholesale access to the local loop fees which were either higher than or too close to what final users had to pay DT for its retail lines. This pricing policy ('margin squeeze') discouraged new entrants from entering the telecommunication market and therefore reduced the choice of suppliers of telecommunication services for final users. The Commission found that the price difference between DT's retail and wholesale prices was insufficient to cover DT's product-specific cost of providing its own retail services.

Transmission to end-users: an example of the new regulatory framework

Television and radio services are accessed through different transmission channels: the masts and sites of the terrestrial transmission network, cable transmission and satellite transmission. Generally, national regulatory authorities consider that cable and satellite transmission are in a different market from terrestrial transmission.

In many Member States, cable and satellite transmission services have regulation in place. In the UK, cable providers have an obligation to carry the public service channels free of charge to all cable viewers. Satellite providers are required to offer conditional access on regulated terms to all broadcasters.[12]

On the basis of the new regulatory framework for electronic communication, national regulators had to review competition in communication markets to ensure that regulation is appropriate, taking into account market conditions. In the UK, Ofcom has considered broadcasting television and radio transmission to end-users. Terrestrial transmission comes in two forms: analogue and digital. In terms of their customer base they are similar but they differ in the transmission equipment used and the capacity of carriage, with digital offering the possibility to carry much more content than analogue. Ofcom analysed the market position of NTL and Crown Castle, the two UK operators of the sites and the antennae support structure (mast and towers) for the purposes of broadcasting transmission in the UK. Its initial views were that Crown Castle and NTL both have significant power (dominant in the sense of Article 82, see Appendix 9.2) in the market for access to their respective masts and sites for analogue and digital terrestrial television broadcasting transmission services. However, for terrestrial radio transmission, Ofcom's views were that no transmission provider is dominant.

Given the ability of Crown Castle and NTL to behave to an appreciable extent independently of competitors and customers for analogue and digital terrestrial television broadcasting, Ofcom proposed to impose conditions on these operators:
- a requirement to provide network access on reasonable request and on fair and reasonable terms that are reflective of cost;
- a requirement to publish a reference offer and not to unduly discriminate.

These conditions will enable third parties (providers of electronic communication services and networks) to access NTL and Crown Castle masts and sites in order to broadcast television programmes in any area in the UK.

9.4 Antitrust and merger control in media markets

In parallel with the use of regulation by sectoral regulators, competition authorities intervene. Antitrust and merger control are instruments that can be applied by European regulators to prevent distortions of competition that may arise as a result of the creation, the strengthening or the abuse of dominant positions in the media markets. Both vertical and horizontal competitive concerns may arise in the media sectors.

Vertical issues

The rationale behind vertical foreclosure

Vertical mergers or exclusive vertical contracts may occur between firms when a firm's product is a component of or a complement to the product of another firm and where products are considered as being traded on two distinct markets. Evaluating vertical integration or exclusive vertical arrangements in dynamic and innovative markets like media markets presents challenges to competition policy. Such behaviour may achieve pro-competitive efficiency benefits. Indeed, vertical integration may undo the effects of imperfect competition at one stage of the vertical chain, eliminating the double marginalisation problem and creating efficiencies that benefit final consumers through lower prices.[13] It may lead to synergistic improvements of current products or to the development of new ones. These incentives may be important in the media business. It may also allow better coordination between upstream and downstream firms, generating cost efficiencies, for example, by streamlining distribution or lowering transaction costs. Finally, knowing that media contents are usually characterised by large sunk costs, vertical integration may encourage media operators to invest upstream, allowing them to keep downstream revenue flows under direct control.

However, competition concerns may arise in vertical integration when a firm has market power either at the upstream level or at the downstream level. This is also the case in exclusive vertical arrangements when contracts exhibit excessive duration or when exclusivity concerns premium contents. Such premium contents may also be bundled in joint selling arrangements and may thus remain inaccessible to potential entrants or current competitors. In these situations, a firm may restrict output in one market by using its market power in the other one, thus leading to foreclosure concerns. By definition, vertical foreclosure may arise when a dominant firm controls an input – the bottleneck segment – that is essential for an adjacent market – the potentially competitive market.[14] The bottleneck segment may be either upstream – on the content side – or downstream – on the distribution side.

The media industry may have characteristics that make foreclosure more likely. In media markets, behaviours that give rise to foreclosure issues are typically situations of leveraging market power from traditional onto new media markets or situations in which a dominant firm (i) denies access to premium content or to scarce distribution network needed by a potential entrant or a current competitor or (ii) grants long-term exclusive licences for premium content to a single operator.

Premium contents in the media business are by definition scarce inputs such as premium sport rights, film rights or music inputs. In a climate of a rapid growth characteristic of a fast-moving market and the emergence of new media markets, access to premium contents upstream is crucial to the developments of current competitors or new entrants downstream. In particular, premium contents are vital for new developing platforms such as mobile, ADSL or DTT,[15] which compete with dominant pay-TV operators. These contents usually boost the growth of innovative services and therefore the market demand. Access to scarce downstream technical platforms is also of high importance for upstream media operators. Without any access to this system and to the provision of related technical services, rivals would not be able to operate vigorously. Enforcers should balance efficiencies versus foreclosure concerns in order to ensure media players' access to key inputs, to promote market opening and innovation and therefore to enhance consumers' surplus.

In general, the European Commission has been concerned about the risks of foreclosure in the media industry. This position has been supported by some economists for whom 'the European Commission has rightly attached great importance to market foreclosure, denying joint ventures where monopolists or firms enjoying very high market power in upstream sectors could create joint ventures with downstream firms' (Motta and Polo (1997)). However, other economists are particularly sceptical about public intervention in the media sector based on a 'vertical foreclosure' argument, first because rapid technological changes in this industry make it very hard for regulators to predict the outcomes of their intervention and second because the effect of technological change is, broadly speaking, to lower entry barriers and therefore firms that appear very powerful today are less likely to be industry leaders in the future.

Merger control in the case of vertical mergers

The Commission has dealt with different foreclosure cases in a series of merger and antitrust decisions in the media industry. Recent merger decisions include AOL/Time Warner (2000), Vivendi/Universal (2000) and Telepiù/Stream (2003).[16] These transactions may reflect the motivation of players to gain access to all stages in the vertical chain with the final aim of deterring potential entry.

AOL/Time Warner

In 2000, the Commission gave conditional approval to the AOL/Time Warner merger. Time Warner is one of the world's biggest media and entertainment companies, with interests in television and cable networks, magazines, book publishing, music and filmed entertainment. AOL is the leading internet access provider in the United States and the only provider with a pan-European presence. In Europe, AOL operates mainly through two joint ventures: AOL Europe, a 50/50 deal with Bertelsmann, and AOL Compuserve France, a venture with both Bertelsmann and Vivendi subsidiaries Cegetel and Canal Plus.

The merger created (i) the first vertically integrated internet content provider, distributing Time Warner-branded content (music, news, films, etc.) through AOL's internet distribution network; (ii) a dominant player through the combination of the music library of Time Warner and Bertelsmann, accounting on average for approximately 30–40 per cent of all music rights at a European level and exceeding 30–40 per cent in a number of European countries. The concentration raised serious competition concerns, in particular because of the structural links and some existing contractual arrangements with Bertelsmann:

- AOL could have refused to carry the content of competitors of Time Warner and Bertelsmann or toughen the terms of trade to bias the market towards them. The latter strategy could have been implemented by AOL charging higher prices or degrading the quality of rivals' content, including making access to rival content slower or more difficult.
- Time Warner and Bertelsmann would have had an incentive to favour AOL and discriminate against competing network operators in Europe. Thus, Time Warner and Bertelsmann could have refused to

supply its content to other internet companies competing with AOL or toughen the terms of trade by means of price or non-price strategies. Therefore, in order to solve the competition problems created by the transaction, it was necessary to prevent AOL from having preferential access to both Time Warner's and Bertelsmann's music rights. To this end the parties gave a number of undertakings aimed at severing all structural links between AOL and Bertelsmann. As a result of these undertakings, Bertelsmann would progressively exit from its European joint ventures with AOL and AOL would meanwhile be precluded from exercising certain contractual rights, gaining preferential access to Bertelsmann's content.

Vivendi/Universal

In 2000, the Commission cleared the merger between Vivendi, Canal Plus and Seagram subject to conditions. Vivendi is a leading French company with activities in telecommunications networks and related services, cinema and pay-TV through its 49 per cent equity interest in Canal Plus and its 25 per cent equity interest in BSkyB (a British pay-TV operator). The Canadian group Seagram is active in particular in the film and music businesses, especially through its subsidiary Universal.

The integration of Universal's premium (films) content with Canal Plus would *per se* have strengthened the latter's market power in the pay-TV market. The transaction would also reinforce Canal Plus's bargaining power vis-à-vis the other US studios, in particular with respect to premium films. As a result, the pay-TV markets where Canal Plus was active would be foreclosed because of its control over the premium input.

Vivendi offered a package of commitments which included access for competitors to Universal's film production and coproduction. In particular, the parties undertook not to grant to Canal Plus 'first window' rights,[17] covering more than 50 per cent of Universal production and coproduction.[18]

Telepiù/Stream

In 2003, the Commission cleared the merger between Stream and Telepiù subject to conditions. Both are Italian pay-TV platforms, the former controlled by the French firm Vivendi/Universal and the latter by Newscorp and Telecom Italia.

The deal created a quasi-monopoly in the Italian satellite pay-TV market. The operation also raises competition concerns regarding:

• the acquisition of broadcasting rights for 'premium' content such as blockbuster movies and football matches;
• the access to TV platform for potential entrants.[19]

Clearance was based on the following opening measures on both content and platform: (i) Newscorp would waive exclusive rights in relation to such content for non-satellite transmission. Cable, DTT and internet operators would thus be able to buy content directly from rights owners (e.g. film producers, football clubs, other sport rights' owners); (ii) non-satellite competitors would be able to buy premium contents from Newscorp by means of a 'wholesale offer' based on the so-called 'retail minus principle'. The wholesale offer would work on an unbundled and non-exclusive basis; (iii) access to content would be facilitated also for potential satellite competitors by allowing rights owners to unilaterally terminate with no applicable penalties their ongoing contracts with the combined platform and by limiting the duration of future contracts (two years for football clubs and three years for film producers);[20] (iv) Newscorp would grant satellite competitors access to its own platform and would offer all related services under fair and reasonable conditions; (v) Newscorp would grant licences for its proprietary CAS technology to all applicants on a fair and non-discriminatory basis; (vi) finally, Newscorp would be obliged to enter into simulcrypt agreements within nine months from the request by competitors willing to adopt a CAS technology other than the one owned by Newscorp.

Antitrust cases
Joint selling of media premium contents or exclusive licensing to downstream TV operators may raise antitrust concerns. In particular, restrictions affecting neighbouring markets and holdbacks of content for new media markets, especially for new entrants, could lead to anticompetitive effects and in particular may raise foreclosure issues.

UEFA Champions League[21]
In 2003, the Commission adopted a formal exemption decision concerning the joint selling arrangement regarding the sale of the commercial rights of the UEFA Champions League, a pan-European club football competition.[22]

Until 2003 UEFA sold all the TV rights to the final stages of the UEFA Champions League on behalf of the clubs participating in the league. The rights were sold, by means of a public bidding process, as a bundle on an exclusive basis for up to four years to a single broadcaster in each Member State, in general a free-to-air television company which would normally sub-license some rights to a pay-TV player.[23]

The Commission identified different patterns of competition concerns:

- The sale of the entire rights on an exclusive basis and for a long period of time would have the effect of foreclosing the market and thereby reinforcing the position of the incumbent broadcasters. It might also prevent the football clubs from individually marketing such rights.
- This, in turn, by barring access to key sport content, would limit the development of sport services on emerging new media markets such as the internet and the new generation of mobile phones.

The main principles of the Commission's decision set up a refined scheme of limitations on the scope of exclusivity based on (i) an open tender; (ii) the unbundling of offers; (iii) no excessive exclusivity/no automatic renewal[24] – with the final aim of keeping markets open to new entrants. In particular, UEFA will continue to market centrally the rights to live TV transmission of the Tuesday and Wednesday night matches. This one-stop-shop for the sale of rights may balance the anticompetitive effects by reducing the transaction costs and fostering the branding image of the UEFA Champions League products. Nevertheless, the main rights will be split into two separate rights' packages, giving the winning broadcasters the right to pick the two best matches. UEFA will initially have the exclusive right to sell the remaining live rights of the Champions League products. However, if it does not manage to sell these within a certain cut-off date, the individual clubs will be able to market the matches themselves. Indeed, the new joint selling system would also afford opportunities to new media operators as both UEFA and the football clubs will be able to offer Champions League content on the internet and operators seeking to launch or boost the new generation of mobile phone services using the UMTS technology. Individual football clubs would also, for the first time, have the right to exploit TV rights on a deferred basis and to use archive content, e.g. for the production of videos, therefore providing their fans with a better and more varied offer.

Horizontal issues

Merger control in the case of horizontal mergers
Under merger control, horizontal competition issues may arise in media markets when regulators face the combination of dominant

positions leading to either single or collective dominance. However, in media markets, one could often observe the emergence of the combination of horizontal and vertical effects. This was particularly investigated in the Sony/BMG (2004) and the Lagardère/Editis (2004) decisions.[25] For the latter, unilateral effects[26] were also a competitive concern.

Lagardère/Editis
In 2004, the Commission gave the go-ahead for Lagardère to acquire part of the publishing business of Editis (former VUP). Editis is the biggest publisher, marketer and distributor of French-language books. Lagardère, through its subsidiary Hachette Livre, is second, just behind Editis. Lagardère also does business in the retail sale of books, television and radio and the publication and distribution of newspapers.

In its inquiry, the Commission examined horizontal, vertical and unilateral effects:[27]

- Through their many publishing houses and their distribution and logistics systems, Lagardère and Editis may dominate the entire book chain[28] in the French-speaking countries of the European Union. In particular, the transaction would have created or strengthened dominant positions both at the upstream level – the purchase and sale of publishing rights – and at the downstream level – the distribution and sale of books by publishers to retailers (notably fiction in hardcovers and paperback, books for young people, practical guides, school books and other textbooks, dictionaries and general encyclopaedias).
- The new entity would also control access to premium input, i.e. well-known authors, whose sales are the lifeblood of publishers.
- In the retail markets of all general literature books (pocket and hardcover formats), from the retailers to the final consumer, the econometric study indicates that, as a result of the merger, prices of the published books would increase significantly. According to the study, which used the bootstrap method to construct confidence intervals, there is only a 5 per cent probability that the price rise due to the concentration could not be included in a significant interval.[29] Consumers' surplus would also fall significantly, accounting for a non-negligible part of the industry turnover in the general literature field.

In its reply to the Commission's concerns, Lagardère undertook to sell Editis with the exception of some assets,[30] which make up around 40 per cent of the total company turnover.

Sony/BMG

In 2004, the Commission cleared the merger between Sony and Bertelsmann, thus allowing the combination of their respective global recorded music businesses in a joint venture to be called SonyBMG.[31] The companies' music publishing, manufacturing and distribution of records would remain separate.

The Commission identified different patterns of competition concerns:

- At a horizontal level, the Commission assessed whether the deal could create or strengthen a collective dominant position between Sony/BMG, Universal, EMI and Warner Music (the other main players in the music industry) in the recording market.[32] The remaining four major players would hold approximately 80 per cent of the recording market, both at a European level and in most national markets in the European Economic Area (EEA). The rest of the market is characterised by a large number of mostly smaller players active on a national level. The Commission focused its attention on the markets for recorded music. An analysis of a large amount of price data in the recorded music markets of the different EEA countries indicated a relatively close price parallelism for CDs released by the majors in some countries as well as certain market indicators that could facilitate tacit coordination. On balance, however, the Commission had to conclude, taking into account a deficit in the transparency of the market, that the evidence found was not sufficient to demonstrate that coordinated pricing behaviour existed in the past.

- At a vertical level, the Commission also examined the merger's impact in the emerging market for online music licences as well as online music distribution, but did not find any serious competition problems.[33] The same applies to the examination of the vertical relationships between Sony/BMG's recorded music and Bertelsmann's downstream TV and radio activities in Germany, France, Belgium, Luxembourg and the Netherlands.[34]

Antitrust cases

In media markets, anticompetitive horizontal effects may emerge as a result of an excessive pooling[35] of media rights. Antitrust concerns may arise when either joint selling or joint purchasing limit or foreclose entry of potential competitors such as TV operators or rights traders or purchasers.

In the media business, joint selling refers to a situation in which a firm, a media rights owner such as a sporting association or a rights trader or seller (i) is dominant in the upstream product markets, the premium media contents, and (ii) sells or bundles media contents to a few large media operators and thereby restricts competition. This may be particularly the case when a rights trader offers exclusive contracts or significant discounts on the purchase of subsequent premium content prior to the purchase of further content. This further content could be either secondary or additional premium content.

Joint purchasing refers to a situation in which a group of firms together purchase premium media content. Competition could be restricted or even eliminated. Rivals could be foreclosed also by making access to contents more costly to them. The restrictive character of joint purchasing could be aggravated by an exclusivity attached to the relevant rights. However, note that potential efficiencies such as lower transaction costs, scale economies or lower risk may balance the final assessment.

As in the case of vertical foreclosure, the incentives to foreclose horizontally are diverse. Firms may protect entry or extend market power from a dominant market to a potentially competitive market.[36] In the UK, the joint selling of football rights by the FAPL, the English football league, to TV broadcasters such as BSkyB raises competition concerns.[37] At a European level, the joint purchasing by the European Broadcasting Union (EBU)[38] of certain 'top' sporting events such as the Olympic Games may restrict or even eliminate competition among EBU members which are competitors on both the upstream acquisition markets and the downstream TV markets.[39] This issue has been under scrutiny by the Commission for a long time.[40]

9.5 Conclusion

Lessons for students: what have we learned?

The media industry has several key characteristics. It is characterised by a small number of actors. It is also a fast-moving industry in which the position of the different players along the vertical chain may change rapidly. Thus, media firms may choose a strategy of forward or backward integration with other players aiming at quickly gaining market power along the vertical chain. Media rights are not a scarce resource.

However, highly valuable media contents such as premium contents appear really to be scarce resources. Premium contents are crucial to the development of new media platforms. However, exclusivity and long-term duration clauses and exclusion mechanisms (such as holdbacks) may prevent potential purchasers from accessing key contents needed to foster their current business or the development of new platforms.

Lessons for researchers: what do we still need to know?

The markets for the selling or the acquisition of media rights, and in particular the markets for premium content, may suffer from a number of market failures, whose effect is to restrict access to premium content. Nicita and Ramello (2005) have argued that 'exclusive dealing in contents distributions acted in Europe as barriers to entry and/or raising rivals cost strategies against new pay-TV operators'. These issues of premium contents and exclusivity are a very promising area for investigation.

So also is the fact that the media industry is characterised by the strong public interest objectives of the national and the European authorities. A particularly important distinction that deserves further investigation is that between the sector-specific framework and the competition law framework.

Lessons for policymakers: what are the priorities for policy in this area?

The media sector remains at the top of the list of concerns of European competition authorities and European regulators. European regulators usually intervene *ex ante* in order to guarantee access to common facilities and to assure a degree of media pluralism and diversity. The new regulatory framework for electronic communication regulates the non-content dimension of electronic communication and the sector-specific framework for TV without borders regulates content-related issues. The priorities for policymakers and regulators are clearly to analyse the pros and cons of regulations in network industries and to see to what extent it is necessary to maintain sector-specific regulatory measures or whether competition law is sufficient.

Ex post intervention is also pre-eminent with merger control regulation. In this industry, considering its constant technological development, difficulties may come in particular from the definition of the product

market. Competition authorities should also particularly look out for
foreclosure concerns which are complex issues. Difficulties may come
from a constant balancing between pro-efficiency and anticompetitive
concerns. A *rule of reason* may then be a good model of analysis to
examine such difficult competitive questions.

References

Aghion, Philippe and Bolton, Patrick (1987) 'Contracts as a Barrier to Entry',
    American Economic Review, 77, 388–401.
Bernheim, B. Douglas and Whinston, Michael D. (1998) 'Exclusive dealing',
    Journal of Political Economy, 106, 64–103.
Bork, Robert H. (1995) *The Antitrust Paradox: A Policy At War With Itself*,
    Free Press.
Carbajo, José, De Meza, David and Seidmann, Daniel (1990) 'A Strategic
    Motivation for Commodity Bundling', *Journal of Industrial
    Organisation*, 283–298.
Carlton, Dennis W. and Waldman, Michael (2001) 'Competition,
    Monopoly, and Aftermarkets', *NBER Working Paper 8086*.
Carlton, Dennis W. and Waldman, Michael (2002) 'The Strategic Use of
    Tying to Preserve and Create Market Power in Evolving Industries',
    Rand Journal of Economics, 33(2), 194–220.
Choi, Jay and Stefanadis, Christodoulos (2001) 'Tying, Investment, and the
    Dynamic of Leverage Theory', *Rand Journal of Economics*, 32, 52–71.
Hart, Oliver and Tirole, Jean (1990) 'Vertical Integration and Market
    Foreclosure', *Brookings Papers on Economic Activity, Microeconomics*,
    205–285.
Motta, Massimo and Polo, Michele (1997) 'Concentration and Public
    Policies in the Broadcasting Industry: the Future of Television',
    Economic Policy, 25, 293–335.
Nalebuff, Barry (1999) 'Bundling', *Yale ICF paper no. 99–14*.
Nalebuff, Barry (2000) 'Competing Against Bundles', *Yale School of
    Management Working Paper no. 7*.
Nicita, Antonio and Giovanni, Ramello (2005) 'Exclusivity and Antitrust in
    Media Markets: the case of Pay-TV in Europe', *International Journal of
    the Economics of Business*, 12(3), November, pp. 371–387.
Ordover, Janusz A., Saloner, Garth and Salop, Steven C. (1990) 'Equilibrium
    Vertical Foreclosure', *American Economic Review*, 127–142.
Posner, Richard (1976) *Antitrust Law*, University of Chicago Press.
Rasmussen, Eric B., Remsayer, J. Mark and Wiley, John S. (1991) 'Naked
    Exclusion', *American Economic Review*, 81, 1137–1145.

Rey, Patrick (1997) 'Discussion on TV regulation', *Economic Policy*, 25, 327–331.

Rey, Patrick and Tirole, Jean (2003) 'A Primer on Foreclosure', in Armstrong, Mark and Porter, Rob (eds.) *Handbook of Industrial Organisation III*, Amsterdam, North-Holland.

Riordan, Michael M. and Salop, Steven C. (1995) 'Evaluating Vertical Mergers: A Post Chicago Approach', *Antitrust Law Journal*, 513–564.

Salinger, Michael A. (1988) 'Vertical Mergers and Market Foreclosure', *Quarterly Journal of Economics*, 345–356.

Segal, Ilya and Whinston, Michael (2000) 'Naked Exclusion: a Comment', *American Economic Review*, 90(1), 296–309.

Whinston, Michael D. (1990) 'Tying, Foreclosure, and Exclusion', *American Economic Review*, 80, 837–859.

Appendix 9.1 – An example of a vertical chain market: the book industry

Books follow a circuit from author to final consumers – the readers. The different players involved at different stages are the authors and/ or their representatives, the literary agents, respectively, the rights holders and dealers, publishers, who play the role of the content producers, the marketers or wholesalers, the distributors and retailers. In the upstream market, the French-language publisher approaches authors or non-French-language publishers, either directly or via the literary agents who represent them. The publisher designs and manufactures books and then sells them (generally via a marketer) to dealers, on the basis of an agreed discount. The publisher determines the retail price.[41] Marketers and distributors respectively then market and distribute the published book to the downstream players, the dealers – booksellers, hypermarkets and wholesalers. The publishers remunerate them for these services on the basis of a percentage of the list price exclusive of taxes, net of returns.[42] The marketer takes orders from retailers. This service is performed by commercial teams consisting of representatives who present new issues, draw attention to existing titles and engage in other promotion operations, and pass them on to distributors. Distributors handle all logistical operations[43] involved in getting books to the final customer. The distributor acts on behalf of publishers who may or may not belong to the same group as the distributor. The wholesaler is a special player who exercises a resale

and marketing function which mainly consists of selling full assort-
ments of books and/or full management of book departments ('rack
jobbing', especially in supermarkets) with smaller retailers not specialising in selling books.[44] Retailers are classified in different categories
depending on their degree of specialisation in book sales, their turnover, the number of titles they keep in stock and their sales area. They
may be class 1, 2 or 3 retailers, hypermarkets or supermarkets. Class 1
and 2 retailers are larger bookshops and smaller local bookshops
respectively. These retailers are supplied primarily by publishers' vertically integrated marketing/distribution units, whereas class 3 retailers,
most of which are small retail outlets and supermarkets, are supplied
by wholesalers. Hypermarkets tend to operate via a central purchasing
facility for their supplies of book titles. Retailers are remunerated on
the basis of a discount on the list price exclusive of tax and sell their
books to final consumers. Furthermore, book clubs, given certain
specific features such as publication dates, tend to be involved in re-
issues and are in any case a separate, independent sales circuit.

Appendix 9.2 – The regulatory framework of electronic communication services

A. Ex ante *regulation*

In the new framework, markets to be regulated are defined in accordance
with competition law criteria and principles. A 'Recommendation on
relevant product and service markets within the electronic communication sector susceptible to *ex ante* regulation' identifies those product and
service markets within the electronic communications sector, the characteristics of which may be such as to justify the *ex ante* imposition of
regulatory obligations.

The governing criteria presented in the Recommendation in order to
provide sufficient reasoning to justify the imposition of *ex ante* regulatory obligations are the following:

Static criteria

These include the existence of high and non-transitory entry barriers
and the existence of natural monopolies (static criteria). Structural
barriers to entry exist when the technology and the cost structures
are such that they create asymmetric conditions preventing or even

impeding market entry by the new entrants (substantial economies of scale and high sunk costs). Legal or regulatory barriers are not based on economic conditions but have direct effect on the conditions of entry (number of undertakings having access to spectrum).

Dynamic criteria

Given the dynamic character of the electronic communications markets, the possibility of overcoming static barriers within a relevant time must also be taken into consideration, e.g. innovations from potential competitors not currently in the market.

Criteria for adequate competition law remedies

The decision to impose *ex ante* regulatory obligations should depend on whether competition law remedies are not sufficient to redress market failures. Where the intervention needed to redress a market failure is extensive, for example because an assessment of costs based on detailed accounting is required (access pricing) or because frequent intervention is needed, *ex ante* regulation could constitute an appropriate complement to competition law.

The list of markets presented in the Recommendation does not prevent an NRA from regulating other markets than those listed in this Recommendation. However, the NRA would need the Commission's prior approval before imposing *ex ante* regulatory obligations. NRAs therefore need to know what the Commission criteria for *ex ante* regulation are before they extend regulation to markets other than those listed in the Recommendation, since the criteria for regulating national markets should be the same.

B. Designation of dominant operators

Under the new regulatory framework, NRAs should impose *ex ante* obligations on operators only if they are in a dominant position within the meaning of Article 82 of the EC Treaty. That new definition of SMP is clarified in the 'Guidelines on market analysis and the calculation of significant market power' in order to assist NRAs. That will put an end to the existing asymmetric treatment of companies which under the old framework were deemed to have significant market power and were thus being subject to *ex ante* regulation. The threshold to impose *ex ante* obligation on operators under the old framework was a market share of only 25 per cent. The application of fundamental competition law notions, such as market definition and dominance, in an *ex ante* environment ensures a smooth transition towards a fully liberalised sector. The Guidelines essentially deal with two main issues: market definition and assessment of dominance in applying the competition rules, in particular, to the telecommunications sector.

C. *Appropriate remedies*

Under the new regulatory framework, once an operator is designated as having SMP, the NRAs shall impose appropriate remedies on the basis of the relevant obligations listed in the directives. The ascending hierarchy of obligations listed in the directives relates to transparency, non-discrimination, accounting separation, access, price control and cost accounting. When NRAs have decided on the appropriate remedy to be imposed on operators, the only recourse available to operators against the choice of this remedy is through the national courts. However, the Commission may intervene when NRAs impose on SMP operators obligations other than those listed in the directive.

D. *Consultation with the EC regulatory authorities*

The NRAs must analyse the product and service markets presented in the Recommendation, determine whether or not there is an SMP operator in these markets, and withdraw, amend or impose regulatory obligations as appropriate. An NRA may nevertheless challenge the Commission's assessment and show that certain relevant markets within its territory have characteristics justifying *ex ante* obligations even if the markets are not included in the Recommendation. The assessment by NRAs in different Member States of SMP operators could diverge since SMP is defined on the basis of dominance in the sense of Article 82. The Commission is able to veto draft NRA decisions on SMP designation where interpretations of the concept of dominance diverge and in new markets not included in the Recommendation. This procedure will avoid NRAs defining an operator as dominant under sector-specific regulations when it is not dominant under competition law and will oblige them to justify the regulation of markets other than those listed in the Recommendation.

Notes

* The views expressed in this article are exclusively the views of the authors and not necessarily those of the European Commission.

1. However, this last point will not be treated in this article.
2. See Appendix 9.1 for a complex example: the book chain.
3. In terms of market size, the European movie production industry turnover was estimated at around €4 billion in 2000, with the fifty leading European film production companies having a combined operating revenue of €2.8 billion. It is a growing market – the production of films increased from 443 in 1995 to 604 in 2000, with France, Germany, the UK and Italy representing together three-quarters of the total European Union film production in 2000. The European television production industry turnover was estimated to be €11.2 billion in 2000 and has also grown over the last two decades. The multiplication of TV channels with growing importance of commercial broadcaster and advertising market, the greater prices for sport rights, the greater prices for US production and the growing demand for local constraints are the most important drivers explaining high growth.
4. See in particular 'Outlook of the developments of technologies and markets for the European audiovisual sector up to 2010' by Andersen, Report to the EU Commission, 2002.
5. AOL/Time Warner, Telefonica, etc.
6. Bertelsmann, Lagardère Group, etc.
7. Bouygues, etc.
8. Sony, etc.
9. The UK communications regulator.
10. 6th amendment of Directive 90/388/EEC IP/99/413, 23/6/1999.
11. O.J. L263, p. 9, 14/10/2003.
12. OFTEL 'Review of Competition: broadcasting transmission services', November 2003.
13. Market inefficiency may be due to the so-called double marginalisation, which means that in the absence of vertical integration each firm aims at setting its price at the level where marginal revenue equals marginal cost, but in doing so it fails to internalise the effect that its production and pricing has on the other firm. By vertically integrating, the upstream and the downstream firms may undo such inefficiency and achieve the volume of production that maximises overall profit.
14. The incentives to foreclose are diverse. First, firms may vertically integrate to protect market power preventing downstream rent dissipation. This concern may arise because the bottleneck owner of premium inputs

faces a commitment problem. He will be able to extract his monopoly rent only if he can commit not to sell to the different downstream firms more than the monopoly quantity of premium input and never to set his price below the monopoly level. Finally, once he makes a deal with a first downstream firm, even though these firms will compete with the first one, he has an incentive to sell the premium good to the other firms, depreciating the value of the first firm's good. See in particular the analysis of Rey and Tirole (2003). Second, firms may vertically integrate to extend market power to another stage of the vertical chain. By integrating backwards, firms may thus lock up the supply of a scarce input and vice versa.

However, according to the Chicago School scholars, there is no rationale for foreclosure as there is only one monopoly rent to extract from the two markets, the one of the monopolised market. Thus, vertical integration or exclusive vertical arrangements should rarely raise anticompetitive concerns. See, for example, Bork (1995) and Posner (1976). Finally, the post-Chicago School literature recognises that, in certain circumstances, vertical mergers or exclusive vertical contracting may produce anticompetitive effects. The basic assumption is that such practices may modify the entity's incentives in its dealings with competitors, both upstream and downstream. Thus, in setting prices to unaffiliated firms the entity would take into account the impact of competition on the profits of its integrated businesses. For an analysis of the rationale and the social costs of market foreclosure, see Rey and Tirole (2003). See also the abundant literature on vertical mergers, among others, Salinger (1988), Ordover et al. (1990), Hart and Tirole (1990), Riordan and Salop (1995), and on exclusive vertical contracting, see in particular: Aghion and Bolton (1987), Bernheim and Whinston (1998), Segal and Whinston (2000), Rasmussen et al. (1991).

15. Digital terrestrial transmission.
16. COMP/M.1845 AOL/Time Warner, COMP/M.2050 Vivendi/Universal, COMP/M. 2876 Telepiù/Stream.
17. Films shown on pay-TV shortly after cinema exhibition and video rental are said to be released on 'first window', that is before they are available more widely on television.
18. This commitment covered France, Belgium, Italy, the Netherlands, Spain and the Nordic countries and had a duration of five years. The notifying party also proposed the divestment of its stake in British pay-TV company BSkyB, which has links with Fox, a major US film studio.
19. Competitive constraints will come in the future from e.Biscom (a cable operator with some capacity resources), from future DTT broadcasters, from satellite TV channels and possibly from an alternative fully fledged

satellite platform. Indeed, it was indispensable that blockbuster movies and football matches be accessible in the future, as premium content is what drives subscriptions to pay-TV. Moreover, specifically as regards potential competition from satellite operators, access to a satellite platform and related services are key. In the absence of corrective measures, Newscorp would be the 'gatekeeper' for the access to the technical satellite platform. The technical platform is a system controlling conditional access and the provision of the related technical services. It deciphers the signals broadcast by the programme supplier and transmits them to subscribers via the set-top box. Newscorp would also be the 'gatekeeper' for the conditional access system (CAS) technology (the software programme which allows set-top boxes to decrypt the encrypted signal) as the new company will most likely adopt the proprietary technology of NDS, a Newscorp subsidiary. New entrants would thus depend on Newscorp to obtain licences. Moreover, potential competitors not willing to use Newscorp's CAS technology would depend on Newscorp's willingness to cooperate for the setting up of simulcrypt arrangements – i.e. systems allowing the same set-top box to 'read' signals encrypted with different technologies.

20. Still to facilitate entry of satellite competitors, Newscorp also undertook not to 'black out' so-called second window movie rights. These are rights relating to the delayed and cheaper (compared with first window rights) release of blockbuster movies on pay-TV. In the absence of these conditions, Newscorp would have been able to decide to buy only first window rights while at the same time preventing potential competitors from buying second window rights. Thanks to this undertaking, barriers to entry have been further lowered and consumers might be able to decide when and at what price to watch movies on pay-TV.

21. COMP/M. 1845 UEFA Champions League (2003).

22. The Champions League is a tournament organised every year between the top European football clubs – seventy-two clubs participate from both European Union and non-EU countries. The last stage, which begins in September, comprises the thirty-two qualifying clubs. The Champions League season ends in May the following year. The regulations of the UEFA Champions League provide UEFA, as a joint selling body, with the exclusive right to sell certain commercial rights of the UEFA Champions League on behalf of the participating football clubs. These rules were notified to the Commission in 1999.

23. One of the drawbacks of the system was that some of the rights, including live footage, were unexploited. In fact, the clubs and possibly other players such as regional television channels or small pay-per-view companies would be happy to use these rights.

24. UEFA will not sell the rights for a period longer than three years and will do so through a public tender procedure allowing all broadcasters to put in bids.
25. COMP/M. 3333 Sony/BMG, COMP/M. 2978 Lagardère/Editis.
26. Unilateral effects refer to situations where two competing firms merge to form a single entity leading to a price increase that results from the firms' individual changes or adjustments following that merger in a particular market. Unilateral effects are now fulfilled with the Commission New Notice on Horizontal Mergers; see Guidelines on the assessment of horizontal mergers under the Council Regulation on the control of concentrations between undertakings, OJ/2004/C 31/03.
27. Unilateral effects were also analysed and included in the final decision, see the econometric study carried out by the Commission: 'Evaluation Econométrique des Effets de la Concentration Lagardère/VUP sur le Marché du Livre de Littérature Générale', by Jérôme Foncel and Marc Ivaldi, revised and increased final version, September 2003. Unilateral effects measure the impact of the concentration between Lagardère and Editis on the public selling prices in the retail market for both hard-covers and paperbacks in general literature (in the absence of reliable data available on the level of the discounts granted to the retailers). Before the merger with Editis, if Hachette Livre (subsidiary of Lagardère) decided to increase prices unilaterally, parts of these final consumers would turn to other competing publishers, among which was Editis. As a result of the concentration with Editis, Hachette absorbs a part of these competitive pressures and can thus recover a portion of these customers.
28. From author to reader a book follows a chain in which various inter-mediate players have a role: the rights holder, the publisher, the mar-keter, the distributor, the wholesaler and the retailer.
29. In addition to the bootstrap method, different elements speak for the robustness of the model: the very high number of observations, the different statistical tests of significance and robustness, the stability of the main parameters (e.g. the marginal utility of a given book and the intra-brand correlation). Overall, the model employed is very robust and is in line with the state-of-the-art of empirical analysis in such a market.
30. That is, the Larousse publishing house and all of its business and its publisher's lists; the Dalloz publishing house and all of its business and its publisher's lists; the Dunod publishing house and all of its business and its publisher's lists; the academic lists made up of the publishers' lists of Armand Colin, Sedes and Nathan Université and the academic jour-nals; the Spanish group Anaya and all of its business and its publisher's lists; the Ivry distribution centre.

31. The decision was overturned by the Court of First Instance in July 2006, a judgment that is under appeal to the European Court of Justice. See Case T-464/04 *Independent Music Publishers and Labels Association v Commission*.

32. The recording market consists of the signing of artists, the actual recording of the songs, the marketing of the artists and their works and the sales of CDs.

33. Since Sony's online music service did not at this point enjoy a dominant position in the market for online music there were no concerns that the merger would create or strengthen a dominant position in the online music market.

34. There will not be a significant impact on competition caused by Bertelsmann's link to the television industry since Bertelsmann does not enjoy a dominant position in the television market.

35. In this section, excessive pooling is non-exclusive. Exclusivity in joint selling or joint purchasing contracts is analysed in Section 9.4.

36. As in the situation of vertical foreclosure, and according to the Chicago School scholars, there is no rationale for horizontal foreclosure. However, the Chicago results are based on strict assumptions such as monopoly in one market – the tying market; perfect Bertrand competition and constant return to scale (free entry) in the competitive market – the tied market; in most cases goods are used in fixed proportions. Departures from the Chicago assumptions may lead to anticompetitive effects. Other motivations for tying/bundling aside from foreclosure are (i) price discrimination and (ii) the softening of competition. Thus, tying/bundling may be an effective price discrimination tool as it may reduce the dispersion in valuations that consumers may have on both goods, thus allowing the firm to capture 100 per cent of the consumers' surplus. In the case of little differentiation in the tied good market, tying/bundling may soften competition by inducing an increase in the degree of differentiation between the firm and its rivals. Indeed, these strategies are clearly motivated by purposes other than entry deterrence effects. For the literature concerning tying/bundling, see in particular Carlton and Waldman (2001, 2002), Carbajo et al. (1990), Choi and Stefanadis (2001), Nalebuff (1999 and 2000), Whinston (1990).

37. Case COMP.38.173 FA Premier League, in cooperation with the OFT, the UK competition authority, and OFCOM, the UK communications regulator. The FAPL gave commitments with regard to its marketing, sale and exploitation of the rights on behalf of the clubs, with effect from (but not prior to) the 2007/8 season.

38. Case COMP/C2/32.150R EBU. The EBU is an association of (mostly public) radio and TV broadcasters.

39. Note also that, due to the exclusivity of the acquired rights, the joint acquisition system may restrict competition as regards rivals (non-EBU members) by foreclosing their access to those rights.
40. The proceedings started in 1989. Among others, the EBU notified a system that provided for the joint acquisition and sharing of sports rights. Since 1989, the Commission has adopted two individual exemptions to EBU. Among others, the exemption was subject to a sub-licensing scheme of the EBU to third parties of the jointly acquired television rights to sport events. See judgment of the Court of First Instance in joined cases T-185/00, *M6 and Others v Commission*; T-216/00, *Antena 3 de televisión and Others v Commission*; T-299/00, *Gestevisión Telecinco v Commission*; T-300/00, *SIC v Commission*. All the Commission decisions were annulled by the Court of First Instance (CFI). Subsequently, there have been extensive negotiations between the Commission and the EBU regarding potential commitments with the view to adopt an Article 9 decision under Regulation 1/2003. In October and November 2004, Pro7Sat1 and Premiere (respectively one of the major commercial free-TV broadcasters and the leading pay-TV broadcaster in Germany) submitted two complaints against the EBU and its German members ARD and ZDF (COMP/C2/39.133 ProSiebensat.1 v EBU and COMP/C2/39.133 Premiere v EBU). Both complaints attacked the exclusive joint acquisition of sports rights.
41. Margins are mainly taken in the form of discounts calculated on the basis of the list price exclusive of tax (French *PPHT*) which the publisher or marketer will negotiate with the various retailers. The discounts are based on quantitative criteria linked to the number of titles stocked and qualitative criteria linked to the nature of the services rendered to facilitate book sales. This marketing system is similar in some ways to large-scale distribution, where the real business negotiations are on 'back margins'.
42. That is to say, net of copies that retailers have been unable to sell and are entitled to return to the publisher at their own expense and on certain conditions.
43. This includes stocking titles, registering and checking orders, preparing and sending orders, managing returns, issuing delivery orders and invoices, managing client accounts and recovering amounts due.
44. He takes his supplies direct from the publishers and generally has a sales depot or salesroom where retailers can come and obtain books if they wish to order small quantities or at short notice. Wholesalers are remunerated on the basis of discounts calculated on the list price exclusive of tax.

10 Competition policy and sector-specific economic media regulation: and never the twain shall meet?

EINAR HOPE*

10.1 Introduction

Against a background of dramatic structural and organisational changes in media markets, most European countries are struggling with reforming their media policies and regulatory regimes to accommodate and comply with those changes, in accordance with stated policy and regulatory objectives. One interesting issue that has come up in this debate is the relationship between competition policy regulation of media markets on the one hand and sector-specific media regulation in general, and sector-specific ownership regulation in particular, on the other. Is it an appropriate and workable policy option to gradually replace sector-specific media regulation by general competition policy regulation or to 'roll back' sector-specific regulation to competition regulation of media markets – to use the expression, and stated intention, of the EU Commission in its proposal for regulatory reform of electronic communications services?[1] There seems to be a general consensus among writers and researchers on media regulation that such a policy proposition is neither workable nor acceptable because of special characteristics of media markets in economic terms and stated public policy objectives of media regulatory policy.[2] At the same time, however, there seems to be a general concern that the regulation of media markets is not working properly in practice; in fact, scepticism and even frustration often come to the surface, both from media regulators and from actors in media markets being exposed to regulation.

There are two aspects, or levels of debate, about the relationship between competition policy and sector-specific media regulation. The first level is the relationship between *general* or 'traditional' media regulation, ranging from measures to safeguard regulatory objectives

310

such as freedom of expression, media diversity, independence of media from ownership and political influence, cultural identity and language, etc. to technical regulation, e.g. of wave frequencies in broadcasting, and *economic* regulation, safeguarding the same objectives and, in particular, the efficient functioning of media markets. The second level is the relationship between sector-specific *economic* regulation and general *competition* regulation. In my opinion, the debate on media regulation would have benefitted considerably from establishing a clearer distinction between the two levels and on that basis identifying properties and characteristics of regulatory measures designed to achieve stated regulatory objectives for the media sector in the best possible way.

The focus of this chapter is on the latter level and more specifically on the relationship between ownership regulation, as generally being the most important instrument of sector-specific economic media regulation, and competition policy regulation. Are the two regulatory policies independent of each other and thus 'never shall meet' in Kipling's sense, or can sector-specific ownership regulation be placed within the realm of competition policy regulation without undue loss of regulatory impact or without sacrificing important regulatory objectives, in particular, media pluralism and diversity? Much of the debate on this policy relationship seems to have been rather 'sector-specific' in the sense that it has originated in the media sector itself from a media policy perspective. This also seems to apply to a considerable degree to the academic literature on media regulation. The competition policy dimension is typically not anchored as solidly in the analysis and evaluation of regulatory media issues. Sometimes one is even left with a feeling that part of the regulatory literature suffers from an incomplete understanding of the analysis and instruments of modern competition policy.

This chapter makes an attempt at striking a balance in this regard, by comparing analytical approaches and instruments of sector-specific economic (ownership) regulation with competition policy regulation of media markets, as a background for a discussion of their 'proper' regulatory relationship. This is the topic of Section 10.3, while Section 10.4 discusses various models for the institutional relationship between sector-specific and competition regulation and the division of labour and responsibility between sector-specific regulatory authorities and competition authorities in media regulation. In Section 10.5, there is a more specific, case-oriented discussion of the Norwegian media regulatory framework and the recent regulatory media reform in Norway, and some lessons that might be drawn from it with regard to the relationship between sector-specific and competition policy regulation. The main policy proposition suggested in the chapter is that competition policy regulation may be substituted for sector-specific ownership regulation without undue loss of regulatory impact, in the context of the Norwegian media regulatory policy framework.

10.2 Some structural and regulatory developments in the media sector

As a background to the discussion of economic media regulation, and the relationship between sector-specific and competition policy regulation, let us list in a summary fashion some relevant, recent developments that have taken place within the media sector.[3] These developments are partly exogenous in relation to regulatory policy in the sense that they take place more or less independently of the regulatory regime, e.g. through exogenous technological change, and so the regime must adjust to them, and partly endogenous, in the sense that developments are deliberately influenced and steered by policy in an intended way, e.g. by merger and acquisition regulations in competition policy.

Market structure and organisation

Media market convergence and network integration on a common digital technological platform have been important driving forces behind the restructuring of media markets in recent years. Network integration has also to some extent taken place over and above digital convergence and integration, e.g. when energy companies with dedicated physical power or gas networks have invested in broadband facilities and started to offer broadband services on the basis of alleged economies of scope in network integration. Under market convergence and integration, market players who formerly have operated in separate markets now become competitors. In order to reap potential efficiency gains from economies of scale and scope, consolidations occur through mergers and acquisitions, leading to increased market concentration. This may have detrimental effects on market competition – a standard problem or dilemma in the welfare analysis of trade-offs between economic efficiency and competition in competition policy regulation.

Concentration in media markets has taken four main forms: (i) mono-media concentration, i.e. integration within a single media sector or business activity, (ii) horizontal integration across different media sectors or activities (multi-media concentration), (iii) vertical integration along different stages in the vertical supply chain from production of media content through packaging and distribution to end-use, and (iv) conglomerate concentration, i.e. expansion into sectors or activities not traditionally understood as media markets, partly facilitated by forces of convergence and integration mentioned above. All forms of concentration can be observed in media markets, with (ii) and (iv) as perhaps the most prevalent ones. The different forms raise different issues and problems in relation to regulatory policy for the media sector.

Market convergence and concentration have paved the way for media product bundling, with potential cost efficiencies on both the supply and the demand sides, e.g. through reduced information search and transaction costs for consumers. However, information technology makes it possible at the same time to target individual consumers and create products and product packages tailored to the preferences of individual consumers. Given the complexities and problems of media regulation as seen from the supply side under convergence, concentration and rapid technological change, this may imply a shift of regulatory focus from supply-side to demand-side regulation, in particular to consumer policy regulation.

Media markets are increasingly moving from predominantly national markets to international and even global markets, especially for the electronic media markets. This has regulatory implications at least along two dimensions: first, a delegation of regulatory responsibility and tasks from national regulatory authorities to overnational or international bodies, in particular to the EU Commission for European member countries; and second, a need for harmonising regulatory policies and approaches among countries to achieve common regulatory goals. It goes without saying that this is a major regulatory policy challenge.

Regulatory policy[4]

With regard to regulatory objectives there has been a shift of focus from broadly defined media policy objectives related to culture, democracy, freedom of expression, pluralism and the like to more emphasis on economic objectives related to industrial and competition policy regulation of media markets. The shift of focus does not imply, however, that the former objectives have been unduly sacrificed, specifically, in the context of this study, the objectives of pluralism of media actors and diversity of media supply.

Following the change in the composition of the hierarchy of media policy objectives, a shift towards more emphasis on economic regulation of the market structure of the media sector, in particular ownership regulation, and gradually to some extent to the regulation of the market behaviour of media actors and content of media supply has taken place. Competition policy regulation has also implied a focus on non-discriminatory competitive aspects of the design and enforcement of media regulations and a critical look at explicit policies to subsidise or give political support to specific media activities or products.

When it comes to the institutional organisation of media regulatory policy and the division of labour between regulatory institutions, a clearer vertical separation of regulatory responsibility for the media sector between the political system and ministerial bodies in government and independent sector-specific regulatory bodies, subordinated to the ministries, can generally be observed. In most countries those bodies have been restructured along with the restructuring of the media sector itself, e.g. by merging mono-media regulatory bodies into multi-media bodies, but often with a fairly long institutional regulatory lag and maintaining the predominantly sector-specific nature of media regulation.

For the question whether sector-specific economic regulation might be replaced with general competition regulation, three aspects of the above-mentioned developments are particularly relevant. First, media market convergence and integration can further competition among media sectors and activities if undue market concentration and restrictions on competition are avoided. Second, modern sector-specific regulatory regimes, particularly for network regulation, make more and more use of competition-like instruments, e.g. incentive regulation, regulation through contracts, auctioning out the right to supply specific activities, e.g. frequencies rights for broadcasting, etc. Third, with multi-media and conglomerate integration, the sector-specific media concept becomes diluted and less 'specific' compared with the traditional mono-media sector concept, making sector-specific regulation less well defined in relation to specific sectors. This is not, of course, sufficient in itself to argue for substituting competition regulation for sector-specific regulation. We must also take a closer look at, and compare, properties and characteristics of instruments and approaches to regulation under sector-specific and competition regulatory regimes. This is discussed in Section 10.3, with emphasis on ownership regulation as a sector-specific regulatory instrument.

10.3 Approaches and instruments

Some of the debate on policy approaches to economic media regulation, in particular the relationship between sector-specific and competition regulation in the composition of the policy 'package', suffers, in my opinion, from misconceptions, or at least an insufficient understanding, about characteristics and properties of policy approaches and instruments of the two policy areas. Therefore, a brief exposition of some important characteristics and properties may be in order.[5]

Ex ante *sector-specific regulation versus* ex post *competition regulation*

Sector-specific regulation is often referred to as *ex ante* regulation, while competition regulation is characterised as *ex post* regulation. The dichotomy is sometimes also referred to as proactive sector-specific regulation versus reactive competition regulation, respectively.

   Such an *ex ante/ex post* dichotomy captures important features of the two policy areas, but is too simplistic both as a characterisation and as a basis for the choice of regulatory policy regimes. There are many examples of *ex ante* approaches to regulation in competition policy, e.g. with regard to exemptions from prohibition rules or regulation of mergers and acquisitions. For merger regulation, criteria for the delineation of relevant market(s) and threshold values for market size or market share are defined by competition authorities in advance, though not legally binding from an enforcement perspective on a case-to-case *ex post* basis. Competition authorities may also *ex ante* enter into a dialogue, e.g. with dominant market players to make them adjust their market behaviour in order to avoid formal proceedings for possible breaches of competition rules, as has often been the case, for example, in telecommunications after deregulation.[6] Similarly, sector-specific regulation is sometimes *ex post* based, in the sense that sector-specific regulatory authorities will wait for market developments or specific market outcomes to materialise before regulations are considered, e.g. price regulation.

Regulation of market structure versus regulation
of market behaviour

Another too simplistic characterisation is that sector-specific economic regulation is *structural* regulation while competition regulation is *behavioural* regulation. True enough, sector-specific media regulation, in particular ownership regulation, is very much about *ex ante* regulation of (ownership) structure. However, competition regulation is not only about regulating market behaviour but to a considerable extent about market structure too. In fact, a fundamental analytical approach to competition policy regulation has traditionally been the SCP (structure, conduct, performance) paradigm, where regulation of market structure has played an important role. This can partly be explained by the analytical belief of economists, based on economic theory, that specific market structures will typically generate specific forms of market behaviour, e.g. competition on price, and partly by a general regulatory lesson in competition policy that it is considerably more difficult to regulate behaviour than structure in practice. But then, of course, being equipped with a box of tools for regulating both dimensions, structure and behaviour, must generally be thought to be better than regulating only one of them.

This can be illustrated by regulatory issues raised by market dominance and market power in the media sector. The approach typically taken under sector-specific regulation has been to place *ex ante* structural restrictions on levels of mono-media, multi-media or cross-media ownership, defined in terms of maximum threshold values for market share, equity or revenue, for various geographic market delineations (national, regional or local) for a given media sector or across media sectors, with the stated intention of avoiding undue media concentrations and securing pluralism of media suppliers and diversity of media output.[7] The upper ceilings on ownership have generally been rather low, typically in the area of 15–30 per cent share, depending on media sector and whether it is mono-, multi- or cross-ownership. Those ceilings have typically been considerably lower than what has generally been defined as market shares for market dominance in competition policy. Recently, media ownership thresholds have been raised in a number of European countries, but still not to the general dominance level defined for other markets.

Under competition policy regulation market dominance is not considered illegal *per se* but rather the *abuse* of a dominant market position to exercise market power to the detriment of economic efficiency.[8] Still, most countries with a market dominance rule in their regulatory regime for competition[9] have defined general dominance standards in terms of market shares, typically in the range 40–60 per cent for unilateral market dominance. These threshold values should, however, be considered partly as a preliminary screening device for the competition authorities for a closer inspection of markets where dominance may represent a competition problem in terms of the potential abuse of market power, and partly as a signalling device to market actors about the regulatory consequences of becoming dominant, i.e. by becoming subjected to a closer scrutiny of their market behaviour by the competition authorities.

Thus, competition authorities must perform a two-way test for market dominance. First, to determine whether the *structural* conditions for market dominance are fulfilled, according to defined dominance standards, and second, to investigate specifically whether the *behavioural* conditions would justify an intervention against the abuse of a dominant position. The competition authorities can, in principle, define structural standards of dominance for individual markets or group of markets, depending on specific competitive features of markets, related for example to network externalities, sunk costs, demand complementarities among products, capacity constraints, etc., which are features associated with information and communications technology markets, to which many media markets belong.

Market dominance standards similar to the ownership thresholds defined in sector-specific media regulation could thus, in principle, be defined and signalled to the markets in competition policy regulation of media markets. A competition authority could also intervene, regardless of whether market dominance standards actually have been defined for a specific market or not, e.g. a local media market, if it thinks that a case of abuse of market dominance position can be raised. Behavioural regulation would thus be a cornerstone of the competition regulatory regime under 'structural' market dominance.[10]

Lately, in telecommunications regulation, the former concept of strong market position has given way to the concept of 'significant market power' (SMP) and has thus moved closer to market and competition concepts in competition policy.[11] Most countries, with the only exception of the Netherlands so far (see Section 10.4 below), have, however, maintained telecommunications regulation as the prime responsibility for a sector-specific regulatory authority, including the demarcation of relevant market(s) on criteria defined by the EU Commission, definition of market dominance or market power criteria, etc. Thus, we see that sector-specific regulation and competition regulation converge, but without the full implications being drawn for the design of regulatory policy and the division of labour between regulatory bodies.

A somewhat different and more general distinction can be made in competition policy analysis between *structural* conditions for the potential exercise of market power and *incentives* for the actual exercise of power. The latter can be termed an incentive-oriented approach to competition policy analysis.[12] The basic idea or contention of this approach is that competition analysis should not be conducted in terms of structural conditions; in fact, the concepts of relevant market and market structure should be considered 'irrelevant' for a proper analysis of competition, which should rather be framed as an analysis of the incentives of business entities to compete. A regulatory implication of this approach is that regulatory authorities should be more concerned with understanding the incentives and strategies for competition at the firm level and not so much with analysing structure as such at the market level, representing a considerable shift of analytical focus in competition policy analysis. In particular, an economic regulatory regime for media markets based on structural ownership regulation alone would become close to meaningless under this approach.

Static versus dynamic regulation

A regulatory issue related to the structural–behavioural dichotomy above is whether the regulatory outcome in terms of economic efficiency will be different under sector-specific regulation compared with competition regulation. An argument often met is that sector-specific regulation is more concerned with dynamic efficiency objectives related to technological change, innovation and growth, and is also better equipped with regulatory instruments to further such objectives, while competition policy, at least the way in which it has traditionally been practised, is steeped in short-run, static economic efficiency considerations and objectives. For the media sector, which has generally been characterised by rapid technological change and market restructuring, especially for the electronic communications part of it, a competition policy based on static competition and efficiency considerations thus could become too interventionistic from a dynamic regulatory perspective.

Again, such a static–dynamic regulatory dichotomy is too crude and simplistic as a characterisation of the two regulatory policies; it may even be directly false. A critique often raised against sector-specific ownership regulation of media is, in fact, that it is too static and backward looking, in the sense that ownership restrictions are not adjusted in the wake of technological and market developments, or they are adjusted with a considerable regulatory time lag. It is also argued that ownership thresholds generally are set so low so that the full potential for cost efficiencies in terms of economies of scale and scope, positive network externalities by network integration and the like may not be realised in practice.[13] Low threshold values might also limit the resources available for innovation for media firms and owners or weaken the incentives for innovation and function as a barrier to entry for new competitors in media markets. In sum, this could represent a constraint on dynamic media competition and a loss of dynamic economic efficiency gains from sector-specific ownership regulation.

Competition policy, as traditionally understood, is vulnerable to a critique of being too focused on static price/quantity competition and static economic efficiency considerations. This is, however, more of a critique of the enforcement practice in competition policy rather than against competition policy as such. Lately, interesting developments have taken place within the realm of competition policy, broadening the scope of competition analysis to include parameters other than just price and quantity competition; in particular R&D and innovation, and placing more emphasis on dynamic efficiency. This reorientation of analytical approach and objective of competition policy has been particularly evident for innovative sectors such as ICT and has, admittedly, not yet permeated the policy field as a whole, neither in theory nor in practice.[14]

This static–dynamic regulatory dichotomy is particularly interesting in relation to the stated media policy objectives of pluralism of media suppliers and diversity of media content. As mentioned in the introduction, it is generally maintained that competition regulation is insufficient or inept to achieve such targets and therefore has to be supplemented by (sector-specific) ownership regulation. This may offhand seem a little surprising on the basis of the discussion above. Competition policy enforcement may have been too lenient with regard to specific cases of media mergers and acquisitions, allowing too concentrated media markets to develop, to the detriment of pluralism from a static competition perspective. If so, however, this could be raised more as a critique of practical policy applications and not necessarily as a fundamental critique of analytical approaches and instruments of competition policy regulation, including dynamic regulation, as mentioned above. Sector-specific ownership regulation, meanwhile, seems to be rather more steeped in a static analytical and regulatory framework, where short-run pluralism may result in less future pluralism through reduced competition and innovation in media markets, compared with dynamic competition regulation.[15] Whether this will be the actual outcome or not is in the end an empirical question, on which little research yet has been done.

Economic versus general or 'non-economic' media regulation

Media regulation is characterised by a number of policy objectives,[16] while general competition policy has just one overriding goal, i.e. economic efficiency.[17] Can a distinction be drawn between economic regulation on the one side and general media regulation, broadly defined as all non-economic regulation, on the other? If so, and as a next step, would it then be operationally possible and meaningful to allocate economic regulation as a primary task for competition policy regulation while 'non-economic' media regulation would be the main task under sector-specific regulation? If such a distinction could be made with a fair degree of precision, this would lead to a clearer division of responsibility and labour between competition authorities and sector-specific authorities, resulting in less regulatory uncertainty for sectors and actors under regulation and more efficient use of regulatory resources.

The crucial issue seems to be rooted in the policy objectives of pluralism and freedom of expression. Media regulators would tend to argue, as mentioned, that competition policy alone is not sufficient to achieve media pluralism and therefore has to be supplemented with ownership regulation to secure diverse media ownership as a means to media pluralism. In addition, measures to safeguard editorial independence and freedom of expression have to be in place, e.g. as self-regulation in the form of written, public editorial agreements to secure editorial independence from media owners, and diversity of content, or legal regulations to the same effect, written into law.

If, therefore, measures can be designed to safeguard those objectives, this part of media regulatory policy could be separated from ownership regulation and from the regulation of supply and demand of media products and services in media markets. The enforcement of the former part of regulatory policy would be the task for sector-specific regulation. Given the rather static and inflexible nature of media ownership regulation compared with the properties of modern competition regulation, as discussed above, there should at least be a presumption for a regulatory policy case of considering to abolish media ownership regulation as a sector-specific regulatory task and replacing economic sector-specific regulation with competition policy regulation, as a basic proposition for the practical approach to media regulation. An empirical discussion of such a regulatory division of labour and responsibility between sector-specific and competition policy media regulation is given in Section 10.5, specifically in relation to the recent Norwegian media regulatory reform.

10.4 Models of the division of responsibilities

The division of labour and responsibility between competition and sector-specific regulatory authorities has a vertical and a horizontal dimension. Vertically, it concerns the division between different levels of government, e.g. between governmental ministries and subordinated sector-specific regulatory bodies, or between supranational bodies, e.g. the EU Commission and national bodies. Horizontally, it is a question of how the division is organised between regulatory bodies at the same level of government, *in casu* between competition and sector-specific authorities, respectively, but also among sector-specific authorities themselves, e.g. between regulatory authorities for telecommunications and media, respectively. Only the horizontal dimension is discussed here.[18]

Along this dimension the division of labour and responsibility between competition and sector-specific regulatory authorities can be organised according to four main types of model:[19]

1. The competition authority has exclusive competence to monitor and enforce competition and (economic) regulatory policies in all sectors and markets.
2. The sector-specific authority has exclusive competence to monitor and enforce competition regulation and sector-specific regulation for the respective sector(s).
3. The two authorities have parallel or overlapping competence (most prevalent in practice).
4. The two authorities both have competence, but in clearly defined competence areas: the competition authority has exclusive competition policy competence and the sector-specific authority has exclusive regulatory competence for its sector(s).

In practice, the models are rarely found in their pure form; most sector-specific regulatory regimes contain elements from more than one model. A common feature of the choice of institutional model in practice, however, is that the horizontal division of competence is vague and unclear, with considerable overlaps and 'grey zones' between competition and regulatory authorities. The third model above thus seems to capture the actual division best in most countries. Such overlaps may create regulatory uncertainty with regard to case handling and outcome, duplication of regulatory efforts and resources, conflicts of competence among regulatory bodies and inertia with regard to adjusting regulatory policies to a changing policy environment.

Some considerations relevant to the choice of model for the horizontal division between competition and sector-specific regulation for the media sector, in addition to those discussed in Section 10.3, are:

- *Form and nature of media convergence and integration*: will convergence and integration result in a well-defined demarcation of media sectors and markets for regulation, applying a common regulatory approach in terms of analysis and policy measures to them, or is the variation across sectors so large that such an approach is not justified? Convergence has, for example, created a much closer regulatory 'affinity' among the electronic media sectors taken together than across-media integration between electronic media and the press.[20] If the variation across sectors is so large that a common regulatory regime cannot be implemented, this would imply an asymmetric regulation of media entities and activities within the media sector. Such regulation might be at variance with the fundamental principles of competition on a level-playing-field basis and non-discrimination of objects in competition policy.

- *Competition and incentives in regulation*: should competition between regulatory bodies (competition and sector-specific bodies) be stimulated as an objective in itself, creating incentives for better decision making and more efficient use of regulatory resources? Is it, specifically, a problem to 'monopolise' all economic media regulation as the sole responsibility for a competition authority?

- *Time aspect in regulation*: is it necessary to monitor and control a sector under regulation more or less continuously – a feature of sector-specific regulation – or is it sufficient to intervene more sporadically on a case-to-case basis when regulatory situations occur – a feature of competition regulation? Is consistency of the regulatory regime over time of importance, e.g. in relation to long-term investment decisions by media investors, and if so, is this more pronounced under sector-specific than under competition regulation?

- *Information, knowledge and communication*: are information and data requirements for regulation different between sector-specific and competition regulation and can they be communicated more efficiently under the typically more continuous and closer relationship between sector-specific regulatory bodies and market actors under regulation than under competition regulation? Is it necessary to have sector-specific knowledge and competence to regulate efficiently and would competition regulation be at a disadvantage in this respect compared with sector regulation? A related question is whether the asymmetric information problem between regulators and regulatees is more pronounced under competition than under sector-specific regulation.

- *Regulatory capture*: is regulatory capture of regulators by regulatees a more serious problem under sector-specific than under competition regulation, partly as a consequence of characteristics and properties of sector regulation discussed above?[21] Surprisingly little empirical research has been done on this issue, in view of the role it plays in the regulatory literature and in the public debate on regulation.[22]

- *Complexity and intensity in regulation*: sector-specific regulation is usually thought of as more detailed and comprehensive compared with the 'minimalistic' and general approach in competition regulation. Is there sufficient proportionality with regard to complexity and intensity in sector regulation, in the sense that the regulatory regime is not overburdened in relation to regulatory tasks and objectives? Is sector regulation susceptible to inertia or sluggishness of adjustment when confronted with rapid changes in the regulatory environment, compared with competition regulation?

- *Resource use in regulation*: are there economies of scale and/or scope in regulatory functions that could be realised by reorganising the regulatory system, e.g. by merging regulatory institutions or making the division of labour among them more transparent and precise? Can regulatory costs be reduced by adopting more effective regulatory measures, including the regulatory cost of market actors being exposed to regulation?

- *Universal service obligations*: USO regulation has been the hallmark of sector-specific regulation, in relation to both regulation of dominant firms in formerly monopolised sectors, such as telecommunications and electricity, and sectors or activities with explicitly stated obligations of universal service, such as public broadcasting and television. Can USO be accommodated in a satisfactory way within a competition regulatory regime so that sector-specific regulation can be replaced by competition regulation even under USO conditions? There is no simple, general answer to this question. The fundamental problem is how to design and impose a universal service obligations regime in a non-discriminatory and neutral way under a competition policy regime, but this problem also remains, in principle, with sector regulation. No fully satisfactory solution can be said to be found for this problem yet, neither from a theoretical nor a practical regulatory perspective.[23]

The issue of universal service obligations illustrates a general point that can be made about the relationship between sector-specific and competition regulation, i.e. that it is not just an either-or question, but that there are complementarities in the relationship. This said, however, the present relationship in practical regulatory policy for the media sector seems to be far from optimal in most countries, the 'grey zones' being too large and ill defined between the two policy areas. Policy improvements can be obtained by making the demarcation between sector-specific and competition regulation more consistent and precise, by harmonising policy objectives and by tapping the synergies between the policy areas with regard to regulatory outcome and resource use.

If competition policy regulation could be substituted for economic sector-specific regulation, competition authorities might have to take over regulatory instruments that could seem 'alien' at first sight in their box of tools, as traditionally understood, e.g. specific ownership regulation of media as practised under the former regulatory regime. This should be considered, however, as a transitory phase, until regular competition policy measures could be imposed.

The institutional setup for sector-specific media regulation and the relationship with competition regulation vary considerably among European countries.[24] Three developments seem, however, to be common to most countries (see also Section 10.2): (a) more focus on competition policy regulation, especially in relation to mergers and acquisitions, (b) more focus on economic sector regulation in terms of ownership regulation, as a task for sector-specific regulatory authorities, and (c) merging mono-media regulatory bodies into multi-media bodies. A full rolling back of sector-specific media regulation to competition policy regulation has not taken place, however, in any European country yet.

The most interesting case in this regard is represented by the Netherlands, where one of the government's stated institutional policy objectives has been to pave the way for a 'sector-specific competition authority' organisational model. Under this model, sector-specific regulation should gradually be transferred to the Dutch Competition Authority (Nederlandse Mededingingsautoriteit (NNa)) and organised as sector divisions within the NNa, as a transitory phase until full integration of the sector divisions into the NNa can be implemented. This is intended to be the model not only for sectors like telecommunications, where the rolling-back intention was stated in the EU directives on telecommunications, but also for sectors such as energy, health and media. According to the chapter on the Netherlands by Kees Brants in Kelly et al. (2004), the Dutch Post and Telecommunications Authority (Onafhankelijke Post en Telecommunicatie Autoriteit (Opta)) was supposed to merge with the NNa in 2005. Brants also mentions that the Opta would like to merge with parts of the Media Authority, 'but as yet that seems politically unviable' (p. 153). The horizontal division of labour and responsibility in media regulation is thus a question of the division not only between competition and sector-specific regulation but also between sector-specific regulatory bodies.

10.5 Sector-specific and competition policy regulation of media – the Norwegian case

Norway presents an interesting case of media regulatory policy in general[25] and media ownership regulation in particular. Some recent developments with regard to Norwegian media ownership policy are as follows:

- A separate Media Ownership Authority (MOA) was established in 1998. The MOA has recently been merged with the former Mass Media Authority and the Film Authority into a common Media Regulatory Authority (MRA).[26]
- The Norwegian government has proposed amendments to the 1997 Act on Regulation of Acquisitions in Press and Broadcasting, and extending the coverage of the Act.
- The government has proposed new legislation with regard to securing freedom of expression and substituting media self-regulation with law-based rules, specifically the Declaration of Rights and Duties of Editors.
- As mentioned earlier, a new Competition Act was enacted in 2004, harmonising Norwegian competition legislation with that of the EU.

Below, I will briefly describe the main developments and the new legislative proposals, as a background for discussing empirically the relationship between sector-specific media regulation and competition policy regulation and, more specifically, whether Norwegian sector-specific media ownership regulation might be replaced by competition regulation, as a long-term regulatory proposition.

Norwegian media ownership regulation – some issues[27]

Media ownership regulation was introduced in Norway in 1997 on the basis of the Act on Regulation of Acquisitions in Press and Broadcasting. A separate, independent ownership regulatory authority, the MOA, was established in 1998 and became operative as of 1 January 1999.

The purpose of the Act was to 'further freedom of expression, real possibilities of expression, and media pluralism'. The MOA was given the right to intervene against acquisitions in the daily press and broadcasting sectors that would give a media firm, alone or in cooperation with others, a 'considerable ownership position in the media market, nationally, regionally, or locally', in conflict with the purpose of the Act. Thus, interventions could be made only against acquisitions of ownership shares and not against established ownership positions before the enactment of the Act, and only in the daily press and broadcasting sectors.

The term 'considerable ownership position' was not explicitly defined in the Act, nor were maximum threshold values for ownership positions defined for the various media markets covered by the Act. However, in the Ownership Proposition to the Storting (Norwegian parliament) (Ot.prp. nr. 30 (1996–1997)), it was indicated that acquisitions resulting in an ownership position of more than one-third of the national daily newspaper circulation in the daily press market would most likely give scope for considering interventions. Meanwhile, a minimum threshold value was explicitly stated in the Act, i.e. that interventions could not be performed against acquisitions resulting in ownership positions of 20 per cent or less of the daily circulation in the national daily press market, defined as the relevant market. If such acquisitions would create considerable ownership positions in regional or local markets, however, interventions could be made in relation to those markets.

Thus, the MOA was given considerable discretion with regard to defining criteria for the delineation of relevant media markets and for ownership threshold values for the various markets. The Authority approached this legal situation by issuing a set of guidelines to create a fair degree of transparency and consistency in its enforcement practice. The guidelines were worked out in close cooperation with the media sector. They are guidelines, however, and thus not legally binding. The final responsibility for decisions in actual cases rests, of course, with the MOA.

According to the Act, the MOA has to perform a two-way test or procedure in actual case handling – first, to determine what would be a considerable ownership position in the actual case, and second, to consider whether the ownership position might be used by the media actors in question detrimental to the purpose of the Act. In practice, the Authority seems to have taken the stance that a considerable ownership position in itself is a sufficient indication of a potential violation of the purpose of freedom of expression and media pluralism; in other words that a one-to-one correspondence can be established between structural ownership positions and legal purpose. Thus, the Authority may be said to have relinquished itself from an explicit interpretation of the purpose of the law in relation to actual cases.

However, situations may arise where an acquisition could result in a considerable ownership position in a specific market, but where an intervention might be considered as a second-best solution in relation to the stated purpose of the Act. This could be the case in a 'failing firm' situation, i.e. where a media firm otherwise would go bankrupt and disappear from the market if it is not allowed to be acquired by another media firm, resulting in less pluralism, even if the acquiring firm would become a dominant player. Under such conditions a trade-off has to be made between ownership concentration and pluralism, implying a specific interpretation of the purpose of the Act. A failing firm argumentation has been used by the MOA in a number of cases, particularly for acquisitions in local newspaper markets.[28] From a competition policy perspective, a failing firm argument in merger and acquisition cases is debatable.[29]

The Acquisitions Act and the enforcement practice of the MOA have been open to considerable discussion and critique from a number of sources, not least from the media sector itself, as may be expected when new regulations are effectuated. The critique has mainly concerned the following issues. First, it has been questioned whether ownership regulation is an appropriate or efficient measure of achieving stated objectives of freedom of expression and media pluralism. When the law was enacted, there was considerable disagreement in the Storting about the need for such legislation and it was specifically argued that competition regulation would be sufficient to achieve objectives of media pluralism and diversity. In fact, in 2001, the government suggested in a White Paper merging the MOA with the Competition Authority, but this was not effectuated.[30]

Second, the considerable discretionary power given to the MOA in the Act and the way the Authority has chosen to use its power have been criticised. It seems to have been a deliberate policy of the Authority to cooperate closely with the media sector and pursue a 'soft' regulatory policy. Still, a majority of its decisions has been appealed to the institutionalised Appellate Body of the Act ('Klagenemnda') and then brought to court after the Appellate Body, invariably, has upheld the Authority's decisions. In a number of cases the MOA has lost its case in the court system.

Third, criticism has been raised against the focus of the MOA enforcement policy and more specifically that it has been preoccupied with acquisitions of newspapers in regional and local markets and not with acquisitions that might matter in relation to the purpose of the Act. A statement by Helge Østbye, media professor at the University of Bergen, may illustrate this criticism: 'It seems as if the Authority lets the big fish pass, but in order for the Authority not to lose credibility and run the risk of being closed down, it catches some small ones and shows them off.'[31]

Fourth, a type of criticism related to the first one is that the Authority seems to be confident with a structural analysis based on a one-way test of media ownership concentration and not with the two-way test as envisaged by the Act, as mentioned above, in relation to the stated purpose of the Act. When the Authority has had to make an explicit evaluation, it has invariably fallen back on a failing firm argumentation, which is open to criticism with regard to the trade-off issue between media concentration and pluralism.[32]

A final, general type of criticism is that there tends to be an inherent bias in a regulatory system based on structural ownership regulation in terms of threshold values towards static economic efficiency considerations to the neglect of dynamic efficiency, as discussed in Section 10.3. The potential efficiency loss from such a system can be particularly large under conditions of rapid structural and technological change, as has been the case for many media markets. This is, however, basically a critique of the chosen regulatory approach as such and not necessarily of the enforcement policy and procedures of the regulatory authority in charge.

Proposed revisions of the Norwegian media regulatory system

The government (Ministry of Culture and Church) has proposed a number of changes in the Norwegian media ownership regulatory framework.[33] The coverage of the Media Acquisitions Act will be extended to include electronic media and the name changed to the Media Ownership Act. However, the extension is supposed, as a first step, to be limited to a market surveillance function of electronic media for the MOA, without the legal right to intervene. In addition, the scope of the Act will be extended to cover cooperative agreements between media firms and not only acquisitions, and also covering multi-media and cross-ownership.

The Media Ownership Authority will be given the right to issue a temporary prohibition against the consummation of an acquisition until the Authority has decided on the case. A similar rule has been introduced in the Norwegian Competition Act of 2004.

Perhaps the most novel and interesting regulatory revision, however, is the proposal of defining 'considerable ownership position' in terms of threshold values and introducing threshold values for media markets explicitly into the Act. The proposed thresholds are:

For *national* media markets:
1. Forty per cent or more of the total daily circulation for the daily press market. The same threshold value applies for the television market, measured in terms of number of viewers, and the radio market, measured in terms of number of listeners (voice).
2. Thirty per cent or more in one of the media markets under 1 above and 20 per cent or more in one of the other markets under 1, or
3. When a media firm controlling 10 per cent or more in one of the media markets under 1 becomes owner or part owner in a firm belonging to another ownership constellation controlling 10 per cent or more within the same media market (cross-ownership).

For *regional* markets:
1. Sixty per cent or more of the total daily circulation of regional and local newspapers in a media region.
2. Forty-five per cent or more of the total daily circulation of regional and local newspapers and 33 per cent or more of the market for local TV or local radio in the same media region, the media regions being defined by the government (the MOA) and introduced by secondary legislation. Note that the concept of local media markets, as a separate geographic market entity, no longer exists in the new law proposal.

In addition to the ownership proposals, the government has, as mentioned, proposed new media legislation to safeguard freedom of expression and media independence and pluralism. First, an amendment to Article 100 on freedom of expression of the Norwegian Constitution has been proposed, following up on proposals from the Commission on Freedom of Expression, appointed by the government in 1996. A constitutional amendment has to be passed by two subsequently elected Stortings. If the proposed amendment is passed, the scope of Article 100 will be broadened and no longer be linked to specific media. It will also make it an obligation for the government to 'create conditions for an open and informed public debate' – an expression coined by the Commission.

A second set of proposals is aimed at trying to separate media own-ership from control to alleviate some of the potential problems asso-ciated with concentrations of media ownership, as a means to safeguard media independence and pluralism. First and foremost is the proposal to write into law the self-regulations in the Declaration of Rights and Duties of Editors ('Redaktørplakaten'), thus formally making them legally binding.[34] This Declaration, dating back to 1953 and agreed on by both editors and owners/publishers, gives a.o. the editors 'full freedom to shape the opinion of the paper' and requires them to 'promote an impartial and free exchange of information and opinion' and to 'strive for what he/she feels serves society'. Writing into law the intentions of the regulations in the Declaration would make infringements by media owners and others liable to legal sanctions and would, intentionally, contribute to a more effective separation of own-ership from control than under the present self-regulatory system.

Vertical relations

Vertical integration has generally not been considered to be a serious problem in the media sector, at least for the traditional sectors, com-pared with horizontal ownership concentrations. This is also the gen-eral position taken by the Norwegian government in its ownership proposals to the Storting and also by the MOA in a contributed Appendix to the Ownership Proposition.

However, the proposed extension of the Media Ownership Act to cover electronic media could pose potential ownership and competi-tion issues with regard to vertical relations, in terms of control of bottlenecks and digital portals in the vertical distribution system.

This is acknowledged by the government, but it is not considered to be a sufficiently serious problem to require regulation for the time being. Measures to control for vertical integration are therefore not proposed to be included in the Media Ownership Act. The government argues that regulating vertical integration would have to be shaped differently compared with horizontal integration, focusing on the abuse of a dominant position instead of structural ownership regula-tion in terms of threshold values for considerable ownership position. Thus, without stating it explicitly, the government seems to relegate economic issues of vertical relations in the media sector to general competition regulation.

A vertical relation issue of a somewhat different nature, but with potentially important regulatory implications, not discussed in the Proposition, is rooted in the 'vertical' division of regulatory responsibility between different layers of government and their relationship to media actors. The issues can be illustrated by the case of allocating the rights to build a new digital, earth-based distribution system for broadcasting in Norway. The only applicant to the concession is Norges televisjon a/s (NTV), a distribution company owned 50/50 by the Norwegian public broadcasting company NRK and the commercial television company TV2. NRK is wholly state owned by the Ministry of Culture. The Ministry is concessionary authority for the allocation and also media regulator of last resort.

This constellation raises two potential vertical regulatory issues. First, how to avoid conflicts of interest for the Ministry and, in particular, infringements on the fundamental requirement of separation of the roles and functions as regulator and owner, respectively, as foreseen, for example, in the EU directives on telecommunications. Second, if the concession is given to NTV under the present ownership structure, how to secure access to the distribution system on transparent and non-discriminatory terms for interested parties, given the strong market positions of NRK and TV2 as media content producers and without extending their positions. With the position, referred to above, on vertical integration taken by the Ministry of Culture in the Ownership Proposition, this should logically be considered an issue to be tackled by competition policy.

The lessons of the Norwegian case

As mentioned, at the time when the MOA was established on the basis of the Media Ownership Act, there was a lot of discussion and disagreement about the relevance and functionality of this type of regulatory model. Some argued that it was unnecessary to establish a separate entity for media ownership regulation and that this function could be performed equally well by the Norwegian Competition Authority (NCA). The experience with regard to the division of labour between the two authorities may be briefly summed up in the following points:

- The authorities seem to have agreed on a division of labour where the NCA has not explicitly considered media ownership positions and issues as such, leaving that to the MOA. However, the NCA has decided on several cases of media mergers and acquisitions on the basis of the legal measures and procedures laid down in the Competition Act.

- The MOA has dealt only with horizontal media ownership issues within the press and broadcasting sectors, given its original legal foundation, while the NCA has also handled vertical relations and covering the media sector on a broader basis, including electronic media.

- Until the new Competition Act of 2004, the NCA did not explicitly deal with market dominance in terms of threshold values, and abuse of market power, but intervened on a case-by-case basis, where market power (unilateral as well as collective market power) could be expected to be exerted on the basis of structural or behavioural indications.

- The principles and criteria for media market delineation and measurement of market concentration (dominance) are somewhat differently defined between the two authorities.[35] The NCA has been mainly preoccupied with the effects on competition in the markets for advertising, when handling exemptions from the Competition Act, for example, or decisions on mergers and acquisitions.[36]

- The legal and institutional system for the appeal of decisions is different between the two policy areas and authorities. For the MOA there is an independent appellant, as mentioned above, while decisions of the NCA have to be appealed to the Ministry to which it is subordinated. The NCA appeal system is an unfortunate one in general, from the perspective of regulatory independence, and perhaps even more so for a sector like media which may be particularly exposed to political influence and pressure in relation to specific regulatory decisions. If competition policy regulation should take over for economic sector-specific media regulation, the present appeal system should be changed to better safeguard independence.[37]

- The revision of the Media Ownership Act to adapt itself to changing regulatory circumstances and media environments seems to have been relatively slow, influencing the ability of the MOA to adjust its regulatory practice to those changes. The NCA, meanwhile, has had the instruments and the powers to deal with a changing media environment, including, in principle, market dominance.

Replacing sector-specific economic media regulation by competition policy regulation?

We may now collect the various strands of argument discussed above regarding the relationship between sector-specific and competition regulation of media to see whether competition policy regulation can be effectively substituted for economic sector regulation, specifically in view of the proposals of the Norwegian government for new media legislation and the newly revised Competition Act.

As mentioned, the Norwegian Competition Act of 2004 is modelled on the EU competition law model and harmonised with EU competition legislation. It contains prohibitions on cooperative agreements and abuse of market dominance positions in restraint of competition, as well as a temporary prohibition on the consummation of a merger or an acquisition by the parties involved until the Norwegian Competition Authority (NCA) has decided on the case. It also introduces a new system of compulsory reporting and registration of mergers and acquisitions above a proposed limit of NKr 20 million (€2.5 million). The Act applies to the media sector.

The measures proposed to control for ownership and cooperation in the new Media Ownership Act are basically the same as the instruments of the Competition Act to control for restraints on competition to the detriment of economic efficiency. Because the objectives of the Media Ownership Act are differently formulated than for the Competition Act, the question remains whether the objectives of freedom of expression and pluralism can be safeguarded under a competition policy regime, combined with legislation to separate ownership from control.

The parallel new legislation on Article 100 of the Constitution and the Declaration of the Rights and Duties of Editors should, in my opinion, instil sufficient safeguards for those objectives into the regulatory system. Making the regulations legally binding and enforceable by sanctions gives a strong signal from the legislators of the importance they attach to media independence and separation of ownership from control. The 'voice' effect in the public opinion of possible infringements on the extended freedom of expression safeguards in Article 100 works in the same direction. It should be the responsibility of the Media Regulatory Authority to address and enforce such aspects of the new regulatory system.

The economic regulatory issue then boils down to whether direct ownership regulation in terms of threshold values etc., as envisaged in the Media Ownership Act, is a better regulatory model than general competition regulation. In my opinion, it is not; cf. the discussion in Section 10.3. Competition policy regulation is more flexible and targeted in comparison; it has a larger box of regulatory tools, it offers more flexibility in terms of market delineation and definition of dominant ownership positions for regulatory purposes,[38] it attacks the issue of abuse of market dominance directly, it handles vertical restraints, it can accommodate dynamic competition and efficiency issues in more consistent and constructive ways, etc.[39]

On this background, I would argue from a position that economic sector-specific (ownership) regulation of the Norwegian media sector could be replaced by competition regulation without unduly endangering objectives of pluralism and freedom of expression, on the condition that the proposed new media legislation is enacted. In this context, the proposed Media Ownership Act thus seems to be superfluous. Parallel sector-specific legislation will in this case overlap with the Competition Act to such a degree that it may result in regulatory uncertainty in case handling and in the division of responsibility between regulatory bodies. It may also result in lack of consistency within the media regulatory system as a whole as well as duplication of regulatory resources and efforts to the detriment of economic efficiency.

An organisational consequence of replacing sector-specific ownership regulation by competition regulation could be that the Media Ownership Authority would be merged with the Competition Authority and its legislative powers and resources transferred there. In a transitory phase, until the direct ownership regulations would be abolished, the activities of the MOA could be organised as a sector-specific competition division within the NCA, based, for example, on the Dutch institutional regulatory model, referred to above.

10.6 Conclusion

The media sector is characterised by rapid structural and technological change. Under such conditions it is important that the time lag in adjusting the regulatory system to a changing environment is not too long and that regulatory measures are designed to cope effectively with changing environments. On a higher policy ambition level, a regulatory regime should also be in the forefront of changes in the regulatory environment, so as to act as a stimulus and a steering device for an *intentional* development and not only as a lagging and controlling device.

The media sector presents public regulatory policies and authorities with a demanding challenge because the sector is so diversified and because such a complex set of regulatory objectives is attached to it. In this chapter a relatively narrow regulatory issue in this complex problem has been discussed, i.e. whether economic sector-specific regulation can be separated from other forms of media regulation and more specifically whether competition policy regulation may be substituted for sector-specific ownership regulation, with a concomitant change of the role and responsibility of regulatory institutions in media regulation.

What are the main lessons to be learned from the practical experience with these regulatory issues? It is important to remember at the outset that the experience necessarily has to be limited because the analysis and evaluation of the relationship between sector-specific and competition regulation of media is of relatively recent origin, stimulated by the EU directives on electronic communications.[40] No European country has as yet, for example, fully implemented the expressed intention of the directives of gradually replacing sector-specific regulation by competition regulation.

Lessons for students: what have we learned?

One important general message for students of media regulation is that there seem to be considerable inertia and vested institutional interests in the transformation of a regulatory regime from sector-specific to competition policy regulation, in this case in economic (ownership) media regulation. Even when the regulatory approach and instruments are basically the same in sector-specific as in competition regulation, the responsibility for designing and enforcing a regulatory regime seems still to be resting within the sector-specific realm.[41] This may create regulatory uncertainty and result in a duplication of resources for regulation.

Another message is that the favoured application in ownership regulation media of setting predefined threshold levels, e.g. for market shares in a structural approach to regulation to secure media diversity and controlling for market dominance, may be questioned. A more flexible approach, including an analysis of market players' incentives and behaviour, is called for in a rapidly changing regulatory environment.

Lessons for researchers: what do we still need to know?

A message for researchers on media regulation is that more research is needed in industrial organisation and institutional theory on the optimal design of the institutional regulatory framework of media regulation. This includes issues such as the division of labour and responsibility between regulatory institutions, broadly defined, complementarities between regulatory approaches and instruments applied in various areas of media regulation under media convergence and integration, the exposure to regulatory capture under different regulatory regimes, and the design and imposition of a universal service obligation regime under media market liberalisation and convergence. A message more specifically in the sector-specific/competition policy regulation context is the need for research on the design and analysis of a regulatory policy for media markets, with dynamic competition and dynamic efficiency as the explicitly stated aim.

Lessons for policymakers: what are the priorities for policy in this area?

The main message to policymakers would be to try to include all of the above-mentioned issues and aspects in their policy design and priorities in the area of media regulation. In a complex and dynamic regulatory environment like media regulation, policymakers should always remind themselves that market failure has to be weighed against regulatory failure in the design and implementation of media policy. Specifically, with regard to sector-specific ownership regulation of media, policymakers should consider replacing it by competition policy regulation and following up with the concomitant institutional rearrangement between regulatory bodies.

References

Beesley, Martin (ed.) (1996) *Markets and the Media: Competition, regulation and the interest of consumers*, Institute of Economic Affairs.

Cave, Martin and Peter Crowther (2004) 'Co-ordinating Regulation and Competition Law – *ex ante* and *ex post*', in Swedish Competition Authority *The Pros and Cons of Antitrust in Deregulated Markets*, Stockholm.

Doyle, Gillian (2002) *Media Ownership. The economics and politics of conver-gence and concentration in the UK and European media*, Sage Publications.

Ellig, Jerry (ed.) (2001) *Dynamic Competition and Public Policy. Technology, innovation, and antitrust issues*, Cambridge University Press.

EU Commission (1997) *Green Paper on the Convergence of the Telecom-munications, Media, and Information Technology Sectors, and the Implications for Regulation. Towards an information society approach.*

EU Commission (2000) *Proposal for a Directive on a Common Regulatory Framework for Electronic Networks and Services*, COM (2000)393.

Fehr, Nils-Henrik von der (2000) 'Who Should be Responsible for Competition Policy in Regulated Industries?', in Einar Hope (ed.) *Competition Policy Analysis*, Routledge.

Fehr, Nils-Henrik von der, Victor D. Norman, Torger Reve and Anders Chr. Ryssdal (1998) *Ikke for å vinne? Analyse av konkurranseforhold og konkurransepolitikk* (Not to Win? Analysis of competition and compe-tition policy), SNF-report 8/98.

Hagen, Kåre P. and Einar Hope (2004) *Konkurranse og konkurransepolitikk i innovative næringer* (Competition and Competition Policy in Innovative Industries), SNF Working Paper 26/04.

Hammer, Ulf (2002) 'EC Secondary Legislation of Network Markets and Public Service. An economic and functional approach', *Journal of Network Industries*.

Hoffmann-Riem, Wolfgang (1996) *Regulating Media. The licencing and supervision of broadcasting in six countries*, The Guilford Press.

Hope, Einar (ed.) (2000) *Competition Policy Analysis*, Routledge.

Hope, Einar (2003) 'Nettintegrasjon – implikasjoner for konkurranse- og reguleringspolitikk' (Network Integration – Implications for Competition and Regulatory Policies), in Helge Godø (ed.) *IKT – etter dotcom-boblen* (ICT – After the Dotcom Bubble), Gyldendal, Oslo.

Hope, Einar (2005) *Market Dominance and Market Power in Electric Power Markets: A competition policy perspective*, Research report 2005:3, The Swedish Competition Authority.

Hope, Einar and Helle Thorsen (1997) 'EC Competition Law: Competition issues with regard to sector-specific regulation', *Fordham Law Review*, Chapter 14.

Humphreys, Peter (1996) *Mass Media and Media Policy in Western Europe*, Manchester University Press.

Hylleberg, Sven and Per Baltzar Overgaard (2000) 'Competition Policy with a Coasian Prior?', in Einar Hope (ed.) *Competition Policy Analysis*, Routledge.

Kelly, Mary, Gianpietro Mazzoleni and Denis McQuail (eds.) (2004) *The Media in Europe. The Euromedia handbook*, Sage Publications.

Laffont, Jean-Jacques and David Martimort (1999) 'Separation of Regulators Against Collusive Behavior', *Rand Journal of Economics*.

Laffont, Jean-Jacques and Jean Tirole (2000) *Competition in Telecommunications*, MIT Press.

Larouche, Pierre (2000) *Competition Law and Regulation in European Telecommunications*, Hart Publishing.

McQuail, Denis and Karen Siune (eds.) (1998) *Media Policy: Convergence, concentration and commerce*, Sage Publications.

Neven, Damien, Roger Nuttal and Paul Seabright (1993) *Merger in Daylight. The economics and politics of European merger control*, Centre for Economic Policy Research.

Neven, Damien, Penelope Papandropoulos and Paul Seabright (1998) *Trawling for Minnows. European competition policy and agreements between firms*, Centre for Economic Policy Research.

Nordic Competition Authorities (2003) *A Powerful Competition Policy. Towards a more coherent policy in the Nordic market for electric power*, Report No. 1/2003.

Norman, Victor D. (2000) 'Competition Policy and Market Dynamics', in Einar Hope (ed.) *Competition Policy Analysis*, Routledge.

Østbye, Helge (1995) *Mediepolitikk. Skal medieutviklingen styres?* (Media Policy. Ought media developments be regulated?), Universitetsforlaget, Oslo.

Østbye, Helge (2000) *Hvem eier norske massemedier?* (Who owns Norwegian Mass Media?), Rapport 25, Makt- og demokratiutredningens rapportserie, Oslo.

Ot.prp. nr. 30 (1996–1997) *Om lov om tilsyn med erverv i dagspresse og kringkasting* (Proposition to the Norwegian Parliament on Act on regulatory surveillance of acquisitions in the daily press and broadcasting).

Ot.pr. nr. 81 (2003–2004) *Om lov om endringar i lov av 13. juni 1997 nr. 53 om tilsyn med erverv i dagspresse og kringkasting* (Proposition to the Norwegian Parliament: Changes in the 1997 Media Acquisitions Act), Norwegian Ministry for Culture and Church.

Persson, Lars (2004) 'Failing Firm Defence', *Journal of Industrial Economics*.

St.meld. nr. 57 (2000–2001) *I ytringsfrihetens tjeneste. Mål og virkemidler i mediepolitikken* (White Paper on Objectives and Instruments in Media Policy).

St.meld. nr. 17 (2002–2003) *Om statlige tilsyn* (White Paper on Public Regulatory Bodies).

Syvertsen, Trine (2004) *Mediemangfold* (Media Diversity), Ij Forlaget, Oslo.

Notes

*   I am indebted to Mats Bergman, Jürgen von Hagen, Paul Seabright, Tanja
     Storsul and Helge Østbye for valuable comments. Remaining errors are
     my sole responsibility. The final version of this chapter was completed in
     January 2005.
1.   EU Commission (2000): COM (2000)393.
2.   Gillian Doyle comments specifically on media ownership regulation in her
     comprehensive media ownership study that 'effective and equitable upper
     restraints on ownership are vitally important tools that no responsible demo-
     cracy can afford to relinquish. Curbs on ownership provide a direct means of
     preventing harmful concentrations of media power and, as such, are indis-
     pensable safeguards for pluralism and democracy' (Doyle (2002), p. 179).
        Likewise, in a recent Law Proposition to the Storting (Norwegian
     parliament) on ownership regulation of media the Norwegian Ministry
     of Culture and Church concludes, after a summary discussion of compe-
     tition and ownership regulation, that the Competition Act is not suited
     for achieving pluralism and securing freedom of expression in media
     regulation, and that ownership regulation therefore is required as a
     policy instrument (Ot.pr. nr. 81 (2003–2004)).
3.   For accounts, see for example EU Commission (1997), Doyle (2002),
     McQuail and Siune (1998), Beesley (1996), Kelly et al. (2004) and
     Syvertsen (2004).
4.   In addition to the references in footnote 3, see for example Hoffmann-
     Riem (1996), Humphreys (1996) and Østbye (1995).
5.   For a more detailed exposition, see Hope (2003).
6.   See Cave and Crowther (2004) for discussion, primarily with reference to
     EU telecommunications and electronic media regulation.
7.   For a detailed account of the UK media ownership policy, and also cover-
     ing European countries, see Doyle (2002). For a discussion of the
     Norwegian case, see Section 10.5.
8.   For a comprehensive analysis of market dominance and market power in
     competition policy, primarily with reference to electric power markets but
     also with a discussion of media markets, see Hope (2005).
9.   Most European countries have by now adopted the market dominant
     position rule and the concomitant prohibition of abuse rule of the EU
     competition policy; consider Norway in the new Norwegian Competition
     Act of 5 March 2004. An alternative to the market dominance test,
     more in line with economic theory, is the 'significant lessening of compe-
     tition' (SLC) test, which, for example, the US competition legislation is
     based upon. The new Merger Regulations of the EU have come closer to
     the American SLC-test concept.

10. In the new Norwegian Competition Act, § 12 on market dominance regulation explicitly states that 'structural measures can only be enforced if equally efficient behavioural measures cannot be found, or if a behavioural measure would be more burdensome for the (dominant) firm'. Similar regulations apply within the EU competition policy in relation to Articles 81 and 82 of the Treaty.
11. See EU Commission (2000).
12. The approach is developed in Fehr et al. (1998) (in Norwegian). An English summary of the main ideas is contained in Norman (2000). For a discussion of the approach and its implications for competition policy analysis, see Hylleberg and Overgaard (2000). See also Hope (2005).
13. See, for example, Doyle (2002).
14. See, for example, Hagen and Hope (2004) and contributions in Ellig (2001).
15. From a more general regulatory perspective it may seem somewhat paradoxical that *ex ante* sector-specific regulation should be better adapted to achieve dynamic efficiency objectives in innovative industries and turbulent markets, with a high degree of uncertainty about outcomes of technological change and innovation, than under *ex post* competition regulation.
16. Syvertsen (2004) distinguishes between the following main categories of objectives for Norwegian media policy: (a) diversity and pluralism, (b) democracy, freedom of expression and public debate, (c) culture, identity and language, (d) protection of minorities and vulnerable groups, (e) safeguarding consumers and efforts against commercialisation, (f) access to media supply on equal terms for all, and (g) support of a national media industry and media production. She groups (a) to (c) into a *cultural policy* regulatory regime, (d) and (e) into a *consumer policy* regulatory regime and (f) and (g) into an *industrial or competition policy* regulatory regime.
17. Consider the opening paragraph of the 2004 Norwegian Competition Act: 'The purpose of this Act is to further competition as a means to achieve efficient use of society's resources.' Under the debate of the Act in the Norwegian Parliament (the Storting), a formulation was added: 'When applying this Act, special consideration should be given to consumers' interests.'
18. Vertical aspects are covered in Fehr (2000), Laffont and Tirole (2000) and Larouche (2000); the latter two primarily with reference to telecommunications.
19. Hope and Thorsen (1997) and Hope (2003).
20. See, for example, Doyle (2002). However, electronic media integration has implications for the horizontal division of labour between media regulation and telecommunications regulation.

21. For some aspects of this discussion, see the analysis in Laffont and Martimort (1999). See also Fehr (2000).
22. An interesting empirical analysis of lobbying, as an aspect of regulatory capture, is Neven et al. (1998). See also Neven et al. (1993) on regulatory capture.
23. For a discussion, see Laffont and Tirole (2000). Hammer (2002) discusses USO under EU regulation, specifically for network regulation in relation to Article 16 in the Amsterdam Treaty, obligating Member States 'to take care that such (public) services operate on the basis of principles and conditions which enable them to fulfil their mission'. Hammer concludes that such regulation 'does not reflect a conflict between public service/universal service and competition. Both aspects can be derived from the new Art. 16 EC. On the one hand, it emphasizes the importance of public service in a situation where state functions are outsourced in several European countries. On the other hand, it does not reflect a conflict between public service and competition.'
24. See Kelly et al. (2004) and Doyle (2002).
25. For a survey of Norwegian regulatory policy for the media sector, see Chapter 14 on Norway by Helge Østbye in Kelly et al. (2004). See also Syvertsen (2004) (in Norwegian).
26. St.meld. nr. 17 (2002–2003). The merger was effectuated as of 01.01.05.
27. For a detailed account, see Syvertsen (2004), Chapter 7.
28. For information, see www.medietilsynet.no and www.eierskapstilsynet.no For most of the case decisions there is an English summary. For competition policy cases, see www.konkurransetilsynet.no, where there normally are English summaries too.
    The majority of the decisions by the MOA have been on acquisitions of ownership positions within the daily press sector. In addition, there have been some cases of acquisitions of ownership positions by newspapers in broadcasting companies.
29. For discussion, see Persson (2004).
30. St.meld. nr. 57 (2000–2001).
31. Østbye (2000) (my translation). This is, in fact, a common, general criticism of regulatory policy not only in sector-specific regulation but also in competition policy. See the discussion in relation to EU competition policy in Neven et al. (1998).
32. A failing firm argument is, for example, insufficient or incomplete without taking into account potential entry and effects of potential competition.
33. Ot.pr. nr. 81 (2003–2004).
34. This proposal rests with the government until the Storting has voted on the amendment to Article 100.

35. For example, the MOA seems to measure market shares for newspapers mainly in terms of the number of circulations, while the NCA typically would measure shares in economic terms, i.e. on the basis of number of newspapers actually sold.
36. In the Ownership Proposition to the Storting (Ot.pr. nr. 81 (2003–2004)) it says, rather surprisingly, that the media markets for readers (newspaper), listeners and viewers are not markets in economic terms according to the Competition Act.
37. Proposals for such a change have been put forward in the legislative process.
38. In competition policy analysis, concentration indices have been developed, taking account of, for example, direct and indirect ownership, and cross-ownership, for the analysis of unilateral as well as collective market dominance. See Nordic Competition Authorities, Report (2003), applied to energy markets. See also Hope (2005).
39. The relationship between sector and competition regulation is discussed rather summarily by the Ministry of Culture in the media ownership Proposition, the conclusion being that the policy fields are complementary rather than competitive, as mentioned in the introduction. It seems to be taken for granted, without discussion, that competition is at odds with media pluralism In a hearing statement to the Proposition, the Norwegian Competition Authority agrees in principle with the complementary relationship argument, but then considered in isolation within an ownership regulatory system alone, and not with the proposed parallel legislation on freedom of expression and media pluralism.
40. For the specific Norwegian experience, see Sections 10.4 and 10.5.
41. This not only applies to media regulation but seems to be a general tendency where sector-specific regulatory regimes have been established, e.g. in the regulation of energy markets and networks. See Hope (2005).

Index